CHOICES IN VICHY FRANCE

CHOICES IN VICHY FRANCE

The French under Nazi Occupation

John F. Sweets

New York   Oxford
OXFORD UNIVERSITY PRESS
1986

Oxford University Press

Oxford   New York   Toronto
Delhi Bombay   Calcutta   Madras   Karachi
Kuala Lumpur   Singapore   Hong Kong   Tokyo
Nairobi   Dar es Salaam   Cape Town
Melbourne   Auckland

and associated companies in
Beirut   Berlin   Ibadan   Mexico City   Nicosia

Published by Oxford University Press, Inc.,
200 Madison Avenue
New York, New York   10016

All photographs are in the public domain and
are courtesy of the Archives départementales
du Puy-de-Dôme, Clermont-Ferrand.

Library of Congress Cataloging in Publication Data

Sweets, John F., 1945–
Choices in Vichy France

Bibliography: p.
Includes index.
1. World War, 1939–1945–France–Clermond-Ferrand–
Case studies.   2. Clermont-Ferrand (France)–History–
Case studies.   I. Title.
D802.F82C627   1986   940.53′44   85–10579
ISBN 0–19–503751–0

Printing (last digit):   9 8 7 6 5 4 3 2 1

Printed in the United States of America

A Alphonse Rozier, un des chefs de la résistance
dans l'Auvergne, ami que j'admire énormément, et pour
Paulette, sa femme, qui a toujours du mal à comprendre
mon français de Tennessee, mais qui m'a adopté
comme "deuxième fils" quand même.

Preface

This book recounts the experiences of some French men and women who lived in or near the city of Clermont-Ferrand during World War II. It is not a history of France under the occupation, nor does it explain the experiences of all the French people—not even of all of those who lived in Clermont-Ferrand or the Auvergne. The uniqueness of circumstances and individual experience inevitably frustrates the historian who hopes to recapture the past in all of its complex detail. The pattern and meaning we discern in the past are the products of an arbitrary logic we have imposed on the chaos of individual experience. Yet the uniqueness of individual experience need not invalidate all extrapolations and generalizations. Human beings, after all, experience life at several levels of reality. Although men, women, and children are individuals, they are also members of communities, residents of particular localities, and citizens of a nation. Local history, at its best, should be able to blend the rich detail and proximity of individual experience with concerns that transcend the local community. Thus, although I have directed the reader's attention primarily to the people of Clermont-Ferrand and the particular circumstances of the war years in the Auvergne, I believe that their experience offers many insights that are valuable for understanding the attitudes and behavior of other French citizens. Indeed, at its most ambitious moments, this account of individuals in one city, and one region, is at the same time a story of the human condition, of human beings reacting to conditions of extraordinary stress, of individuals confronted with choices.

I have tried to keep these ambitions of historical synthesis to modest proportions, arguing for general applicability only where the evidence available to me or the work of other scholars validates comparable conclusions. Without question I know much more about Clermont-Ferrand and the Auvergne than about other regions of France. During the course of several years of research, I have become particularly fond of the Auvergne and its people, both past and present, and I believe that merely to describe their experience would be interesting and valuable in itself. Still, as I pieced together the threads of Clermont-Ferrand's reaction to the defeat and the German occupation, I discovered many surprising things that bring into question some of the conventional wisdom about France during World War II.

My research has confirmed that the Vichy government was, or had ambitions to be, the sort of regime portrayed in the excellent accounts of Henri Michel, Yves Durand, and Robert Paxton. Many Frenchmen in positions of highest authority during the years of German occupation believed that Germany would remain dominant for a long time and sought to take advantage of the defeat of France to remake the country in a new, authoritarian mold. I have discovered that it is often necessary to make clearer distinctions than have sometimes been made between the French government and the people of France. While Marshal Philippe Pétain enjoyed substantial support from the French people at the time of the fall of France, his following was at no time unanimous, and Pétain fell out of popular favor much earlier than has been generally recognized. At no point did the French people exhibit much enthusiasm for the Vichy government's efforts to remake France.

The regime's attempts to build a "New Order" at Clermont-Ferrand—the city closest to France's wartime capital and most subject to all of the pressure that could be brought to bear by handpicked followers of the government—demonstrated how little resonance the ideals of the Vichy government found in the population. My research suggests that authors dealing with themes of collaboration and resistance must be especially careful in examining evidence regarding the size of those two phenomena. New definitions of collaboration and resistance are needed that will incorporate a consideration of public opinion and levels of popular support for collaborators and resisters. One of the most important contributions that research at the local level offers the student of wartime France is the ability to measure popular response to the multiple choices required by a foreign occupation that dislocated the normal pattern of life in so many ways. I found that more people chose to oppose the Vichy regime and fewer people actively collaborated than I had anticipated. The experience of Clermont-Ferrand and the reactions of the Clermontois testified to the ingenuity and resourcefulness of individuals under extreme conditions and produced some examples of reprehensible behavior, but also evoked no small measure of integrity, courage, and sacrifice.

My attention was drawn to Clermont-Ferrand, in part, by the Marcel Ophuls film *The Sorrow and the Pity*. Although it was a huge success in France and other countries, the film is highly unsatisfactory from a his-

torical perspective. The examples chosen by Ophuls for dramatic or enter-
tainment value often abuse the historical reality beyond recognition. Without great illusions about the influence of the written word in competition
with a celluloid medium, I have addressed and attempted to correct several of these distortions in my text. In addition to its proximity to the capital of wartime France, another (and more crucial) consideration for my
choice of Clermont-Ferrand as a case study was the possibility of access to
local archives.

I could not have completed this study without the warm welcome and
generous assistance offered to me by archivists at Clermont-Ferrand. Monsieur René Sève, Conservateur en chef des Archives de la Région de
l'Auvergne, was extremely cordial to me and always helpful, even at a time
when he was fighting a fatal illness. His death was a great loss not only to
his profession in France, but also to American specialists of French history
who had grown accustomed to his enthusiasm for and encouragement of
our research. His successor as Conservateur en chef, Francine Leclercq,
was the assistant director of the Archives when I was working in Clermont-
Ferrand. I could not have asked for a better reception or more helpful
assistance than I received from Mademoiselle Leclercq. She was the person who introduced me to the holdings of the Archives and spent many
hours answering questions and guiding me through inventories of available
documentation. I would like to thank the following members of the staff at
the Archives départementales du Puy-de-Dôme who good humoredly tolerated my French, spoken with a Tennessee accent, and were unfailingly
helpful and courteous: Monsieur Jean Crespin, Monsieur Emmanuel Ar-
minjon, and Madame Nicole Boivin.

As has been true since my first research trip to France for an earlier
book, Henri Michel generously offered encouragement and support for this
project. His associates at the Comité d'histoire de la deuxième guerre mondiale (now a branch of the Institut d'histoire du temps présent in Paris)—
including Claude Lévy, Dominique Veillon, Françoise Mercier, Marianne
Ranson, and Michel Rauzier—all offered advice, assistance, and encouragement at various stages of my research. In Freiburg, Germany, Hans Umbreit greatly facilitated my work at the Militärarchiv. The staff at England's
Public Record Office at Kew were superbly efficient. Among American
scholars I am indebted to Robert Paxton for his support in obtaining fund-
ing for this project and for several discussions of the Jewish question in
France, and to Howard Sachar and Irwin Wall for thoughtful criticisms
of parts of the manuscript. In that respect, and closer to home, I wish to
thank those of my colleagues in the Department of History at the University of Kansas who participated in Hatchet Club sessions involving two
chapters of the book. In particular, I appreciate the comments of Professors

x

Preface

Benjamin Sax, Rita Napier, and Ted Wilson, who have taken the time to read and discuss with me substantial portions of the manuscript. I am most indebted to my colleague Cliff Griffin, who read every word and subjected the text to thoughtful and meticulous scrutiny. The book is much better because of his unselfish commitment to collegiality.

The friends I have made in the Auvergne—both those who lived through the German occupation and shared their memories with me and those born since the war or too young to remember the 1940s—are too numerous to mention individually, but I sincerely appreciated their expressions of interest in my work and the warm hospitality they offered my family on many occasions. My wife, Judy, and my son, Craig, shared two research trips to France with me, partially compensating for numerous material difficulties by recourse to a steady diet of French pastries. I thank them for their patience and companionship.

Research for this book was made possible by a National Endowment for the Humanities Individual Research Grant during the 1978–1979 academic year. The University of Kansas provided a sabbatical leave during the fall of 1980, and supported this book with several smaller grants from the University of Kansas, Office of Research Administration General Research Fund. The American Philosophical Society awarded the project a summer research grant in 1973 that partially funded the original stage of research. Finally, I would like to thank Penny May and Pam LeRow for their expert typing of the original manuscript.

Lawrence, Kansas   J. F. S.
June 1985

Contents

CHOICES IN
VICHY FRANCE

1

War, Occupation, and Society

Sprawled beneath the foot of the Puy-de-Dôme to its west, bounded on the south by the Plateau de Gergovie, and flanked by the mountains of the Livradois and the Forez to the east, Clermont-Ferrand is most accessible to a visitor (or invader) from the north across the fertile Limagne plain, traversed today by Route Nationale 9. Over the centuries, through this narrow funnel facing north, Paris has attracted thousands of emigrants from Clermont and the hills around it, making the nation's capital the "second city" of the Auvergne. Clermont-Ferrand is the Auvergne's regional capital, and in 1940 it was France's seventeenth largest urban center with a population of slightly more than 100,000. Historically, the city has numerous claims to fame from a rich and varied tradition. The Gallic chieftain Vercingetorix, whose statue dominates Clermont's main square, the Place de Jaude, inflicted a dramatic though short-lived defeat on Julius Caesar on the nearby Plateau de Gergovie in 52 B.C. Gregory of Tours, one of the best-known chroniclers of the early Middle Ages, was a native of Clermont. In 1095 Pope Urban II launched the First Crusade from a pulpit erected on the site of the present-day Place Delille. The city's lycée is named for Blaise Pascal, one of Clermont's most brilliant native sons, who, in a famous experiment carried out in 1648 on the Puy-de-Dôme, proved that the atmosphere has weight. Since the Napoleonic era Clermont-Ferrand has been a university town, and in the twentieth century it is perhaps most widely known as the home of the Michelin Company, one of the world's foremost manufacturers of rubber tires.

In recent years there has been much talk in Clermont-Ferrand and the region about *désenclavement* (a "breaking-out") of the Auvergne, bypassed by the earliest French autoroute-building programs and desirous of more rapid and reliable communication with Paris, Lyon, and the larger world beyond.[1] The outsider is struck by a pervasive emphasis on this theme that Clermont-Ferrand and the Auvergne have been isolated from

3

the mainstream of France's rapid postwar modernization. The same term, *cloisonné* ("isolated"), is employed frequently with regard to the purported outlook of the Clermontois (and Auvergnats in general) toward the outside world. Often the Clermontois describe themselves and their fellow Auvergnats as suspicious and inhospitable toward strangers and seem to think of their town as ugly. A visitor,* who appreciates the many charming corners to be found in Clermont and the surrounding countryside and finds the local people to be extraordinarily helpful and welcoming, may suspect the Clermontois of a curious inferiority complex. Readers of local newspapers at Clermont-Ferrand in 1942 were confronted by a strikingly similar image in references to the "reputation for coldness," the "legendary coldness," the "well-known coldness," and so forth, of the Auvergnats.[2] One might speculate as to whether or not this persistent stereotype of the people of the Auvergne as cold and inward-looking and of the region as cut off from the rest of France, physically as well as temperamentally, was more valid in 1942 than in the 1980s. In any case, with the French government established at Vichy, a mere fifty-nine kilometers away, Clermont-Ferrand found itself thrust uncharacteristically close to the heart of the tragic course of French history between the summers of 1940 and 1944.

Indeed, for a fleeting moment, barely forty-eight hours of glory, Clermont was the capital of France. The first day of July 1940 local newspapers noted a beehive of activity as carpenters and decorators scrambled to refurbish the hotels and public buildings of Clermont-Ferrand and the adjoining suburbs of Royat and Chamalières. "Everywhere people are cleaning, polishing, washing, mending their rugs . . ."[3] The city was putting on this new face to accommodate President Albert Lebrun, Premier Philippe Pétain, Vice-Premier Pierre Laval, and other dignitaries of the French government, who, along with their staffs and services, were to be relocated at Clermont-Ferrand. Uprooted by the military disaster of 1940, the government had moved to Clermont following its departure from Bordeaux, an earlier temporary haven on the wandering road that was to lead from Paris to Vichy. Bordeaux had become unsuitable because it was included in the area of permanent occupation by German troops, but almost immediately Clermont-Ferrand also proved unacceptable because of a lack of adequate housing. Government officials concluded that concentration of most of the ministries at the resort town of Vichy was preferable to the inconvenience of spreading out government agencies from La Bourboule to Royat to Chatel-Guyon if the capital remained at Clermont-Ferrand.[4]

Undoubtedly, local boosters who, along with *Le Moniteur*'s editor, had been confident that the city was worthy of "this magnificent promotion"[5]

---

* Here, at the risk of a slight abuse of poetic license, I take my case to be typical.

to the rank of national capital were dismayed when a government spokesman announced that the ministers would be moving to Vichy. He added, perhaps as a sop to local sensibilities, that Clermont-Ferrand would remain the "official seat" of the government.[6] In fact, the administrative offices of several ministries, notably the headquarters of the military services, remained in the city until the liberation in 1944. Two days after the government left Clermont-Ferrand, *Le Moniteur's* editor, still grasping for straws of recognition, came up with this happy formula:

> The two cities are in reality one, the political capital of nonoccupied France, just as long ago when the High Court sat at Versailles, Paris and Versailles formed the French capital.
> It will be from Clermont-Ferrand–Vichy, double capital, that the government of Marshal Pétain will undertake the task of administering France, putting the country back to work, and rebuilding it.[7]

The editor of a competing newspaper, *La Montagne,* seeming to accept the disinvestiture more stoically, concluded:

> . . . The capital of the Auvergne reigned barely two days, hardly the time to savor the intoxication of power.
> What a disappointment![8]

In retrospect, Clermont-Ferrand was probably lucky to have avoided the distinction of serving as France's wartime capital. Its reputation for "coldness" and its isolation from the rest of France were enough to live down without the added opprobrium by association that might have resulted from hosting the governments of Pétain and Laval. In any case, the proximity of the French government during the German occupation of their country meant that the people of Clermont-Ferrand would experience those years as if they were at the center rather than on the periphery of national affairs.

In the summer of 1940 the flurry of activity surrounding the temporary presence of the government at Clermont may have helped to sweeten the bad taste left in Clermontois mouths by the brief German occupation of their city during the week of 21–28 June. This temporary visit by German troops, which had followed minor skirmishes outside of the town, was Clermont-Ferrand's closest encounter with the war in 1940, and it gave little indication of the ultimate consequences for the local population of France's defeat. Until November 1942 Clermont was to remain in the unoccupied or "free" zone, under French sovereignty without the direct supervision or intervention of German occupation authorities. Even during 1943 and 1944, with German police and troops stationed in the city, it might be argued that Clermont-Ferrand was *relatively* unscathed by the occupation. To be sure, Clermont was an important center for the resistance's shadow war against the Germans. Occasional attacks on the occupying troops led to the imposition of curfews and more serious reprisals, including arrests, deportations, and executions. In the spring of 1944 Allied aircraft bombed the airfield at Aulnat and destroyed a substantial part of the Michelin factory, entailing the loss of civilian lives. The occupation authorities could, and did, act with brutality, as in their raid on the University of Strasbourg's faculty and students in the fall of 1943. However, measured by the destruction of whole sections of a town—as was the case for Marseille's Old Port and the coastal towns in the path of the Allied invasion in 1944—Clermont-Ferrand and its residents bore less of the *direct* costs of defeat and occupation than was the case for those French cities more exposed to large-scale military engagements and four years of total occupation.[9]

Placing Clermont's wartime experience in such a comparative perspective is not intended to minimize the hardships or suffering faced by the city's population. As will be demonstrated, these were enormous. The designation *Zone Libre* did not mean that the populations of Clermont-Ferrand and the other cities in southern France were free from the consequences of France's defeat. The impact of the war and defeat were felt most directly and immediately in the absence of more than 3000 prisoners of war from the city and its suburbs. More than 16,000 POWs were from the department of the Puy-de-Dôme.[10] Fewer than one-fifth of these men were released and returned to Clermont-Ferrand before the liberation. Uncertainty and fears about the well-being of husbands, sons, and fathers were constant companions for the families of those who did not come home for five long years. In terms of the city's population, these men were "replaced" at once by a flood of refugees from the north.

Le Moniteur of 22 August 1940 described the exodus of May–June 1940 as "the largest population movement recorded in many centuries" and noted that the population of the eight departments of central France had almost doubled because of the influx of 1.4 million refugees. By mid-July thirty-five welcome centers and hundreds of individuals at Clermont-Ferrand were offering food and shelter to 27,000 refugee families. Within several months, most of the more than 180,000 refugees who arrived at Clermont-Ferrand during the exodus returned to their homes or went elsewhere. In the fall of 1940 the Vichy government supplied free rail transportation for those who wished to return to northern France. Notices published in local newspapers through the fall and even later, however, indicated that many children separated from their families in May and June still had not located their relatives. The thousands of refugees who remained in Clermont-Ferrand throughout the war, when added to the staffs of the newly arrived ministries, seriously taxed the abilities of the city to house and feed them all. Despite Vichy's eventual attempts to expel Jewish and foreign residents[11] and frequent fluctuations in population, Clermont-Ferrand was overcrowded throughout the war with between 30,000 and 60,000 new inhabitants.[12]

In addition to the absence of the prisoners of war and the overcrowding of cities, one of the most visible and disruptive signs of France's defeat was the line of demarcation that separated occupied France from the area controlled by the Vichy regime. The major crossing point closest to Clermont-Ferrand was located at Moulins, north of Vichy. Before its suppression on 1 March 1943 (after Pierre Laval's announcement in February 1943 that French men would be drafted for labor service in Germany), this boundary was a major irritant to the French. Because their country was divided by closely watched internal frontiers, they were forced to communicate with friends, relatives, or business associates on regulation postcards and letters subject to German interception and censorship. During the first year of the occupation, travel between the two zones was restricted severely by German authorities, and occasionally traffic was cut off entirely to pressure the French in negotiations concerning the application of the Armistice terms. The removal of the demarcation line was hailed by Laval as concrete evidence of the benefits of Vichy's policy of collaboration with the Germans. In fact, the Germans had realized for some time that although manipulation of the line might be useful for blackmail in negotiations with the French, its existence, by disrupting the normal flow of commerce within France, hampered their ability to milk the French economy to Germany's benefit. Therefore, this "concession" was no more than Germany's recognition that the line no longer made sense in view of the total occupation. Their "magnanimous" gesture followed directly from what their economic specialists had realized for months to be in their own interest.[13] All the same, residents of Clermont-Ferrand welcomed the change after more than two and one-half years of limited access to the north, and in March 1943 police reported "a stampede of clients" requesting validation or renewal of identity papers required for travel.[14]

Concerned about the POWs, burdened by refugees, and annoyed by the demarcation line, the Clermontois were nonetheless pleased that their city was free from occupation troops until November 1942. Although psychologically significant, this fact temporarily obscured the extent to which the city's economy and society would be affected by the defeat and occupation of France. During their brief passage through the Puy-de-Dôme and the Allier in June 1940, German troops had confiscated large stocks of rubber from the Michelin, Bergougnan, and Dunlop tire factories and had taken a few cattle from local farmers. These direct seizures were of little consequence to the local economy when compared to the indirect impact of occupation payments, currency manipulation, and other methods by which the Germans harnessed the French economy to their war effort. Other writers have demonstrated how successful Germany was in exploiting French resources on a national scale.[15] By one estimate, in 1943 France had become "the most important supplier of raw materials, foodstuffs, and manufactured goods to the German economy," supplying goods and services roughly equivalent to one-quarter of Germany's gross national product.[16] The French often misunderstood the mechanics of this not-so-subtle pillage of their country, but they were soon acutely aware of its meaning for their everyday lives.

If the collective memory of the war years in Clermont-Ferrand could be reduced arbitrarily to one word, that one word might be shortage (*la disette*). The most important shortages, in terms of their effect on the local economy, were of raw materials, energy, and labor. Influenced by shortages in these three domains, industry and agriculture both experienced a marked decline in productivity from prewar levels. The Michelin Company, the area's most important industrial concern, is one example; even before it was shut down in 1944 by Allied bombs, Michelin employed less than two-thirds of its prewar work force, and production was down by at least 40 percent.[17] Counting a high percentage of the department's POWs among their number, in 1942 farmers in the countryside surrounding Clermont-Ferrand produced only two-thirds as many horses, one-half the pork, and one-half of the potatoes and wheat that they had in 1939.[18] Engineers at St. Eloy and La Bouble reported mining productivity per working day down 14 and 17 percent respectively from prewar levels.[19] A complete survey of every component of industry and commerce in the Puy-de-Dôme would reveal variations in performance, but the overall pattern was one of significant decline.

Although in a fundamental way the Clermontois were not mistaken in their belief that the Germans were responsible for France's economic woes, the situation was more complex than the popular image of thousands of railroad cars hauling off tons of booty to Germany.[20] Already during the period of the "phony war" (*drôle de guerre*), the disruption of the normal flow of commerce and the requirements of the war effort had begun a transformation of the local economy that was to be accelerated dramatically as a consequence of the defeat and occupation. The relative prosperity or failure of a given business was linked more or less clearly to these changing conditions.

In some cases, there was simply no longer a strong demand for the goods or services offered. The health spas at Royat, La Bourboule, Saint-Nectaire, and other thermal centers in the region experienced precipitous drops in the number of clients and their families who were so crucial to the economic well-being of the hotels, restaurants, and related facilities that depended on the tourist business. In September 1942 the police commissioner for Chamalières-Royat reported that during the past summer season only 2000 guests had come to Royat for treatment, in contrast to a prewar average of 8000; the mayor of La Bourboule said that business in his town was off by one-half for that same period. Appealing to the prefect of the Puy-de-Dôme for economic assistance, hotelkeepers and representatives of the thermal business at Saint-Nectaire claimed that health spas in the Auvergne had lost almost 80 percent of their clientele in 1940 and 1941. Later reports confirmed this state of affairs, and only the influx of refugees from the north and the resettlement of Jewish families in several of the spas maintained to some extent the economies of those communities dependent on "thermalism."[21]

In other cases, the demand for products remained high, but critical shortages of raw materials and electricity prevented adequate production. At Clermont-Ferrand this situation was characteristic of the garment industry. Recognizing that France produced few of the raw materials necessary for making textiles, the minister of industrial production had begun rationing of these products even before the fall of France. After the institution of the Vichy regime and throughout the war years, the shortage of cotton and other raw materials for textiles remained acute. Month after month local police reports noted that Conchon-Quinette, Benech et Maury, Peyronnet, and other garment manufacturers at Clermont were unable to secure the materials necessary to maintain their normal production. On those rare occasions when stocks of raw materials were satisfactory, production was hamstrung by restrictions on electric power. Thus, in February 1942 Conchon-Quinette, which employed more than 500 workers, was operating only 25 hours per week, and its sales department was open only three out of six days because of shortages of materials. In October of the same year stocks of material were considered adequate, but the sewing shop was closed three days a week because of a lack of power. By August 1942 the rationing of energy for factories had restricted consumption of electricity to 65 percent of the normal levels. Small wonder, then, that shopkeepers complained they had nothing to display in their stores, and even when they had the obligatory ration coupons, consumers often learned to their dismay that they could not buy clothing and shoes. A persistent shortage of consumer goods meant that an unrelenting malaise plagued Clermont-Ferrand's shopkeepers throughout the war years.[22]

The printing business was another example of an industry affected by shortages of raw materials. The shortages of paper were reflected not only in the problems of book and newspaper publishers but also in the scarcity of writing tablets for schoolchildren, directives ordering government officials to reduce the length and frequency of reports, and sarcastic comments from the public about the flowering of *affiches* (posters) on the city's walls when the government was calling for conservation of paper. On the other hand, the Banque de France's 1700 well-paid employees at Chamalières worked overtime, printing the francs needed by the Vichy government to pay the heavy occupation costs; and some of Clermont's printers—notably *Le Moniteur,* owned by Pierre Laval—benefited from the relocation of several newspapers from the occupied zone that used the presses at Clermont-Ferrand.[23]

Many other organizations and enterprises moved to Clermont from Paris or elsewhere in northern France during the exodus. One of the most important was the transfer, during the "phony war" period, of the faculty, staff, and students of the University of Strasbourg to Clermont, where they shared facilities with the city's own university. Some of these newcomers brought employment or revenue opportunities to the area, but in purely economic terms, the benefits probably were outweighed by problems associated with the overcrowding of the city.

When local officials looked to the French government for relief and assistance with their multiple economic problems, they were usually disappointed. With its ability to influence developments in northern France extremely limited, and facing huge occupation payments of 20 million reichsmarks a day,[24] Vichy had few resources to commit to public works projects of any sort. Moreover, one idea behind the regime's administrative reforms was to shift more economic responsibility back onto the local and regional governments. Consequently, appeals for assistance, from requests for wood to make coffins for public burials to grandiose schemes to rebuild large sections of Clermont-Ferrand (as proposed by the head of the Légion des Combattants at Clermont), were routinely met with rejections beginning with the phrase, "due to present shortages."[25]

Unable to provide concrete assistance to its people, the Vichy regime urged them to be ingenious and inventive. The French are reputed to be masters of the system "d"—from the word *débrouiller,* "to make do," "to get by," or "to improvise." Seeking to draw on this trait, in May 1941 the minister of the economy and finances instructed his representatives in southern France to urge local industrialists to innovate by introducing new raw materials, new products, and new methods of production, to create "replacement industries" as one way out of France's serious economic crisis; the minister concluded that "obviously we have to adapt."[26]

According to the prefect of the Puy-de-Dôme, entrepreneurs at Clermont-Ferrand had not awaited this exhortation from the government to begin transforming and diversifying their businesses. In December 1940 the prefect cited local production of *gazogènes* (charcoal-burning engines mounted on automobiles), bicycle accessories, and woodstoves, and the exploitation of local forests for charcoal and reeds for cellulose.[27] By January 1942 Conchon-Quinette had begun to produce an artificial fiber, *Fibranne,* as a substitute for unobtainable raw materials, and local officials hoped that this would breathe new life into the depressed garment industry.[28] The Puy-de-Dôme is heavily wooded, so a turn to the forests for fuel was one logical expression of the system "d" at work in the Auvergne, but because police reports continued to note shortages of fuel throughout the occupation, this example also points to the limits on France's capacity to make do.

In the fall of 1941 the prefect of the Puy-de-Dôme instructed a committee charged with the regulation of coal and gas distribution to devise a comprehensive system of coal coupons to control more effectively the distribution of fuel. The committee's solution was to divide consumers into three residential categories: forested communes, semiforested communes, and nonforested communes. The system was designed to force the rural population to turn to the forests for fuel if they had not done so already. No coal was to be alloted for the first category except for hospitals. Consumers in the second category would have their allotment reduced by one-half, and only consumers in the nonforested category would continue to received the full allotment. This solution seemed to be reasonable, but it overlooked the shortage of the labor necessary to transform *potential* fuel into heating for homes and factories. The head of the Departmental Coal Committee reported that 72 million tons of coal had been consumed in the Puy-de-Dôme in 1937–1938, but a significant part of that had been imported and was no longer available. Current production covered at best 62 percent of the department's requirements. Therefore, in recommending obligatory coal coupons for all consumers, the official advised: "We must have a 'Controlled Distribution' for an extended period of time."[29]

The rationing of gas, food, clothing, and other essential consumer goods responded to this same inescapable logic. Confronted with serious shortages in every domain, lacking the funds to stimulate a depressed economy with public works, and finding that synthetic, ersatz substitutes were at best partial palliatives for major declines in productivity, the Vichy regime was forced to resort to a sort of "distributive socialism" (although Vichy's leaders surely would not have called it that), in which the aim became to allot relative degrees of suffering in a more or less equitable manner.[30] This move, of course, enhanced the importance and visibility of the various regulatory organizations, which, not surprisingly in a period of extreme hardship, were severely criticized by an unhappy public. From this perspective one might argue that what passed for "economic planning" at Vichy originated not so much from the fertile minds of theoreticians in Vichy's

Economic Ministry as from the needs of local communities whose representatives were calling urgently for such measures.

There is bitter irony in the fact that where visible improvement in the local economic situation could be seen, it often came from the hands of those who were responsible for the problems to begin with—the Germans. In a monthly report for June 1943, Clermont-Ferrand's central police commissioner observed that "only those industries working for the public administration or for the Occupation Authorities are relatively healthy."[31] This observation was confirmed by an informant who told British intelligence officials in Lisbon that when he left Clermont in 1942, the Michelin factory was very quiet, whereas Bergougnan was busy day and night, reconditioning rubber and retreading tires. His explanation for this contrast was that members of the Michelin family were serving with de Gaulle. Consequently the firm was receiving no orders from either French or German authorities.[32] In fact, the informant's evaluation was only partially, or temporarily, correct. Although British intelligence and the Germans seemed to agree that "one of the strongest leaders of resistance in the country was Monsieur Michelin,"[33] as early as October 1941 the Michelin Company was negotiating with German authorities for contracts that would provide German *buna,* an artificial substitute for the rubber Michelin could no longer obtain from plantations in Indochina and Malaysia. By the time Allied bombers struck the factory in March 1944, German orders accounted for 80 percent of Michelin's production.[34]

What was true for the rubber industry, the region's most important business, was equally valid for other manufacturing establishments. Businesses that produced goods of value to Germany found markets open to them; others did not. Among the relatively prosperous industries were several cutlery manufacturers at Thiers and mechanical and metalworking plants such as Ducellier at Issoire, Aubert et Duval at Les Ancizes, and Ollier at Clermont-Ferrand. Even some nonindustrial concerns did fairly well, such as the region's confiture, candied-fruit, and chocolate producers, whose products appealed to the German soldier's sweet tooth. In April 1942 one of Clermont's police commissioners noted that Ollier had more orders than it could fill. Indeed, German economic officials in the area reported that there was seldom a problem finding parties to contracts for German orders. Instead, the problem from the German point of view was that low productivity meant that orders were rarely filled completely or on time. After they had occupied Clermont-Ferrand, the Germans designated certain establishments as priority factories in hope of increasing productivity (and thus their capacity for exploitation). As was true in the rest of France, these factories were favored in obtaining raw materials, rail transport, and electrical energy, and they were shielded from the loss of skilled workers to the forced labor draft. Even before the occupation of southern France, the situation was in essence fixed. An active business meant a business that was in some way, directly or indirectly, working for Germany.[35]

This fact complicated the task of postwar courts, as it does that of today's historians, in dealing with the sensitive issue of collaboration. By the time the work of the Committee for the Confiscation of Illicit Profits for the department of the Puy-de-Dôme was finished in 1948, it had examined almost 1500 cases of individuals or companies accused either of black-market profiteering or economic collaboration with the Germans. The committee levied fines totaling more than 840 million francs. Almost one third of that amount was assessed for a single blackmarketeer, and fines ranged from a few thousand to 250 million francs. Individuals and enterprises of all sorts were touched by these decisions. One list of 281 persons affected in the Puy-de-Dôme included 47 cutlery manufacturers, 36 persons involved in agriculture, 20 butchers, 16 auto mechanics, as well as the Michelin and Bergougnan rubber works. The evidence available makes clear that postwar judgments concerning economic collaboration varied widely from locality to locality. In the Puy-de-Dôme, for instance, many more cases were brought before the courts for Clermont-Ferrand and Thiers than for Issoire, a fact that cannot be explained readily by differences in size or industrial activity. Clearly, investigators and courts differed about what constituted economic collaboration; but in general black-marketers were viewed much more negatively than were owners of factories who kept their establishments running in the interests of the local economy and attempted to protect their workers from deportation to Germany.[36]

Such a judgment was consonant with the opinions of most local police officials who during the era of the occupation portrayed local industrialists favorably for their behavior with regard to their employees. In 1941 and later, when factories were forced to shut down for weeks at a time because of power shortages, Michelin and other companies in the area paid 85 percent of the normal salary to workers who had to be laid off, for which they were later reimbursed by the government. When the Germans occupied southern France, one officer at Clermont-Ferrand remarked: "Certain employers are making praiseworthy efforts to avoid the shutdown of their plants and unemployment for their workers: for example, they credit their workers with forty-two hours of labor, when in fact these employees are working only about twenty hours."[37] He added that several companies were giving bonuses to their workers to try to compensate for the sharp rise in food prices, but all of them did not have the means to make that kind of a sacrifice.

An investigation of the metallurgical factories at Clermont-Ferrand in

the summer of 1943 revealed that relations between workers and management resembled a peculiar sort of honeymoon in contrast to their normally
stormy relationship. The conditions of the occupation and the economic
dislocation it had brought to Clermont-Ferrand meant that they approached
the situation from a similar frame of mind. Neither group liked political
collaboration and both were resolutely opposed to the forced labor draft,
which they hoped to defeat through passive resistance.[38] In reality, what
practical alternative did a French factory owner have to keeping his business going by taking up German contracts? Refusal to cooperate might
mean confiscation of the factory's material stocks and equipment for shipment to Germany; by 1943 it definitely would have threatened the workers
with transfer to Germany under the forced labor draft. For now, suffice it
to say that choices were not simple and without consequence in occupied
France.

We have seen in brief outline how the local economy was affected by the
defeat and occupation of France. Serious shortages of raw materials and
electric power, substantial reductions in the production and circulation of
goods, dependence on German orders—all contributed to a precarious state
of affairs. How did these circumstances relate to the day-to-day life of the
average citizen who spent the war years in Clermont-Ferrand? In May
1941 a police commissioner at Clermont wrote: "One can say without
reservation that the chief preoccupation of the public—a matter that certainly will have a vital importance—is the question of food supply."[39] And
in the fall of that year the minister of the interior, commenting on public
opinion concerning conditions in all of southern France concluded that

> it is dominated essentially—some prefects go so far as to write in their re-
> ports "uniquely"—by material concerns, centering always on the same ob-
> jects: food, heating, clothing, shoes.
> How will we make it through the winter?[40]

These same concerns were expressed again and again throughout the occupation era, and they point to a fundamental aspect of the history of
wartime France. These were years of extreme hardship for most French
citizens.

One should not be misled by the amusing but completely atypical example in *The Sorrow and the Pity* of the pharmacist who claimed to have
made his son fat by overfeeding him as a baby during the occupation.[41]
Most Clermontois, and most of the French, had no means for such indulgence. As indicated by a report on the status of food supplies at Clermont-
Ferrand, the milk available in August 1943 for baby bottles was more apt
to make children sick than fat!

> During these past few months two so-called *fresh* eggs were allotted per
> person, but many homemakers were forced to throw out their allotment

because the eggs were rotten. Once again the ration tickets for butter and oil were not fully honored. The milk which is distributed to children arrives many times completely sour and the young children are deprived entirely of their principal source of nourishment. The mothers of these children are highly critical and demand that very energetic measures be taken to remedy this situation.[42]

In March 1941 local officials calculated that 62 percent of an average household budget in Clermont was spent on food, but even with such a disproportionate expenditure, families were unable to obtain balanced or adequate meals.[43]

Evidence for a significant problem with malnutrition in the Puy-de-Dôme was abundant. A report from the rector of the academy at Clermont-Ferrand documented a drop in the average weight of the city's school children. Therefore, beginning in December 1942 vegetable soup was served at eleven o'clock in local schools to supplement the students' diets.[44] Schoolchildren were also given cheese crackers, vitamins, evaporated milk, and chocolate supplied by the French Secours National and the American Red Cross.[45] Children were not the only ones to suffer from food shortages. The departmental medical service, reporting on its activity for March 1943, cited levels of tuberculosis twice the prewar totals and noted the generally poor health of workers in their twenties: "Can one see already in the 46 cases of tuberculosis and in the 72 cases of workers exempted for generally poor condition (weight below 45 kilograms) the first consequences of the restrictions?"[46] Work-related accidents, blamed on fatigue and undernourishment, were on the rise.[47]

After the occupation of southern France in November 1942, popular resentment about food shortages and high prices was often directed at the German officers who ate in restaurants whose prices placed them out of the reach of most French citizens; many people grumbled about the special treatment received by French government officials and officers of the Armistice army who seemed to be fed well in the mess halls provided for them.[48] As a police agent at Vichy remarked, "People are beginning to ask whether or not there are two categories of persons: those who eat in the mess halls and are well fed, and those who eat at home and are poorly fed."[49] The basic problem of food shortages in a region that, after all, had an important agricultural sector was that production of food was down by at least 30 percent at a time when the population of the region had increased dramatically. There simply was not enough food to go around.

The government sought to cope as best it could with this problem by instituting a rationing system. Begun in 1940 and expanded rapidly, it applied eventually to virtually all foods and other consumer goods. Expectant and nursing women, workers in jobs requiring heavy physical exertion, and returning prisoners of war were among those who were granted supplementary rations. Identification cards in a variety of categories, coupons, and tickets were required in order to purchase each month's allotment of eggs, bread, butter, meat, vegetables, and so forth, but having the proper coupons was no guarantee that one could obtain these products.[50]

At six o'clock early one morning in March 1941, approximately 100 people were waiting in line outside the butcher shop at N° 45, boulevard Lafayette in Clermont-Ferrand. Monsieur Licheron, the owner, opened his door at six-thirty, and by seven o'clock all of his meat was gone and most of his customers had to be turned away empty-handed. Earlier the butcher had gone to six different markets in towns around Clermont to secure what little meat he had to sell. Recounting this incident, a local police officer warned that the food situation was potentially a very serious threat to public order.[51] Indeed, the regional *L'Humanité* of 6 April 1941 reported a demonstration at Montferrand by angry housewives demanding food. Witness to numerous such incidents in the following months, by early 1942 the Vichy government was seriously concerned about food riots. In January Pierre Pucheu, minister of the interior, issued firm orders for the energetic suppression of any disturbance of that sort.[52]

At the local level, officials prohibited newspapers from publishing anything about the food riots, attempted to spread the hours of food distribution over a longer period of time in order to reduce conspicuous waiting lines, and stationed police guards in the Marché Saint-Pierre, Clermont-Ferrand's central market, to keep order in the lines and report daily about conditions in the market. In view of the recurrent failure of local markets to fill ration quotas for staple items, police at the Marché Saint-Pierre marveled at the patience of shoppers who were turned away repeatedly and told to return the next day. Even though these daily reports from Clermont's central market emphasized the admirable restraint of the city's often frustrated shoppers, local police remained very nervous about the potential for food riots.[53]

Elaborate security precautions ordered in March 1942 for ceremonies intended to highlight the work of the Secours National in collecting food for the needy illustrated both the seriousness of food shortages and the government's anxiety about them. Noting that perhaps 150 trucks filled with food would arrive in Clermont-Ferrand for the ceremony, local police feared: "Such an apparent abundance of food of every sort, if we do not take certain precautions, might arouse diverse reactions from a population which, this winter, has often found itself before empty shelves in local shops." Consequently, police were ordered to observe the following rules:

1. Avoid all stopping of loaded trucks on public streets.
2. Keep all food in a closed and guarded depot.
3. Explain through the press that

"(a) this impressive quantity is only a drop of water in terms of the general food supply for the country.

(b) it is destined only for the needy.

(c) it represents the effort of farmers from all over France and it must be distributed widely."

4. Noticeably improve the soup kitchens and the distribution of food-stuffs during the following days.

5. Publicize this event *after* rather than before ceremony.[54]

Hoping to avoid serious disturbances, in subsequent months the prefect occasionally intervened to release emergency stocks of food from the Secours National depots at Royat after reports of incidents or rising tensions in local markets.[55] Riots might not have been avoided had the public at Clermont-Ferrand realized in October 1943 that there were 400 tons of foodstuffs, "for the most part products that were impossible to find in the marketplace" (patés, chocolate, coffee, etc.), in warehouses at the Casino of Royat.[56]

If the Clermontois complained most often about food shortages and the poor quality of the food they did receive—by February 1943 the "coffee" they were drinking was only 10 percent coffee[57]—shortages of other consumer items were equally severe, if less critical from a health standpoint. Particularly during the harvesting season, but throughout the year as well, local authorities registered complaints about restrictions on wine, and tobacco shortages infuriated smokers. As indicated by the earlier discussion of problems of garment manufacturers in the city, clothing was in short supply. Shoes were especially difficult to replace, despite a resort to leather substitutes. Each Christmas season during the occupation, parents grumbled hopeless, pathetic protests about their inability to find toys for their children.[58]

Had products been more abundant, many families would not have been able to purchase them. Confronted by shortages of all goods, the Vichy government was much less successful at controlling prices than it was at regulating wages. Consequently, the gap between wages and prices was an ever-widening one, and the average family experienced a steady erosion of its standard of living. The uncertainty of statistical evidence for the occupation era makes a precise mathematical calculation difficult, but police and Légion officials at Clermont-Ferrand agreed that by the end of 1942 the average worker had lost roughly 80 percent of prewar purchasing power.[59] Based on the situation of workers at the Michelin Company, Légion officials concluded that a minimum budget for a family of four in Clermont-Ferrand as of December 1942 would require 3500 francs per month.[60] Assuming the conclusions of the Légion study to be reasonably accurate, and comparing them to the wages earned in 1942 by workers in a wide variety of occupations (see table), it is obvious that most workers

Examples of Wages at Clermont-Ferrand, 1942–1943
(wages given in French francs)

Banque de France/Chamalières (1650 employees)
   Printers of the French currency, these white-collar workers were in essence civil servants (*fonctionnaires*) and were very well paid
           15,000–25,000F per month

 Apprentices at the Banque de France received 6F25 per hour

Brewery: Grand Brasserie et Malteries d'Auvergne (35 employees)
   Driver/deliveryman   1900F per month
   Brewer/supervisor   2500F per month
   Mechanic   1814F per month
   Worker   6F25 per hour
   Barrel maker   10F50 per hour

Chocolate Manufacturer: Chocolaterie de Royat
   Boys up to 18 years old   4F30–6F20
   Girls up to 18 years old   3F45–4F60
   Women more than 18 years old 5F30–5F40

Food Products: Banania (57 employees)
   Female worker   6F per hour
   Male worker   8F per hour
   Office worker   1350F per month

Casino
   Truck driver   1705F per month
   Male hourly worker   9F30 per hour
   Female hourly worker   7F20 per hour

Garment Workers: Conchon-Quinette (521 employees)
   Seamstress/tailor   1280–1470F per month
   Sewing machine operator 1350F per month
   Liner   1200F per month
   Male hourly worker   10F50 per hour
   Female hourly worker   6F50 per hour

Manufacture des Chapeaux (135 employees)
   Male officer worker   1300–1800F per month
   Female office worker   1300–1600F per month
   Male hourly worker   11F per hour
   Female hourly worker   8–9F per hour

Hydroelectric workers: Cie. Hydro-Electrique (1070 employees)

   Office employees   1665–2646F per month
   Workers   7F86–11F per hour

 This company gave its employees a 3000F "avance d'approvisionnement" plus an 8 percent salary advance in 1943

Journalism:　*L'Avenir* (170 employees), *La Montagne,* and *Le Moniteur* (375 employees)

Editor-in-chief	8850F	per month
Editor with bylines	5700F	per month
Photographer/reporter	4750F	per month
Printer	2640–5000F	per month
Engraver and offset print operator	3315–5000F	per month

In general, workers at *Le Moniteur* were at the top end of the scale, while workers for the other newspapers were less well paid; this was be-because *Le Moniteur*'s presses were used for other publications and were in operation more hours

Metalworkers:　Ollier (500 employees) and Ateliers de Construction du Centre (407 employees) had the same wage scale

Unskilled worker	7F99	per hour
Highest-skilled worker	12F63	per hour

Ateliers de Mécanique du Centre (metallurgy and aeronautical construction) (200 employees)

Low to high-skilled worker	7F99–11F81	per hour

The company gave a 12–15 percent bonus to all personnel in 1943

Pingeot (metal and automobile accessories) (200 employees)

Male worker	7F98	per hour
Female worker	6F93	per hour

Personnel at the Prefecture

Range from 1400F (women) or 1500F (men) to a maximum of 3250F per month for an employee with 17 years service, covering all sorts of office workers from typists to machine operators

Retail Sales Personnel:　Galaries de Jaude (220 employees)

Salesman	1500F	per month
Saleswoman	1250F	per month
Department supervisor	2000–2600F	per month
Floor supervisor	2500–3500F	per month

Rubber-Working Companies:　Michelin (7000 employees)

Clermont-Ferrand's largest business, traditionally a paternalistic, family-run organization with elaborate benefits for workers (including housing, with reduced rent for families with several children; medical care; schools; daycare; and so forth), that were well beyond the norms for France, but base salaries were not high, as the management admitted in 1943

Unskilled or low-skilled worker	10–16F	per hour
High-skilled worker	2000F	per month

SEA (rubber contractor) (150 employees)

Male worker	9F50	per hour
Female worker	7F	per hour
Upkeep personnel	10–11F	per hour

The company paid two bonuses of 500F to its workers in 1942

required two incomes, or means beyond their monthly pay, to feed, clothe, and house their families. To meet the minimum requirement a worker had to make between 13.5 and 17 francs per hour, assuming an eight- to ten-hour workday, six days per week. With the exception of highly skilled metalworkers, some printers, and the best-paid Michelin employees, few workers at Clermont-Ferrand made more than 10 francs per hour. Bank clerks, sales personnel, and employees in the garment industry and in food processing were particularly disadvantaged. The chocolate factory at Royat seemed to have paid the lowest wages in the area; like every business without exception, it paid girls and women less than boys and men.

Even when supplemented by occasional cost-of-living bonuses and modest "family allocations" (in keeping with Vichy's emphasis on the family), wages never caught up with the rapid rise in prices. Among the most striking reflections of the seriousness of the problem of rising prices were instructions sent out in the fall of 1943 to schoolteachers concerning a revision of their mathematics texts. Observing that a glance through the old math problems where one bought and sold land or cloth at discount prices and eggs by the dozen was, in the present circumstances, "at once amusing and heartbreaking," the author of *L'Ecole et la famille* indicated that after several efforts to adjust figures in the examples to conform with actual prices, the editors had given up. The latest edition would leave to the students the task of assigning values to the products used in their homework and examinations. Finding virtue in shortcoming, the author seemed delighted that this change would bring the student closer to real life: "He will know the price of things, and starting from there, how important it is to economize."[61]

Filling out the picture offered by abstracts from the available statistical data, throughout the years of war and occupation, police reports bore eloquent witness to the difficult material circumstances of the average family at Clermont-Ferrand. Recurrent references to the black market, to barter, and to family gardens underlined the variety of strategems employed by the Clermontois and other French people to cope with a persistent shortage of income, services, and goods. In November 1941 the minister of the interior, summarizing conditions in all of southern France, wrote: "The tendency already noted of substituting barter for the normal sale of products seems to be spreading and extends currently to individuals: merchandise for food, food for labor, such is the system used more and more, an alarming sign of the depreciation of our currency."[62] A few months before the arrival of occupation troops at Clermont-Ferrand, a local official noted: "The situation of numerous households, workers or lower civil servants has become truly precarious in the face of the unbroken rise in the cost of living. . . . The situation would be disastrous had there not been created happily at Clermont-Ferrand numerous workers' gardens which are helping to overcome many difficulties."[63] He added later: "For many products the black market has become the only market. . . . Potatoes are impossible to find. One never sees them in the regular markets because of the regulated prices that have been set . . . really much too low. What is abundant is sold at very high prices, what is rare is still higher."[64]

A month after the Germans arrived in town, another police officer reported: "The working class . . . and in a general manner . . . those retired on modest incomes . . . are suffering more and more. . . . The basic necessities are being sold at higher and higher prices and will soon be entirely beyond their means."[65] The following spring Clermont-Ferrand's central police commissioner remarked: "Modest households, which are the most numerous, wonder anxiously how they will be able to provide for themselves if this vertiginous rise in prices is not stopped."[66] A year later the commissioner recorded further deterioration: "Salaried employees of every class complain bitterly that their pay is no longer in line with the cost of living."[67] The commissioner passed along to the regional prefect a subordinate's indignant comment concerning the "véritable scandale" of women's hats priced in excess of 2000 francs, more than a month's wages for many workers.[68]

These crucial issues of food, minimum income for basic necessities, and a host of problems related to them plagued the French and their local governmental and administrative representatives throughout the occupation era. Everyone knew that the black market existed and was flourishing.[69] One observer even claimed that by the fall of 1942 the black market was "the only market at Clermont-Ferrand."[70] What was to be done about it? From time to time the Vichy regime attempted to crack down on the black market, and in a given month, the number of arrests, fines, and internments for black-marketeering might be impressive.[71] In January 1943 police at Clermont-Ferrand rushed to the municipal theater to warn Jean Maupoint, a popular entertainer, that he absolutely could not sing verses with references to the black market. Maupoint had improvised a song entitled, "Old Memories: Letter from a Clermontois in 1953 to one of his Parisian friends who long ago (1943) was a refugee in the Auvergne," which included this refrain:

> In that sad time long ago
> We bought one evening
> A beautiful ham
> 3000 francs on the Black Market . . . ![72]

Presumably unable (or unwilling) to curb his wit entirely, poor Maupoint was arrested two months later by the Germans for singing verses "offensive" to the occupation troops. But controls and searches by the economic police antagonized many French men and women—all the more when it appeared that only the minor offenders, a censored *chanteur* like Maupoint or Jean-Pierre returning to the city from his cousin's farm with a dozen eggs, were being punished, while the major black-marketers went their way unscathed, occasionally with protection from influential German or French clients.

Stressing that the government opposed anything that disturbed or agitated the country unnecessarily, and reacting to widespread criticism of the behavior of its economic police, in the spring and summer of 1942 Vichy announced a major reorganization of that service and ordered its agents to ignore "benign infractions" of the ration control laws and to concentrate on important cases. Admitting "regrettable errors which have led to the abuse of searches and domestic visits," René Bousquet, Vichy's general police secretary, decreed that only the prefects could authorize searches of private homes.[73] Failure to obey this regulation would mean immediate removal from office of any police official. This decision represented a compromise with the reality of an era of hardship. The government was in essence recognizing that circumstances influenced and limited behavior and choices. If the local butcher or grocer could not supply meat or potatoes to satisfy the meager allowances of the ration tickets, one looked elsewhere.

Circumstances were such that farmers were often suspected of reaping huge profits from the black market, and in 1941 the prefect at Clermont-Ferrand feared threats to public order from growing tension between urban and rural residents.[74] In fact, although there were surely exceptions to the rule, most farmers were hard-pressed to make ends meet even when they disposed of a part of their produce on the black market. Légion surveys of agriculture in the Auvergne indicated that the costs of production for agriculture rose more sharply than the official prices, and that overall agricultural production was down by as much as one-third during the occupation era. The cost for fodder to nurture cattle and hogs exceeded the official prices allowed by the government for the sale of those animals, which explains why farmers either stopped producing them or held them off the official market. While government ministers were calling for discipline and respect for the law, farmers complained that those same men were sending out trucks whose drivers hectored farmers in the Allier and the Puy-de-Dôme to deliver illegal food for the tables of the ministers and their friends at Vichy. Unable to receive a fair return for their fresh milk through legal sales, small wonder that many farmers preferred to turn it into cheese that could be more easily disposed of on the black market. Police officials and mothers of children in the cities who needed the milk were upset, of course, but farmers also had to try to make a living for their familes.[75]

Meanwhile in the cities many people sought to supplement their diets by setting out small vegetable gardens or fattening rabbits in their homes. Michelin and some of the other large employers owning land in Clermont-Ferrand and the region provided garden plots for cultivation by their workers. Although these gardens undoubtedly benefited many families, they led to new problems of law and order for the local police. In August 1942 the intendant de police informed the mayor of Clermont-Ferrand that he had ordered increased surveillance for garden plots in and around the city.[76] This decision followed reports of a sharp rise in thefts of food from the gardens and threats from owners of the plots to take the law into their own hands. Police at Clermont-Ferrand were convinced that a dramatic rise in the number of petty crimes was a "direct consequence of shortages." One officer claimed: "The curve representing thefts of food, clothing, or bicycles would be parabola."[77]

Less widespread, but more serious, and reflecting the potential for vicious behavior in an exceptionally distraught society, was the appearance of letters of denunciation, usually unsigned. Most of these letters concerned matters of food supply or the black market, and their authors often suggested that the persons in question were communists or Jews. In later stages of the occupation the German police offered 5000 francs for the denunciation of forced labor draft deserters or persons involved in the resistance. The French police did not encourage anonymous denunciations, in part because the majority of such tips, upon investigation, were revealed to have originated in personal jealousies or commercial rivalries and seldom led the police to the discovery of serious criminal behavior. In January 1942 the regional prefect sent a letter to the mayors of the Auvergne urging them to discourage such actions: "These practices create an unacceptable environment of suspicion and risk to sow discord among the French people at a moment when the country needs to preserve intact all of its moral forces to ensure its recovery."[78] In February the prefect ordered local newspapers to publish a notice warning that anonymous denunciations were to be treated as serious offenses and that the police would track down the authors with all means at their disposal. At that time (early 1942) the prefect stated that these letters were "happily very few in number," but according to an estimate by postal workers at Chamalières (headquarters for the German Gestapo and the French Police Judiciaire), perhaps as many as 1800 denunciations were received during the occupation from the four departments of the Auvergne.[79]

As serious as were the myriad problems associated with the absence of the prisoners of war, the shortages or inadequacy of all basic goods and services, the overcrowding of the city by refugees from the north, and the arrival of occupation troops in 1942, nothing affected the Clermontois and their fellow Auvergnats quite so dramatically as the imposition of the forced labor draft by the Vichy regime. Even before the occupation of southern France, German labor recruiters had been allowed to operate in the "free zone," soliciting voluntary enlistments for work in German factories from offices (designated Offices de Placement Allemand—OPA) such as the one established at Clermont-Ferrand in June 1942.[80] In particular these recruiters were permitted to visit the encampments for foreign workers (Groupements de travailleurs étrangers—GTE), although French authorities told the camp commanders that they should not be allowed to meet with skilled workers whose services were needed in France.[81] By 2 July at least sixty-two persons, including nine women and several foreigners, had signed contracts with the OPA and had left Clermont-Ferrand for Germany.[82]

In late June 1942 Pierre Laval announced that he had negotiated an exchange program with the Germans whereby French prisoners of war would be released in return for *voluntary* engagements by skilled workers, especially those in metallurgy, to work in German factories. This was the origin of the so-called relève program, presented by Vichy spokesmen as an opportunity for French workers to demonstrate their patriotism by helping out the long-suffering prisoners of war. Strict limits to the attractiveness of such patriotic appeals were soon evident, especially when people learned that the Germans expected *three* skilled workers for each prisoner to be released. Police at Clermont-Ferrand reported that a brief period of interest in the relève and momentary enthusiasm at the thought of the possible return of local prisoners of war was replaced almost immediately by the unmitigated hostility of all concerned. As the head of the gendarmerie for the region wrote: "The 'relève' finds warm supporters only among those who do not risk being sent to Germany."[83]

The actions of the Vichy government made it clear that the relève was no more popular elsewhere in France. Lacking genuine volunteers, in October 1942 the regime began to manufacture them. Businesses in the region were given quotas of workers to supply for the relève. Michelin and Ollier at Clermont-Ferrand were ordered to furnish respectively, 165 and 60 sixty men, and similar designations of "volunteers" followed in the region's other industrial plants during November and December.[84] Some volunteers were found in the area, many of them foreign workers, possibly duped by promises of better pay or working conditions in Germany. But most French workers viewed the relève as a "véritable déportation," and they were determined to avoid "volunteering."[85] The central police commissioner at Clermont-Ferrand reported that only 2 of the 489 workers designated in the Puy-de-Dôme as of 25 November 1942 had agreed to go to Germany, and in neighboring Thiers officials reported that *none* of the 167 workers ordered to sign contracts had left as anticipated on 9 December.[86]

Months before 16 February 1943—when compulsory labor service was made obligatory for all French males under a law instituting the Service du Travail Obligatorie (STO)—workers at Clermont-Ferrand had responded to the notion of being drafted for German factories with a flurry of strikes at the train station, Michelin, Ollier, Chartoire, and other plants.[87] Those workers who were arrested and forcibly put on trains for Germany left the station singing the "Internationale" and shouting "Hang Laval!"[88] While acknowledging that several departures of workers from the train station at Clermont had taken place "in a stormy atmosphere,"[89] the regional prefect seemed pleased that no "serious incident" had occurred there by the end of January 1943. Not far away, at Montluçon in the Allier, a large crowd had invaded the train station on 6 January, overwhelming guards and allowing all of the "volunteers" assembled for departure that day to escape into the surrounding countryside.[90] Later the police would be better prepared. On 17 February 336 policemen were on hand at Montluçon to supervise the departure of a mere 27 workers.[91]

The use of substantial detachments of police and reducing to a minimum the time spent by the drafted workers awaiting departure in the train stations cut down on violent incidents in the spring and summer of 1943, but from its inception the forced labor draft proved to be an onerous burden for the French police. They could expect little or no help from their fellow citizens in tracking down deserters from labor service, and parents and friends of the young men who did leave for Germany resented the manner in which the draftees seemed to be treated as though they were criminals. Instructions given by the regional prefect to his subordinates in December 1942 revealed just how little "volunteerism" was involved in the relève process. If designated workers did not respond to convocations, they were brought by police or gendarmes to holding stations. There, "after having given the draftees several hours for reflection and having told them what penalties they faced should they refuse, those who decided to go [to Germany] would be authorized to leave, the others would be sent to a concentration camp."[92] No wonder the Clermontois referred to labor service under the relève as "deportation" long before Vichy decreed it "obligatory" with the STO.

The more the government increased police powers for tracking down STO deserters, the stronger became the resistance to the labor draft. Of the 630,000 Frenchmen who were drafted for labor service in Germany, almost half of them left before the STO was officially in place, and the numbers of departures dwindled steadily after the spring of 1943.[93] All of the government's pleas, bribes, and threats of force were of little avail in face of massive public disobedience and hostility. Judging by the statistical evidence in other reports, Clermont's central police commissioner certainly understated the extent of resistance to the relève when he stated in late

RECENSEMENT

ET VISITE MÉDICALE

des Jeunes Gens de la Classe 1945

Nous PRÉFET de la Région de Clermont-Ferrand, Officier de la Légion d'honneur,

Vu la loi n° 869 du 4 septembre 1942 sur l'utilisation et l'orientation de la main-d'œuvre,
Vu le décret n° 2390 du 26 août 1943 (article 2),
Vu la circulaire n° 912, ET du 20 avril 1944, du Chef du Gouvernement,

ARRÊTONS

Article premier. — Recensement

Tous les jeunes gens, de nationalité Française, sans distinction, nés entre le 1er Janvier 1925 et le 31 Décembre 1925, devront, pour se faire recenser, se présenter à la Mairie de la Commune où ils se trouvent aux dates fixées pour le recensement.

Ils devront présenter à la Mairie les documents suivants :

Carte d'identité, récente ou validée ;

Carte d'alimentation ;

Certificat de travail, ou une attestation d'emploi légalisée, authentifiés par un bulletin de paie ou de traitement, datant de moins d'un mois.

Les Etudiants seront tenus de présenter le récépissé numéroté attestant qu'ils ont été recensés comme tels en Mars - Avril 1944 à l'établissement d'enseignement où ils sont régulièrement inscrits pour l'année scolaire 1943-1944.

Les jeunes gens qui, pour raison de maladie, seraient immobilisés à la chambre, à la date du recensement, devront se faire recenser par un tiers qui présentera en leurs lieu et place leurs pièces d'identité, et un certificat médical légalisé.

Dans ce cas, le certificat de recensement sera remis à leur représentant.

Art. 2. — Les opérations de recensement auront lieu aux dates suivantes :

Vendredi 19 Mai, Samedi 20 Mai, Lundi 22 Mai, Mardi 23 Mai Mercredi 24 Mai, Jeudi 25 Mai, Vendredi 26 Mai, Samedi 27 Mai 1944

Le recensement sera clos le SAMEDI 27 MAI, à 18 h. 30 définitivement.

Art. 3. — Les jeunes gens ayant satisfait aux obligations du recensement recevront un certificat dont ils devront être CONSTAMMENT PORTEURS. La présentation de ce récépissé sera exigée en diverses circonstances, et en particulier au moment de la visite médicale.

Art. 4. — Les sanctions prévues par les lois n° 869 du 4 septembre 1942 (article 12), n° 342 du 11 juin 1943, sont applicables aux jeunes gens qui ne se sont pas soumis à la date fixée par le présent arrêté aux obligations du recensement.

Art. 5. — Visite médicale

Tous les jeunes gens nés en 1925 seront convoqués à une visite médicale de sélection.

Le lieu et date de cette visite médicale seront indiqués ultérieurement.

Art. 6. — Le présent arrêté sera affiché et publié par les soins des Maires dès sa réception, dans toutes les communes des Départements de la Région.

Art. 7. — Les Secrétaires Généraux des Préfectures, les Sous-Préfets, les Maires sont chargés, chacun en ce qui les concerne, de l'exécution du présent arrêté.

Clermont-Ferrand, le 23 Avril 1944.

Le Préfet Régional,
Paul BRUN.

Imprimerie spéciale Clermont-Fd   C O T A C L   N° JH 2411   P 9500   19-4-44 (2000)   Dépôt légal imprimeur 108   Dépôt légal éditeur 148   Visa de censure du 8-8-44

Twenty-year-olds ordered to register and take medical exams for the Forced Labor Draft (STO)

December 1942 that 50 percent of those requisitioned for Germany had refused to go. But he admitted: "The obligatory character of the relève has produced a very unfavorable impression. . . ."[94] Moreover, the commissioner emphasized that opposition to the relève was by no means confined to workers, observing: "Let me underline once more the full concordance of views of management and workers with regard to the relève. There can be no doubt that some heads of industry have recommended that their workers disappear rather than go to Germany!"[95] Michelin's directors were singled out as particularly active in cooperating with workers to sabotage the relève.[96]

After the liberation a man who had been among those responsible for supervising the STO in the region claimed that a Free French radio broadcast from London, congratulating the young men of the Auvergne for their low rate of compliance with the labor draft, had created problems for local officials with the occupation authorities.[97] In fact Paul Brun, the regional prefect, was summoned to Paris in July 1943 and called on the carpet by German labor officials for his region's consistent failure to fill its quota of draftees.[98] It seems that as many as 60 percent of those convoked for physical examinations at Clermont-Ferrand were receiving medical exemptions. Could it have been simply that traditions died hard in the Auvergne? One historian has demonstrated that during the revolutionary and Napoleonic periods, the French government had a difficult time obtaining either volunteers or conscripts at Chamalières-Royat, communes adjoining Clermont-Ferrand, and false medical certificates of incapacity were common.[99] Later in the nineteenth century, the Auvergne was one of the areas in France with the highest rates for failure of men to appear before army recruitment boards, and the region was among those most frequently cited for large numbers of fraudulent medical exemptions.[100]

If tradition favored resistance to conscription for the labor draft, so did the region's terrain. The mountains and forests of the Auvergne offered shelter to several of France's first maquis groups. Local farmers and foresters were quick to hide and feed these STO deserters in exchange for their labor. According to police at Clermont-Ferrand: "The whole population is demonstrating a passive complicity in all matters involving the deserters."[101] Potential draftees were also "sheltered" in an ironic way by a polio epidemic that struck the Auvergne in August 1943, leaving several dozen deaths in its wake, but canceling STO departures from the region for the remainder of that year.[102] Finally, quarrels between competing German labor authorities and the passive resistance of Vichy's own STO bureaucracy cut down substantially on the number of men ultimately sent to work in Germany.

The STO apparatus and, in particular, mixed French-German selection committees were responsible for designating workers for a whole spectrum of tasks. The draftees might be sent to Germany, selected for work in France in factories filling German contracts, ordered to join the TODT organization, which was charged with construction projects such as the Atlantic Wall defenses, or they might be drafted as supplementary guards for critical railroads, all of which fell under the purview of the STO administration. French representatives on the joint committees had orders from Vichy to do their utmost to protect the local economy from a depletion of skilled workers.[103] Some German delegates strove to channel more workers into those French factories supervised by their superior, Albert Speer, while others, responsible to Fritz Sauckel sought to extract as many men as possible for shipment to Germany. These tensions and rival ambitions contributed to frequent arguments and delays that allowed numerous workers to avoid transfer to Germany.[104]

Ultimately, by the end of the German occupation, fewer than 4000 Frenchmen had left the department of the Puy-de-Dôme under the various labor draft schemes.[105] The number who had been classified as "deserters" far exceeded that total. Although resistance to the forced labor draft was certainly strong, Clermont-Ferrand and the Auvergne were not exceptional in this regard. In January 1944 the German Military Command in Paris complained to French labor authorities that only 5920 workers of the 33,000 demanded from France for the TODT organization had been delivered.[106] Later that year, with the whole operation visibly grinding to a halt, Vichy's general labor secretary (Secrétaire Général à la Main d'oeuvre) reported that instead of the 273,000 workers requested that year, only 13,000 had arrived in Germany as of the beginning of April.[107] Thus, Clermont's experience and that of the Auvergne mirrored the situation found elsewhere in France. The French response to the forced labor draft demonstrated the extent to which passive and active resistance could be successful, despite foreign occupation and authoritarian government at home. Probably more than any other single factor, the relève and the STO drove increasing numbers of French men and women beyond simple dislike and into active resistance to the government of Pierre Laval and Philippe Pétain.

We have seen that war and occupation meant hard times for almost everyone in France. Uncertain employment; shortages of food, clothing, and most consumer goods; restricted mobility; unwelcome regulations and controls from both German occupation authorities and their own government; and other problems contributed to the discontent of most French citizens. Although it was probably too much to expect that the French (or anyone else for that matter) would have accepted these conditions with good humor, the material discomfort of the occupation era, possibly even the dislocation caused by the STO, might have been endured stoically as the unfortunate but unavoidable consequence of the disastrous military defeat of 1940. Responsibility for these unhappy circumstances might have been laid solely at the Germans' doorstep, with perhaps some share of the blame going to those leaders of the Third Republic who were accused of weakness and failure to head off the catastrophic defeat. The Vichy regime, of course, placed much emphasis on this latter theme. That the public discontent engendered by the conditions of the occupation era was *not* focused exclusively on the Germans and the leaders of the late Republic is best explained by the actions of the Vichy government. Going far beyond the role of shield and protector for France, prostrate victim of military defeat, the new regime's leaders chose to seize the opportunity offered by the exceptional circumstances of the occupation era to remake French society in an image more congenial to them. This critical choice, made very early in Vichy's history, aggravated an already disturbing situation and ultimately was to channel toward their own government much of the rage felt by the French people as they struggled to survive the distressing consequences of foreign occupation.

2

The New Order at Clermont-Ferrand: Political and Moral Renewal and the Mobilization of Youth

Not unlike other new political orders in France and elsewhere, in the first months of its existence, the Vichy regime sought to mark a break with the past and perhaps to suggest new directions for the future by changing the names of public thoroughfares. In a letter to the mayor of Clermont-Ferrand, the prefect of the Puy-de-Dôme wrote:

> There are a certain number of streets in your city whose names represent homage to those who by their errors or their faults have contributed to driving our country to its ruin.
>
> Is it really opportune, at the present time, to have a street named Emile Combes, another Jules Guesde, a Boulevard Jean Jaurès?
>
> I ask that in these circumstances you decide upon new names for these streets. There have been enough incontestable glories in French history so that you should have no difficulty giving new names to these public thoroughfares.[1]

Probably unwittingly, but prophetically, in neighboring Riom the boulevard "La Liberté" was renamed the boulevard Maréchal Pétain; towns all over southern France witnessed similar transformations until late March 1941 when Marshal Pétain requested that no further streets be named for him—unless they were newly constructed ones and they were major thoroughfares.

In itself a minor episode in the history of Vichy France, symbolically the renaming of these streets was highly instructive about the nature of the new regime. In announcing the government's decision to sign the Armistice, Pétain had presented himself as a shield to protect France from the anticipated harsh demands of the victorious Germans, but the Vichy government was never merely a caretaker regime. Evident from the earliest days were a forceful rejection of the Third Republic (whose institutions, leaders, and ideals were held responsible for France's defeat) and the determination to recast French society in a new mold. The very day that

30

French representatives were signing the Armistice at Rethondes (to Hitler's delight), Pétain, speaking in Bordeaux, claimed that honor had been saved, adding: "A New Order is beginning."[2] One week after the vote of full powers to Pétain, an agent of the ministry of information at Thiers—criticizing the French for their selfishness and lack of patriotism and civic spirit, allegedly fostered by "godless schools" and a corrupt press—claimed that "French public opinion is in great need of being informed . . . and reformed."[3] Two months later the prefect of the Puy-de-Dôme was calling for reports from the mayors of the department on those civil servants whose "physical, intellectual, or moral weaknesses render them incapable of collaborating in the creation of the *new order*."[4]

Politically, Vichy's New Order represented a distinct shift to the right. The presence in the government of several "nonpolitical" technocrats and of René Belin, an anti-Communist syndicalist, as minister of labor may be cited to illustrate the "pluralism" of Vichy; contemporaries as well as some historians have drawn distinctions among the Vichy of Pétain, the Vichy of Laval, and the Vichy of Darnand. But if there were interminable quarrels at Vichy about particular policies or the extent to which changes should occur, all the factions agreed that France should be restructured significantly. Participation in the government and administration by some representatives of the prewar left did not change the fact that Vichy policy and ideology were aimed in part at the elimination of what was considered to have been the pernicious influence of the French left. It was no accident that the names of the two most prominent founders of the French Socialist Party, Jules Guesde and Jean Jaurès, along with that of Emile Combes, one of the most important anticlerical figures in modern French history, were the ones chosen by the prefect for elimination from the streets of Clermont-Ferrand. The new regime sought to restore Catholicism to a prominent role in the public and private life of French citizens and hoped, with a melange of planning, corporatism, and paternalism, to seduce the working class away from its traditional attachment to pacifism, internationalism, and socialism. Notwithstanding several disclaimers made by government officials at the time and later, in simplest terms Vichy represented to a considerable extent a revenge by the French right for the Popular Front. In his excellent history of the trials staged in early 1942 by the Vichy regime to cast the blame for France's defeat on carefully selected political and military scapegoats, Henri Michel accurately termed the Popular Front "the number one defendant at Riom."[5] Another vivid illustration of this anti–Popular Front spirit was provided at Thiers where the newly baptized rue Saint Roch replaced the street named for Roger Salengro, Léon Blum's minister of the interior who had committed suicide in November 1936 in the wake of a vicious press campaign launched against him by the extreme right. According to the prefect of the Puy-de-Dôme: "Even though former Minister Salengro did not belong to the Third International, it does not seem at the present time that a street should be named for him."[6]

Personalities, policies, and circumstances at Vichy were in a constant state of flux, and the regime's evolution over time makes it difficult to generalize about its nature. To some degree the rapid turnover of personnel and the modification of policies were a result of internal considerations, the consequence of feuds among rival French factions. Although power shifted progressively from its more moderate to its more extremist expressions, the evolution of Vichy remained broadly within the framework of the French right. It might be argued convincingly that these shifts followed the logic of Vichy's earliest attitudes and policies, but the growing authoritarianism of the government and ultimately, in the face of massive popular hostility, the desperate turn to brutal repression under Joseph Darnand's Milice were influenced strongly by events beyond Vichy's control. To cite only the most obvious example, in 1942 Germany's need for labor led directly to a forced labor draft (the Service de Travail Obligatoire—STO) that was to spawn the maquis whose presence and activities would force the government into an actively repressive posture. Acknowledging that competition among various factions and the intervention of the Germans contributed to certain fluctuations and ambiguities in Vichy policy, as Yves Durand has argued, there was nevertheless a certain unity to Vichy because of the personal nature of the regime. While others shared or exercised power from time to time, Marshal Pétain remained from the beginning to the end of the regime, and all of Vichy was indeed "Pétain's Vichy."[7] To the extent that it is possible to speak of an "essence" of the Vichy regime, it is best discovered by a consideration of the goals and policies of Pétain's "National Revolution." In the first year or so—before the return to power of Pierre Laval in the spring of 1942 and the German occupation of the south in November 1942, while Vichy was freest to act on its own initiative—the government most systematically pursued its ambition of remaking France. Even though, as will be shown, almost nothing permanent was accomplished by the National Revolution, the slogans that accompanied it, the organizations created to sponsor it, and the policies attempted in its name all define the basic contours of Vichy's projected New Order.

In contrast to the alleged weakness of the Third Republic's parliamentary regime, torn by the partisan strife of political parties, Vichy planned to build a forceful, authoritarian state in which the pettiness of politics would be transcended by a new national union around the figure of the head of state, Marshal Pétain. A new moral order was to emerge in which duties would precede rights; discipline, order, and respect for authority would be stressed; and a new community would emerge based on work, family, and country (*Travail, Famille, Patrie*). This new trilogy had replaced the former republic's Liberty, Equality, and Fraternity. Alexandre Varenne, the maverick editor of Clermont-Ferrand's *La Montagne,* pointed out in a letter to Pétain that the initials in his new motto, TFP, had an unfortunate correspondance to those used by the judiciary for *Travaux Forcés en Perpétuité* ("forced labor for life"), but there is no evidence that such satire deflected Pétain or his colleagues from the pursuit of their goals.[8]

A poster entitled "Principles of the Community," signed by Pétain and ordered displayed in all French schools, captures something of the spirit of the National Revolution. The following excerpts suggest the flavor of the sixteen principles enunciated:

> 6. Any citizen who pursues his own interests outside of the common interest goes against reason and even against his own interests.
> 7. Citizens owe their labor, their resources, and even their lives to the fatherland. No political conviction, no doctrinal preference relieves them of these obligations.
> 8. Every community requires a leader. Every leader, being responsible, must be honored and served. He is no longer worthy of being a leader from the moment he becomes an oppressor.
> 10. The state must be independent and strong. No group can be tolerated that brings citizens into conflict with one another or that discredits the authority of the state.
> All cliques imperil the unity of the nation. The state must smash them.
> 12. The school is the prolongation of the family. It must make children aware of the benefits of the human order that surrounds and supports them. It must make them sensitive to the beauty, grandeur, and continuity of the fatherland. It must teach them respect for moral and religious beliefs, in particular those that France has professed since the origins of its national existence.[9]

A survey of several of the kinds of activities that fell generally under the rubric of the National Revolution will indicate the concrete form taken by these ideals as applied under the Vichy regime.

Within days after France's destiny was placed in his hands, Pétain issued a decree permitting the removal by administrative action of civil servants who could not be penalized under existing legislation or because of professional shortcomings. The next month this procedure was extended to cover municipal or communal employees as well. The prefect of the Puy-de-Dôme informed the mayor of Clermont-Ferrand and the other mayors of the department that this preliminary purge of unreliable civil servants was necessary to ensure the success of the reform of the French administration. The purge of personnel was followed by a restructuring of the ad-

Principles of the Community: Vichy rewrites the Declaration of the Rights of Man and the Citizen

ministration. The Third Republic's conseils généraux, commissions départementales, and conseils d'arrondissement were replaced by commissions administratives départementales and later by Laval's conseils départementaux; a conseil national was named to substitute for the popular representation formerly embodied in the Chamber of Deputies. Of much greater importance was the enhanced centralization of executive authority and the increased power delegated to the prefectures. In April 1941 Vichy created a network of regional prefects who were assisted for matters of law enforcement by regional intendants de police. The jurisdiction of the regional prefect at Clermont-Ferrand extended over the four departments of the Auvergne region—the Puy-de-Dôme, the Allier, the Haute-Loire, and the Cantal.

The impact of these changes in the various agencies of government included a marked increase in influence and power of the prewar right and of "nonpolitical" technicians, the substitution of appointment for the elective principle, an attempt to redefine representation following the National Revolution's idea of natural and moral communities, and in general the elaboration of a pattern of organization to buttress an authoritarian regime. A cursory glance at the statistics concerning Vichy's reorganization of the administration at Clermont-Ferrand and in the Puy-de-Dôme would indicate a relatively modest purge. Only 14 percent (65 of 473) of the department's municipal councils were dissolved and replaced by "special delegations" or "appointed municipal councils." Instead of a wholesale removal of former municipal officials, the vast majority were retained in office, and there was no massive transfer of power into the hands of the reactionary or extreme right. The designation "Radical modéré" is probably the most common indication of political nuance for those newly or reappointed municipal officers for whom a political affiliation is ascertainable.[10] This pattern would seem to conform to the prewar political situation of the Puy-de-Dôme in which at the local level the Radical Party held the balance of political power. In 1939, of the department's mayors, 206 were Radicals, 50 were Radicaux Indépendants, 111 were representatives of parties to the right of the Radicals (Républicains de Gauche, URD, or Conservateurs), and 100 to the left (Socialists—SFIO, Républicains-Socialistes, Socialistes de France, and Démocrates Populaires). Cities like Clermont-Ferrand and towns like Thiers and Issoire where the Socialists were strong were exceptional, and even at Clermont-Ferrand the mayor had been a Radical although the conseillers d'arrondissement and the conseilleurs généraux who represented the city were mostly Socialists. The composition of the last conseil général elected before the war for the Puy-de-Dôme included twice as many moderates or conservatives (27 Radical

Socialists, 4 Radicaux de Gauche, 3 URD) as Socialists (11 SFIO, 4 Socialistes de France, 1 Républicain-Socialiste).

In the Puy-de-Dôme, as in France generally, conservatives and moderates, often through the agency of the Radical Party, had maintained a
predominant influence in local politics, even though the department had
turned increasingly to Socialist candidates in national elections. Six of the
Puy-de-Dôme's eight deputies were Socialists, with one Radical (a supporter of the Popular Front), and one Républicain de Gauche. There were
two Radical senators, one of whom supported the Popular Front, in addition to the independent Pierre Laval, and one Républicain de Gauche. The
senators were, of course, elected through indirect suffrage and, as in the
country at large, were generally more conservative than the deputies.

So, if one overlooked the dissolution of the elected Chamber of Deputies with its former Popular Front majority, its left wing already reduced
before the Vichy period by the exclusion of the Communists, the maintenance of most of the personnel of local government with an apparently
slight shift to the right in political coloration would seem to suggest a substantial continuity with the past. According to one former Vichy prefect:
"In the provinces above all the average Frenchman . . . really did not
realize that there had been a radical change in the political system."[11] At
first Pétain's government seemed not dissimilar to those of Poincaré or
Doumergue who earlier had been granted extensive powers in emergency
situations. Therefore, the former prefect argued, most of the population
had not perceived the coming of the Vichy regime as a "rupture" with the
past. In a similar vein, speaking four decades after the events and down-
playing the significance of the purge, a high administrative official in
Vichy's secrétariat général à la jeunesse commented: "Speaking of the
arrival of certain men at Vichy, people have often spoken of taking revenge; there was no revenge to be taken on anyone."[12]

On closer examination, the facts do not support such a benign interpretation. Although only 14 percent of the municipalities in the Puy-de-
Dôme were replaced or modified in Vichy's original purge, this 14 percent
included all of the cities with large populations and most other population
centers of any significant size. Of the twenty-eight towns of 2000 to 10,000
population, eighteen mayors considered loyal to the new order were maintained, but ten new ones were named by Vichy, and the municipal councils
of many of these were remade even if the mayor remained in place. In
other words, a substantial proportion of the population was placed under
new local leadership despite the relatively small numbers of changes with
regard to the total number of communes. At Clermont-Ferrand, Pochet-
Lagaye, a moderate Radical, was retained as mayor; but only one third of
Clermont's municipal councilors were maintained, with twenty-two re-

moved from office. Just as ministers were constantly being shuffled at Vichy, modifications in the composition of the municipal governments continued throughout Vichy's history. In the Puy-de-Dôme over 100 persons resigned from municipal office in 1942 and 1943. Some of these resignations were because of health or age, but almost half were clearly politically motivated, and reasons such as "poor administration" sometimes given by the prefect probably concealed political motives in several other cases.[13]

It was true that Vichy's purge was not *solely* a political phenomenon, in the sense of an unabashed attack on former supporters of the Popular Front. Among the sixty-five dossiers of municipal employees in the Puy-de-Dôme removed as "incapable or unworthy to collaborate in the work of revival undertaken by the Government,"[14] only a few specify political motives for dismissal. Of the twenty-nine employees fired in October 1940 by the mayor of Clermont-Ferrand, two workers at the municipal hospitals were fired because of their political viewpoint (Communist—PCF); but others, policemen, firemen, gardeners, and so on, lost their jobs because of "immorality" (one report noted, "His debauched life-style is a detestable example"; three others mentioned "deplorable appearance and morality"), laziness, drunkenness, "insubordination," and one because he was partially paralyzed even though well noted for his work.[15] In the selection of the municipal councils and other new creations, in line with Pétain's idea of recognizing certain "natural" communities of interests, attention was paid to the representation of various social categories, such as labor, management, agriculture, and the professions, as well as to political viewpoint. At a conference with the regional prefects in response to a question about publicity concerning the reordering of municipal councils, the minister of the interior left to the discretion of the prefects the task of explaining to the public that the changes were for failures in administration, not attempts to "judge people because of their beliefs."[16] In one of his first instructions concerning the appointment of mayors and the replacement of municipal councils, the minister of the interior, Marcel Peyrouton, had claimed: "It would be to misunderstand the thinking of the Government to select persons exclusively from 'the right,' who under the old regime were called 'reactionaries.' Just as the Marshal of France, Head of State, declared in a message to the Country, one will not discover in the new order 'the features of a sort of *moral order* or a revenge for the events of 1936.' "[17]

Declarations were one thing, but actions were another. When one examines the application of the new municipal laws in the Puy-de-Dôme and the prefect's interpretation of the instructions to "oust here and now any municipality incontestably opposed to the national revolution on the basis of their members' past associations or their present actions,"[18] the specter of the Popular Front is visible at every turn. This situation was possibly unavoidable at Clermont-Ferrand, where enthusiasm for the Popular Front had been very high. Throughout the 1930s—but especially in the middle and last years of that decade—a lively political atmosphere had been evident at Clermont with frequent, well-attended political rallies of all sorts, ranging from avowedly fascist groups, to the Croix de Feu whose leader Colonel Casimir de la Rocque lived nearby, to pacifist, Socialist, and Communist organizations. In a massive demonstration to celebrate the victory of the Popular Front coalition, on 14 June 1936, 25,000 people marched through the streets of Clermont-Ferrand from the train station on the east to the place de la Liberté on the western side of the city—a crowd more than twice as large as any that turned out to greet Marshal Pétain on several visits to the town during the Vichy era, and larger even than the crowds that celebrated the liberation in August 1944.[19] No less evident than the popular enthusiasm for the initial victory of the Popular Front had been the bitter disappointment at its relative failure in the economic realm. In the fall of 1938 the workers in Clermont-Ferrand brought to a standstill virtually every industrial or manufacturing firm of any size and many commercial establishments by massive sit-in strikes whose legacy, of more recent vintage, was, if anything, more sharply engraved on public consciousness than that of the warm enthusiasm of 1936.[20]

Subsequently, one's statements and actions at the time of the events of 1936 and 1938 became the touchstone by which one's probable attitudes toward the Vichy regime might be reckoned. Belying the regime's public statements advocating political appeasement, direct references to the Popular Front were frequent in requests for police investigations and explanations for dismissal from office. Among many such cases were a tobacco-shop clerk at Trezelle, fired because he was still a *propagandiste* for the "régime of Léon Blum"; an individual called "quarrelsome, obstinate, partisan of the occupation of factories and of the Popular Front"; a professor at the University of Strasbourg, suspect because as a boy he had gone to school with Blum, and had been a leader of the Popular Front at Strasbourg, considered "a bitter, vindictive and scheming man"; and although nothing improper had been observed in the conduct of a visitor to Riom, the prefect at Clermont-Ferrand reported to the minister of justice that because the man had been a zealous advocate of the Popular Front, the prefect would investigate further to see "whether or not he was not involved in some reprehensible activity during the few days he spent in Riom."[21]

The boundaries delineating political suspects were fuzzy. Although, as will be discussed later, the Vichy government was at times at odds with groups to the extreme right, its chief enemies were perceived to be on the left. The Communists were, of course, excluded from the new national community, and often Socialists were viewed in the same light. Frequently, because of Popular Front activities, civil servants who had been members of the SFIO were falsely accused of being Communists. But *any* overt, forthright identification with the "old regime" might bring censure. The sub-prefect at Issoire, following protests from the local Légion, demanded the resignation of the mayor of Neschers because he had worn the traditional republican tricolored scarf around his waist to a public funeral.

Although desiring to mark a break with the old order, the Vichy government did not desire to cut itself off entirely from those constituencies represented by France's former political parties. After all, more than half of those Frenchmen who had voted in the last parliamentary elections had voted for candidates who adhered to the now much-maligned Popular Front. In explaining the government's intentions with regard to representation on the conseils départementaux, Laval insisted that no former deputy or senator should be appointed president of a conseil and that only a small number should be included on the conseils "in order not to give the country the impression that we are returning to the mistaken ways of the old regime."[22] Parliamentarians were not to be systematically excluded if their attachment to Pétain's regime was certain, however. Georges Hilaire, Laval's secretary-general at the Ministry of the Interior, specified: "It is fitting not to leave out the socialists who have rallied to us, and notably the Paul-Fauristes."[23] One assumes that the "Léon-Blumistes" were not so welcome.

At Clermont-Ferrand the prefect had some difficulty finding such *"ralliés."* When Admiral François Darlan's directeur de cabinet asked why a man who had been condemned by a court at Riom for his part in the general strike of November 1938 had been nominated for Clermont's conseil municipal, the prefect responded that the individual in question had only been caught up in the strike because of his position as Secrétaire de l'Union Départemental des Syndicats, claiming "he has never gone beyond a trade-unionist viewpoint and his actions have always been in a moderating direction." Moreover, added the prefect with a plea for the retention of his nominee, "he was in fact one of the only workers qualified to represent the workers in an assembly of municipal councillors from Clermont-Ferrand."[24] As with this case of the syndicalist municipal councillor, one was not *automatically* excluded by the Vichy regime from a role in public life or from employment by the mere fact of having adhered to the Popular Front. Apparently, one might even be "cured" from the debilitating influence of the Popular Front. In recommending his employment as a custodial worker at the prefecture, the intendant de police at Clermont-Ferrand noted that the candidate "passionately fell under the influence of the agitators of 1936. However, he was always an excellent worker, and he appears now to be completely rectified."[25] As illustrated by the case of René Belin at the national level, at the local level one occasionally found former adherents of the prewar left in both minor and relatively important functions under the Vichy regime. The significant factor was whether or not they were believed to "understand the new situation"[26] and were willing to acknowledge the error of their former ways. Those who were not willing to do this—and it should be emphasized that such individuals were among the vast majority—remained suspect of "hostility to the work of national renewal"[27] and were excluded.

That the "correct" political viewpoint was essential to selection for appointment to the various local, departmental, regional, or national commissions and conseils established by Vichy is evident from the reports, recommendations, and other information that accompanied all nominations for such posts from the mayors and the prefect. Moreover, in the Puy-de-Dôme those councils whose composition was considered to be ideal from the government's perspective followed a predictable pattern that included conservatives or Radicals of a "moderate" persuasion, several "nonpolitical" personalities, often a large number of légionnaires, and few, if any, outspoken Socialists. For example, Thiers, traditionally a Socialist stronghold, was represented by an appointed municipal council termed by the subprefect, "Very homogenous municipality offers all [desirable] guarantees." The mayor named by Vichy was the "nonpolitical" commander of the Légion, his first adjoint was a Radical, "entirely won over to the National Revolution," and among the seventeen other councillors there were ten légionnaires and one prisoner of war.[28] In other parts of France where the right had been stronger before the war, the *number* of changes of personnel was often less than in towns like Thiers or Clermont-Ferrand. But an overview of the administrative reform for all of France reveals that the changes brought about by Vichy were virtually always in the *same direction* as the pattern for the Puy-de-Dôme—an elimination of the influence of the prewar left replaced by a strengthening of the right and an increase in representation of "nonpolitical" elements believed loyal to the values of the new order.[29] Beyond reorganizing or replacing traditional organs of popular representation with commissions and councils "oriented" in a political shape in conformity with the government's outlook, the new regime insisted on *appointment* of those individuals who might wield effective power within the new bodies. In a letter to the prefects concerning officers for professional organizations within the various ministries, the Secrétaire d'Etat à l'Intérieur noted "the risks that might be posed by the election of civil servants whose loyalty is not certain";[30] and Laval decided to appoint the presidents and the members of the bureaus (the executive committees) for all of the conseils départementaux "in order to avoid all political competition."[31]

Clearly, Vichy's political reorganization of France entailed a determined effort to purge "undesirable" elements, especially those who because of their past political viewpoints were known or expected to be hostile to the New Order. Yet, curiously, having gone to great lengths to purge and juggle personnel at all levels, the regime seemed virtually to ignore most of its new political creations, and the various local commissions and councils had little or no impact in practical terms. They were consultative bodies only, they met infrequently, and for all intents and purposes they did little other than endorse the actions of the administration, or send occasional greetings and formal expressions of confidence to Pétain and his government. A new political elite was indeed selected, and the regime's political preferences may be discerned by an examination of the composition of the newly appointed councils of regional, departmental, and local government; effective power, however, was maintained in the hands of the central administration, whose agents, the prefects and subprefects, carried out the regime's wishes free from the challenges or contradictions by locally elected representatives of the people that had been an integral part of the previous republican system.

It was perhaps natural that a regime that emphasized authority, hierarchy, and the importance of leadership by chiefs at every level should relegate to a minor role representative councils, even though these had been carefully oriented in hopes of ensuring "proper" attitudes and predictable behavior. Beyond conformity to Vichy's ideology, the restrictions placed on local institutions under the new political system reflected the fears and insecurity of the regime in the face of a public opinion that Vichy's leaders knew to be indifferent, if not hostile, to many of its designs. In January 1942 the minister of the interior ordered a confidential investigation of all persons who were believed to exercise "a moral influence" on the population, including politicians, labor leaders, and other notables. Of the forty-seven leading notables cited for the Puy-de-Dôme, as many were considered "hostile," "doubtful," "reserved," or "indifferent" as were classified under "seemingly favorable," "loyal," or "certain."[32] The imprecision of some of the information submitted to the minister limits the usefulness of this survey, but most striking is the fact that the prefect could report that the loyalty to Pétain of only thirteen of the forty-seven was "certain," with seven others considered "loyal"; the corresponding figures for the government were seven whose loyalty was certain, with nine others termed "loyal."

As will be demonstrated later in detailed examination of public opinion, the mass of the population was, if anything, more skeptical about and hostile to the Vichy regime and its National Revolution than were the "notables." In April 1941 the commissaire de police, chef de la Sûreté, for Clermont-Ferrand reported that all of the changes in governmental personnel were producing "an unfortunate impression" and that the purge had been ordered "less in the interest of purifying the administrations, and more in order to satisfy certain clans desirous of settling personal vendettas."[33] Two years later another police official at Vichy remarked: "The citizenry observes once again that the unity forecast by the government, and a goal of the Marshal's policies, is still in the planning stage, and that on the contrary the parties and groups of the right seem to be reviving their quarrels."[34] If Pétain had felt it necessary to assure the French that the purge and the New Order were not simply a revenge for the Popular Front, did he not do so because so many people were convinced that that was precisely what was taking place? The new regime was aware that significant changes in attitudes were necessary if its ambitions for the creation of a New Order in France were to be realized with any semblance of popular support.

The New Moral Order

Along with an emphasis on those "faults" of the past that allegedly had brought France to its ruin, and were now to be recognized and cast aside, Marshal Pétain and other leading spokesmen for the National Revolution stressed the necessity for a moral renewal of individual French citizens and the country as a whole. Contrite in the fact of its crushing defeat, the French nation was to rebound from disaster and humiliation through the efforts of a new generation, unblemished by the faults of the past and brought up under the influence of a new morality. According to a brochure, "L'Ecole et la Famille," distributed in 1943 to the schools by the propaganda service of the Commissariat Général à la Famille, the greatest danger for France was not the war, the invasion, the loss of colonies, the army, or the navy. "The greatest threat to France is depopulation."[35] The rich and strong nations were those with large and growing populations. "Not enough children,"[36] the Marshal said. The first step along the road to recovery for France was to remedy this situation by encouraging and rewarding large families.

Although the occupation and the special economic conditions associated with it limited the possibilities for a systematic program to promote births, many initiatives were inspired either directly or indirectly by the regime's concern with the family. Mother's Day was celebrated with great pomp and circumstance, the newspapers usually carrying elaborate accounts of ceremonies in which Pétain or lesser dignitaries of the regime distributed medals to mothers of large families. Of more practical consequence, tax benefits were provided for households with several childrern, and proposals were made for the extension of family allocations to ensure better coverage. If the government's recommendations were followed, women, whose proper place and most natural role was believed to be in the home, were among the first to be laid off in the days following France's defeat when most industries were forced to cut back their operations for several months. Exceptions were to be made for widows of soldiers, those whose jobs were the only source of income for the family, or those in "traditionally feminine" industries.[37]

If the government might have preferred to keep women at home, conditions would not allow this. In the summer of 1943, citing shortages resulting from the transfer of male workers to Germany and the desirability of training new men for skilled positions, a high official in the labor ministry urged the regional prefects to "substitute a woman for a man in every case where such a change is not counterindicated because of the muscular force required, the special fatigue associated with the job, and so on."[38] By the spring of 1944 Laval had ordered the drafting of women 18 to 45 years old, who might in some cases be sent to work in centers away from their homes. In such cases special housing would be provided for them. According to Laval, "This center, distinctly separated from the masculine residence, will be directed and watched over by a woman of high morality and a clearly established social character."[39] Married women and girls younger than 25 were to be sent to work only in locations from which they could return home each night.

In addition to attempts to keep women out of factories or to oversee their "virtue" when this was not possible, Vichy initiated campaigns to fight prostitution and abortion. The law of 15 February 1942 on the repression of abortion was considered "an essential element in the family policy of the government";[40] like attempts to control prostitution, which floundered because police had so little time or manpower to devote to it during the occupation, the regime's efforts to stop abortions evidently did not succeed. Indeed, police at Vichy reported a sharp rise in the number of abortions and complained bitterly that doctors refused to cooperate, "systematically hiding behind professional confidence." (The officer submitting that particular report felt that this situation presented a "gap to be filled"–the police must be given the power to force doctors to talk!)[41]

The theme of a return to the soil and to the countryside was also associated with the government's ideal for the French family. Champions of the National Revolution believed that farmers were especially prolific. Industrialization, urbanization, and the progressive abandonment of the countryside were seen as major contributors to the drop in the French birthrate. Consequently, in addition to being encouraged to talk about the future when they would be "fathers" and "mothers," children should be told stories about the attractions of the countryside ("the little father-land"): "This is perhaps one of the best ways to counter migration to 'cosmopolitan areas' so dangerous for the body and the soul."[42]

Particular emphasis was placed on the education of French youth—France's hope for rebirth—who should be taught in conformity with the regime's ideals of order, discipline, and love of country. Because of the potential influence their position allowed them, schoolteachers, both in and outside the classroom, were of great concern to the Vichy regime. In addition to his crucial role in the guidance of youth, particularly in the smaller communes where teachers often served as secretaries to the mayor, the schoolmaster was considered simply as "he who knows" and was asked for advice on countless matters from the choice of career for one's children to the interpretation of legal documents. In the Puy-de-Dôme, as in many other parts of France, a problem was posed by the fact that before the events of 1939 a majority of the teachers had shown "much sympathy for socialist ideas and those of the leftist parties."[43] Therefore, hostility to educational reforms, especially the introduction of religious instruction into the curriculum, and to other aspects of the new regime's ideology was to be feared. The essence of this issue was captured well in the report of an agent of the Police Spéciale who was sent to investigate complaints about the teachers at La Roche Blanche, a little village on the southern slope of the Plateau de Gergovie, a few kilometers from Clermont-Ferrand. "In essence," he wrote,

> there exist in La Roche Blanche as elsewhere two clans who are opposed to one another and clash over political and religious issues. The teacher was a socialist, therefore he is a "red"; and the "whites" will never admit that he could now be "without color."
>
> The teacher is headmaster of a "laic" school; and in one clan, they are resolutely hostile to laic schools that they hope to see replaced or superseded by a denominational school.[44]

A partial solution to the problem of loyalty was to remove from the ranks of the profession those teachers who were the most outspokenly leftist, and quite a few instances of this, especially involving alleged Communists, occurred in the Puy-de-Dôme. But almost one-fifth of the department's teachers had been eligible for mobilization in 1939, and many were prisoners of war during the Vichy period. In these circumstances a whole-sale purge that might have created a serious shortage of teachers was rejected. To be sure, administrative authorities were never especially confident about the teacher's enthusiasm for the New Order. In 1941 the Secrétaire d'Etat à l'Instruction Publique noted that it had been brought to Pétain's attention that "a large number"[45] of teachers were acting against the spirit of the National Revolution by not following the scheduled hours for the catechism, arriving late for religious instruction, and so forth. The military commander for the Puy-de-Dôme argued that a careful watch should be kept on teachers who had held leftist ideas, and, he believed, might still have them beneath the surface appearance of support for the government. The prefect recommended surprise visits to classrooms to check on the teachers from time to time. In addition to the initial purge, at least twenty or thirty teachers were investigated in 1942 and 1943 for "Communist" or "extremist" ideas and were reprimanded, transferred to other locations, forced to retire early, or fired.[46]

Although never entirely dropping their general suspicions about teachers, and admitting that "almost all of the teachers in the public schools of Clermont-Ferrand have retained certain republican convictions"[47] and continued to question some of Pétain's decisions in the realm of education, the authorities took heart from the fact that most of the teachers seemed to be acting as loyal servants of the state, observing a strict political neutrality in the classroom. While a few exceptions were noted, the prefect of the Puy-de-Dôme and the regional prefect both claimed in early 1942 that most of the teachers were behind the government's efforts for a "National Renewal." If "several members of the teaching corps still retain a certain neutrality with regard to the actions of the Marshal's government," nevertheless "they do not demonstrate, openly at least, any hostility toward the work of revival that it has undertaken."[48] The regional prefect was pleased that teachers were engaged actively in organizing their students' participation in campaigns to help the needy (refugees from other parts of France, victims of bombings, the families of prisoners of war, and so forth) and other activities related to the government's effort for "national solidarity." Of course, schoolchildren had undertaken similar activities under earlier regimes; in a sense the Vichy regime benefited from the former republic's well-known penchant for promoting patriotism, as well as its credo of "scholarly neutrality"—partisan politics were to be left outside of the classroom.

Soon the regime would decide that "neutrality" was not sufficient for the guardians and molders of France's future generations. As witnessed by the increasingly dogmatic instructions issued by the Ministry of Education, the creation of youth groups dedicated to the glory of the New Order, and the active intervention of the state in the role of moral censor, Vichy aspired through increasingly authoritarian techniques to mold the rising French generation according to the ideological bent of the National Revolution. As with so many of Vichy's ambitions, the experiment was a dismal failure, but that should not obscure the reality of the attempt. We shall see that in addition to the limited means at its disposal and restrictions on its freedom of action, due to the circumstances of the occupation, Vichy's desire to control the formation of the youth of France ran into substantial and effective opposition from the French people.

Perhaps exaggerating the influence exercised by teachers over their young charges, Jerome Carcopino, Vichy's education minister in 1941, reminded France's educators that theirs was the highest mission of all in the New France. Outside of the classroom, teachers should be exemplars of good conduct and loyalty toward the regime, and even more so in the classroom where their every word "may arouse in your students profound reverberations . . . the slightest doubt may trouble them."[49] Teachers were urged to exalt the French nation and above all the figure of Marshal Pétain, "who, alone among so many, from 1914 to 1918, had acquired enough glory to win the admiration of the victors, to stop the invasion of 1940, and whose presence at the head of the government symbolizes and guarantees the unity of France and its empire."[50] Students should be inspired with the cult of heroism and protected from harmful, divisive propaganda. An active role was expected from the teachers: "Today, teachers cannot be permitted to isolate themselves in an abstention that our circumstances condemn. I invite you to take effective action on your students: an action for truth, for patriotism, for public safety."[51]

Carcopino's "invitation" presumably having been insufficient to evoke the desired response, his successor as minister of education, Abel Bonnard, *ordered* the teachers to take an active role as propagandists for the National Revolution. In transmitting the minister's instructions to the teachers, the Inspecteur d'Académie de Clermont-Ferrand required that every teacher in the Puy-de-Dôme initial a copy of Bonnard's *circulaire* of 13 May 1942, "so that no one can claim that he has not seen it."[52] In the combination of exhortation and barely veiled threat that was increasingly visible in the public pronouncements and private orders of this regime, whose plans were turning sour, Bonnard argued that teachers, because of their intelligence and the nature of their profession, "must be ahead of the bulk of the nation," which had still not grasped the meaning of France's defeat, "if only because they still have in their heads the very errors that led them to defeat." Teachers could not simply stand aside as spectators while Pétain, Laval, and others remade France. "Any man who pretends to hold himself in reserve reveals himself, inertia is only a cover for resistance. The Marshal said it clearly, life is not neutral. The teaching of neutrality amounts to the teaching of nothing. It will not furnish our children the nourishment they require." Lacking proper advice from their teachers, the young French had come under the influence of "abominable English propaganda" that had found occasionally "an underground echo" in the classroom. If this was understandable in the immediate disarray caused by the defeat, "nothing of the sort will be tolerated any longer." Although it may have been reasonable under the republic to avoid plunging schoolchildren into "political controversies," times had changed. Words changed meaning in different circumstances:

> In the past politics was for the French a dreadful routine of disharmony, an opportunity to fight among themselves. . . . Politics today has become once again what it should never have stopped being, the art of rebuilding France with the cooperation of all the French people.[53]

Obviously pleased with this insight about the changing meaning of words, the minister returned to it a few months later in a speech broadcast by radio to elementary teachers. Claiming that he was not concerned with their past opinions, *provided, of course, that they had changed them,* Bonnard proclaimed:

> Any Frenchman who remains today what he was yesterday is too small for today's drama.
>
> You, teachers, you have been moved and impassioned by the word Revolution. I do not ask that you drop the concept of Revolution, but that you understand it better. As you have loved it falsely in the past, I ask that you love it correctly today. Revolution, according to an outworn ideology and condemned with a vanished era, was an appeal that the impotence of man addressed to the evil-mindedness of the crowd. . . . Revolution in our new age is on the contrary the best led, the best controlled, the best mastered of all historic events, one in which the will of the leaders responds to the needs of their people, one which is nourished by discipline not by abuse, it is no longer a threat, it is a promise, it is no longer an adventure in which a nation tears itself apart, it is one in which brothers come together; confronted by a loathsome communism, which represents the greatest danger, not only of evil but of abasement, that has ever threatened the future of mankind, this National Revolution will be the triumphal entry of a living order that will replace a dead one.[54]

It was to be the duty and the honor of the nation's teachers to explain the National Revolution to French youth and to lead them along the path to national regeneration.

Because of their position in society, schoolteachers were called on frequently to perform functions outside the classroom that almost automatically involved them in apparent support for the regime. In the public ceremonies celebrating the memory of Joan of Arc, what was more natural than that the local schoolmaster should be the one asked to give a brief description of her achievements? Similarly, a teacher might be the best qualified (possibly, the *only* choice in some rural communes) to act as secretary for the local Légion organization. There is some evidence that such visible public activities created occasional problems for teachers after the liberation, but generally their opinions and political viewpoints were well known to students and parents alike; purge committees were careful to look beyond surface appearances, usually concluding, along with the Inspecteur d'Académie for the Puy-de-Dôme, that with regard to moral and civic education "it is unnecessary to note that the personnel of the elementary teaching corps never forgot . . . the traditional conception of its duty."[55]

Some activities sponsored by the schools and heralded as important "moral lessons during which French solidarity was exalted,"[56] supposed fruits of the new ideology, were in line with well-established traditions. For example, collection of gifts, money, blankets, clothing, food, and so forth, for the Secours National continued the practice of the Third Republic, which had created the organization in 1939, reviving a similar institution active during World War I. Campaigns to assist in the salvaging of metals, to pick nuts and wild fruits, or to fight insect pests were in this same tradition. More distinctive, though not entirely without precedent in French history (one thinks of the catechisms in praise of Napoleon I), were those activities that contributed to the fostering of a "cult of the Marshal."

In the fall of 1940 teachers were instructed to prepare the first "Christmas surprise" for Marshal Pétain in what was to become a regular component of each year's school program. In February 1941 the minister of education reported that 2,200,000 drawings had been sent by the children to Pétain and that the Marshal was very moved by this *"spontaneous* demonstration by French young people."[57] For Christmas celebrations in 1941 and 1942 delegations of students went to Vichy bringing letters written to the Marshal by students from all over France. These letters were to be *"freely* composed" as part of their schoolwork by the students, although teachers were told, "Only you can judge the best procedure to obtain the largest possible number of *sincere* testimonies."[58] For the 1942–1943 school year, the minister of education ordered that teachers adopt the theme, "The France that we love," using examples of the great heroes of France to inspire the students. Materials sent along with the instructions included a series of brochures illustrating the exploits of great leaders, from Vercingetorix—described with notable poetic license as a "valorous and *undefeated* leader" who had surrendered to Caesar to save his soldiers—to Pétain, who, "of all the great warriors, of all the great diplomats, of all the great organizers our country has produced,"[59] had done the most for France. Students were to be reminded that Pétain had often said he counted on the young people of France to help him in his immense task of reconstruction of the country, and to be exhorted: "Be worthy of him!" Classrooms were to be decorated in keeping with the year's theme—drawings of "Marshal Pétain's visit to the school," "Marshal of France, Head of State," the French colonial empire, "return to the soil," and so forth. Students would be left *free* in their choice of decorations; however, "You might . . . put at their disposition some leaflets that would give them suggestions."[60] What better evidence could be found to confirm Bonnard's observation about the flexibility of language? As is evident from these few examples, along with *politics* and *revolution, spontaneous, freely,* and *sincere* had been transformed to accommodate the New Order.

If this attempt to manipulate young minds through blatant propaganda for the Marshal is almost amusing in retrospect, it underlines the degree to which apparent enthusiasm for the regime was manufactured and orchestrated by the government. "Loyalty leagues" were created as part of regular school activities. Traveling expositions, "The Life and Work of the Marshal," toured cities in southern France, and students were taken in groups to see them. The best students received brochures, photo albums, or "Marshal's commendations" as a reward for their hard work, not unlike their parents; artisans who won contests with their handiwork or mothers for their exemplary fertility were given medals engraved with Pétain's likeness. Those who entered "the best letter" competitions or debates with themes such as "How will the French youth save France?" or "Christmas 1942" knew that numerous references to Pétain were de rigueur if they hoped to win.

Much of the regime's hopes for national renewal through changing attitudes rested on the cooperation of teachers in the classroom, but Vichy's propaganda in favor of the Marshal seemed to address the adult French population as if they were children, too. For example, given the tone and simplemindedness of this advertisement for a calendar illustrated with photographs of Pétain, one is almost surprised by the use of the formal *vous* instead of the more familiar *tu* used when addressing children.

The Marshal's Calendar

You haven't heard about it yet? You don't have one? Without delay, you must remedy the situation, because every Frenchman should have this calendar in his home. In the family home, at the office, in the workshop, in the store, everywhere one can find a use for this handy object, which in fact is doubly useful, because at the same time as you learn the date you are seeking, you will be able to follow, month after month, in a striking photograph, the life of the Marshal in his functions as Head of State.[61]

From the early months of the regime, photographs of Pétain were ordered displayed in all public buildings with one in every classroom, and the country was inundated with a flood of Pétain memorabilia of all sorts.

The omnipresence of the words and images of Marshal Pétain has often been cited in discussions about the "unanimity" of support for Vichy in its first years, but what did this evidence of hero worship amount to in reality? In early February 1941, only seven months after the vote of full powers to Pétain, the members of a club for science students at the University of Clermont voted on the question of whether or not to put up a picture of Pétain in their meeting place. The results were: sixteen for, sixteen against, and five abstentions. The photo was not put on the wall.[62] Leaving until later a fuller discussion of the level of popular support for Pétain and the Vichy regime, we must admit that we cannot know how many people, *given a choice,* would have demonstrated their enthusiasm for the regime by displaying photos of Pétain. We do know that no such free choice was available for most people.

In its determination to promote a new morality in French society, the Vichy regime took up an active role as moral censor, purging school libraries and public bookstores of objectionable books and intervening in other ways to influence the public and private behavior of children and adults as well. The words *order, discipline, authority,* and *morality* were constantly on the lips of the regime's spokesmen and their subordinates at the local level. In December 1940 in the little town of Pont-de-Dore near Thiers, a young Swiss woman was denied permission to organize a sports club for girls because her conduct was said to be "rather loose."[63] In the summer of 1941 a journalist was denied the renewal of his driver's permit because he had been seen using his car and wasting gas for Sunday meals in the company of "young girls of questionable morality."[64] Public balls, even on private property, were forbidden in the Puy-de-Dôme because authorities believed public gaiety was inappropriate to France's circumstances, and particularly because, "Too often wives whose husbands are prisoners of war let themselves go and join in. . . ."[65] Requests to Pétain to serve as honorary godfather to French children were always followed by thorough police investigations of the parents; if any question about the family's morality arose, permission was refused. Because a certain woman at Randan had outdone herself in terms of the regime's ideal of large families—she had given birth to *seventeen* children—Pétain agreed to be a godfather to the latest of her children in the fall of 1943; but the police who had investigated the family nevertheless expressed their concern about one of the other children. Marie-Antoinette was considered a flirt whom the gendarmerie should perhaps keep an eye on: "This young woman needs to be watched and held in check; her mother, despite the punishments she inflicts, is not capable of handling her."[66]

Vichy was especially anxious that representatives of public order embody the ideals of the National Revolution. Pierre Pucheu, minister of the interior in 1941, informed the intendants de police of his desire to be "precisely informed about the *moral character* and the degree of loyalty toward the Government as well as about the physical aptitude and professional competency of each civil servant."[67] The intendant at Clermont-Ferrand, unintentionally testifying to the lack of success of his exhortations by periodic repetition of the same orders with additional threats of sanctions, called on the local police to wear clean uniforms, use proper salutes, stay out of cafés and bistros and away from drink while in uniform. Faithfully echoing the regime's favorite watchwords, he proclaimed: "Disciplined myself, as much as anyone, I believe that at the present hour discipline is a necessity for it is the mother of order and authority, indispensable factors for the renewal of the country."[68]

The private behavior of policemen was subject to scrutiny, and their wives were also watched closely; the approval of one's superior officer was required for marriage. In November 1941 a Gardien de la paix in the GMR (Gardes Mobiles de Réserve) d'Auvergne was refused permission to marry and ordered to stop living with his intended bride, accused of having "loose morals." The intendant de police instructed the unit's commanding officer to see that his orders were obeyed, adding that if not: "I will demand that he resign."[69] Vichy was not the first or last government in history, of course, to desire discipline or require temperate behavior on the part of its public servants, but one is struck by how persistently, almost fanatically, the regime clung to and attempted to apply the guidelines of its particular "morality" right down through the last desperate days of the occupation. Only a few days before the Allied landings in Normandy, when it was extremely difficult to find anyone who would fight willingly to support the crumbling Vichy regime, police at Clermont-Ferrand refused to accept three out of the five men proposed by the directors of the Ateliers de Construction du Centre as armed guards to protect the factory from resistance sabotage. All three men were certified as politically "correct" with good work records, but one was rejected because of a tendency to drink and the other two eliminated because of the suspected loose morality *of their wives!*[70]

On a much smaller scale than in Nazi Germany, and without elaborate public participation in or celebration of the fact, but with a similar intention of thought control through prohibition, there were book burnings in Vichy France. In April 1941, in what was described as a contribution "to the action of the Government against communism and in favor of the moral revival of the Nation,"[71] the first of several lists of books to be withdrawn from public libraries was sent out over the signature of Admiral Darlan, along with the announcement of the creation of an interministerial committee to decide about further exclusions of works judged "of extremist political viewpoint, or contrary to the fundamental notion of morality."[72] The government was dismayed by the lack of cooperation from teachers in this procedure, complaining in January 1942 that nine months after being ordered to do so, "only a dozen departments"[73] had provided lists and brief descriptions of those works recommended for removal. The committee nevertheless selected several hundred additional titles for extirpation, including bookstores as well as libraries in their ban on circulation of the offensive literature.

Most of the books selected were either political or pornographic in content. The authors designated as having written "tendentious books" were almost all Socialists, Communists, or Anarchists. The "viewpoint" under attack was easily discerned. The works of Marx, Engels, Lenin, Bakunin, and Kropotkin were joined by those of Blanqui, Guesde, Liebknecht, Lassalle, Kautsky, Blum, and many others, including not only major political treatises but books like *L'Oeuvre littéraire de Léon Blum* and biographies of various Socialist thinkers. Several anticlerical books (*La Peste religieuse, Vers l'idéal laïque et Républicain,* and so forth) were banned, as were titles that were clearly erotic or suggestive of sexual themes (*Cléopatre voluptueuse, Nuits de la casbah, La Danseuse de Singapour, La Volupté éclairant le monde, L'Ile des seins nus,* and so forth); occasionally the two themes were combined (*Femme et prêtre, La Passion amoureuse de Jésus de Nazareth*). Authors of little apparent literary merit shared the honor of exclusion with some figures of greater prominence, such as Zola (*Nana, La Terre, Pot Bouille*), Gide (*Le Procès d'Oscar Wilde*), Lawrence (*Lady Chatterly's Lover*), Rolland (*Jean-Christophe*), and Scott (*Ivanhoe*).

The reasons for selection of a particular work were not entirely clear. "Les Tribulations d'un pêcheur à la ligne" was deemed unsuitable for children, and *Jean-Christophe* and *Ivanhoe* were withdrawn because they were termed "mediocrities." The literal destruction of books seems to have been restricted to those classified as pornographic and ordered "turned into pulp." Those presenting a "historical, scientific, or documentary character" were to be placed in separate locations, with access obtainable by special permission for the use of scholars or others with serious reasons for consulting them. School libraries were supposed to have been reclassified and supervised closely by the teachers, with special sections for children and adults, although the Inspecteur de l'Enseignement Primaire for the Puy-de-Dôme seems to have believed that the adults were in as much need of "protection" as the children. Arguing that the works of Renan, Lamarck, Anatole France, and others should be put on separate shelves, he claimed: "The readers who use the school libraries usually lack the necessary minimum of philosophical sophistication to avoid being unnecessarily disturbed by such books."[74]

This particular official might have had a particularly low opinion of the intelligence of his Auvergnat neighbors, but the tone of his admonition that teachers should be especially careful in making decisions about lending library books was typical of the Vichy regime, much of whose propaganda, as mentioned earlier, addressed the French as if they were infants. Acting along these same lines, the government stepped in to prohibit the sale of certain board games that were considered "potentially corrupting to young people." The characters in the games *Big House* and *Chicago* were gangsters who won the game by robbing the most banks, jewelry stores, and so forth, avoiding capture by the police. According to the Ministry of the Interior: "This brief description will make it sufficiently clear the unhealthy influence such a pastime could exert on children and young men, awakening and developing in them the worst instincts."[75] (Ironically, at that very moment, August 1943, many young men, members of the burgeoning maquis groups, were in fact out in the countryside, robbing banks and avoiding the police; but one doubts that *Big House* or *Chicago* had much to do with it. Police at Clermont reported that the games were not on sale locally!) Similarly, "motivated by a concern to reeducate the public and restore, in matters of musical selection, the best traditions of French taste,"[76] jazz was exorcised from the list of records that were allowed to be played in public places, and only orchestras that had expunged jazz from their repertoire were given authorization to play concerts.

The Vichy government was not the first nor the last French regime to attempt to influence public taste or morality, but Vichy officials exhibited to a remarkable degree the apparent belief that they could mold behavior and attitudes through the selection of what passed before the eyes and ears of the French public. In this sense Vichy's New Order contrasted sharply with its republican predecessor. Jules Ferry, midwife of the Third Republic's public education system, writing in October 1880 about the choice of books to be used in the schools, said that there were two possibilities, "the path of authority and the path of liberty," noting that the republic had chosen the second way. In July 1913 Louis Barthou, as Ministre de l'Instruction Publique et des Beaux-Arts, had reaffirmed the liberal principle for selection of books to be used in the schools:

> The State has not for an instant considered reserving for itself the easy but dangerous privilege of drawing up an official catalog of books to be placed in the hands of teachers and students. It has not wished to impose a doctrine, a system of morality, a historical dogma, or a scientific method. It believes that liberty alone can animate, fertilize, and enliven teaching, that any imposed doctrine results in formulas taught without faith and learned without the vital adhesion of the intellect and the heart.[77]

To be sure, the examination system, readings selected independently by teachers, and so on, inevitably had restricted choice; certain works deemed "contrary to morality, the constitution, or the laws" or considered a threat to "scholarly neutrality" had been proscribed from the Third Republic's classrooms.[78] But the democratic procedure through which such censorship decisions had been taken, and the extremely limited number of times such a practice was utilized for a few works—some proclerical works were banned at the height of the controversy over the formal separation of church and state—were in marked contrast to the Vichy regime's assumption that such actions were a desirable, routine responsibility of government.

Religion and the Organization of Youth

The regime's encouragement of religious education was another area in which Vichy's New Order broke conspicuously with the evolution of the Third Republic whose leaders had forced through the separation of church and state and had substituted "civic instruction" for religious instruction. Few of the leaders of the Vichy regime were fanatically religious, but— not entirely unlike those supporters of the Falloux Law following the revolutionary disturbances of 1848, who believed that a small dose of religion might be a good thing for French youth—many of them felt that French Catholicism's support for order and discipline, and its respect for the family and the established political hierarchy, was in keeping with their design for a more disciplined, obedient nation. Pétain told children that they should go to mass because they would learn "good things"[79] there. His government allowed clergy to teach in their habit, ordered religious instruction to be incorporated into the curriculum of public schools, and offered financial aid to private as well as public schools. Nurtured in a long tradition that had associated "clericalism" with "obscurantism," many French teachers, who might not have hesitated to celebrate the legend of Marshal Pétain as Victor of Verdun and savior of the nation, were alienated from the Vichy regime by the imposition of religious instruction in the schools. Quite possibly the church lost more in public esteem than it gained by its public association with the regime; in practice Vichy promised more than it delivered to the French Catholic church.

Statistics for school attendance in the Puy-de-Dôme and for France in general during the 1940s suggest a slight relative increase in students attending private elementary schools that may reflect the influence of Vichy's support for Catholic education.[80] Public écoles maternelles continued to gain at the expense of the private schools, and when one considers the number of Jewish children and other refugees uprooted by

the war and occupation who received private tutoring outside of the regular system, no significant impact of the government's policies was discernible in terms of patterns of attendance. One reason for a lack of any dramatic alteration of the balance between public and private schools was that the state's direct subvention to Catholic schools amounted to very little. Although the bishop of Clermont-Ferrand had celebrated Vichy's educational reforms as "a just return to equity," proclaiming, "With the Marshal Equality is no longer simply inscribed on the facades of public monuments, it will reach the people and children of France,"[81] the funds that would have been necessary to produce a meaningful transformation simply were not available. Many directors of private schools who had greeted the school reforms as a potential bonanza were bitterly disappointed, grumbling that Pétain's promises of a New Order were not being kept when their requests for public funds to pay for utilities, food, and school supplies were denied by the government.

In response to several such requests in the Puy-de-Dôme, the prefect explained that a law of 6 January 1941 had specified, "Communes *may* share in the expenses for heating, lighting, equipment, and kitchens for private institutions," but *"no obligation* is placed on the communes to support the private schools . . . the *possibility* is simply *left open to them to do it."*[82] Because the communes, which bore the chief responsibility for financing public education, were at least as short of funds as the central government, only rarely and then with parsimony did they award subsidies to private schools. Almost a year after orders were issued for their creation, more than half of the communes in the Puy-de-Dôme still had not formed the caisses des écoles, which were designed to encourage the children of poor families to attend school. Even where these caisses existed they provided only "a drop in the bucket"[83] for the most destitute, and almost all of the limited funds were attributed to public rather than private schools. Although the church apparently was pleased to be given more consideration and respect by Vichy than it had enjoyed under the Third Republic, the bishops probably would have welcomed higher levels of material, not simply verbal, sustenance.

For its part the government made no bones about the fact that it expected an enthusiastic endorsement from the Catholic church for the New Order. Noting that some confusion existed because of orders issued by several bishops that clergy in their dioceses should not become involved in politics by serving as municipal councilors or accepting offices in the Légion, a government spokesman stated, "The intent of the Government is to associate the religious forces in the reconstruction of the Country while avoiding giving them an exclusive role which could only favor the birth of an anticlerical reaction in public life."[84] Prefects were encouraged to use their control over public funds for education to induce the clergy to support the New Order. In July 1942 Pierre Laval directed the prefects to inform him at once should they hear of any member of the clergy whose attitude or words were "incompatible with the Government's policies," reminding them that the government's "generosity" toward the church schools "must entail on the part of the clergy an understanding attitude."[85]

It is unlikely that any such leverage was necessary to convince the bishop of Clermont-Ferrand to support the New Order. Monsignor Gabriel Piguet was among the Vichy regime's most outspoken and loyal champions. At the outbreak of the war and throughout the Battle of France, Monsignor Piguet had joined his fellow clergymen in praying that God would bring victory to French arms and in condemning the Germans, those "Motorized Ostrogoths of the twentieth century," of whom, following the invasion of France, he said: "Never in the history of the world have barbarians such as these come to desecrate our land."[86] Immediately following France's defeat, even before Pétain was voted full powers, the bishop was talking about a "new order"[87] that was to be established in France. His calls for penitence, for a recognition and cure of the faults that had led to disaster—these included materialism, sectarianism, false ideologies, immorality, dechristianization, and so on—echoed many of Vichy's favorite themes; often Piguet simply used Pétain's words to express the "necessary lessons. . . . The spirit of pleasure has overwhelmed the spirit of sacrifice. We have demanded more than we have served. We have wished to avoid effort. Today we are reaping the calamity. . . ."[88] Subscribing wholeheartedly to most of the goals of Pétain's projected National Revolution, Piguet incited the priests of his diocese to be "apostles for teaching, for saving, for rebuilding . . .";[89] he urged Catholic teachers to become "the best artisans of the rebirth of our dear Fatherland";[90] and he admonished all good Catholics to offer their spiritual support "to French renewal,"[91] insisting that "the National Revolution must not remain simply a phrase."[92] For the celebration marking the first anniversary of the Légion, Piguet ordered bells to be rung in all of the churches under his jurisdiction to indicate the Catholics' attachment to Marshal Pétain and the national unity he represented. Celebrating mass for those festivities, the bishop stated clearly and unequivocally his position with regard to the Vichy regime and toward those who might oppose France's New Order:

> In the troubled times through which we live and in which people seem bent on dividing, misleading, stirring up opinion in our country, I am fulfilling my role as religious leader and Father of your souls in saying to you, outside of and above any partisan spirit, that in the present circumstances any dissidence, in the interior or the exterior, camouflaged or avowed, in whatever place it may be found, is a misfortune and a transgression.

It is a transgression against the Christian spirit, because Catholic morality teaches submission to the legitimate secular authorities. . . . It is a
transgression against good sense, because we must not forget either the
causes of our misery, or the noble and wise words of the providential Head
of State . . . there can be no French unity other than around the Person
and the Government of the Marshal.[93]

As time passed, Piguet's insistent appeals for unity around Pétain
betrayed the fact that many Clermontois were not following his advice;
occasionally his despair over conditions in occupied France burst to the
surface, as in his 1943 Christmas address, when amid prayers for an end
to war, suffering, and the destruction of the human personality, he lamented: "Alas, justice has deserted the earth."[94] But until 28 May 1944
when he was arrested on the basis of uncertain evidence by the Germans
for his alleged involvement in the hiding of a fugitive priest, Monsignor
Piguet clung to his belief that Pétain was France's only possible savior and
persisted in his public condemnation of those involved in resistance to
Vichy, accusing them of following "slanted, suspect and criminal directives" drawn from foreign sources or false ideologies. It is true that *La
Semaine religieuse,* the church's newsletter, was subject to both French
and German censorship, and some articles were imposed directly by the
government. This would explain why the items published under the "general chronicle" that refer to atrocities, the horrors of war, or destruction
of the human spirit all refer to Allied bombings in France and Italy or
conditions in Soviet prison camps. It is also true that some articles published in *La Semaine religieuse,* notably the passages quoting a collective
letter from the French episcopate and similar statements by the Pope
calling for the defense of "the human person,"[95] could be read between
the lines as criticism of nazism or fascism. But when the bishop of Clermont-Ferrand mentioned *by name* the offenders responsible for "hundreds
of deaths of innocent people, . . . an odious and treacherous aggression,"[96] and the doctrines responsible for the development of hatred and
the "contempt for the human person,"[97] these inevitably turned out to be
the Americans or the English and communism. So fervent and consistent
was Monsignor Piguet's public support for Pétain and the Vichy regime,
as was his condemnation of their opponents, that one may speculate
whether or not his fate might have been different in liberated France had
he not been deported to Dachau and thus welcomed home warmly with
other survivors of the concentration camps.

Aside from higher visibility—Piguet, as did lesser priests in local Légion
ceremonies, frequently joined Pétain, Darlan, Laval, and other dignitaries
of the regime in the front rank of viewing stands set up on the place de
Jaude for the parades that were an important part of Vichy's celebrations

of various sorts at Clermont-Ferrand—there is little evidence that the church reaped significant benefits from its close public association with the government or from the bishop of Clermont's outspoken loyalty. Piguet, probably expecting some cooperation, or at least some sympathy, from the government in such enterprises, attempted to play an active role as the champion of a conservative concept of "virtue" and "morality" in French society. For example, in June 1941, upset by women dressing informally for church services in the diocese's recreational areas, he called on Catholics to "denounce the indecency of immodest attire and to insist on the application of the law," claiming: "There can be no serious renewal of our country in the perversity of morality and the indecency of clothing styles."[98] Similarly, in September 1942, insisting that "the physical and moral future of French youth was endangered by mixed schools," those in which boys and girls shared the same classrooms, the bishop, citing his duty as "Representative and Guardian of Christian Morality," ordered Catholic parents to approach their city councils and local magistrates to demand that such classes be abolished. Parents and priests in several communes in the vicinity of Clermont-Ferrand responded to the bishop's exhortation with protests about the mixed classes to their local authorities, but they were turned away with flat refusals, and in some cases even received lectures in a different sort of "morality" from these officials. One mayor told a curé pointedly that "in a moment during which the country is passing through somber hours, it is perhaps a poor idea to raise problems which really have no foundation in fact."[99] A few months later the minister of education told the prefect of the Puy-de-Dôme to ignore requests for the suppression of mixed classes, noting that parents and academic authorities agreed that the impact of "gemination" since 1933 had been positive and that he had never received *spontaneous* complaints about these schools. As an afterthought, perhaps intended to demonstrate that he was as concerned with "morality" as anyone, the minister added that "children of different sex must not sit on the same row of seats, recreation classes will remain separate, as will restroom facilities."[100]

Overall, the relation between church and state at Clermont-Ferrand and the activity of the clergy during the Vichy era were not particularly out of line with the situation in the country at large, except perhaps that in his reverence for Marshal Pétain, Bishop Piguet was more outspoken and persistent than ecclesiastics elsewhere who more rapidly began to mark their distance from the regime with a more neutral public posture. In the vicinity of Clermont-Ferrand as in France generally, many priests, acting in line with traditional conceptions of Christian charity, were involved in activities that contributed to the preservation of human life whether or not they were directly linked to organized resistance movements. This protective, helping, and saving behavior, which contrasted with the public position of most of the church hierarchy, was no secret to many French people, and helps to explain why there was not a massive anticlerical reaction following the liberation. In the Puy-de-Dôme several motions were presented to the new authorities to repeal religious instruction in the schools and prevent priests from wearing their habits in the classroom; the ties of a couple of priests with collaborationist groups were investigated; and the Commissaire de la République, citing plans for a counterdemonstration at the time of bishop Piguet's return from Dachau, did report evidence for the persistence of the traditional animosity between "laic circles"[101] and the Catholics. A general survey drawn up for the minister of the interior describing the actions of the clergy in the Puy-de-Dôme during the occupation, however, stressed a popular recognition of the contributions of the church to the resistance, concluding: "These actions motivated by patriotism and Christian charity were not played up by publicity or fanfare, but the silent resistance was by no means ineffective."[102]

In one significant area the attitudes of the Catholic hierarchy diverged from the wishes of at least some high officials at Vichy. Although strongly advocated by collaborationist journals in Paris, and finding several champions among the ministers and high civil servants at Vichy, the idea of a "jeunesse unique"—one large, unified youth movement organized and run according to the principles of the National Revolution—did not become a reality in wartime France. Rival conceptions of an overall strategy for a new system that in conjunction with the schools would be called on to mold French youth, the clash of personalities, the suspicions of the German occupation authorities, the lack of firm support from Pétain, and the spirit of independence of long-established organizations such as the Scouts—all contributed to the failure of a united French youth movement. In addition to these factors, the opposition of the Catholic church certainly played an important part in undermining any possibility that French children would be grouped into an authoritarian formation along the lines of Germany's Hitler Jugend. Addressing a congress of the Jeunes d'Action Catholique (JAC) in May 1941, Monsignor Piguet, faithfully echoing the French episcopate's position, told his young auditors: "Remain true to yourselves. Keep the JAC independent. The unification of the various youth movements would be an absurdity, and it is not desired by the government. The JAC must retain its full vitality, assured by the originality of its methods."[103]

Along with control of information, frequent addresses and appeals to the public by leading government personalities, and the orientation of education, the mobilization of youth movements as living incarnations of the government's propaganda themes represented an attempt by Vichy to institutionalize support for the New Order. According to the Auvergne's regional delegate of the secrétariat général à la jeunesse, the government's goal was no less than the rebirth of France through the moral and physical education of French youth. By improving sports facilities and organizing participation in outdoor sports and group singing, local representatives of the secrétariat général à la jeunesse were to "give a helping hand to the Marshal" by seeing to "physical development and the moral revival of our race."[104] The idea of centralized supervision of such activities by the secrétariat made little progress in the area, however. Not until the summer of 1943 were male and female departmental chiefs for the Puy-de-Dôme appointed to constitute teams of young men and women for various civic and social services, and the projected local network of delegates was never put into place, nor was anything of substance achieved. In the spring of 1942 the Ministry of Education under Abel Bonnard had attempted to push the organization of French youth in a more rigorous, authoritarian line, sponsoring an organization called the Jeunes du Maréchal. Three divisions were planned for these groups. The Cadets, 8 to 12 years old, would mostly play games, and emphasis on the cult of the hero was to help them develop the "taste for the marvelous." The Jeunes du Maréchal, 12 to 14 years old, would be given a "stoic training," utilizing group activities, physical education, and patriotic demonstrations, and stressing unity, discipline, and a sense of hierarchy and community. Finally, the Gardes du Maréchal, those above age 14, would be ready for "involvement in collective life" after political training had taught them "orderly reflexes, understanding of order, defense of order."

In the Puy-de-Dôme, responses to Bonnard's initiative in favor of the Jeunes du Maréchal ranged from indifference to hostility. Headmasters of the schools argued that nothing could be done before the next fall term because students were off studying for examinations and teachers were busy with grading. Several teachers pointed out that such groups would compete with already existing organizations so that recruitment of members would be difficult. Others said that there were already too many groups in the schools, and an inspecteur primaire at Clermont-Ferrand flatly opposed forming groups of Jeunes du Maréchal, claiming that the students were already attached to Pétain without the need for "more or less artificial creations." The inspector claimed that a large number of the best students were already in Scout groups that they had no intention of leaving, and added that "many families are expressing more and more their discontent at seeing introduced in the schools a host of new things to the detriment of instruction and regular work schedules." Other groups—Equipes et Cadres de la France Nouvelle, Les Compagnons de France, and La Jeune Légion, to name only a few—made sporadic attempts to organize French youth, but none succeeded in supplanting the traditional Scout and Catholic Action groups within whose framework were continued as before the war the group activities and physical education that the secrétariat général à la jeunesse had hoped to boost.[105]

One organization created by Vichy that did have a meaningful impact on the lives of thousands of French youth, or young adults, was the Chantiers de la Jeunesse. Born of the inspiration of General Paul de La Porte du Theil, whose experience in both scouting and the army was reflected in their organization and activities, the Chantiers de la Jeunesse were first organized to take care of the class of 100,000 men who had been called up for military service in the spring of 1940 just as France was being defeated. La Porte du Theil hoped to create a reserve for the future of men who, without military training per se because this was impossible under the terms of the Armistice, would be physically and morally prepared to form the disciplined core of a new French army when circumstances would permit it to emerge. In the following years the Chantiers were turned into an obligatory substitute for military service for all 20-year-olds, who were to serve an eight-month *stage* in one of the encampments that served as home to from several hundred to 2000 men. The young men were given a heavy dose of physical exercise, camping, and exposure to nature and the open air—the mountains and forests of the countryside being considered a far more healthful environment than the corrupt cities. Hard work, especially in forestry and agriculture, was demanded of the Chantiers, and a community spirit was fostered by working, playing, and singing in groups.

In 1943 a physician who had examined a large number of men 21 to 24 years old for possible incorporation in contingents required by the Service du Travail Obligatoire (STO) remarked that in contrast to his image of prewar youths, almost all of them had been "exceptionally proper." He wondered: "Can one already see the influence of the camps de Jeunesse?"[106] A skeptic might note that fear of deportation for work in Germany was at least as great a motivation for proper behavior in those circumstances, but the doctor's question did reflect accurately one of Vichy's hopes for the Chantiers. Their experience in the Chantiers was expected to "ingrain in young people the spirit of discipline and respect for authority."[107]

Overall, the Chantiers de la Jeunesse made an important contribution to the French economy, affording cheap labor for forestry (cutting wood for use with charcoal-burning motors and planting new trees), agriculture, and the upkeep and improvement of the road system in rural areas; undoubtedly they served to enhance the physical fitness of thousands of young men. But the Chantiers were not conspicuously successful in winning over French youth to the ideology of the National Revolution. Most young men seem to have experienced their stay in the Chantiers in much the same manner as young men in all times have reacted to obligatory military service—some recalling the bad food, poor housing, and isolation; others appreciating the camaraderie with other young men who in some cases became lifelong friends. Levels of enthusiasm for the Vichy regime varied somewhat from camp to camp, often closely related to the ardor of individual commanders, but the Chantiers were far from forming a united phalanx in support of the New Order. The same individuals might well sing "Marshal, here we are" while marching in file through a village near their camp, and yet desert to resistance maquis when faced with transfer for service in the forced labor draft. After the occupation of the southern zone, the Chantiers, already under close surveillance by the Germans who suspected their leaders of conducting camouflaged military training in the camps, fell easy prey to maquis bands who stole from them clothing, food, and other equipment, almost at will, rarely encountering serious opposition to their actions.

Ultimately, early in 1944 the Chantiers de la Jeunesse were closed down at the Germans' insistence, and something of a scramble developed to see whether the agents of the STO or the resisters would capture the young men and whether the French government, the resistance, or the Germans would take over the equipment being abandoned at the Chantiers' campsites. Long before the dissolution of the Chantiers, considerable evidence of their political unreliability had surfaced. German officers had complained about their lack of respect for the führer when newsreels of Hitler shown in cinemas at Chatel-Guyon had been greeted with whistling and howls of laughter from members of the Chantiers. A report on attitudes and behavior in the Chantiers of the Auvergne, submitted after an inspection visit through the area during the summer of 1942, noted that the commanders of the camps were listening to the BBC and commenting favorably to the young men about the British-Canadian commando operation at Dieppe. The observer indicated that for the typing of his report he had been forced to use the secretary of the regional propaganda officer, because he did not trust the staff of the Commissariat de la Jeunesse who had intercepted earlier reports and recommended that he no longer be allowed access to the camps for "spying," concluding: "Unhappily, I fear that the anti-German sentiment is much stronger in the Chantiers than we thought, and this Germanophobia borders on Anglophilia, not to mention Gaullism."[108] Perhaps not surprisingly, the regional head of the Chantiers for the Auvergne was one of those most suspected by the German police of resistance sympathies, and he as well as La Porte de Theil would be arrested during the winter of 1943–1944 and deported.

As the demand for laborers to work in German factories grew strong in 1943, groups from the Chantiers were ordered to go directly from the camps (one-sixth of the STO contingent for February and March 1943 were selected from the Chantiers), and the young men designated for departure became virtual prisoners. Police reports stated: "These departures are not always well accepted, and one must admit that the precautionary measure of preventing the youths scheduled to depart from going home to see their families is generally considered to be inhumane."[109] At the very least, by such treatment of these young men the regime's actions reflected its frank acknowledgment that the Chantiers had failed to create disciplined cohorts ready to obey their leaders' commands whatever the consequences might be. Despite the regime's best efforts, a "moral renewal" in the sense desired by Vichy simply had not taken hold.[110]

3

The New Order: The Légion Française des Combattants and the Mobilization of Adults

With Philippe Pétain's appeal to French veterans to join a united Légion Française des Combattants, Vichy came closer to creating a mass movement for the mobilization of enthusiasm for the National Revolution than it did in its attempts to regiment French youth. But even the Légion, which was the regime's most successful creation in terms of numbers of adherents, fell far short of the hopes placed in it by its organizers and their most committed followers. Clermont-Ferrand and the department of the Puy-de-Dôme were associated closely with the birth and development of the Légion. Clermont and the neighboring Plateau de Gergovie were selected as sites for elaborate ceremonies commemorating the second and third anniversaries of the founding of the Légion; and several of the most prominent directors of the Légion were from the area. Dr. Vimal de Flechac, chef régional for the Auvergne, was a member of the Légion's national directory, and in the summer of 1942, Raymond Lachal, the mayor of Ambert, a friend and protégé of Pierre Laval, became the directeur général of the Légion.

Even before the signing of the Armistice, the leaders of Clermont-Ferrand's prewar veterans organizations had published an "Appel des Anciens Combattants" in the local newspapers calling on all veterans to offer their full support to Pétain—"The illustrious leader who incarnated French resistance at Verdun," who had offered "all his soul, all his courage, all his glory to the service of France."[1]—requesting specifically that they cooperate with local authorities to assist in welcoming and housing refugees. In late June 1940 when Clermont was selected to become—for only a few days, as it turned out—the seat of the new French government after it left Bordeaux, the same leaders sent a message of welcome to Pétain affirming their loyalty to him and seeming to suggest their anticipation of an altered destiny for France under Pétain: "Please accept the homage and welcome to the Auvergne from your soldiers of Verdun who share your pain, understand your actions, and quiver in your hopes."[2] Expectations that a government under Pétain might be sensitive to their concerns must have been strengthened by Laval's promise to Raymond Grasset, the first head of the Légion for the Puy-de-Dôme and later minister of health in the Vichy government, of a "privileged position in French reconstruction for the War Veterans."[3] Grasset claimed that Laval had pledged this in a conversation at Clermont-Ferrand the day after full powers were voted to Pétain, but without specifying the form or manner in which this special role would be assured.

After the Légion was formally established on 30 August 1940, in accordance with the model drawn up for Pétain's approval by Xavier Vallat, Grasset was involved in a letter-writing campaign to secure the adherence of all of the former veterans associations to the idea of a single, united organization. Although a unified veterans organization was now imposed by the government, differences of opinion, conflicts of personality, and other factors that had defeated prewar attempts to unify the veterans associations did not disappear at the snap of Marshal Pétain's fingers, as some champions of fusion had hoped they would. Responses from many regions of southern France to Grasset's letters indicated a warm reception for the idea of a "légion unique,"[4] but widespread objections to the direct transfer to the Légion of all of the funds of the former organizations and opposition to the appointment instead of election, as in the past, of local, departmental, and national directors for the new Légion. These issues and the political coloration of those men appointed as presidents of local and departmental units help to explain why the Légion's initial recruitment campaign fell well below the director's original expectations.

Although the Légion was touted as a nonpartisan organization and most often "nonpolitical" but usually conservative officials were named, where political viewpoints were identifiable right-wing affiliations were predominant. Vimal de Flechac, representative of the Auvergne region on the directorate, had belonged to the URD and held a "very decidedly right-wing viewpoint." In the Puy-de-Dôme Grasset was a former Radical, but a safely conservative one, "never having expressed his adherence to the Popular Front," according to a police report. The chief for Clermont-Ferrand, Gilbert Sardier, a popular World War I air force hero, had "decidedly right-wing opinions," and one of the vice-presidents and another important leader of the Légion for the city of Clermont were former members of Colonel de la Rocque's PSF (Parti Social Français).[5]

In a report to François Valentin, national director of the Légion, about the first three months of Légion activity in the Puy-de-Dôme, Grasset, calculating that on the basis of membership in the prewar associations of World War veterans alone, the Légion should have been able to enroll a minimum of 40,000 adherents in the department, reported dejectedly: "In fact *we have not reached the total of 15,000 légionnaires after a vigorous effort of two and one-half months*. One must know how to recognize a failure. This is one."[6] The situation was perhaps the worst in the city of Clermont-Ferrand, Grasset's hometown, where "the working class remains indifferent, if not hostile."[7] In the largest population center of the Auvergne, a city of 110,000, the Légion had not yet reached a total of 2500 légionnaires, and enthusiasm was on the wane ("Membership is increased only with difficulty").[8] According to Grasset, the principal cause for this disappointing beginning was that a certain *tendance* was being given to the Légion:

> The Légion is disappointing certain people, is treated with suspicion by others. They say it is "oriented," too sharply oriented. Instead of playing the role of a national assemblage! . . .
> It is for me an obligation of conscience to say that the Légion which carried so much hope, is in danger of becoming simply the instrument of *one part* of French opinion. . . . The initial conception which shaped the formation of the Légion, that envisaged a unified national party of fervent support for the policies of the Marshal, is already deformed. If we do not watch out, it will soon be no longer recognizable . . . we must not alienate or push aside a notable part of the French people. One cannot govern against public opinion.[9]

The Légion's outlook improved and recruitment was buoyed somewhat in February 1941 when Admiral François Darlan stated officially that the government intended to promote an "intimate collaboration"[10] between public authorities at all levels and the légionnaires. Eventually, almost 30,000 adherents were enrolled in the Puy-de-Dôme (29,632 according to a report in September 1941).[11] At its apogee in mid-1941, for all of the unoccupied zone, the Légion counted within its ranks 1.5 million veterans. On the surface, at least, Vichy would seem to have succeeded in creating a mass movement of imposing dimensions; there can be little doubt that, especially among the older veterans, the Légion reflected an outpouring of genuine admiration for Marshal Pétain and a willingness to march at his command. Thus, it is not surprising that descriptions or photographs of Légion ceremonies often figure prominently in accounts that emphasize the unanimity of public opinion behind Pétain during the first years of the occupation. Still, one should recall the perceptive commentary offered by Jean-Paul Cointet, a leading French authority on the Légion, who cautioned that these maximum totals include: "extremely variable levels of participation and commitment; many saw in the Légion, in joining it, either the assurance of 'having no problems,' or the opportunity to benefit from certain advantages."[12]

Certainly there would seem to have been potentially no more fruitful ground for recruiting servants for the National Revolution than the veterans. What more promising field could a national military hero like Pétain hope to find? Yet, the fact remains that for almost every veteran who chose to join the Légion, another veteran chose not to participate.[13] Enrollment in the Légion of an impressive number of veterans clearly indicated a significant reservoir of support for the New Order, or at least for Pétain, but the abstention of almost half of those eligible for participation from among the most favorably inclined segment of the population suggests a limit to the validity of the thesis of a "unanimity of opinion" behind Pétain.

In the Puy-de-Dôme as elsewhere, membership varied greatly from commune to commune. Among those communes for which such statistics are available, the range in levels of adherence to the Légion is suggested by the contrast between Orcines where 140 of 150 veterans were légionnaires and St. Genès Champenelle where only 37 of 130 joined. The personality or reputation of the local Légion president seems often to have been critical in determining whether or not most or very few veterans would join. At least this was a common explanation given by officials who sought to account for the relative success or failure of the Légion in different towns. For example, based on the observations of the secrétaire général of the prefecture during an inspection in February 1943, the préfet délégué at Clermont-Ferrand explained why fewer than half (100 of 250) of the eligible veterans participated in the Légion at Bourg-Lastic. The good work of the Légion president at Bourg-Lastic was being sabotaged by the syndic (of the Corporation Paysan), who was described as "demagogic and mocking." So the prefect concluded that this man must be eliminated "if we wish to accomplish good Légionnaire work."[14]

One pattern that was common to the Légion in the Puy-de-Dôme and in France generally was that the younger veterans, those of the 1939–1940 campaign, were much less likely to participate than were the World War I veterans. The subprefect at Ambert reported that in the commune of Viverols 80 percent (40 of 50) of the World War I veterans had signed up for the Légion, but only 10 percent (4 of 40) of the recent Battle of France had done so, noting: "As is true everywhere else, the young soldiers of the 1939–1940 war have not joined the Légion."[15] Photographs of Légion ceremonies at Clermont-Ferrand with rank after rank of middle-aged men, chests covered with medals, and reports from every region of the unoccupied zone confirm this impression that the veterans of World War I—those whose sentimental attachment to Pétain was stronger, more visceral—were the ones who swelled the Légion's ranks.

Not unlike the local liberation committees following the liberation of

Veterans at Clermont-Ferrand for Légion ceremonies

France, the local Légion sections, eager to play a significant role "in the service of French rebirth,"[16] were hamstrung from the beginning by the ambiguity of their legal status. Recognized as the chief publicists and propagandists of the National Revolution, many légionnaires aspired to be the instruments of its direct application as well. Therefore, they were extremely dismayed not to have been appointed in greater numbers to prominent posts during the government's early administrative reorganization. In February 1941 Vimal de Flechac asked Xavier Vallat how the légionnaires could act as the base of the National Revolution if they were not put into positions of authority. Arguing that this was the last chance to reverse an already serious morale problem, Vimal urged Vallat to do everything possible to obtain for the Légion a major share of the seats on the soon-to-be named municipal councils.[17] Although illusions to the contrary were occasionally nurtured by the public statements or private confidences of leaders of the Vichy regime, the Légion Français des Combattants was never given the effective political power it desired. The encouragement fostered by Marshal Pétain's statement of 30 June 1942 ("I wish to see, at every echelon where the general interests of the Nation are represented, those organizations stuffed with légionnaires. The légionnaires must be everywhere"[18]) was dashed by the hard reality of repeated instructions to the prefects from Darlan and later Laval that the public authorities should listen to the *advice* and *suggestions* of Légion dignitaries, but the "representatives of the Central Power are the only responsible holders of the constitutional au-

thority of the government."[19] Prefects were told emphatically that cooperation with the Légion "must not hamper your authority."[20] It was not quite
accurate to say, as their leaders often complained, that the légionnaires
were not being listened to; but it was a fact that their opinions could be,
and often were, ignored with impunity by government officials.

In these circumstances, the role of the Légion in Vichy France became
something like a self-appointed moral watchdog over the implementation
of the New Order. In a rousing oration for the constituent assembly of the
Légion in the Puy-de-Dôme, Raymond Grasset claimed that, unlike the opportunity for purge and reform that they had missed with the *Chambre
bleu* (the Chamber of Deputies elected immediately following World War I
and including many veterans), "the Légion française will be something different." The légionnaires were admonished to be "fully imbued with the
idea that things have changed in France" and exhorted to embrace the Légion's goals: "To remake a people, to restore a soul to France."[21]

In carrying out its mission of renewal, the Légion engaged in multiple
activities at the local level. During the first two years of the Vichy regime,
no organization was more in the public spotlight than the Légion Français
de Combattants. Of course, the banning of political parties and the dissolution of the prewar labor organizations meant that few competitors were allowed, thus emphasizing the presence of the Légion. The first work of the
Légion in the Puy-de-Dôme, and the domain of its most worthwhile accomplishments, was the effort made in favor of the French prisoners of
war and their families. In conjunction with the Secours National and the
Red Cross, the légionnaires were tireless in their campaigns to raise money
and collect clothing, food, books, and so forth, for packages to send to the
department's 14,000 POWs and to ease the burden on the prisoners' families who had been left behind in France. As of 1 January 1942 the Légion
in the Puy-de-Dôme had sent 65,807 packages worth 3.5 million francs to
prisoners of war from the department. Occasional problems with packaged
food spoiling, and complaints about details of the administration of the
Maison du Prisonnier or the savings accounts established to facilitate the
prisoners' homecoming and adjustment to life in France cropped up, but
there was virtually unanimous appreciation of the Légion's actions in this
realm. Long after its political activities and pretensions in other regards
had alienated most citizens, the French continued to respond favorably to
Légion activities concerning the prisoners. Describing an outdoor fair sponsored by the Légion in July 1943 at the city's largest public park, the Jardin
Lecoq, the commissaire central de police at Clermont-Ferrand reported:
"It was a great success as is true for anything involving the prisoners of
war."[22]

The Légion was engaged in several other activities that might fall under the heading of civic action. A Légion committee collected information about the cost of living and the status of certain professions at Clermont and worked with officials at the prefecture to propose possible solutions to the area's economic difficulties, especially those regarding food supply. In 1942 the Légion, calling for solidarity between veterans in the countryside and the city, helped organize volunteers to assist with harvests and to transport wheat and other products to the cities to alleviate severe shortages. Local and regional Légion leaders at Clermont-Ferrand were particularly sensitive to the concerns of farmers, who constituted a large majority of the effectives of the Légion. For a lead article in the *Légionnaire* in the spring of 1942, Grasset criticized sharply the alimentary and agricultural policies of the Vichy government which were increasingly vexatious to the farmers. Arguing that "it will not be by multiplying inquisitions, statistics, prohibitions, requisitions, controls, fines, and so forth, . . . that we will improve the production of French soil," Grasset called for new policies based on the ideas "from men of the soil, from those who work it in fact, not from theoreticians who have been kicked out of the University."[23] Similarly, the president of the Légion section at Veyre-Mouton, complaining that his earlier reports had been ignored, warned Gilbert Sardier: "If in high places they persist in not wishing to see the peasant situation clearly, they will be preparing a revolution, but it will not be the national revolution as conceived by the Légion. And the Légion is the first one to suffer the consequences, for its members observe the organization's impotence and wonder if this is what is meant by the new order."[24] In this case, as was true of their attitude toward the operation of the Service du Travail Obligatoire at Clermont-Ferrand, local Légion officials, although staunchly loyal to Pétain and the Vichy government, were willing to take strong stands in opposition to particular policies to which they objected.

In the late fall and winter of 1942–1943, when the relève and then the STO began to transfer thousands of young men to German factories, the Légion counseled obedience to the government's orders and supported its propaganda about the requirements of national solidarity. But Légion directors at Clermont-Ferrand argued strenuously for "equity" of treatment, advocating that veterans be selected after the "affectés spéciaux," those men who had been retained for work in factories instead of being sent to join the fighting men at the front during the 1939–1940 campaign. Sardier and others sent repeated bitter protests about irregularities in the operation of the STO and about legal exemptions that seemed to them to be unfair to veterans. After the liberation some Légion leaders claimed to have saved individual veterans from deportation to Germany by finding them protected jobs in the region; but from correspondence preserved in Légion files at Clermont-Ferrand it appears that Légion leaders at Clermont in most cases stood firmly for application of the STO equitably to all persons. On several occasions they refused to intercede on behalf of sons of légionnaires who had asked for help, even chiding the fathers for failure to exhibit the proper civic attitude.[25]

Critics of the Légion regarded it as a source of special favors, "a sort of placement office, or a recommendation bureau";[26] and, in fact, Légion leaders were very active in attempting to promote the interests of veterans and their relatives or friends. The correspondence of Grasset, Sardier, and Lachal is full of examples of requests for appointments or assistance to veterans. This activity does not seem to be anything beyond the normal practices of veterans groups or other special-interest organizations seeking political patronage on behalf of their members; and intendants de police, prefects, and other officials usually seem to have rejected such propositions when the candidates appeared to be unqualified. Indeed, from the number of times that Légion officials were forced to reply to requests by admitting their failure to obtain favors, one suspects they may have been embarrassed by the frequent revelation of their impotence in this domain. After the German occupation of Clermont-Ferrand, the Légion's lack of real influence was further apparent in its utter failure to obtain information of any sort on behalf of the relatives of those arrested by the German police or military, despite hopes that as former soldiers they might receive a sympathetic hearing from the German military authorities. As if to underscore this situation, Gilbert Sardier was forced to evacuate his apartment and garage to make room for a German officer.

The Légion Française de Combattants presented itself most often before the public in various guises as champion of the National Revolution. The first public demonstration staged by the Légion at Clermont-Ferrand took place in June 1941 on the place Jaude, where 2000 légionnaires passed in review before General Emile Laure, Pétain's secrétaire général. The second and third anniversaries of the founding of the Légion were commemorated in ceremonies at Clermont-Ferrand in August 1942 and 1943; and a monument erected on the Plateau de Gergovie, containing samples of soil from all parts of France mixed together by Marshal Pétain during these festivities, was among the Légion's most cherished shrines. In addition to major patriotic celebrations, the Légion organized sporting events and sponsored drawing, speech, and writing contests with appropriate patriotic themes directed particularly toward the younger generation. In early 1944, undoubtedly too late and with a conspicuous lack of success, the Légion offered "information and documentation sessions" for teachers, hoping to clarify the goals of the National Revolution. Despite a dispensation from their classes and the fact that the Légion offered to pay all of their expenses, *no* teachers from Clermont-Ferrand attended these sessions, and only fifteen

Pétain and Laval visit Clermont-Ferrand, August 1942

of the eighty places available were filled by teachers from other communes of the Puy-de-Dôme.[27]

The légionnaires themselves were called on to demonstrate their loyalty by filling the rows of auditoriums or theaters when various speakers advocating the government's position were scheduled to visit Clermont-Ferrand. On some occasions they were even coached to be sure they applauded loudly and at the proper moments. In preparation for ceremonies to be highlighted by the visit to Clermont of the head of state, Grasset instructed leaders of the local Légion sections that their units must show enthusiasm upon the Marshal's arrival by "prolonged and rousing cheers." Légionnaires were to pay close attention to Pétain's words, providing further "rousing cheers" at appropriate moments and a long ovation at the conclusion of the speech.[28] One is reminded of the regime's attempts to cultivate "spontaneous" enthusiasm in the classrooms of elementary schools. It is particularly striking that Légion officials apparently believed that in the spring of 1942 it was necessary to stimulate fervor, *even from veterans,* in the presence of the illustrious hero of Verdun.

Had the Légion's activities been restricted to well-received efforts in favor of the prisoners of war, largely unsuccessful attempts to wrest a meaningful share of political power from the administration, and public appearances in a multitude of forums in hopes of bolstering the faltering appeal of the policies and programs of Vichy's National Revolution, the French at the time and historians later might have been satisfied with the rather sad commentary of a légionnaire from the section of Courpière, who attempted to summarize the situation of the Légion a few days before Christmas 1942: "After so many great betrayals, what more can one say? That a weariness has invaded Légionnaire circles, which have the impression the National Revolution is nothing more than a phrase. That the veterans may be suitable for parades, but in practical terms they should be put in storage."[29] Such a description might evoke sympathy for what in retrospect seems a pathetic experiment that had failed by the end of 1942, in part derailed by a minority from within its ranks, the more aggressively authoritarian Service d'Ordre Légionnaire (SOL), core of the hated Milice. But long before its effective demise, beneath its carefully cultivated public image of patriotism, unity, and service to an ideal, the Légion Française de Combattants was all too often involved in deleterious action having serious repercussions.

Légionnaires in the Puy-de-Dôme and elsewhere were among the purveyors of anti-Semitic literature, and some of their leaders were quick to denounce the administration's "deficiency" in not acting firmly enough to eliminate Jewish civil servants. Moreover, the Légion—or more accurately, some légionnaires and their hierarchical superiors—was the source of numerous denunciations of fellow French citizens or foreigners for alleged antinational behavior. Sometimes this involved petty matters with results of no particular consequence. For example, when an individual who re-

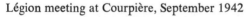

Légion meeting at Courpière, September 1942

fused to make a written statement and insisted that he remain anonymous complained to Légion officials at Clermont-Ferrand that three persons at Martres d'Artières were listening to the BBC, the police, after investigation, decided not to prosecute the individuals involved because they were listening to the radio in their own homes and were not "consciously" spreading antigovernmental propaganda. (One of the men was a "grand mutilé de la guerre 1914–1918, Chevalier de la Légion d'Honneur," who had responded sharply to the question of whether or not he listened to the BBC: "Of course I do!")[30]

In many other instances both the charges and the consequences were more severe. In February 1943 Gilbert Sardier, president of the Légion for the Puy-de-Dôme, received the following note from the president of the Légion in a small community just south of Clermont-Ferrand.

> Monsieur C——, President of the Communal Légion Française at Romagnat, has the honor of pointing out to you a certain G——, of the class of 1927, one of the leading communists at Romagnat, this person deserves your attention, always picking quarrels in the area, a bachelor, 35 years old, perhaps a good choice for Germany, although he complains about a weak arm, it doesn't keep him from fighting. I am confident that you will take care of this matter and the countryside will be a little cleaner.[31]

This letter was passed immediately to the préfet délégué, who ordered a police investigation, and was ultimately sent on for action by the regional prefect. Because relatively few written records remain concerning the ultimate disposition of similar cases, it is impossible to establish exactly how many individuals were deported, were sent off for forced labor, or underwent lesser hardships as a result of denunciations that originated with the Légion. Still, ample evidence survives in the departmental archives to demonstrate that, contrary to some of their statements at the liberation, several leaders of the Légion at Clermont-Ferrand and in the Puy-de-Dôme were directly involved in denunciation of Jews, Gaullists, Communists, Socialists, and of others considered guilty of antinational activities.[32] Understandably, then, a police commissioner at Clermont reported in February 1942: "The public seems to distrust the Légionnaire Movement which it considers to be a political organization for surveillance and spying in the service of the Government."[33] Two years later, trying to explain why the Légion had become a fiasco, Sardier attempted to shift much of the blame onto others.

> The Légion no longer interests anyone; the SOL and the Milice have killed it. To speak of a new spirit and a national revolution when the

whole country is occupied is ridiculous. The Légion has been discredited. It bears the weight in the view of public opinion of having supported the foreign policy of Laval: "one-way collaboration."[34]

Still, the Légion's problems had not all come from the outside, and Sardier admitted candidly: "It was occasionally the instrument of petty village rivalries, of electoral revenge, indeed even of false accusations."[35]

The evidence of denunciations is only one indication of the general sense in which the Légion experiment went sour, corresponding in large measure to the failure of the Vichy regime's attempt to erect a New Order in France. The path that the légionnaires chose to follow was in many ways parallel to the evolution of the Vichy regime. Originally hoping to carry out its National Revolution with popular backing, the regime, confronted early with undeniable and substantial public hostility, turned to elitism and to blatant authoritarianism, deciding to impose by force what it could not obtain through persuasion. One example of this was the utter failure of the Charte du Travail, which was to have rallied French workers to the New Order by demonstrating that the Marshal's government was to be "boldly social," as the Légion's propaganda claimed. Class conflict was to be eliminated and replaced by national solidarity, an idea dear to the hearts of those in many fascist movements of the era of the 1920s and 1930s.

In April 1941 a police official at Clermont-Ferrand noted: "Workers' attitudes are bad. They demand above all from the Government *work and bread*. They do not believe in the national revolution. The new regime leaves them skeptical or indifferent."[36] The definition of a new place for the workers in French society according to the guidelines set out by the Charte du Travail in October 1941 did little to change the workers' outlook toward the Vichy regime. Response was negligible to meetings organized by the Légion to explain the significance of the Charte, with reports that they had drawn "from workers circles especially, only a very feeble attendance, far from being as numerous as one might have hoped for from an industrial region like Clermont-Ferrand."[37] After the return of Laval in 1942, the government through the Ministry of Information tried to establish better relations with French workers by assigning special propaganda delegates to each region. Their primary objective was stated by Paul Marion, the minister of information, in his first general directive to these delegates: "Restore the confidence of the working class in itself by demonstrating that the National Revolution is not a revenge by management against the social reforms of 1936, but that on the contrary, it is . . . a social revolution destined to reintegrate workers into the national community."[38] They failed miserably, as was apparent in the title of a program sponsored by the Légion at Clermont-Ferrand in December 1943, more than two years after the proclamation of the Charte du Travail: "Why are you ignoring the Charte du Travail? Why is it not yet being implemented?"[39]

In fairness to the Vichy regime, the serious deterioration of the conditions of workers in France would in large measure have been beyond the capacity of any French government to control satisfactorily. The serious economic problems and the extraordinary obligations that resulted directly from the German occupation and German insistence on rigorous wage ceilings had made it impossible for wages to keep up with the dramatic rise in the cost of living. Few governments would have been popular in such trying times, and when Laval agreed to sponsor the relève and later the STO, any chance for sympathy from French workers vanished completely. The decision to send out special propaganda delegates to convince the workers that the government was on their side corresponded almost exactly with the opening of a campaign to recruit workers for voluntary transfer to Germany under the relève. At Clermont-Ferrand, workers pointedly walked out of meetings where government representatives were discussing the Charte du Travail and appealing for support of the relève; in several factories workers staged symbolic strikes in protest. The management of the Michelin factory flatly refused to allow propaganda delegates and representatives from the Ministry of Labor to enter the plant to address the workers, and company officials made little effort to hide their advice that workers refuse to leave for Germany.

By the end of the occupation, "comités sociaux d'entreprises," as provided for by the Charte du Travail, were established in ninety firms in the Puy-de-Dôme; but often they existed only on paper, were made up of the same people, did the same work as preexisting workers' delegations, or, as in the case of Michelin, never met. According to information in a police dossier concerning the comités sociaux, the directors of Michelin had selected workers' representatives, almost all of whom were former members of the CGT (Confédération Général du Travail), but they had never called a meeting "because, it seems, the Direction fears that by obliging these representatives to meet they would discredit them in the eyes of their comrades."[40] In 1941, at the height of its success, the Légion had succeeded in creating a workers' section at the Michelin factory with more than 100 members, but before long these members drifted away, and after the institution of the STO, the few diehards who remained were actually taken aside, harrassed, and beaten up by their fellow workers. As the central police commissioner for Clermont observed in March 1943: "The massive departure of workers for Germany has relegated all other social questions to secondary concerns. . . . The 'Charte du Travail' seems very definitely buried."[41]

Workers at the Michelin plant and in Clermont-Ferrand generally, with a tradition of well-organized support for the left, may have been more politically sensitive than others to the potentially negative consequences of Vichy's Charte du Travail, but studies that include all of France have demonstrated that the regime's labor policies found very little support from workers anywhere.[42] Even without the external factor of a pressing demand for workers to work in German factories, it is difficult to imagine how Vichy might have won the loyalty of French workers. After all, Pétain's government, not the Germans, had imprisoned or outlawed many syndicalist leaders and numerous politicians from the Communist and Socialist parties, the traditional speakers for the working classes, had taken away the right to strike, and had abolished the political parties and trade union organizations that had done the most in past years to promote the workers' interests. Reminded month after month by the prefects' recurrent reports of the workers' manifest scepticism and hostility to the regime, the government responded by further restrictions on the right of assembly and increasingly firm instructions commanding an immediate resort to force to suppress the slightest hint of agitation in the factories.

More surprising, at least on the surface, was a similar phenomenon of alienation and hostile reaction to the Vichy government from much of the French peasantry. In a major public demonstration organized in March 1942 at Clermont-Ferrand to help the Secours National, on the same platform with Marshal Pétain and Admiral Darlan, a speaker declared: "In the New Order, the farmers will be in the front rank."[43] One could not hope to find a more succinct statement, issued before the approving glance of the head of state and the head of the government, of a favorite leitmotif of the Vichy regime. Yet, just as the government's promises to the workers dissolved before the constraints of the occupation and the demands of the forced labor draft, so the economic realities of the epoch undercut the rhetoric of the New Order with regard to the agricultural community. With the government's failure to fulfill many of its promises to the peasants came bitter resentment caused by unrealized ambitions and a sense of betrayal. Reports of police and administrative officials offer some indication that the Vichy regime was originally able to generate a higher level of enthusiasm in French rural society (including many small towns that may have been classified technically as "urban" but whose residents were predominantly involved with agriculture) than was possible in the urban areas. Fueled by public ceremonies and effusive speeches that underscored the regime's ideological favoritism toward men who tilled the earth and their allegedly fruitful spouses, this "honeymoon" was short-lived.

Although many of their fellow citizens in the cities believed French farmers to be relatively well off, perhaps even accumulating secret fortunes

on the black market, the circumstances of war and occupation confronted
the farmers with serious problems and forced many of them to make
difficult adjustments in order simply to make ends meet. Along with the
possibility (particularly on the black market) of higher prices for the
farmers' produce must be reckoned the shortages and inflation in price
of fuel, fertilizers, and other commodities necessary to agricultural production. According to a study undertaken by the Légion's Agricultural
Committee, a comparison of 1939 and 1943 prices in the Puy-de-Dôme
revealed that the average selling price of the department's chief agricultural
products had risen by 216.9 percent, but the price of goods necessary to
agricultural production had risen by 308 percent.[44] The committee explained shortages of beef and veal by noting that prices that farmers could
obtain for raising cattle were not keeping up with the rise in the cost of
production. Another report, apparently drawn up in late 1942, said:
"There is no longer any question of pork, the fixed prices for this meat
have been set so low that the selling price has fallen far below the cost
price, which explains the total absence of pork on the market."[45] With
government officials trying to hold down inflation by fixing prices, farmers
naturally shifted production toward those items for which they might expect some return and very often resisted delivering produce on the legal
market at prices arbitrarily fixed at low levels by the government. Reports
about attitudes in the countryside of the Puy-de-Dôme during the Vichy
years offer a striking resemblance to Eugen Weber's impressive portrait
of the French peasantry at the end of the nineteenth century.[46] Despite
Vichy's glowing "peasant as salt of the earth" rhetoric, in many practical
day-to-day dealings, the peasant viewed the government's legal representatives as the enemy.

When various units of the Légion were transported to Vichy to celebrate that organization's first anniversary, farmers in the area around
Clermont-Ferrand, including some légionnaires, complained that the gasoline expended might better have been distributed to them for use during
the harvest; and the chef de la Sûreté at Clermont feared that their comments posed a threat "to the work of national renewal undertaken by the
government."[47] The following year the farmers were very upset when, after
they had cooperated in a campaign to collect copper, the government failed
to live up to its part of the bargain by returning quantities of copper sul-
fate to the farmers for use with their crops. The Légion's Agricultural
Committee reminded the intendant des affaires économiques that the government's promises had been published in the newspapers several times
and warned him that if something was not done rapidly, "the results would
be disastrous in our countryside where the farmers would lose all trust."[48]
From every indication, though, by the time the légionnaires made this

appeal to the intendant, most of the farmers already had lost their faith in the government.

Describing their inspection visits to rural communes in the summer of 1942, administrative officials in the Puy-de-Dôme reported scathing indictments of Vichy's agricultural policies from local notables, including many whose loyalty to the regime was unassailable. For example, a friend and supporter of Pierre Laval, the mayor of Ris, a small town not far from Laval's residence at Chateldon, charged the government with absolute ignorance of peasant affairs and blamed what he considered to be unfair and idiotic impositions for alienating everyone. Most observers agreed that in addition to shortages of certain commodities—agricultural workers in the Puy-de-Dôme seemed to be dismayed especially by the restricted availability of wine—farmers resented most of all the host of government agents, particularly those employed by the Ministry of Food, who sought to regulate forcibly the kind and quantity of goods they produced. In a ten-page report entitled "Psychological Study Concerning Relations Between the Peasantry and the Food Ministry,"[49] Raymond Grasset postulated that the more regulations and controls were applied, the more the peasants would find ways to get around the rules. Grasset remarked that traditionally in the region peasants had slaughtered a pig each Christmas and given parts of it to their relatives in the town. Now that it had been made illegal to slaughter a pig privately on their farms, the peasants continued to do it, but killed two or three instead of one as in the past, leading Grasset to conclude: "It is thus that overly strict regulations, too brutally applied, are leading men to the 'black market.' "[50] Echoing the judgment of an officer of the Puy-de-Dôme's Corporation paysanne who wrote in May 1943 that the farmers "are beginning to switch loyalties [*tourner casaque*], as we said in the good old days,"[51] Grasset warned that Pétain's plans for national renewal were seriously endangered: "At the present time, the discontent in the agricultural class that has not ceased to grow during the past months has reached a level that those who live outside agricultural circles cannot imagine."[52]

The ultimate futility of the Légion's attempt in 1943 and 1944 to organize Groupes Légionnaires Paysans (GLP) provided an interesting example of that organization's turn to elitism in face of popular hostility to the National Revolution, and at the same time it constituted a frank recognition that Vichy's campaigns to ensure the support of the peasantry had failed. In the spring of 1943 the Légion in the Puy-de-Dôme had begun naming individuals in each section to be responsible for action in the rural domain, but the program was very slow to develop. After several months of effort, only twenty-nine sections (out of more than 400) had submitted names of the local representatives, so the Civic Service Committee issued orders to try to speed up the process. Almost a year after their creation had been decided, however, many of the GLP had still not held their first meeting. Of course, it was difficult to hold meetings without members! In February 1944, in response to letters from various communal Légion heads who had reported disconsolately that "there is nothing to be done with the peasants," Monsieur A. Mallet, departmental inspector for the GLP, exhorted the local officials to push on with their attempts to organize.

> It matters little that you have so few members in the beginning. This is not a question of the mass, far from it, this is a question of the elite. You must bring in several active, committed légionnaire farmers who will become involved in our movement. Perhaps, you may have trouble finding them because of the disturbed times in which we live but they do exist, if only three or four of them.[53]

For the time being it was necessary to forget about the mass "too amorphous and transfixed in anticipation of hypothetical and miraculous events that will restore to our country the grandeur, well-being, and riches of yesterday, without effort on its part." Despite the attitudes of the overwhelming majority, "a small number of farmers of good will—oh, a very small number," had retained their attachment to Pétain and his doctrine. These men should be sought out one by one and instructed "in such a manner as to constitute the leaven that will regenerate the France of tomorrow."[54]

In other words, Vichy's National Revolution was being postponed. Perhaps the leaders of the Légion had come to accept the verdict of their former head, François Valentin, who, ousted following Laval's return and having gone over to the resistance, wrote that the Légion's error was to believe that a country could be renewed before being liberated: "One does not rebuild his house while it is burning!"[55] Or perhaps here is an outline of the emergence of what was to be one of the most common themes of Vichy's apologists: it was simply too much to ask of the Marshal's government that it both protect France from Germany's insatiable demands and at the same time create a new society.

Without denying in the least the enormous difficulties faced by the Vichy regime, the contents of this chapter are evidence that Pétain's government had indeed attempted to create a New Order in France. As has been demonstrated, this attempt was an abortive one. It would be only a slight exaggeration to conclude that everything the Vichy regime tried failed. As Yves Durand stated so perceptively: *"Vichy,* one might say, or *much talk and little action."*[56] Recalling the anecdote with which the second chapter began—when the boulevard Jean Jaurès at Clermont-Ferrand and other streets with names deemed ideologically displeasing to the regime's new leaders were ordered renamed—the reader should not be surprised

to learn that, in fact, the changes did not occur. Although the mayor selected the names and the prefect ordered them changed, municipal employees simply did not take down the old street plaques, and both German
and French police reports throughout the occupation continued to describe
various incidents that took place on the (proscribed) *boulevard Jean
Jaurès*. Historians, of course, should be wary of reading too much into one
amusing anecdote, but beyond Vichy's inability to enforce its will in so
little a matter as this, a remarkable consistency in failure is revealed in
a review of the full range of initiatives undertaken by Vichy in order to
recast French society. As applied at Clermont-Ferrand and the Auvergne,
the administrative purge, censorship of books and music, attempts to regulate the private behavior and morality of French citizens, the labor charter
and Vichy's agricultural policies, state orientation of schooling, youth
groups, and veterans organizations—all created more enemies than friends
for the regime. Vichy did not succeed in creating a New Order tailored to
its designs in part because of severe economic and political constraints
that had resulted from the defeat and occupation, and in part because of
the shortcomings and rival purposes of the regime's leaders; but perhaps
the fundamental reason that a French New Order did not emerge was
simply that most French citizens did not want one—at least not the one
prepared by Vichy.

4

The New Order at Clermont-Ferrand: Collaborationism

The two preceding chapters have considered the Vichy government's actions in favor of a National Revolution, generally emphasizing the period before the German occupation of southern France in November 1942. This emphasis resulted from the fact that the first two years of the regime were the ones in which the greatest energy and enthusiasm were expended in the name of the National Revolution. As we have seen, by 1943, confronted with unmistakable public hostility, even a substantial number of the regime's warmest supporters had begun to despair of the present and talked of a future revolution to be spearheaded by a dedicated core of loyalists. Admitting that the National Revolution had miscarried, a Légion tract, quoting Pétain's comment "I am not unaware of the weakness of the echoes aroused by my appeals," insisted in the fall of 1943 that the Légion still had a role to play. "[The Légion] knows that France can save itself only if a minority of ardent revolutionaries appears. . . . It commits all of its forces to the search for and formation of that revolutionary elite."[1]

Long before some légionnaires were driven to adopt this position by the public's refusal to rally willingly to Vichy's National Revolution, other individuals and groups, believing Vichy's National Revolution too moderate, had called for a forceful transformation of French society along decidedly authoritarian lines. Most outspoken among these groups were various collaborationist groups whose main strength and headquarters were in Paris; but in the south, the Service d'Ordre Légionnaire (SOL), transformed in 1943 into the Milice Française, aspired to lead a more energetic and virile crusade for the renewal of French society. As opposed to Marcel Déat's Rassemblement National Populaire (RNP), Jacques Doriot's Parti Populaire Français (PPF), or the much smaller Franciste movement headed by Marcel Bucard, the SOL and later the Milice emanated directly from the Vichy government. As such, the SOL and the Milice represented in simplest terms the regime's acknowledgment that their New Order could

maintained a residence nearby, and Jacques Doriot addressed crowds numbering in the thousands at Clermont; and because of frequent violent clashes provoked by the presence of counterdemonstrators at such political rallies, the police occasionally banned public meetings or parades where the threat of violence was great. When the so-called Cagoulard conspiracy was unraveled by the police early in 1938, several engineers employed by the Michelin company were found to be among those responsible for dynamiting the offices of the Employer's Federation at Paris. Local police at Clermont had at first minimized the seriousness of the activities of the CSAR (Comité secret d'action révolutionnaire—the Cagoule). In November 1937 the commissaire divisionnaire had assured the prefect:

> If it is incontestable that an embryo of a CSAR group exists in our region, it does not seem to have much importance and it would be appropriate to accept with prudence, and serious reservations, the numerous bits of information sent to diverse administrative or judicial services by anonymous correspondents and others.[6]

Nevertheless, following the confession in January 1938 of a Michelin engineer named Locuty to having made and planted the bombs in the rue de Presbourg, two of his co-workers and at least fourteen other Cagoulards were arrested at Clermont-Ferrand; substantial weapons caches containing automatic rifles or machine guns, bottle bombs, grenades, and so forth, were discovered. Among those arrested were men who during the occupation were prominent in the PPF at Clermont-Ferrand.

The police observed repeatedly that the Paris-based collaborationist groups in particular were having no luck recruiting adherents,[7] so the conspiratorial past of some of their members, not the size of their organizations, concerned local authorities the most. In April 1943 an officer noted:

> The local section [of the PPF] at Clermont-Ferrand, although very few in number, since it includes no more than fifty members, including sympathizers, is nonetheless dangerous in view of type of activities of its adherents. The militants who compose it are used to illegal and underground action because most of them come either from the CSAR movement or the Communist Party.[8]

At Clermont-Ferrand, the type of activities in which they engaged differed somewhat, but the various collaborationist groups shared a common futility in their attempts to gain converts to their cause.

Possibly because one of the local leaders, Roger Godonneche, was involved in the publicity business, Francisme concentrated most of its efforts on the distribution of its newspaper, of which it sold a maximum of 650 copies in the department (four times more than the PPF's *Emancipation*

Nationale could manage). Francisme does not seem to have sponsored public meetings, possibly because of its limited following (sixteen members were noted for arrest and investigation at the liberation); but according to local police, the regional inspector for Francisme, Monsieur Mechler, was kept busy drawing up lists of suspects to be "neutralized in case of a takeover of power by the leader BUCARD."[9] Déat's RNP was virtually nonexistent at Clermont. Only one member was included on the lists of collaborators to be arrested at the liberation. Older rightist groups such as the Action Française and de la Rocque's PSF showed some—though modest—signs of life. Although about 200 men, women, and children attended a commemorative mass at Clermont-Ferrand in January 1943 marking the execution of Louis XVI and possibly indicating a flickering of hope for a restoration of the monarchy, lectures sponsored by the Action Française during the occupation drew no more than ten to fifteen people, mostly young students. Colonel de la Rocque firmly separated himself from the Parisian-based collaborationist groups, and although publicly supporting Pétain he did not favor Laval. For all intents and purposes his organization, regrouped as the Auxiliaires de la Défense Passive and later as Auxiliaires du Devoir Patriotique (ADP), limited itself to nonpolitical social activities in favor of the prisoners of war. De la Rocque was himself suspected of resistance activities by the Germans, and they arrested and deported him in 1943. Individual members of the former PSF joined and were active in the PPF and the Milice, but the ADP was not considered a collaborationist organization, and its local leaders were not prosecuted as such at the liberation.

Of those groups linked with the major collaborationist organizations in Paris, Doriot's Parti Populaire Français was by far the most active at Clermont-Ferrand, with a few more members, but no more substantial success than the others. At Clermont, as was often the case elsewhere in France, the small band of truly active collaborationists were involved in several movements at once; a significant proportion of the leaders and members were to be found on multiple membership rosters. Antoine Charamel, one of the principal PPF directors, was at the same time departmental director of the Légion Tricolore, formerly regional delegate for the anti-Bolshevik LVF (Légion des Volontaires Français), president of the local "Groupe Collaboration," and secretary of the Cercles Populaires Français (the last two organizations were sponsors of "cultural" activities directed toward Franco-German understanding). All of these organizations operated out of headquarters in buildings at N° 5, rue Gonod and N° 14, rue Abbé Girard, chez Laurent (Laurent was another of the directors of the PPF at Clermont); all required heavy police protection for any of their activities because they were among the favorite targets for resistance bombing attacks. (In May 1942 Laurent's home was bombed; in June 1942 and on later occasions LVF, "Collaboration," and PPF offices were attacked; Charamel was killed by resisters a month before the liberation of Clermont-Ferrand.)

Interesting insights into the standing of collaborationist groups at Clermont-Ferrand may be gleaned from the response of local authorities to a request by the Cercles Populaires Français to stage a meeting, 2 June 1942, at the Salle Saint-Genès. Abel Bonnard, Laval's minister of education, was the président d'honneur of the Cercles Populaires, so the prefect was unable to deny authorization for the meeting (as was occasionally done for specifically PPF functions), but police anticipated trouble. Noting that this organization was inspired by the PPF and that "most of the members of this organization are also members of the other groups cited ["Collaboration," Union Populaire de la Jeunesse Française, and the LVF]," police inspector Bellon reported: "At Clermont-Ferrand these groups meet with serious opposition, which has been expressed on various occasions by noisy counterdemonstrations, by boycotts, and even by acts of terrorism (lecture at the Rialto Cinema, lecture by Monsieur Georges Claude, bombing attacks, and so forth)," adding that "it may be worth recalling that for many years at Clermont-Ferrand, every manifestation of activity on the part of the Parti Populaire Français has led to occasionally violent incidents."[10] Therefore, the organizers of the meeting were asked to speak only before a friendly audience—"that is to say the meeting will take place only by invitation and those attending will be screened at the entry"[11]—and a heavy police guard was provided before, during, and after the presentation. The day after the meeting was held, police seemed relieved to report that except for a smoke bomb thrown into the lecture hall at four o'clock in the afternoon but discovered in time for the room to be aired out, this first public appearance of the Cercles Populaires Français had passed without serious incident.

Less detailed accounts of similar meetings held in the spring and summer of 1942 for lectures, films, or other fare sponsored by the LVF, the Groupe Collaboration or other collaborationist organizations indicate that audiences usually ranged from two to five hundred people. The Salle Saint-Genès was watched over by fifty to sixty policemen, and those in attendance were mostly légionnaires, members of the SOL and their handpicked guests. Describing the proceedings at the 2 June Cercles Populaires meeting, a police observer commented:

> The audience included a significant percentage of retired military officers. Two-thirds of the audience, always the same ones moreover, applauded those passages of the speech condemning England and the Allies or in favor of collaboration.

The speakers carried on in the language of the political meetings of the past when they were speaking to a popular audience, but the audience, by its clothing and comportment, gave the impression of belonging to a milieu above the level of the masses.[12]

In terms of membership, the Groupe Collaboration was the most successful of those organizations that drew their local inspiration and direction from the PPF at Clermont-Ferrand. According to various lists drawn up by the police following the liberation, ninety-five individuals had adhered to Collaboration. This total included many of the thirty-two regular PPF members, but its cultural emphasis and the theoretically non-political aspect of the organization allowed the Groupe Collaboration to attract adherents who hesitated to involve themselves in the direct political activism of the PPF. Youth groups sponsored by or associated with the PPF had virtually no luck in a town where the majority of students from a very early date had been considered by the police to be Gaullist sympathizers. The Jeunesse Populaire Française (JPF) in February 1943 had twenty-four members (apparently including ten girls in an "almost non-existent" Jeunes filles française section); according to the police, many of these resigned in the spring of 1943 to join the Milice, "in order to penetrate that organization,"[13] which was in accordance with PPF policy at that time. These young people, like the handful who belonged to the Jeunes de France et d'Outre-Mer (JFOM) were called "young Hitlerians" and experienced "a hard life" at the hands of other young people of their age, especially from the Alsatian students from the University of Strasbourg who were prominent among those who shouted down speakers or set off smoke bombs, hounding and disrupting the fruitless efforts of the young collaborationists to win new recruits.[14] Similarly, the LVF in its various incarnations—Légion de Volontaires Français contre le Bolchevisme, Légion Tricolore, and Phalange Africaine—despite relatively lucrative incentives (local recruitment fliers emphasized the material benefits, salary, pension, clothing allowances, and so forth), received no response except for hostility and "sarcastic comments."[15] Only eleven individuals in the Puy-de-Dôme were cited for investigation at the liberation as former members of the LVF or the Légion Tricolore, including their leaders who were the PPF chieftains at Clermont-Ferrand.

The suspicion of Vichy authorities about their activities on some occasions combined with popular antipathy to check the collaborationists' ambitions. This was particularly true of the PPF, whose leader, Jacques Doriot, was considered by Laval and others at Vichy to be potentially their most serious political rival should the Germans choose to back him. Consequently, local police were ordered to watch carefully all PPF activities. Issues of Doriot's newspaper, *L'Emancipation Nationale,* were withdrawn from circulation, and PPF posters were ordered torn down when they were too critical of the Vichy government. In the summer of 1942, when the PPF laid plans for a "congress of power" which they hoped might serve, along with German assistance, to catapult Doriot into power, Laval ordered the regional prefects not to allow the PPF to hold departmental congresses in the areas under their jurisdiction; he stated clearly the government's attitude toward the PPF:

1. The PPF is not a Government party.
2. The Government gives it no support.
3. The activity of the PPF must not be exercised in the street *nor in the administrations.*
4. The PPF is not authorized to possess arms.
5. Members of the PPF must not appear in uniform in public.[16]

When Doriot returned from service on the Eastern Front, a small departmental PPF delegation was authorized to travel to Paris to welcome him home only after agreeing that they would "observe a perfect discipline during the trip" and wear no "obvious insignia or uniform."[17]

These precautions undoubtedly reflected the government's hostility toward the PPF, but they also derived from genuine fears that public order might otherwise be disturbed by counterdemonstrations. In view of the consistently hostile reaction of public opinion to them, it is unlikely that without government harrassment the PPF and the other Paris-based ultra-collaborationist organizations would have attracted a significantly wider following at Clermont-Ferrand. All together, when allowances are made for duplicate memberships, they could claim scarcely more than 100 adherents out of a population in excess of 500,000 in the department of the Puy-de-Dôme. Such groups may have constituted in numerical terms something more than a negligible factor elsewhere in France, but at Clermont-Ferrand they may appropriately be considered the lunatic fringe of political reality during the occupation. To summarize the importance of the ultra-collaborationist organizations at Clermont, one can do no better than to repeat the judgment of Clermont's central police commissioner, who in February 1943 concluded: "Collaboration has experienced a total failure."[18]

The Paris-based movements with pretensions to a national audience and influence were not the only expressions of an extreme right-wing authoritarianism during the Vichy era. Of greater consequence in the southern zone, both in terms of the size of their following and the serious repercussions of their actions, were the Service d'Ordre Légionnaire (SOL) and its successor, the Milice Française, under the leadership of Joseph Darnand. These organizations were distinguished from the PPF, the RNP, Francisme, and so forth, by the fact that (although they sprang up independently in southeastern France through the efforts of Darnand and other activists within the Légion Francaise des Combattants) they received the official endorsement of the Vichy regime. Despite Darnand's increasingly independent initiatives after he was named Secrétaire Général au Maintien de l'Ordre in December 1943 and then Secrétaire d'Etat à l'Intérieur in May 1944, the Milice remained under the orders of the French government. This official patronage no doubt helps to explain in part the Milice's relative advantage in recruitment in southern France over its Paris-based competitors; it was no less extremist or authoritarian in ideology, however, and did not refrain from admiration of German models, nor hesitate before what came to be its principal role, direct participation with German troops and police in military actions against the French resistance.

Even before the SOL was transformed into the Milice in January 1943, Joseph Darnand, proudly describing his shock troops as a "conquering minority," had argued that nationalism, socialism, and authoritarianism were as much a part of the French "race" as of others. Speaking in Marseille in October 1942, Darnand admitted that his values and ideals were not shared by most French people ("by the crowd")

> because they fear to find in them foreign methods. And why not! we declare clearly that the safety of the Fatherland is at stake and we refuse to compromise it by rejecting under a false pretext the methods which have furnished elsewhere striking proof of success.
>
> We are determined to save FRANCE despite public opinion and against it if necessary. . . .[19]

The emergence of this activist minority from within its ranks was disquieting to many leaders of the Légion. At Clermont-Ferrand, as elsewhere, the creation of the SOL and, later, the formation of the Milice brought about a serious crisis in the Légion, many of whose members were traditional nationalists who wished to see collaboration with Germany limited strictly to the requirements of the Armistice agreement. Even though his replacement as director general of the Légion was their fellow Auvergnat Raymond Lachal, several local Légion chiefs were unhappy when François Valentin, who disliked the SOL, was forced out after the return to power of Pierre Laval. Commenting on the developing split within Légion ranks, local police distinguished between the partisans of a "policy of collaboration that was *submitted to*" in contrast to a "policy of collaboration that was *desired.*"[20] The principal leaders of the Légion at Clermont-Ferrand were conspicuous by their absence at the meeting held 28 February 1943 to organize officially the Milice at Clermont. Subsequently, local Légion spokesmen went out of their way to separate the actions of the Légion from those of the Milice, claiming that the two organizations had nothing in common.

In these circumstances, although individual légionnaires joined the SOL

and the Milice, there was little continuity of leadership from one organization to the next, as was sometimes the case in other regions of France. At
Clermont-Ferrand, in addition to new, politically inexperienced recruits,
the influence of former PPF adherents was important, as in the case of
Robert Bonnichon, an extremely violent man who was one of the most
hated of the local Milicians at Clermont. In discussing the Milice one
should be aware of the danger of overemphasizing the role of individuals
on the margins of society, the violent, extremist types. Studies of various
fascist movements have demonstrated that many apparently "normal"
persons have been attracted to them, and no doubt changing circumstances
may dramatically alter the behavior of any given individual. Still, at
Clermont-Ferrand, even before the SOL and the Milice were armed and
associated so closely in actions and popular imagery with the Gestapo,
observers stressed the questionable reputations of many of their adherents.
The SOL were called "SS" or "SA" at Clermont-Ferrand, and according
to police, their recruitment "was achieved with great difficulty but without
discrimination or concern for morality. People say that habitual criminals
are among their members. The public which detests them considers them
militarized and fears the worst acts of violence from them."[21] In late
October 1942 the commissaire central de police at Clermont-Ferrand sum-
marized the development of the SOL to that point. Noting that recruitment
had come to a halt, he argued that this was to be explained "by the presence in the center of the SOL of a certain number of adventurers and
unscrupulous characters who are in the movement out of personal interest
rather than conviction. In these circumstances honest and sincere men
naturally hesitate to adhere to a movement that is tending to become a
party, contrary to the Marshal's directives."[22] Predicting that the growing
impopularity of the SOL and interior divisions would soon lead to numerous resignations, he concluded:

> Wishing to carry out the National Revolution through violence and for
> its own benefit, the SOL risks becoming the instigator of internal troubles
> and seeing the calm and serious-minded members escape it. Certain lead-
> ers have the impression of being overrun by their own movement; dis-
> couraged, they are ready to resign, thus giving the public yet another ex-
> ample of the disunity that is so undesirable today.[23]

Unfortunately, gaps in the available documentation make it impossible
to discuss with the desirable precision all aspects of SOL and Milice membership at Clermont-Ferrand, but we do know enough to validate at least
some of the contemporary impressions and predictions of this particular
police commissioner. Indeed, a spate of resignations and purges ensued.
The first regional chief of the SOL was forced to retire, according to his
successor, because of "a divergence of views not in conformity with the

party's doctrines";[24] and further shakeups in the leadership followed. For the mass of the membership, as seems to have been true in other departments, a core of committed Milicians eventually emerged from a much larger pool of adherents who at one time or another, by choice or without their knowledge and consent, found themselves enrolled in the Milice. Following the liberation a total of almost 1000 names appeared on various lists of individuals suspected of membership in the Milice in the Puy-de-Dôme, and 500 or 600 individuals were investigated in view of possible arrest and trial as Milicians. More thorough examinations by police and purge committees revealed that the number of persons in the Puy-de-Dôme who had participated *actively* in the Milice was far smaller than the lists of suspects had suggested. Included in the papers of the Departmental Liberation Committee's Purge Commission is an evaluation of the membership of the Puy-de-Dôme's Milice at its height in the summer of 1943. The Franc-Garde at Clermont was composed of three "groups of thirty," including the youngest and most active elements who were "les durs," the only truly reliable members. Those called the Milice per se were usually the older "lukewarm" members. In theory there were 300 of these, but "these numbers hardly exist except on paper, for the most imperative convocations bring out no more than 30 to 50 members."[25] Outside of Clermont-Ferrand there were perhaps 100 other Milicians in the Puy-de-Dôme, but only a dozen or so who were active Franc-Gardes. In other words there were probably 150 to a maximum of 200 active members of the Milice in the Puy-de-Dôme (or about 50 to 100 fewer than the maximum strength that the SOL had reached).

A purge committee staffed by resisters was not apt to understate the numbers of the Milice—they had no interest in letting their enemies escape retribution—and their figures offer solid confirmation to the suspicions of German officers who believed that Milice chieftains (who had turned to them with urgent requests for arms) had exaggerated the number of their active members. Membership figures as of 30 June 1943 supplied to the Germans by the Milice showed 850 members (610 Milice and 240 Franc-Garde), four or five times more than their actual effectives. Given this evidence for the Puy-de-Dôme and the results of local studies concerning other departments (for the Isère approximately 250 rather than 620; for the Loire a maximum between 250 and 500—in February 1944 there were 230—rather than 700); Jacques Delperrie de Bayac's estimate that 10,000 to 15,000 "real militants" had participated in the Milice for all of France seems reasonable.[26] Inflated Milice membership lists, even when pared down to eliminate many former members of the Légion or the SOL who were enrolled without being consulted and whose resignations were ignored, included a large number of individuals who had little or no interest in politics or the creation of a French New Order, but were attracted to the Milice by what often proved to be a shortsighted perception of self-interest. Jean-Marie Guillon, noting that political enthusiasm was largely confined to the leaders of the organization, has estimated that 40 percent of the Milice in the Var joined "for reasons of personal interest," notably to obtain employment or escape from the STO.[27]

Documentation concerning those who joined the Milice in the Puy-de-Dôme is available for too few individuals to permit confident generalizations about their motives, but a desire to avoid working in Germany under the STO is among the most frequent explanations where specific causes for adherence are known. Among those Milicians from the Puy-de-Dôme who had their property confiscated temporarily at the liberation because their names had been on Milice membership rosters was one young man from Dore l'Eglise who had signed up in 1943 for the Milice on the advice of his lycée professor in order to avoid the STO. He had sent in a letter of resignation, ignored a summons to join his Milice unit (whose leaders at Clermont-Ferrand had ignored his resignation), never paid dues, and never attended any Milice function. An agricultural laborer at Villars par Orcines, a village overlooking Clermont-Ferrand, was pressured into joining by the proprietor of the land he worked, but only attended early organizational meetings of the Milice. Another example was a hapless young man of mediocre intelligence who, according to police reports, had joined the Milice to escape the STO so that he could stay at home to care for the elderly grandparents who had raised him since he was abandoned at birth by his parents. Unhappily, he had been taken by the STO anyhow, and was still in Germany when the Provisional Government's authorities reviewed his case after the liberation, concluding: "It seems unreasonable then to penalize him today in the same manner as those who, enrolled in the Milice out of conviction, followed its policies until the end committing all of their activity to the movement."[28] Purge committees at the liberation were generally lenient toward those whose participation in the Milice had been minimal or purely nominal. Nonetheless, several hundred such persons were arrested and spent three or four months in prison before their cases were investigated and their situation clarified. A smaller number, whose fate was ultimately more tragic, had chosen the apparently "easy" road to security from deportation for labor service by joining the Milice, and had wound up with weapons in their hands to be used against their fellow French citizens.

During the first five or six months following its creation, the specific mission of the Milice had been uncertain. To be sure, the Milice was to be in the vanguard of the fight against "Communism, Gaullism, the Jewish leprosy, Freemasonry," and the other targets of the Milice's Twenty-one

Points, but what did this mean in practical terms? At Clermont-Ferrand little use was made of the Milice in the early months of its existence. Projects for their employment as auxiliary firemen or in passive defense were considered, and local Milice chiefs pressed for involvement in the fight against the black market and participation on boards supervising the selection for the STO. Many professional policemen resented competition in their domain of peacekeeping from men, some of whom had unsavory pasts, and whom the regular police considered to be little better than irregular vigilantes. But the government brushed aside these objections and sent directives ordering prefects and intendants de police to cooperate with Milice leaders. As early as the summer of 1942, following widespread disturbances on Bastille Day in the towns of southern France, Vichy had decided to reinforce public security forces by calling on the SOL to provide assistance for the repression of public demonstrations. At Clermont-Ferrand the SOL chief agreed to put at the disposal of the intendant de police three units of fifty men, "on condition that we be powerfully armed by your services."[29] French police and German military authorities were both reluctant to arm the Milice in a significant manner, however. Only late in 1943, after they had proved their mettle in action against the maquis, did the Germans decide that the Milice were worthy of confidence as allies in the fight against the French resistance.[30] Thereafter, they were more heavily armed and became frequent participants in antiresistance activities alongside the German police and military units: their true vocation as auxiliaries of the SD had been found.

The special powers granted to Joseph Darnand in January and February 1944 permitted him to name courts-martial before which the defendant's rights were minimal. Both guilt and penalty were decided by the court-martial; there was no right of appeal, and death sentences were executed immediately. Ultimately, the Milice paid scant attention to even those remnants of legal procedure by which their actions were in theory limited. For example, in July 1944 when two Milicians burst into the Michelin factory and were criticized by the personnel director for not informing the company's management or following proper formalities, one of them replied: "We are in a revolution and we will enter the factory whenever we see fit."[31] Jean de Vaugelas, Darnand's appointee as Directeur des Opérations, Maintien de l'Ordre at Clermont-Ferrand, responded to inquiries from the regional prefect about this incident by agreeing that in the future a representative of the firm might be present at such arrests, but claimed that the high-handed manner of his men had been justified.

In June and July 1944 local French executive power at Clermont, as exercised under German control, was effectively in the hands of the Milice, undercutting the authority of the regional prefect. Jean de Vaugelas was responsible for the Milice, and Lt. Colonel Hachette was in charge of the regular uniformed police forces. Because Clermont was an important regional center, the Groupement des Forces de Clermont concentrated its attention on that city, and reinforcements including 500 Milice and some extra GMR units were dispatched to strengthen preexisting local elements. With this influx of outsiders, the proportionate responsibility of local Milicians in Milice activity is impossible to determine in these months in which the levels of violence and internecine strife reached their height. Some of the most flagrant examples of cruelty and brutality were the work of newcomers to the region, such as Jean Roger Thomine, ultimately arrested by his superiors and ejected from the Milice because he had raped a female prisoner, a teacher at Clermont-Ferrand; and Maurice Peyronnet (called Lucas), an exceptionally brutal torturer and chauffeur for Jean-Paul Filliol (called Denis at Clermont-Ferrand), earlier chief of the Second Service of the Milice at Limoges. Along with these outsiders, local Milicians, such as Jean Achon, chef régional of the Milice at Clermont-Ferrand, Robert Bonnichon (known as "Captain Bob"), head of the Second Service at Clermont, and others, had a direct hand in the robberies, murders, deportations, and torture for which the Milice were justly notorious in the region.

The Milice were very active in the Auvergne. Occasionally, they participated in regular military operations against maquis formations under the supervision of German troops, who would use the Milice to set up roadblocks, guard prisoners, and so forth. Far more often the Milice operated in small groups on their own or in conjunction with German police or the strong-arm bands hired by the German Labor Service to track down individuals for deportation for work in Germany. Frequently, their actions could hardly be distinguished from those of common criminals—extortion, robbery, acts of vengeance against rivals, and much seemingly senseless violence. In the spring and summer of 1944 the Milice's Franc-Garde headquarters on the rue Torrilhon at Clermont-Ferrand was the scene of torture, rape, and brutality of the basest sort, often directed against persons who had little or no connection with the resistance. Well might the average citizen ask what these actions had to do with the "maintenance of order" for which Darnand had been made responsible by the Vichy regime.[32]

If the reprehensible behavior of the Milice can in large measure be attributed to the violent temperament and unsavory character of some of its members, their propensity toward violence was perhaps nurtured by the circumstances in which they found themselves. As the occupation wore on, they became increasingly frustrated, isolated, and desperate creatures, loathed by the vast majority of their countrymen. This isolation and hatred of the Milice was apparent from the earliest days of its existence at Clermont-Ferrand. In February 1943 one observer had noted:

> The creation of the French Milice has in general received little enthusiastic echo. People are apprehensive about revolutionary actions on the part of this milice in which they see a superpolice charged with the brutal repression of working-class agitation. The civil servants too are very hostile to the French Milice, which they see as an organization for the surveillance of the Public Service in general.[33]

In late March 1943 the Ministry of the Interior, fearing counterdemonstrations, requested that the regional prefects provide security for any public meeting of the Milice. A special report drawn up by German Armistice Commission personnel in November 1943 stressed the extent to which Milice doctrine and actions aroused the hostility of most French people: "Whoever joins the Milice can expect only *trouble* and *the greatest danger*."[34] Not only did the Milician risk harm personally—through October 1943, 20 Milice had been killed and 135 wounded, and the number slain in southern France by the resistance rose to 85 by March 1944—but his family and children were ostracized at school or work, and along with him they were potential victims of the frequent bombings of the offices, stores, or private homes of Milice adherents.

No one was more aware of their uncomfortable position than the Milice themselves, and their own words offer perhaps the best testimony to their extreme isolation from the national community. A month before the liberation of Clermont-Ferrand, Jean Achon, head of the Milice for the Auvergne, requested publication in the local newspapers of an article in which he deplored the lack of appreciation by the public for the Milice's work against the "terrorists." Claiming that the selection process for Milicians was "much more rigorous than people pretend," Achon argued that many Milicians were giving their lives for the safety of those French people who were insulting them, concluding bitterly: "At least they could better respect their memory!"[35] In the last desperate weeks of the occupation, reacting in the manner of a trapped animal striking out in fury at his tormentors and sounding very much like a man who saw enemies and treason everywhere, Joseph Darnand issued harsh orders for tightened discipline ("The leaders must, in the first place, lose their taste for discussion") and demanded immediate application of severe sanctions to slackards. Darnand's directives for the operation of Milice units in the French countryside included the terrible phrase: "seizing of hostages if the latter [the local population] shows itself to be hostile."[36] Had the Germans not taken enough French hostages by themselves? It was as if the Milice were operating on foreign soil.

In a bitter and tragic irony, particularly for those who had joined the

SOL or the Milice from political commitment, considering themselves superpatriots pledged to save France from ruin, they had become in essence men without a country. At the liberation several thousand of the survivors and their families sought temporary haven in Germany, leaving in the baggage train of the German troops and police in whose presence they were safer than in that of their compatriots. Thus was laid bare the stark reality, the ultimate logic, of the Vichy government's decision to collaborate with Germany. The actions of the Milice had been the most obvious example of the validity of Robert Paxton's argument that step by step the Vichy regime was drawn "into trying to do the Germans' dirty work for them."[37] The intensity of the hatred and vilification of the Milice by the overwhelming majority of the French population suggests the ultimate backruptcy of ultracollaborationist schemes to remake France according to a fascist mold. Because the Milice and the other ultracollaborationist organizations were most closely identified in the popular mind with the German cause, the retribution that followed the liberation not surprisingly fell swiftly and most heavily on their heads. But the patent and unequivocal rejection of the programs and actions of the Milice and the ultracollaborationist organizations should not obscure the fact that the more modest authoritarianism of Vichy's New Order had also been rejected decisively.

The Milice was only the most extreme expression of a regime gone sour; it is essential to recall that the Milice was an official government organization, no matter how emphatically (in postwar trials) many of the regime's dignitaries might try to separate themselves from that organization's "excesses." No less than Milice, the Vichy government, evolving over time in an increasingly authoritarian direction, had become the creature of the German Reich, with whose fate Vichy's destiny was inextricably bound. We have seen that at least in part, as with various attempts to create politically oriented youth groups, the failure of certain aspects of Vichy's National Revolution was linked to their association with German models. The heavy material cost of the occupation undoubtedly hampered Vichy's attempts to create a French New Order, but the apologists for the regime—who, in the summer of 1944, argued that "it is difficult to build on an erupting volcano!"[38] and claimed that Pétain and Laval would have succeeded if only peace had come—missed the most essential point. Fundamentally, the National Revolution had not succeeded in France, and could not succeed, because very few French citizens wanted the kind of New Order proposed to them by Vichy.

As will be demonstrated by a systematic evaluation of public opinion under the Vichy regime, the actions of the Milice alone had not discredited Vichy in most French minds. Indeed, most people had reached a negative verdict about the regime long before the Milice existed. Little more than a year after Pétain had taken power, the chef de la Sûreté at Clermont-Ferrand reported to the regional prefect:

> As a whole, the population is discontented in a high degree. It no longer believes in much. Contrary to what is printed in the newspapers, whose articles people insist are imposed and therefore do not represent the exact truth, which never miss underlining the adherence of the public each time a new reform is presented, the public in fact remains indifferent. Having many things to complain about, including policies concerning food supply as well as the politics currently pursued which tend, many fear, to restrict liberty of conscience, the public seems to be holding itself back for the day when it will regain its right of criticism. It notices the clergy's attempt to regain importance and is suspicious, fearing an underhanded revenge to be taken on its [the clergy's] former adversaries. Also, the idea of democracy remains much stronger in people's consciousness than one might have imagined. Very objectively, it is my duty to stress particularly this last point.[39]

This reminder about the strength of the democratic tradition in France, our discussion of the almost total failure of the National Revolution, and the analysis in Chapter 6 of public opinion may suggest that some modification is necessary to a widely held assumption that the Vichy government enjoyed massive popular support for several years.[40] At Clermont-Ferrand, the largest city within close proximity of the seat of government, there was little evidence of genuine mass enthusiasm for the regime beyond the first few months of its existence. Given the extraordinary deprivation and hardships of the era, probably any French government would have had great difficulty in generating public enthusiasm for its programs. Given the particular programs embodied in Vichy's National Revolution, there was virtually no chance at all that the French people would rally to the proposed New Order.

5

The Outcasts

Without discussing at length a popular question concerning the nature of the Vichy regime—was Vichy France fascist?—one may suggest that many elements contributed to the creation of a police-state environment in wartime France. Vichy's concern with order, its attempts to distinguish between the "good" and "bad" French, and its fear of "foreign" influences led the regime to establish a system of laws and administrative practices that withdrew many traditional liberties previously enjoyed by several French generations. Some of the repressive apparatus employed by the Vichy government was inherited from the Third Republic, notably anti-Communist legislation and measures concerning the movement of foreigners and domestic suspects designed to cope with the exceptional demands of a wartime situation. But Vichy augmented the scope of government initiatives in these matters, added substantially to the number of potential "enemies" or suspects, and severely restricted for those involved the possible recourse to due process in the redress of grievances. Certain measures that had been used in times of crisis or exceptional emergency by republican regimes were considered to be desirable, normal procedures under Vichy's New Order. In this regard, the Vichy regime may be said to have differed in kind, not simply in degree, from its republican predecessors and successors in modern French history. Following a brief discussion of several measures that fostered a repressive atmosphere in wartime France, we will turn to an examination of the experience of Communists, Spanish republicans, and Jews, the three groups most seriously affected by Vichy's repression.

As will be seen in a discussion of the evolution of public opinion during the war, Vichy had good reason to be pessimistic about the extent of its popular support. Not surprisingly, the regime was suspicious about the attitudes and activities of many French citizens. For Vichy, domestic enemies were an ever-present concern. A ministerial directive of 9 October 1941 announced a further extension of the powers of Vichy's regional prefects to include the right to nocturnal searches and control over weapons sales. Appropriately, in a symbolic way, for its legal precedent, the decree referred back to a law of 9 August 1849 and an epoch in French history when another insecure regime wanted desperately to prevent the renewal of popular agitation.[1] In order to watch over its citizens, the Vichy government used telephone and postal interceptions, paid police informers, revised and updated various lists of suspects, and carefully regulated movement of foreigners around the country and of citizens across national frontiers. What seems to distinguish the Vichy period from the Third Republic in the surveillance of its citizens was not so much an originality in practices for gathering information, but an expansion of government prerogatives in this realm and a marked increase in attention paid to those individuals believed to be hostile to the regime.

Information about private citizens was obtained in a variety of ways. As early as September 1934 the Third Republic had resorted to the interception of mail and telecommunications for soundings of public opinion, indicating the growing possibilities for government control.[2] In the 1930s formal instructions specified that names and addresses were not to be conveyed to the authorities. Under Vichy these same instructions remained valid in theory, but in fact names and addresses were turned over to the police, who used the postal and telephone interceptions to track down specific individuals. The use of paid informants is probably at least as old as the institution of regular police forces, but the Vichy regime particularly emphasized the need to recruit and encourage informers and allocated substantial sums to this end. Similarly, regular police of all ranks were urged to be attentive during their off-duty hours to information that might come their way in their local neighborhoods.[3] One of the unpleasant facts about wartime France was that denunciations, anonymous or otherwise, were not infrequent. The police often found these to provide false leads or to have been based on personal vendettas, and so they tried to discourage anonymous denunciations by announcing that persons responsible for them would be sought out and punished.[4]

However accumulated, information, once received, was put to various uses. Lists of suspects to be watched and arrested immediately in case of "troubles" were drawn up and periodically revised. The famous, or notorious, "Carnet B" was brought up to date in the summer and fall of 1941 and then replaced in 1943 by new "Listes S." Most of the thirty or forty names included for the Clermont area were individuals believed to be Communists, many of them workers at the Michelin company.[5] For dealing with such suspects, Vichy granted its regional prefects extensive administrative powers that allowed them to bypass traditional legal obstacles, such as proof of guilt. Among many possible examples was the case of Monsieur

Dassaud, a tobacco store operator at Courpière, about whom the subprefect at Thiers reported to the intendant de police at Clermont-Ferrand. Local members of the Parti Populaire Français (PPF) had accused Dassaud of distributing Gaullist propaganda and saying nasty things about Pétain. Even though the courts had not been able to establish Dassaud's guilt, the subprefect wrote: "The gendarmerie at Courpière is convinced that the individual in question is worthy of no consideration, and in the circumstances, personally I see no problem in your taking any action against him that you judge opportune."[6] In passing, the subprefect noted that Dassaud had been active in a local committee for aid to the Spanish republican refugees and had been a supporter of the Popular Front.

Although we will show that Vichy's police were at times ineffective, the feeling on the part of a French citizen that "Big Brother is watching" would not have been misplaced in wartime France. Imagine the surprise of René Picard, an electrician at Saint-Nectaire, who in August 1941 received the following letter from the intendant de police at Clermont-Ferrand:

> It has come to my attention from several sources that you have made numerous thoughtless remarks in conversations concerning the present Government.
>
> The information I have been furnished about you is not excellent, you know.
>
> On several occasions already my attention has been drawn to you, in particular you are reproached with many slips of the tongue about Marshal Pétain, both when you were sober and after drinking.
>
> This letter is to warn you to put a lid on your fashion of thinking in public and your conversation, for otherwise, even though you are the father of a large family, I will be forced to intern you.
>
> This warning from me, mark my words, will be the first and the last.[7]

The warning about possible internment contained in the letter to Picard was not simply an idle threat. Under Vichy more than 300 persons from the department of the Puy-de-Dôme were administratively interned, at least 259 for political reasons and lesser numbers for black-market offenses.[8] Although the evidence used to justify such actions might be more substantial in some cases, in one case Ayzyk Gorny, a mathematics teacher at the University of Clermont-Ferrand whose professional record was unblemished, was recommended for internment because a search of his room at the Cité Université had turned up a copy of Trotsky's *History of the Russian Revolution* and a 1938 membership card for the "French Association of the Friends of the Soviet Union."[9] Because internments resulted from an exceptional administrative action, there was no normal procedure for repeal or review of the decisions. On two or three separate occasions, once following negative reports by International Red Cross officials about conditions in the camps, Vichy authorities acknowledged the desirability of reexamining the cases of each internee. Yet, as late as February 1943 the regional prefect at Clermont-Ferrand admitted that many internees had been held in the camps for several months and occasionally even for two or three years without any serious review of their situation.[10]

Although the minister of the interior had written that "ill-considered internment is as blameworthy" as the "inopportune liberation of an individual who is dangerous in terms of public order,"[11] the evidence suggests that review of one's case, and (even more so) release from internment was exceptionally difficult to obtain. Vichy was more willing to consider the conditional release of ordinary criminals than of its political opponents. In September 1943, in order to make room for those arrested or suspect for resistance activities, and citing the necessity of a quick resolution to "the problem, crucial from the point of view of public security, of the overcrowding of prisons,"[12] René Bousquet, Vichy's Secrétaire Général à la Police, urged the prefects to speed up the process of release on probation of common criminals, particularly those who agreed to go to Germany under the Service de Travail Obligatoire (STO). The prefects were made personally responsible for tightening security precautions for the guard of these individuals and other political prisoners. After January 1942 those rare administrative internees who were lucky enough to obtain release needed the personal approval of the minister of the interior, and were required to sign an oath swearing on their honor "to rally to the new social order and to respect the work and the person of the Marshal of France, Head of State."[13]

Short of internment, one might be assigned to a residence—preferably at a safe distance from one's normal home and associates—with the obligation to report weekly to the local police. When prefects complained that suspects, especially Gaullists or Communists, were released by the courts for lack of proof before the prefects had had time to arrange for their confinement by administrative order, the minister of justice ordered the public prosecutors to inform the prefects immediately of any court order for the release of suspects and to hold such individuals until the prefect had had enough time to take any desired administrative action.[14] Emphasizing one distinction between Vichy regime and the Third or Fourth republics, at the liberation when ordering the rapid processing of the cases of administrative internees, Adrien Tixier, the minister of the interior, pointed out that Vichy's practice of administrative internments for criminals or suspects, often tacked onto terms already served to satisfy legal penalties, was contrary to republican legality.[15]

In addition to filling jails and camps with convicted or suspected opponents, two other means by which Vichy sought to maintain order were the prevention of strikes or public demonstrations and careful surveillance of domestic and international travel. In the days preceding any major holiday, particularly those with revolutionary or patriotic significance, elaborate security precautions were observed and impressive numbers of police deployed. Following incidents in Clermont-Ferrand and several other towns around the unoccupied zone on Bastille Day in 1942, the government issued detailed and rigorous orders to the prefects that any sort of public or private demonstration that risked troubling public order was to be forbidden. If, despite precautions, a situation got out of hand, the orders authorized the police to use units of the Service d'Ordre Légionnaire (SOL) as auxiliaries and instructed them to make massive arrests that after identification might lead to internments. With reference to the prohibition of strikes, Bousquet ordered the prefects to act firmly to oppose any attempted strike, using arrests, internments, and even (for extreme cases) deportation to work camps in southern Algeria. Bousquet's choice of language lent credence to those who considered Vichy to have been to some extent a revenge of those opposed to the Popular Front. Exhorting the prefects to be firm, he concluded: "Above all, you must not tolerate for a single instant any incident that might recall, directly or indirectly, those events from which France suffered so much during the months of 1936."[16]

To some extent, Vichy's control over the movement of foreigners was a product of the Armistice arrangements made with Germany, and specific measures of an exceptional nature were made in conjunction with developments on the world's battlefields. For example, following the German invasion of the Soviet Union, the intendant de police at Clermont reported that eleven Russian citizens in the area had been arrested and sent to an internment camp in the Pyrenees. At the same time the finance minister had ordered the blocking of bank accounts, safety deposit boxes, and other resources of Soviet citizens in France. Similarly, after the American and British landings in North Africa in November 1942, Vichy ordered strict surveillance over the activities of British and American citizens, and early in 1943 26 of the 206 British and American adults living in the region of the Auvergne were sent to camps in northern France.[17]

Immediately following the Allied invasion of North Africa and the consequent German occupation of southern France, all foreigners were required to obtain police permission for travel outside of their place of residence. Affecting both the French and foreigners until its removal in the spring of 1943 was the line of demarcation that separated Vichy France from the other two-thirds of the country. Legal passage of this internal frontier required permission from both French and German authorities; depending on the nationality of the person involved or the current state of Franco-German negotiations about the Armistice obligations of the French, the proper papers could be difficult to obtain. While the demarcation line disrupted the economy and presented many other difficulties for the French, it also provided the government opportunities for control over movement. In a similar way the rationing system, as refined over time, offered a chance to keep close watch over both the French and foreigners, and various population censuses were carried out on the basis of lists provided by the services involved with the distribution of food coupons.

Dozens of ministerial circulars and a host of periodically revised guidelines attest to the fact that the Vichy regime was most preoccupied with the regulation of movement of foreigners, but the regime was also concerned about the movement of the French, especially those who sought to leave the country. In some cases the reasons were fairly obvious. In February 1943, worried about defections to Giraudist or Gaullist camps in North Africa, Pierre Laval requested that the regional prefects establish lists of prominent political personalities who were apt to try to leave France secretly or act in a manner that might embarrass the government. These individuals were to be watched carefully and handled with "tact and discretion"[18] should they try to leave. A standard form used by the police for the examination of requests for exit visas ordered a thorough investigation to determine the applicant's political leanings, his attitude toward the regime, and whether or not his departure might be detrimental in some way to France's economy. Occasionally, special notices would be circulated concerning the movement of an individual, as occurred, for example, when General Jean de Lattre de Tassigny escaped from the prison at Riom. The government's motive for prohibiting the travel of specific individuals was not always so clear as that, however—at least not to those ordered to stop it. For example, without explanation a curious note from the minister of the interior of 5 March 1942 ordered that Edith Gassion, called *Edith Piaf,* not be allowed to leave France.[19]

As suggested by these few illustrations of the use of its police powers by the Vichy regime, everyone in France, whether of high or low station in life, was susceptible to surveillance and control, but certain categories of French citizens and foreigners were especially suspect. In theory, and in the words of some leading spokesmen at Vichy, the Freemasons were among those groups considered most dangerous to the regime. Their lodges were dissolved, and those holding public office were obliged to repent by breaking completely with their old ways and pledging support for the New Order. Should they refuse, they were to be removed from office. In practice, although a few schoolteachers at Clermont-Ferrand were temporarily dismissed because of Masonic ties, the consequences of anti-Masonic attitudes and legislation were far less dramatic than actions taken against Communists, Spanish republicans, and Jews. By and large, local officials shared Pierre Laval's skepticism about theories of a Masonic conspiracy, and the delegate appointed to Clermont to supervise the repression of secret societies seems to have spent most of his time in joint activities with his colleagues in Jewish Affairs and the Milice. Attracting the particular displeasure, and thus the special attention, of the authorities at Vichy, French Communists, Spanish republican refugees, and Jews were the *outcasts* of Vichy France. Each of these three groups, for a variety of reasons, was considered a threat by the regime and suffered extraordinarily in comparison to others trying to survive in the universally difficult circumstances of a divided and occupied country.

The Communists

Whatever else they might disagree about, leaders of the Vichy regime were virtually unanimous in their hatred of communism. No theme is more consistent in the history of Vichy than anticommunism. In this attitude Vichy was building on well-established foundations in French political life, dating back to the Bolshevik victory in Russia in 1917 and the creation of the French Communist Party (PCF) at the Congress of Tours in 1920. In France hostility to communism was not the exclusive preserve of the political right. At the Congress of Tours and later, Léon Blum had argued that the Russian model of communism was incompatible with French traditions and feared for democracy should it triumph in France. During the interwar period the French Communist and Socialist parties often seemed more concerned with fighting one another than their avowed class enemy, the bourgeoisie. Although French governments were concerned about the effect Communist agitation and propaganda might have, especially in the army, during the interwar period they seem to have been more worried about the extreme right. In January 1929 André Tardieu, minister of the interior, wrote to the prefects: "If the Communist Party is attempting principally to hamper national defense measures, the Action Française seems to be preparing a true movement of force against the Government of the Republic. These activities must be watched attentively."[20] The prefect of the Puy-de-Dôme at Clermont-Ferrand concurred that the Action Française posed a much more serious immediate threat. Later in the mid-1930s, local authorities at Clermont were more apt to prohibit potentially disruptive demonstrations by the right than those planned by the left. Even after the outbreak of the war, officials at Clermont-Ferrand did not believe that in the Auvergne sabotage or Communist opposition to the war effort was a real menace.[21]

Communist support for the Nazi-Soviet pact had sharply altered attitudes toward the party. Earlier abrupt changes in party policies had fostered the conviction among rivals or opponents that the French Communist Party was directly controlled by Moscow, but the party's decision to support the Nazi-Soviet pact provoked a major offensive to crush the Communist Party in the last years of the Third Republic. The party's stance and some instances of "defeatist" propaganda placed the PCF outside of the patriotic fold. Edouard Daladier's government closed down hundreds of PCF organizations, banned all publications associated with the Third International, and arrested and imprisoned thousands of Communists during the drôle de guerre. Although some leaders, notably Blum, feared that the government's strident anti-Communist campaign might win sympathy for the Communists and ultimately boomerang contrary to the government's desires, there is little evidence of popular sympathy for the Communists before the fall of the Third Republic. Perhaps, as intelligence observers for the British Foreign Office speculated, most French people considered the PCF endorsement of the Nazi-Soviet pact to have been antipatriotic.[22] This, more than opposition to Communist ideas about French society, was the basis of the general hostility to the party. Certainly, the wartime situation contributed to the ease with which the government attacked the party with exceptional severity.

Without question, then, before Pétain came to power, the French Communist Party was to a significant degree divorced from the French national community. The Vichy regime was to carry this separation still further. Already considered misguided prodigal children under the Third Republic, the French Communists were to be eliminated completely from the national family by Vichy. When Pierre Pucheu, Vichy's minister of the interior, selected Communists rather than "good" Frenchmen to be executed before German firing squads at Chateaubriand and Mont-Valérien, the process can be said to have been completed. Because of the strength of the Communist Party in the north and in the vicinity of Paris, not surprisingly the most extensive repression took place in those areas. Nonetheless, the example of Clermont-Ferrand demonstrates to what extent anti-Communist attitudes in Paris and later at Vichy found forceful echoes elsewhere in France.

On 27 September 1939, the day after a government decree ordering dissolved all Communist and affiliated organizations, the police at Clermont-Ferrand went to the headquarters of the local Communist Party, 6 rue de la Treille, carried out a thorough search, seized books, pamphlets, and documents, taking seventeen boxes of them to be used as evidence in judicial proceedings. Later even the office furniture would be auctioned off with the proceeds going to the state. In addition, five affiliated organizations at Clermont (Jeunesses Communistes, Paix et Liberté, Le Secours Populaire de France, Les Jeunes Filles de France, and Jeunesses Communistes de Montferrand), together with twenty-seven communal Communist Party cells and eight syndicats in various locales of the Puy-de-Dôme were disbanded. The goods of the syndicats were often turned over to CGT affiliates whose leaders had denounced the Nazi-Soviet pact. Newspapers, periodicals, and all publications sponsored by the Communist Party were forbidden when the party's organizations were dissolved in August 1939. An original list of twenty of these for Clermont-Ferrand was drawn up at the end of August and many others added later.[23]

Individuals as well as party organizations and publications were the object of anti-Communist measures. In September 1939 the police of the Sûreté at Clermont-Ferrand began drawing up lists of Communist leaders and militants to be placed under surveillance. The first report noted eleven men, including the heads of both party and syndicalist organizations, labeled "very dangerous leaders," nineteen "dangerous militants," and five Communist civil servants, in addition to hundreds of simple militants from various communes in the Puy-de-Dôme who were considered suspect. Other lists drawn up in October 1939 and February 1940 for the commanding general of the 13th Region (headquartered at Clermont-Ferrand) noted 395 Communists from the area who had been mobilized for the war and underlined in red the 33 considered "most dangerous."[24] Following the law of 20 January 1940 that unseated all elected officials who had not disavowed publicly the Communist Party's endorsement of the Nazi-Soviet pact, four municipal councillors in the Puy-de-Dôme were removed from office. In a corollary action, the various ministries moved to purge Communist civil servants from their ranks. Although teachers, for example, were required to fill out a questionnaire indicating whether or not they belonged to the Communist Party and, if so, had now ceased all such activity, the prefect of the Puy-de-Dôme reported 17 May 1940 to the minister of the interior that "no civil servant or agent of the public services or of services related to them in the department of the Puy-de-Dôme has been dismissed or deprived of any sort of mandate."[25] Nevertheless, police checks were run on several persons who had been mobilized for the war. Upon the return from the front and demobilization of these suspects, the Vichy regime purged many of them from the civil service and often interned them in prison camps.

According to British intelligence sources, by March 1940, for all of France (not counting the top party officials who had been tried and imprisoned), 2778 Communist town councillors and 300 town councils had been suspended by the Third Republic; 443 officials and employees had some administrative action taken against them; 159 newspapers had been supressed; 620 trade unions and 675 political groups were dissolved; and 3400 arrests had been made.[26] The decree of 18 November 1939 allowing prefects to intern persons believed dangerous for national security had been used mostly against Communists. The bulk of those affected by these measures lived in Paris or elsewhere in northern France. Although a handful of arrests for Communist propaganda seem to have been made in the region, pre-Vichy repression of individual Communists can be said to have been slight at Clermont-Ferrand. Following the defeat of France, however, both military and civilian officials in the Auvergne would make up for lost time. Making good use of those lists of suspects prepared under the Third Republic, they would eliminate that "softness"[27] allegedly derived from the lingering influence of the Popular Front and complained of in November 1939 by the Second Bureau of the Etat-Major du Commandant Militaire of the 13th Region.

From the first months of the Vichy regime, an almost obsessive "tracking down of Communists" began that was to remain one of the principal preoccupations of the regime's spokesmen and their local subordinates in the various police services. At the highest levels of government, this obsession was perhaps most visible, at least in its most strident, exaggerated form, in the last years of the occupation. A rapid glance through the files of the Office Français d'Information (OFI)'s propaganda directives or an examination of the texts of the radio speeches of Philippe Henriot for 1944 suggests that the theme of anticommunism was omnipresent as the German armies reeled backward before the Red Army. Pierre Laval, in a much-noted speech, had justified his hope for a German victory on the grounds that "without it, Bolshevism would tomorrow install itself everywhere."[28] Communism was not only, or primarily, seen as a threat from the exterior, though. The "General Regulations for the organization of the French Milice," published in February 1943 to define the tasks of that newly created organization, included a message from Joseph Darnand who proclaimed: "The interior danger exists. It would be vain to enumerate all of the causes for trouble or revolt that might arise. They can all be subsumed in a single threat: Bolshevism." The first duty of the Milice was "to save France from Bolshevism."[29] Earlier, in the summer of 1942, Laval had described the obligations incumbent on the reorganized gendarmerie: "The first of these duties is the desperate struggle against Communism, destroyer of all civilization and enemy of social and national order."[30] Possibly the hysterical vilification of the Communists toward the end of the occupation reflected the fact that, more aware by then of the dangers confronting them, the Communists had become harder to catch!

Local officials at Clermont-Ferrand had not required the excited encouragement of their superiors to goad them into action against the Communists. Much of the serious damage to Communist militants in the Auvergne was carried out in the early months following the defeat of France before anticommunism came to be so blatantly and publicly the chief leit-motif of a desperate regime. The day before the vote of full powers to Pé-tain, military authorities had decided that all "demobilized undesirables" would be sent to a "guarded camp" unless the departmental military com-mander and the prefect recommended otherwise.[31] In the weeks that fol-lowed, local police were ordered to run checks on all demobilized Com-munists believed "susceptible to becoming involved in activities harmful to the national interest."[32] In the late summer of 1940 as the Communist mili-tants returned home, having served their country under arms during the Battle of France, they were called in before local commissaires de police and warned "that they would be the object of careful surveillance and that at the slightest hint of agitation on their part, they would be interned."[33] Having listened to the commissaire's lecture, and signed a document ac-knowledging that they had been duly warned, these men, war veterans yet suspects, were free to go—but not for long. Within weeks, and in some cases despite police reports indicating that they were "above all preoccu-pied with their material circumstances"[34] and not active politically, many of these men had been thrown into internment camps or were in hiding. Thus many French Communists were forced immediately into an under-ground struggle which they may or may not have joined had they been given a choice.

According to a French police report, between September 1939 and 31 January 1941 in the unoccupied zone alone, 21,152 searches had been car-ried out, 8872 persons had been arrested, and 4014 interned in camps for Communist activities.[35] A later report following the Allied invasion of North Africa, alerting police to the danger of their possible attempted re-turn to metropolitan France, listed over 400 French Communists who had been deported to work camps in North Africa.[36] The British Foreign Office research department noted that as of May 1941 Vichy officials claimed 30,000 Communists were imprisoned (18,000 in the north and 12,000 in camps in the south).[37] These figures must be accepted with some caution because of the looseness with which the term *Communist* was used by Vichy officials. Those suspected of Communist activities, upon investiga-tion, frequently turned out to be Socialists, Pivertists, or even Radical So-cialists whose real "crime" had been active support for the Popular Front. And, of course, the Germans, but also Vichy spokesmen, often used *terror-ist* and *Communist* as interchangeable terms, possibly because non-Commu-nist Gaullist resisters might be viewed more sympathetically by the public as patriots. Despite any possible misconstruction of the statistics (both at the time and after the war for other purposes) about the repression of the French Communist Party, what is certain beyond any question is that the Communists were in theory and in practice considered to be *the* chief opponents of the Vichy regime. They were therefore singled out as political enemies for persecution whose severity was matched only by Vichy's treatment of the Jews. Moreover, the shrill anticommunism of many of Vichy's leaders more frequently found willing accomplices at the local level than was true for its anti-Semitism.

Police at Clermont-Ferrand were energetic and persistent in their attempts to track down Communists. Although he claimed that Communist propaganda was having no effect on the population, in January 1941 the chef de Sûreté at Clermont-Ferrand noted that he had assigned four inspectors to "concern themselves especially with communist propaganda."[38] In the fall of 1941 a major investigation of more than 100 suspects headed by a special agent of the Police Judiciaire sent from Vichy led to the arrests of forty-nine people in the region who were involved in the production or distribution of Communist underground newspapers.[39] To cite all of the major operations, much less the day-to-day searches and arrests of Communists, would be monotonous and unnecessary in this limited discussion. Suffice it to say that the police at Clermont-Ferrand had no more pressing interest than the fight against communism. When lists were established of suspects for preventive arrests or whose residences were to be searched in the event of "disturbances," or when propositions for internment of political opponents were made, the Communists always headed the lists. In one of many examples, when in June 1943 the commissaire central sent the regional prefect four lists of suspects (Communists, Gaullists, anglophile students at the University of Strasbourg, and common criminals) whose homes were to be searched in case of "disturbances, riots, or terrorist attacks," more than twice as many names of Communists appeared than of any other category.[40] For the country as a whole, Vichy was convinced that the Communist OS (Organisations Spéciaux) were responsible for most of the terrorist attacks since the entry of the Soviet Union into the war. Although this was not true of the earliest bombings at Clermont-Ferrand, the commissaire central at Clermont nonetheless asserted in February 1943 that "Communism is more and more Enemy No. 1. . . ."[41]

As the resistance became more and more active, even though most resisters in the Auvergne were certainly not Communists, the police persisted in stressing above all the Communist menace. Moreover, in marked contrast to the more lenient treatment of Gaullist and other non-Communist resisters, Vichy's leaders were unwilling to extend to French Communists the benefit of the doubt that they might have been acting from patriotic motivation. In August 1942 René Bousquet exhorted the regional prefects to intensify their struggle against communism and terrorism. Acknowledging that Gaullist activities also had become a serious problem, he nonetheless distinguished between two cases. For those Gaullists who were clearly determined to tear down the work of renewal undertaken by the government: "It is important to prevent them from harmful actions by attacking them in an inexorable manner just as for the communists and terrorists with whom their action coincides."[42] The implication was that until that time, the Gaullists had not been treated as severely as the Communists. The time had come to act against those who were unwitting agents of foreign propaganda, following "orders that they believe to be inspired by a national sentiment."[43] The government's idea was to intern several well-known personalities who were considered to be Gaullist sympathizers in order to intimidate others. For Clermont-Ferrand the nine names proposed included the Doyen de la Faculté des Sciences de Clermont-Ferrand (who had joined a demonstration at the Place Jaude in singing the "Marseillaise" on Bastille Day), a law professor, a philosophy teacher at the Lycée Blaise-Pascal, and some students from the University of Strasbourg at Clermont. Interestingly, General Gabriel Cochet, considered by the Service de Renseignements Généraux to be among the most active Gaullists and anglophiles, was not chosen at this time. Bousquet had stressed: "The measures envisaged must be essentially of an exemplary character, and consequently it is important to weigh the consequences carefully."[44] Presumably, in terms of possible adverse reactions, academics could be attacked with greater impunity than generals.

As hostilities between the resistance and Vichy accelerated in the last year of the occupation, and the Germans, along with Vichy's Milice, bypassed the regular French police and increasingly took initiatives in the repression of opposition, these distinctions between Communist resisters and others were less apparent, but they never entirely disappeared. In postwar testimony, police officers in defending their comportment during the war claimed always to have been patriotic and anti-German, but occasionally specified that their aid to the resistance had not included Communists.[45] The head of the gendarmerie for the region around Clermont-Ferrand became, posthumously, a hero (the gendarmerie headquarters at Clermont are named for him) because he died in deportation. But at the time of his arrest by the Germans he was marked for execution by the Front National.[46] Allegedly, he had distracted the Germans' attention from non-Communist groups by revealing to them the locations of Francs-Tireurs et Partisans (FTP) units. This same official had acted to protect individual Jews from persecution. His story should sound a note of caution for those students of ethics or morality who would see the history of wartime France in clear shades of black and white—the good resisters versus the bad collaborators. To sort out the interwoven threads of heroism, treason, good, and evil is exceedingly difficult. In wartime France *everything was complicated.*

The Spanish Republicans

Given the tendency on the part of the French right to identify the government of the Spanish Republic with communism, as well as the reality of Soviet aid to the Spanish Republic and the consequent increase in influence of the Spanish Communist Party in the final years of the Spanish Civil War, the more than one-half million Spanish republican refugees who fled to France following Franco's victory were tarred with the same brush of suspicion as the French Communists. French attitudes and actions toward the Spanish refugees reflected generosity and a measure of atonement for not having aided the Spanish Republic in its hour of need; at the same time there was suspicion and not infrequent hostility to these uninvited guests whose presence was in many ways awkward for the French. Dealing with the refugees had taxed the ingenuity of those agencies responsible for them and severely strained the resources of those areas where they first settled. Although the government welcomed the Spanish refugees in adherence to a French tradition of sanctuary for political exiles, officials hoped to be able to return most of the Spaniards to Spain as rapidly as possible. In the spring of 1939 the police at Clermont-Ferrand tried to prevent the circulation of a Spanish newspaper, *Voz de Madrid,* in the local refugee camp because it had contained articles describing a "ferocious repression" of those republicans returning to Spain. The prefect of the Puy-de-Dôme feared that such articles would "inhibit" the repatriation of the Spanish refugees.[47]

After the war broke out, battle-hardened Spanish veterans who would agree to serve against Germany in the Foreign Legion were encouraged to stay, but negotiations with Franco were continued to try to arrange for the return of most of the refugees. Veterans of the International Brigades who had found refuge in France along with the Spanish were, if anything, less welcome than the Spanish. The minister of the interior ordered that they be given only transit visas and be actively encouraged to leave France.[48] Perhaps 200,000 Spanish refugees returned to Spain either soon after their exodus or over the course of World War II, but more than 300,000 remained in France during the war and beyond.

Originally the refugees had been herded into several large, overcrowded camps on the beaches of the Mediterranean in the department of the Pyrénées-Orientales bordering Spain. The camp at Argelès-sur-Mer, at one time holding more than 100,000 refugees, was notorious for its unsanitary conditions and lack of facilities. In the Pyrénées-Orientales, refugees out-numbered residents by two to one in early 1939.[49] Acknowledging the mis-erable conditions in the camps and recognizing the necessity of relieving pressure on the border areas, the government soon began to transfer the refugees to smaller camps in other parts of France. Clermont-Ferrand, which had already sheltered around 1000 noncombatant Spanish refugees (all but 30 were women and children) in 1937, was one of the towns chosen for a refugee camp. If the first wave of refugees had been viewed in humanitarian terms as people in need of help, the later arrivals were considered primarily in terms of their economic impact on the region.[50]

As war with Germany approached in 1939, Spanish workmen from the camps were recruited both as individuals and as part of workers' companies and used to increase French production. After the Battle of France, with two million French POWs in Germany, France experienced a labor short-age that was aggravated dramatically in the 1942–1944 period by the STO, which sent hundred of thousands of men from France to work in Germany. In these circumstances, tens of thousands of Spanish refugees concentrated in camps by the Third Republic, seen originally as a burden, now provided an opportunity to help alleviate Vichy's labor problem. While some refugee camps were retained as such for invalids, in September 1940 Vichy began organizing fit male workers into groups of foreign workers—Groupements des Travailleurs Etrangers (GTE). There they were joined by Dutch, Bel-gian, Polish, and other foreign refugees who had been part of the exodus from northern France. At Clermont-Ferrand the Spanish far outnumbered other foreigners, comprising roughly 80 to 90 percent of those incorpo-rated into the labor groups.

It is difficult to determine how many Spanish republicans came to Cler-mont-Ferrand because of frequent fluctuations due to transfers and de-portations to the north or to Germany, and because transport lists did not always distinguish between Spanish from other departments and those from the local camps who were shipped out by train from Clermont-Ferrand. At least 1500 Spanish republican refugees remained in the Puy-de-Dôme dur-ing the war, but several thousand others passed through and worked in the area's economy for varying periods of time. These workers were highly valued by their French supervisors, who singled them out for praise as the most reliable and productive among the foreign workers. When not threat-ened with deportation to Germany or northern France, the Spanish were considered to be cooperative, even docile, in contrast to the Dutch and Belgians who were considered troublemakers, thinking only of escape and a second chance to fight the Germans.[51]

Although local labor officials at Clermont-Ferrand viewed the Spanish with favor, government policy, both consciously and unintentionally, at times conflicted with this sympathetic attitude. Although most of the refugees were not political activists, they were unable to escape the onus of having supported what was perceived as a left-wing cause. Already under the Third Republic suspected troublemakers among the refugees, whether Communists or anarchists, had been sent to special disciplinary camps at Le Vernet, Collioure, and elsewhere where conditions were extremely harsh. According to some witnesses, conditions were worse even than similar camps found at the same time in Franco's Spain or in Germany. Vichy's leaders were less inclined than the Third Republic's had been to make distinctions among the Communists, anarchists, and other refugees; suspicion of them as well as repression increased. Discipline and surveillance in the camps were tightened, and those considered most dangerous were now sent to labor camps in the North African desert along with numerous French Communists. In 1942 a central card file was constituted of all Spaniards suspected of communist or anarchist activities, and special reports were required for "Spanish subversive activities."[52]

Local labor supervisors pointed out that treating the Spanish with such suspicion was dangerous for morale and risked driving them into the mountains to join maquis bands. In his "Report on the Morale and the Activity of Foreign Workers" of 18 August 1943, the chief labor supervisor for the Clermont area reminded his superiors that all of the dangerous individuals had long ago been sent to internment centers or to "trans-Saharan worksites" and added that all local employers agreed with him that those Spanish remaining were at most "pink-tinged" in memory of the cause for which they fought, "but without desiring a new red revolution, which has done so much harm to their country."[53] Since local officials regularly repeated these same appeals until the liberation, such councils of moderation probably had little impact on their superiors at Vichy.

Still, when Vichy perceived an economic advantage for itself in so doing, the government acted at times in the interest of certain categories of Spanish refugees. In October 1941 and again in May 1942 local officials were ordered to hide those Spanish already working for French employers from German recruiters for the TODT organization.[54] The possibilities for keeping Spanish workers out of German hands were reduced, of course, when the Wehrmacht occupied southern France in November 1942. Moreover, faced with the obligation to send hundreds of thousands of *French* workers to Germany, Vichy was not receptive to the suggestions of one local defender of the Spaniards who argued that, viewed from a perspective of productivity for the local economy, it would be better to send "these young people called the 'swing generation' "[55] to the TODT organization and keep good Spanish workers where they were. Laval and others involved were well aware that it was politically expedient to force foreign workers to Germany or into TODT before sending Frenchmen. Ordering the regional prefects to arrange for Frenchmen to replace foreigners in factories working for the Germans in France so that they (rather than the French) could be sent to Germany, the Secrétaire Général à la Main d'Oeuvre assured the prefects: "You will certainly find public opinion around you unanimous on this point."[56]

Massive police sweeps through the Auvergne were ordered in conjunction with authorities in the neighboring Correze and the Dordogne in the summer and fall of 1943. All healthy Spaniards "who entered France following the Spanish events of 1936"[57] were to be arrested and placed in internment camps in preparation for their deportation to Germany. These major operations were rarely as successful as the police had hoped, but on a daily basis Spaniards found without proper identification and many others brought before the various committees set up to select workers for the STO were added to the totals of those sent to Germany or to the north where, for example, they provided much of the manpower to construct Hitler's defenses along the Atlantic Wall.

Certain factors inhibited the French government's plans to use Spanish rather than French workers to satisfy the inexorable requirements of Germany for more labor. Spaniards protected by Franco's consul at Vichy were not supposed to be drafted. False papers were fairly easy to obtain, thanks to the complicity of local officials, employers, or resistance organizations, so Vichy was often unsure of which Spaniards were the republicans. Repeated complaints by the Spanish consul suggest that many nonrepublican Spaniards were taken despite their legal protection.[58] French officials from other ministries might interfere with the police. For example, the Ministry of Industrial Production, concerned with the completion of a hydroelectric project at l'Aigle in the Auvergne, desired to retain its largely Spanish work force and objected to the arrest of the workers.[59] Similar attitudes were found at the local level where employers of fewer Spanish workers were suspected accomplices in the absence of these men when the gendarmes appeared to arrest them. Finally, the Spanish might take matters into their own hands as when the prefect of the Cantal had to report to the regional prefect at Clermont-Ferrand that he had been unable to carry out his orders to round up 400 Spanish workers near the Correze. Warned in advance and aided by maquis from the surrounding area, the Spanish workers had resisted by force, disarming the gendarmerie unit sent to arrest them.[60] Although in smaller numbers than in the Limoges area to the west and especially the region of Toulouse to the south, many Spanish republicans disappeared from labor camps in the Auvergne and joined French maquis groups or formed their own Spanish resistance units. One such group participated in the liberation of Montluçon.

The area's GTEs were not housed in internment camps, which meant that flight to the surrounding hills was a relatively simple matter. Monitored by supervisors from headquarters at Vic-le-Comte and Riom, the Spanish workers in the Puy-de-Dôme were scattered all over the department. Some were contracted individually or in small groups to farmers who might house them in barns or an extra bedroom; others worked and lived in logging camps near Ambert; still others worked in private industry and were responsible for their own lodging. Labor supervisors complained that with only a handful of guardians to oversee thousands of workers, effective control was simply impossible. For example, eighteen men were assigned to control almost 1300 workers in the two GTEs regulated from Riom. In these circumstances failure to meet quotas imposed for TODT was inevitable. As a remedy for the situation, the head of the foreign labor services in the Puy-de-Dôme called for a strengthening of the civilian staff who, he claimed, would have better success than the gendarmes in rounding up the Spaniards, noting, "The sight of one uniform is the best way to make them run away."[61] The Spanish workers, who according to their supervisors "had a proud character, accepting poorly to be treated like criminals,"[62] began to feel more and more "hunted" in late 1943, and more than 300 deserted from the GTE of the Puy-de-Dôme in the first three months of 1944.

The Spaniards were particularly upset by the attempts to transfer large groups of them to the north and to Germany because they were, at first, singled out as the only foreign workers being sent from the region. Local labor officials seemed delighted when in the fall of 1943 they could tell the Spanish workers that a shipment of Jewish workers had been arrested for transfer to a TODT project at Marseille.[63] Given the relatively slight numbers involved, one suspects that the Spanish were not particularly impressed by this attempt to appease them.

In view of the increasing threats to their security and the local conditions (mountainous, forested terrain and lack of effective control) that favored desertion to the maquis, it was doubly surprising that most of the Spanish workers stayed at their assigned work sites. To some degree this may be explained by the influence of local labor supervisors who were without question favorably disposed toward the Spanish and tried to protect them whenever possible. But the actions of the Spaniards are probably best understood in a broader context of their general situation in wartime France. Most of the leaders and activists of the republican cause had been deported or interned and were not in the GTE; those who remained relatively free to choose, while surely sympathetic to the Allied cause versus Nazism, had had enough of fighting in Spain in the late 1930s and were not particularly eager to take up arms to help liberate France, a country whose treatment of them, after all, had not been in every way exemplary. By 1944 most Spaniards believed that the Germans would be defeated eventually and hoped that a new regime in France would be sympathetic to their plight; for the present their problem was to survive as best they could. In this attitude, of course, they were not so far removed from the position of many of the French, although the latter might feel a stronger emotional commitment to and have a more direct stake in the outcome of the liberation of France. Most of the Spaniards, as was true of the French, had not really objected to working for Germany in local industry. Only when they were treated as suspects because of their alleged leftist politics and, more important, rounded up for deportation to Germany or for TODT projects where they would be exposed to Allied bombings had the Spanish workers rebelled and deserted in substantial numbers. Labor officials in the area repeatedly argued that if treated fairly and left alone to work, the Spaniards would remain loyal to their supervisors. Therefore, with obvious satisfaction in seeing his predictions vindicated, the chief labor supervisor for the Puy-de-Dôme reported that with deportation suspended, only fifty-eight workers were illegally absent during the second trimester of 1944.[64] This drop to less than one-third the number of deserters for the preceding three months had occurred despite frequent recruitment attempts by local resistance groups at the time of the Normandy landings, and despite the Vichy government's lack of any means of effective control over the countryside in the Auvergne.

However pleased the supervisor might have been with this "proof" of his argument, the fact remained that for most of the past five and one-half years the Spanish in France had not been left alone. Without counting those considered politically dangerous who were treated the most severely, more than 4000 Spaniards were taken from the Auvergne region to Germany or to TODT projects elsewhere in France. Although they often received sympathy and support from individual French citizens it was the misfortune of the Spanish, because of their circumstances as refugees, to have been grouped together in camps or assigned en masse to labor groups. Consequently, they provided an irresistible target for both Vichy and German authorities. If deportation were taken as the only measure, in proportion to their numbers, the Spanish can be said to have suffered more than any other single category of people in the Auvergne. Happily for them, the odds of escaping death from Allied bombings at TODT work sites were far better than those of return from the death camps to which French and foreign Jews were sent.

The Jews

Any discussion of the "Jewish Question" in France during World War II must start with the recognition that although German pressure was at times a factor in French actions, Vichy's anti-Semitism was homegrown. There is a hollow ring to the claims of the regime's apologists who stress that relatively few French Jews died in the Holocaust. Aside from over-looking the fate of those foreign Jews who were rounded up and turned over to the Germans by Vichy, such arguments obscure the fundamental point that the relatively happy situation of French Jews, particularly in southern France, reflected Vichy's failure, its inability to implement policy. Except for a few minor instances (for example, Jews in the south were not obliged by Vichy to wear the yellow stars imposed by the Germans in northern France), only with the most tortured logic can one find in Vichy policy a desire to protect Jewish interests. Varying degrees of enthusiasm were evident in Vichy administrative circles, but from the beginning to the end of the regime, many eager anti-Semites were active, pursuing measures that were discriminatory, humiliating, and ultimately fatal for many Jews, both French and foreign.[65]

In contrast to the harsh anti-Semitism of official Vichy policy, the response of the French population, at least that of the Auvergnats in the region surrounding Vichy itself—if not exemplary in every respect—may provide some solace to those who see in this tragic period of French history all too much evidence of inhumanity. At first indifferent, insensitive, or perhaps unaware of the implications of Vichy policy toward the Jews, the population as a whole became disturbed about and then hostile to government policy as life became increasingly precarious for the Jews with each new action against them. After massive deportations were ordered in the summer of 1942, Jewish refugees were given false identities and warned of roundups by friendly gendarmes or civil servants, and they found safe haven in villages all over the Auvergne. To be sure, not every-one escaped. Just as massive popular hostility to the STO could not stop hundreds of thousands of French from being taken to work in German factories, so widespread opposition was insufficient to prevent a partial ac-complishment of Vichy and German anti-Semitic designs. But without ex-tensive popular complicity, combined with the determination of the Jews not to be caught and led away passively, far greater harm would have been done.

Vichy's attention had been turned to the Jews from the first months of the regime's existence. In October 1940 "Jewishness" had been officially defined by Vichy authorities in a manner more stringent than the German's had planned for France, and Jews were banned from several professions.

In June 1941 this "Jewish Statute" was revised and exclusions extended, as explained by the prefect of the Puy-de-Dôme to his subordinates, so that Jews could hold no jobs other than manual labor or minor office positions allowing no advancement that might "confer any influence or authority whatsoever."[66] The impact of these first measures at Clermont was relatively small. Exemptions were possible (for example, veterans with good records and refugees from Alsace-Lorraine), and a certain discretionary power was left to local officials. In this sense, being in southern France instead of the occupied zone, where anti-Semitic measures were applied directly by the Germans, unquestionably reduced the immediate threat to French Jews. Also, the number of Jews in the region with prominent positions in the professions who were affected by the first decrees was slight.

Probably the most important development in 1941 was the census of all French and foreign Jews ordered by Vichy in June and carried out in late July in the Puy-de-Dôme. Around 3000 people declared themselves to be Jewish, of whom 1238 were at Clermont-Ferrand.[67] Police had estimated that perhaps twice that many Jews were in the area, and we know that many refused to cooperate. As was later the case for those who came in to have their identity papers stamped "Juif" in January 1943, those who made these declarations at their local city or town hall had their names and addresses included in card files and on alphabetical lists that were to serve as the statistical base for later actions against the Jews. In addition to information of a personal and family nature (relatives, addresses, and so forth), a statement of personal wealth was required for the census. One of the most damning aspects of Vichy policy was that later, upon request, these lists were turned over to German military, police, and labor officials, apparently with little or no hesitation. The lists for Clermont were first given to the Germans in May 1943.[68]

Although the prospects of systematic anti-Semitic actions were enhanced with the establishment of the Commissariat Général aux Affaires Juives in March 1941, and Jews in southern France were increasingly alarmed by reports of treatment of Jews in the occupied zone (spoliation of Jewish property, obligation to wear the yellow star, and so forth), only in 1942 were Jews in the unoccupied zone exposed to the full brunt of Vichy's anti-Semitic policies. In the south there was a relative moderation in the application of some of the earliest measures, so many Jews, especially French Jews, tended to believe that they might escape truly serious consequences from the troubling anti-Semitic bent of Vichy policy. Jews whose families had lived many years in France, including men who had won distinction fighting on the battlefields of World War I and in the recent Battle of France, often thought of themselves as French first and Jews only by religious profession. That Germans, beguiled by Nazi demagoguery, posed a threat to them was certain, but surely a government headed by Marshal Pétain would not fall into line with such folly. Foreign Jews and the most recently naturalized French Jews were most frequently and seriously affected by Vichy actions, thus seeming to justify such a belief in the relative safety of French Jews.

That faith in Vichy's protection was misplaced was only slowly perceived by many Jews. A turning point for many French Jews at Clermont-Ferrand, when danger to them was perceived as immediate, came in October 1942 when Jewish merchants were obliged to display yellow-colored posters on their storefronts indicating "Jewish Enterprise" for all passersby to see. A few weeks later all Jews, French and foreign, were ordered to have their ration cards and identity papers stamped "Juif."[69] By this time the perceived threat of persecution had become a stark reality for thousands of foreign Jews and for many French Jews as well. At the risk of oversimplifying an exceedingly complex issue, an examination of the application at Clermont-Ferrand and the surrounding area of three major anti-Semitic programs, resettlement or relocation schemes, deportation, and "Aryanization" of Jewish property, will be used to illustrate the seriousness with which Vichy pursued anti-Semitic goals, and will permit an assessment of popular response to the government's official anti-Semitism. These three policies were not the only discriminatory actions taken against Jews in southern France, but they had the most dramatic impact on large numbers of French and foreign Jews, and they represented the most visible expressions of Vichy's attempt to deal with what it called the "Jewish Question." All of these policies were begun and indeed enjoyed their most successful application *before* German troops arrived in southern France in November 1942. That this was true suggests the extent of French responsibility for the mistreatment of the Jews. The relative lack of success later testifies to the greater awareness of both Jews and non-Jews and to the far wider network of support available after the German occupation of the south.

Resettlement and Relocation

The sudden and unexpected defeat of France had been accompanied in the summer of 1940 by a tremendous exodus of French and foreigners from the north. At Clermont-Ferrand, as elsewhere, facilities to house and feed the refugees had been strained to the maximum. More than 100,000 people flooded into the Puy-de-Dôme in a few weeks, and although most returned to their homes shortly after the Armistice, many remained. Among them were numerous Jews who preferred not to live in the zone of German occupation; in any case, they were refused reentry to the north by the Germans, who had found it more convenient to take over Jewish property in the absence of the owners. Although a rapid turnover of the population made such figures impossible to verify, a year after the defeat the police estimated that 60,000 "foreigners"[70] were in residence, by which they meant non-Clermontois French as well as those of other nationalities. At least 3000 of the newcomers were believed to be Jewish. The absence of perhaps 14,000 prisoners of war from the department provided some extra space, but the authorities felt that their town was seriously overcrowded. The most evident reason for this situation was Clermont's proximity to Vichy and the fact that many government agencies, along with the University of Strasbourg, had been established at Clermont and its neighboring communes. In seeking to alleviate the problem of overcrowding, the gov-

Jews ordered to report changes of address to the police

MINISTÈRE DE L'INTÉRIEUR

DIRECTION GÉNÉRALE
DE LA POLICE NATIONALE

Direction de la Police du
Territoire et des étrangers

4° Bureau

DÉCLARATION
DES
changements de résidence
DES
JUIFS

Les Juifs français et étrangers qui changent de résidence doivent en faire la déclaration au Commissaire de Police (ou à défaut de Commissaire de Police, au Maire), de la commune de leur domicile si la durée du déplacement prévu dépasse 30 jours.

Les intéressés sont tenus d'effectuer la même formalité au cours des 48 heures qui suivent leur arrivée dans la commune du lieu de destination.

Tous renseignements complémentaires peuvent être recueillis auprès des autorités de police ou administratives compétentes.

Les présentes instructions sont applicables à partir du 25 septembre 1942.

ernment's first thought was to evacuate all excess foreigners, particularly the Jewish refugees.

Through the summer of 1941, on an individual basis local authorities had refused to permit at least 100 foreigners to settle in the Puy-de-Dôme, most of whom were Jewish.[71] In one particularly striking case, a Mr. Kohn Felsenberg had requested that he and his family be liberated from an internment camp to join his brother-in-law's family at St. Sauves. They hoped to spend together the two or three months that remained before all of them were scheduled to emigrate to the United States. The local gendarmerie had strongly endorsed the request; the mayor, citing several substantial contributions made by the family to national and local refugee assistance groups, vouched for the brother-in-law's ability to support the Felsenbergs. Still, the subprefect at Issoire explained to his superior, the prefect at Clermont-Ferrand, that he had denied the request. "These foreigners can await their departure for America in the camp at Riversaltes."[72] Besides, he added, the brother-in-law was among those recently naturalized Eastern European Jews from whom Xavier Vallat, the recently appointed Commissaire Général de la Question Juive, planned to withdraw their French citizenship.

Despite their immediate disappointment about the subprefect's decision, the Felsenbergs later must have counted themselves fortunate—considering the ultimate fate of many other foreign and recently naturalized Jews—to have been among the approximately 10,000 Jews who escaped before the Germans occupied southern France. From 1940 until the winter of 1942 roughly 350 to 400 (presumably wealthy) Jewish refugees received exit visas and passports from the prefectures at Clermont-Ferrand.[73] In February 1942 Vichy encouraged prefects to facilitate departure of those who chose to leave France and could afford to pay their own expenses. But bureaucratic procedures, requiring purchase of tickets for passage in advance, were complicated, and there is no indication that the rate of departures increased through government efforts. In the desperate circumstances of those grim days, police at Clermont-Ferrand uncovered at least one criminal scheme involving attempts to prey on gullible Jewish families by offering to arrange for passage to the United States at exorbitant rates.[74] This avenue to safety was closed, and no further legal departures took place after the arrival of German troops in November 1942.

In August 1941 the prefect of the Puy-de-Dôme complained that piecemeal actions were insufficient to "preserve Clermont-Ferrand, Riom, and Thiers . . . from the influx of certain types of Jews,"[75] and he asked the minister of the interior whether or not some more effective general action might be taken, such as a prohibition against foreigners traveling through or settling in the area. By December the police were sounding out various localities about accommodations since the regional prefect was considering ordering certain Jews there, because he hoped "to *air out* some towns in the department that really are becoming too full of Jews."[76] A few days after the return to power of Laval, the prefect's wish was granted.

Undeterred by the central consistory's appeal for cancelation of the project since 65 percent of the Jews at Clermont-Ferrand were refugees from Alsace-Lorraine, Vice-Admiral Charles Platon ordered certain categories of Jews expelled from the administrative region of Clermont-Ferrand. He cited the shortage of housing for government employees as the reason. The instructions were applied beginning in late June, and those affected were given two weeks' notice to pack and leave. A police report of 4 September 1942 indicated that 356 Jews had been ordered to leave Clermont-Ferrand, and three weeks later the prefect of the Puy-de-Dôme informed Platon that about 70 percent of the cases examined had resulted in expulsion. Exemptions had been given to refugees from Alsace-Lorraine, those assigned to foreign labor groups, veterans with outstanding records, those with French or "Aryan" wives native to the region, and those who had established residence in the region before 1 January 1938. The government also took this opportunity to expel from Clermont the Ecole Rabinique de France, the Consistoire Israélite, and other major Jewish organizations.[77] Since such a large number of Jews were being ordered out of Clermont, reasoned the government, why keep their organizations there? By mid-October Platon pronounced himself satisfied with the operation, claiming that "the maximum effect that could have been reasonably expected" had been obtained for Vichy and Clermont-Ferrand. He admitted that the work "had hardly begun in other localities of the two departments," and that it was "evidently necessary to continue it," but from the point of view of his principal concern, housing, the operation no longer had the same "immediate urgency."[78] The committee charged with expulsion of the Jews, though handling fewer cases, continued to meet periodically through May 1944. Focusing their energies almost exclusively on those Jews who had arrived during or after the "Exodus," they granted very few exemptions.[79]

The aftermath of this affair was distressing for some of the Jewish families who found themselves shunted around from department to department when various prefectures refused them permission to settle. In despair over this situation, the Union Général des Israélites Français beseeched the prefect at Clermont for "written assurance or at least advice" that could permit that organization to recommend "a path leading to some security" for their "unhappy fellow Jews."[80]

Ultimately, most of these displaced persons were more fortunate than other categories of Jews affected by different measures that included assignment to a specific residence. In perhaps an oversight on Vichy's part, the government had ordered the Jews out of Clermont without specifying destination. In any case, the officials from Jewish Affairs were soon upset to realize that many (and probably most) of the families ordered out of Clermont in the summer of 1942 were still living in the area in 1943. The director of the Clermont Section d'Enquête et Contrôle (SEC), the local representative for the Commissariat Général des Affaires Juives, complained bitterly that most of the foreigners expelled had relocated in neighboring villages with convenient transportation to Clermont, and "thanks to travel permits given them much too readily" by local officials, "these foreigners continue in effect to live permanently at Clermont."[81] The same was all the more true for the French Jews who were not obliged to have special travel permits. Consequently, the delegate for Jewish Affairs demanded the imposition of strict controls on travel and insisted on actual expulsion for those involved. The regional prefect ordered such measures, but local police, who (as we shall see) were on very bad terms with the Jewish Affairs people, denied that they issued travel passes too freely. The Jews, now keenly aware that they were better off absent from police registers, lived under false identities and avoided contact with the authorities. Thus, most of them were sheltered from the ominous threat of deportation that confronted other Jews grouped in labor camps and special regional or national centers.

Even before the fall of France, the Third Republic had established concentration camps, complete with barbed wire and mail censorship, peopled by Spanish republicans, political and racial refugees, and suspect foreigners of various sorts. These measures dictated by emergency conditions and intended as a temporary expedient were greatly extended by Vichy. Shortly after taking power, Marshal Pétain decreed that all foreign Jews were liable to arrest and imprisonment in special camps on a prefect's administrative order.[82] By January 1942 the minister of the interior had established forty-nine internment camps for common criminals and black-marketers, political opponents (especially Communists), and foreigners. Seven of these camps were specially designed for Jews, five in the north—most notoriously, Drancy, the way station of deportation for tens of thousands—and two in the south, the camps at Gurs and Rivesaltes.[83] But these forty-nine camps were only the major ones administered by the minister of the interior. Hundreds of other temporary or semipermanent labor camps, refugee centers, shelters, or prisons, with tens of thousands in detention, were established at the departmental level and controlled by different ministries. In the Puy-de-Dôme at least twelve of these camps held perhaps 4000 people for varying lengths of time during the four years of the Vichy regime.[84]

In November 1941 the minister of the interior decided to reorganize and coordinate the relocation of "undesirable refugees." He had begun the process in April, but now he hoped to "substitute . . . a controlled relocation for a disorganized dispersion."[85] To this effect four national relocation centers were established; three of them, La Bourboule; Le Mont-Dore, and St. Nectaire, were in the mountains of the Puy-de-Dôme. Located near one another, they were 40 to 60 kilometers away from Clermont-Ferrand. Therefore, the police and other officials in the area around Clermont were to play an important role in the concentration of foreign Jews by the Vichy regime.

The original measure had spoken of "undesirable refugees"; in practice this meant principally foreign Jews. The major category affected by the relocation schemes were Jewish refugees who had entered France since 1936, including many naturalized French. Those Jews with sufficient means to support themselves were assigned to residence in the national relocation centers, while those without resources were incorporated into work groups or, if they were unfit or too old for work, placed in centers supervised by the Service du Contrôle des Etrangers. As enforced at Clermont-Ferrand, the measure was applied almost exclusively to those who had arrived during the "Exodus" and those who had illegally crossed the line of demarcation. The prefect ordered that "only very exceptionally"[86] should the measure be applied to those who had come to Clermont before June 1940. Consequently, of 233 cases considered in February and March 1942 only 27 individuals were ordered into the (GTE), 18 others were incorporated nominally into the GTE but remained at jobs they held already, and just 40 were assigned to residence in the relocation centers.[87]

Jews might be required to move to relocation centers under a variety of pretexts. The government's apprehension about possible demonstrations in favor of Léon Blum at the Riom trial led it in February 1942 to order the evacuation from Riom of sixty-one Jews and their assignment to various relocation centers.[88] The actions of a "Commission de révision: étrangers en surnombre"[89] added others at regular meetings that were held almost every month until the liberation. By the summer of 1942 when the first deportations from the unoccupied zone began, several hundred Jews had been assigned to the relocation centers of the region. Later a special relocation operation accompanied the visit of Pétain to La Bourboule for a thermal cure in the summer of 1943. In five days (2–6 June) 332 persons were transferred to other towns in the region so that the venerable head of state might not be troubled by the sight of them.[90] On the official pretext that they were occupying quarters needed for "curists," but probably because their rooms were coveted by government bureaucrats, fifty-two Jews and sixty-one other foreigners were driven out of Chatel-Guyon in May 1943. On a smaller scale, as early as September 1941, seven Jews from Puy-Guillaume, the village closest to Laval's chateau at Chateldon, were expelled and placed in camps as a security measure, even though Laval was not in the government at that time.[91]

The experience of one Jewish family that had come to La Bourboule by its own choice may serve to illustrate the dangers and uncertainties that faced even those Jews in the Puy-de-Dôme who were not on the lists of those assigned to residence and were not among the most recently naturalized. Cecile Rotkeil Wechsler, born in Warsaw in 1905, was a physician trained at Basel and Montpellier who had been a French citizen for several years. Her husband, Marcel Wechsler, a professor of mathematics and languages, was of Rumanian nationality. When German troops approached Paris in June 1940 the Wechslers had taken their eight-year-old son to La Bourboule in search of safety in southern France. At La Bourboule Dr. Wechsler was hired by the Baronne Rothschild to serve as physician, hygienist, and nurse to several hundred children at the Maison de La Guette, an orphanage founded in the 1930s by the Rothschilds for children from German Jewish families that had been transferred from the north to La Bourboule at the time of the "Exodus."

When the director of the Maison de La Guette learned of a possible raid by the Germans, the children were spread around the area in private homes until many of them were able to be shepherded to refuge in Switzerland. Dr. Wechsler remained at La Bourboule after the closing of the Maison de La Guette working as an assistant to local French doctors. Since, as a Jew, she could not practice medicine officially, she was given all "the dirty jobs for the doctors, night calls, emergencies, caring for the paralyzed and dying . . . even doing massages and podiatry."[92] Her husband taught mathematics and languages to help prepare students for their baccalaureat degrees.

Even though the Wechslers were performing valuable services in the community, when Pétain came to the town for a cure in the summer of 1943, they were ordered out of La Bourboule along with the more than 300 "undesirable refugees" who had been forcibly sent to La Bourboule as part of the relocation program. After several months' stay at Massiac in the Cantal, in November 1943 they were among the minority of those Jews who were allowed to come back to La Bourboule, thanks in part to strong letters of recommendation from two doctors at La Bourboule, one of whom was the former mayor, and from Professor Wechsler's students. Despite such support and the friendly attitude of local police, who when possible gave advance warning of raids, the family, already having had two narrow escapes, was not able to feel secure until the liberation. Once, Dr. Wechsler managed to prevent her husband's deportation during a roundup of foreign Jews by putting a large cast on his right leg and refusing to dress him when the police wanted to take him away. At the time of their stay at

Massiac, one morning at five o'clock Professor Wechsler had been arrested by labor draft agents but was reprieved when a cooperative medical committee exempted him on the basis of his teaching responsibilities. Dr. Wechsler was given a pass permitting her to travel around the commune late at night, and although not a member of any particular resistance movement, occasionally she was able to perform valuable services by transmitting messages and false papers in emergency situations. In the summer of 1944 she joined a Russian surgeon, Dr. Finikoff, in setting up an emergency clinic for the Forces Françaises de l'Intérieur (FFI). They successfully performed thirty-five operations in spite of primitive conditions and won the gratitude of the young men they treated who had discovered that many French doctors in the area were less willing to help.

These examples from the Puy-de-Dôme may suffice to demonstrate one fundamental condition of existence for all Jews in Vichy France. They were at any moment subject to banishment from a given town at the government's whim, and so lacked any semblance of security in their residence. More significant in the case of those affected by the relocation actions was the fact that they were physically isolated; their names and addresses were known and checked regularly. Therefore, not surprisingly, among those deported, particularly those rounded up by the French police in the summer and fall of 1942 and early 1943, a very high percentage were from the internment or relocation centers, or in the GTE.

Deportation

In turning to deportation, we come to what was surely one of the most sinister episodes in the history of the Vichy regime. In all of France 70,000 to 80,000 Jews were deported to Germany and to concentration camps to the East. Very few of them survived the Holocaust. Although most were trapped in areas under direct German occupation, and many were arrested by German police or the military in reprisal for various incidents during the occupation, a substantial number were rounded up by French police and handed over to the German authorities. At least 400 Jews were deported from the Puy-de-Dôme, and 60 percent of these men, women, and children were deported *before* German troops occupied the area or afterward in operations carried out exclusively by the French.

The experience of deportation at Clermont-Ferrand was no less tragic for having been on a relatively small scale. The three major operations carried out by the French police were in August 1942 and February and March 1943. Deportation operations, called "roundups" (*ramassages*), were carried out in raids launched simultaneously in different parts of the Puy-de-Dôme in the middle of the night or very early in the morning (most often starting at 4:30 A.M.) involving units of the police, gendarmerie, and the Gardes Mobiles de Reserve (GMR). Those arrested were brought to assembly points at Clermont-Ferrand, including the Quartier Gribeauval, l'Ecole Amédée Gasquet, and "Camp F," a demobilization center for former prisoners of war near Gerzat, where they underwent physical examinations and might be kept for a few days before they were herded into cattle cars for shipment to the north. In addition to those trapped by French police during the major roundups, other Jews were deported in isolated follow-up actions to these raids, or as a result of reprisals. Thirty-eight foreign Jews were deported 26 June 1943 after the killing of two German police, and perhaps twenty Jews were among those deported at the time of the action against the University of Strasbourg in November 1943. Other deportations followed arrest by the German police or military (at least sixty-six).

The amount of documentary evidence preserved for the whole process at Clermont is astonishing. Local archives contain everything from receipts to reimburse the tramway company of Clermont-Ferrand 2088 francs for transporting deportees 174 kilometers to the train station; to 1290 francs to Dr. Pierre Gourdan, his *"honorarium"* for physical examination of forty-three Jews; to payment for "four bales of hay" to *"garnish* a railcar for the transport of foreigners." In the archives are lists, marked ominously by underlining, red crosses, or blue dots, indicating those to be arrested. Along with accounts of physical examinations (contrary to the guidelines suggested by authorities, at least one Polish Jew was deported from Clermont despite evidence of pregnancy), and orders for the provision of two tins of fish, 100 grams of seasoning, 60 grams of jelly, 700 grams of bread, and one-half liter of wine for each deportee's journey, is the grotesque indication that the trains and their garnished cattle cars of human cargo were to leave Clermont-Ferrand from the *"quai des béstiaux."*[93]

Aryanization

In contrast to relocation operations and deportation, the process of "Aryanization" of Jewish property at Clermont-Ferrand, the third example of those most visible anti-Semitic policies, was one of an outwardly dramatic appearance belied by a more subtle, and less damaging, reality. Here again, the Vichy government acted before the arrival of German troops. Virtually every Jewish business in the Puy-de-Dôme and its neighboring departments was taken over by the Commissariat Général des Affaires Juives and given an "Administrateur Provisoire" charged with supervising the business or liquidating it in the event its operation was not deemed vital to the local economy. As early as June 1942, seventy Jewish businesses in the Puy-de-

Dôme, most of them clothing establishments with a few financial institutions, had been "Aryanized" to the extent of having non-Jewish administrators appointed. By the end of the Vichy regime, some 334 for the whole region were affected, by far the greatest number at Clermont-Ferrand and Vichy.[94] On 3 October 1942, the intendant régional de police at Clermont ordered all police stations in the area to see to it that yellow colored posters were displayed prominently on storefronts to indicate "Entreprise Juive" for those that had been "Aryanized"; and, perhaps anticipating trouble, he added: "Take every possible step to avoid their being torn down."[95]

Vichy officials had learned that "Aryanization" in northern France had provided a cover for the transfer of French wealth directly into German hands, and partially because of this the Service de l'Aryanisation Economique desired to control Jewish wealth in southern France. In Clermont-Ferrand at least the regional director of the "Aryanization" program for the Auvergne consistently argued that his intention was for the temporary administrators "to assure the direction of the business *en bon père de famille,*"[96] letting the Jewish owners in fact run their own concerns as long as they followed all of the laws. Only a small minority of the businesses were actually closed down and sold. On one occasion the local director of "Aryanization" even opposed deporting Jewish workers from the region on the grounds that the local economy would suffer from it.[97] While there were possible exceptions to these guidelines—many Jews certainly suffered financial spoliation through arbitrary actions of those connected with the Jewish Affairs police (the SEC)[98]—most Jewish businessmen *who survived the occupation* were able to recover their property in reasonably good shape after the liberation. As with all other measures affecting the Jews, this was most valid for those families long established in the area. The refugees or recent arrivals were most likely to suffer. One example is that of Paul Ulmann, director of La Maison Rouge, whose family had been in business at Clermont since 1891.[99] Ulmann gave his shares in various financial concerns to a trusted employee who hid them throughout the occupation in a small village and returned them at the liberation. La Maison Rouge's Administrateur Provisoire hardly ever came into the store, and then only to sign checks or other documents as indicated by Ulmann. Only five or six of the twenty-two Administrateurs Provisoires for the Puy-de-Dôme were investigated for mismanagement at the liberation, suggesting that Ulmann's case was not exceptional.[100]

The Ulmann family's experience also illustrates that even those Jews long established at Clermont-Ferrand with friends in the local administration could never feel secure under Vichy. Because of favorable recommendations from local officials, Ulmann's firm had originally been exempted from "Aryanization," but the reprieve had lasted only a few months. Although a Swiss passport and a friendly consul at Vichy had provided an avenue to safety for the senior Ulmanns, their son, Jean, was forced into hiding in the last months of the occupation to escape arrest by the German labor service, the Office Placement Allemand (OPA). In the summer of 1944 La Maison Rouge was slated for sale by the Commissariat Général des Affaires Juives. In other words, many French Jews in southern France benefited *temporarily* from the fact that foreign and recently naturalized Jews were attacked first by Vichy and German anti-Semitic measures. But outside of the liberation of France, there was no prospect of security on French soil for any Jew.

Having outlined the results of some of the most significant actions taken against Jews in the Clermont area, what can be said of the local response to these policies? Among those most directly responsible for Jewish Affairs, Mr. Suramy, the local director of the "Aryanization" services, was the only one who apparently acted at times in a fairly correct manner. Otherwise no redeeming feature seems evident in the personnel associated with Jewish Affairs at Clermont. They were hoodlums, thugs, brutes of the most despicable sort, who interwove their activities as agents for the Commissariat Général des Affaires Juives with participation in the Milice, and as Gestapo or German labor service auxiliaries. Georges Bonnichon, for example, who was one of the two or three most feared local Milice officials, was involved in many actions against Jews. As director in charge of the repression of secret societies, he shared an office with the Jewish Affairs police, and believed that Jews, Freemasons, and Gaullists were working hand in hand to destroy France.[101] Jewish Affairs officials themselves acknowledged an inability to recruit responsible, qualified investigators as employees. Even before the liberation, when several Jewish Affairs people were executed or received stiff penalties for their actions, Vichy's police had brought criminal charges against many of the local agents for false arrests, extortion, fraud, theft, and a host of other illegal activities. There seems to have been quite a bit of competition among the Jewish Affairs delegates, the German labor service employees, and the Gestapo to see who could pillage the apartments of arrested Jews first.

From the beginning, the regular police were suspicious of the Jewish Affairs employees, some of whom they had arrested for criminal activities in the 1930s. In his notes for a 16 December 1941 meeting with the prefectorial staff at Clermont-Ferrand, the local Secrétaire Général pour la Police described the recently appointed delegates for Jewish Affairs and for Secret Societies: "ignorant of police methods and knowing nothing about proper procedures or the criminal and penal codes,"[102] adding that it would be well for the local undercover police to keep an eye on them. It was extremely fortunate for the Jews, and perhaps one thing that should be credited to the Vichy regime, that the delegates of the Section d'Enquête et Contrôle in the south (unlike those in the occupied zone) were not given full police powers, notably the right to arrest suspects, until a month before the liberation when Darnand and the Milice were dominant. Therefore, the Jewish Affairs agents had to depend on the regular police to have their charges investigated and sanctions applied. The normal result of this circumstance was that Jewish Affairs would demand severe sanctions (expulsion, internment, confiscation of property, and so forth) on the basis of the flimsiest of charges (in at least one case, only because they desired an apartment for a friend), and the police would throw out the case for lack of evidence or recommend far more lenient treatment. As time passed, without question the regular police came to look on the agents of Jewish Affairs with undisguised contempt. The SEC, of course, saw this as sabotage and complained bitterly that regular police were calling their inspectors "liars," systematically siding with Jews, and treating their agents discourteously. The regular police were apt to use "absurd" phrases such as "his good faith can be accepted" when referring to Jews; in short, bemoaned the director of Clermont's Jewish Services, the employees of the prefecture "are trying to reduce to nothing the work of the Section d'Enquête et de Contrôle by warning Jews of our action."[103]

Despite the impression of Jewish Affairs agents, it would be an exaggeration to see every policeman at Clermont-Ferrand as a guardian angel for persecuted Jews. Several certainly were. For example, the commissaire de police for the First Arrondissement at Clermont, Mr. Azier, died in deportation partially as a result of his actions in favor of Jews.[104] Most policemen seem to have applied the law more or less thoroughly, often with some leniency to those willing to comply. To cite one instance, those who agreed that they were Jewish after all were allowed to have their identity papers stamped "Juif" after the deadline, instead of being interned as the SEC demanded. Some gendarmes were commended for acting with courtesy to those Jews they were rounding up for deportation, but nonetheless, they put them into the cattle cars. Of course, these same men also arrested non-Jewish resisters and escorted thousands of French citizens to labor service in Germany or along the Atlantic Wall. In these matters they seem to have been acting with a conviction that they were behaving as responsible professionals fulfilling their duty.

As for the general population, individual expressions of hostility to anti-Semitic policies were fairly frequent before deportation began in the summer of 1942, but widespread popular opposition was most evident and effective when the regime began to deport Jewish men, women, and children. Even for the first major operation in August 1942, most of those scheduled for deportation from the Puy-de-Dôme were not caught. Ordering rigorous measures to try to catch the fugitives, the regional prefect indicated to the four departmental prefects for the Auvergne that "more than 50 percent had escaped."[105] For the Puy-de-Dôme, of 226 persons on the lists just 59 were deported. The central police commissioner at Clermont-Ferrand suspected that someone from the Red Cross had warned them, or perhaps a foreign radio broadcast had alerted them about the roundup. Each succeeding operation netted fewer captives as secretaries refused to type lists or conveyed warnings, and mysterious telephone calls or personal messages from friendly gendarmes arrived before the police could carry out the raids. Some policemen began to complain that they were being made a laughingstock.[106]

The commissaire de police at Issoire reported that the mother of a Jewish boy who had avoided being arrested had even told them with obvious satisfaction that her son "had well-placed friends at Vichy, and he was warned about this roundup," adding: "It was very clear that all of the Jews we were to have rounded up had been warned well before we were of the measures taken against them."[107] In February 1943, 36 Jews who were in labor camps were caught, but only 18 of 184 others were found in the Puy-de-Dôme. In September 1943 only 13 of 286 foreign and 8 of 170 French Jews sought were deported, although 50 had been discovered. In still another case, a German labor draft official was extremely upset because he was forced to explain to his SS superiors in Paris why, at his request, they had routed a special train to Clermont-Ferrand to pick up only three men when 250 had been promised.[108] In short, thanks to the support of many individual civil servants or government employees and the sympathetic aid of other people in the local population, as well as to their own determination not to be trapped, most of the Jews scheduled for deportation from the Auvergne avoided that fate.

The complicity of hundreds of people that made such escapes possible did not preclude the existence of anti-Semitism among the Auvergnat population. As elsewhere in France, anonymous denunciations occurred—most frequently, allegations that Jews were involved in black-marketeering—windows were broken in several Jewish shops at Clermont-Ferrand, Légion chiefs expressed regret that exemptions were permitted in the purge of Jews from government jobs, and occasionally virulent anti-Semitic statements were made by local officials. For example, the mayor of La Bourboule, appointed by Vichy to replace an outspokenly republican predecessor, was dismayed that his town had been selected as a relocation center.

Begging for repeal of the government's decision, Mayor Mille noted that La Bourboule was famous as an excellent thermal station for children, thus requiring exceptional hygienic precautions. "A city upon which in part depends the future of the race," appealed the mayor, "must be sheltered from all risks of contamination. The health of French youth will not permit us to expose it to avoidable dangers."[109] Here was one Frenchman who needed no lessons in anti-Semitism from Adolf Hitler.

Poignant as such examples may be, insofar as one can measure public opinion in such extraordinary times, the majority of the evidence seems to indicate a rejection of Vichy's anti-Semitic propaganda and a steadily growing opposition to the implementation of government policies. As was true elsewhere in France, little visible opposition was apparent at Clermont-Ferrand to the Statut des Juifs and the earliest discriminatory measures taken against the Jews. Although Alexandre Varenne, editor of *La Montagne,* wrote privately to Pétain in February 1941 to protest indignantly against the application of the Statut des Juifs, and particularly against the lack of consideration being given to Jewish prisoners of war and their families, censorship made it impossible for him to publish such criticism in his newspaper.[110] Administrative notices calling on Jews to report to police stations to fulfill certain obligations (announcements about the census of Jews, stamping of identity papers, and so forth) were published in the newspapers and posted by *Affiche,* and posters indicating Jewish shops were visible to all; but newspapers at Clermont-Ferrand did not report anything about the roundup and deportation of Jews. Police noted that the public seemed unaware that these operations had taken place locally, but there can be no doubt that the arrests and deportations soon became known by word of mouth. The general public, as was true of many local French officials and the Jews themselves, was not immediately aware of what deportation would mean for those sent from Clermont to "unknown destinations."[111]

Although there were acts of kindness and assistance from local clergy to individual Jewish families, the Catholic Church and the bishop of Clermont-Ferrand were not among the leading outspoken critics of Vichy's anti-Semitism. In March 1943 the bishop of Clermont ordered read to all Catholics a joint letter of the French episcopate inspired by the massive deportation of Jews that presented a clear, but general, defense of "the human person."[112] But even though Gabriel Piguet would eventually be deported for alleged assistance to a fugitive priest, his voice was not publicly joined to that minority of prominent French Catholics, such as Monsignors J.-G. Saliège, bishop of Toulouse, or Théas of Montaubon, who courageously protested the government's anti-Semitic actions. In October

1942 *La Semaine religieuse de Clermont-Ferrand* printed a contrived "mise au point" attributed to Saliège, in which he affirmed his support for Pétain's government, acknowledged the church's condemnation of communism, and expressed concern that certain people had misconstrued his ringing protest against persecution of the Jews. (". . . Jews are men and women. . . . There is a limit to what can be permitted against them, against these men, these women, against these fathers and mothers. They belong to the human race. They are our brothers, like so many others . . .")[113] It is striking that the bishop of Clermont, despite publishing the "retraction," had not seen fit to publish the original appeal of Saliège in *La Semaine religieuse*. That the *mise au point* was published by the church hierarchy within six weeks after Saliège's public protest against deportation of the Jews also testifies to the rapid spread of news around southern France despite Vichy's rigorous censorship of the media.

Quite a few Clermontois, offering letters of guarantee, and so forth, had tried to intervene to help individual Jews avoid relocation or resettlement measures, but it was clearly the beginning of massive deportations that first notably awakened an important segment of the population to the necessity of active complicity with the Jews. Supervisors of the vicinity's foreign labor services acknowledged that the deportations were causing "a profound malaise among the agents responsible for carrying them out."[114] Police reported that the government's heavy-handed anti-Semitic propaganda was counterproductive, creating more friends than enemies for the Jews. For example, few Clermontois took seriously the government's allegation that Jews were behind President Roosevelt's "theft" of North Africa. While noting less critical reaction in some parts of France than others, the Ministry of the Interior's "synthèse" of the prefects' reports for August 1942 admitted: "The measures of regroupment and expulsion taken against foreign Jews have provoked a very clear disturbance in public opinion. A good number of Prefects have noted in this regard reactions of sympathy from the public. It seems that everyone agrees in placing the responsibility for these measures on the German authorities. However, these massive arrests, widely exploited by the opposition, have aroused, in certain departments, a disapproval that is not dissimulated."[115] Clermont-Ferrand was among those areas cited where opinion was seen as favorable to the Jews. Contemporary British intelligence surveys cited a "considerable number" of French military and police officers in southern France who had refused to carry out orders for the arrest of Jews, and claimed: "It seems beyond doubt that the French population in general strongly disapproves of the campaign."[116]

Some writers have suggested that this negative popular reaction to the deportations forced Laval's government to retreat from a vigorous prosecution of Vichy's anti-Semitic designs.[117] Although the evidence is not conclusive on this point, some indications support such a hypothesis as applied to the Auvergne. At the very least, a change in tactics for the accomplishment of anti-Semitic programs was evident after the first deportations. Immediately following the August 1942 roundup of foreign Jews, Vichy officials, angered that more than half of their targets had escaped, ordered the prefects to intensify searches for the fugitives, employing all means at their disposal. In September 1942 the préfet délégué for the Puy-de-Dôme drew up instructions for the apprehension of ninety-three foreign Jews who had escaped deportation from Clermont in August. The original draft ordered his subordinates to push their investigation "to the farthest removed farms or dwellings of the department,"[118] but, interestingly, this phrase was crossed out and not used. The actual order sent to the police and gendarmerie called only for an "active search," and by late October several of the instructions related to searches for fugitive foreign Jews said seek "discreetly" to find their new addresses.[119] In March 1943, when ordering the third major deportation operation to be carried out by the French police in the Puy-de-Dôme, the intendant régional de police at Clermont-Ferrand instructed the commander of the GMR units involved that his forces were to leave Clermont-Ferrand for La Bourboule under cover of darkness, "avoiding to let themselves be seen by the public";[120] and the men were not to be informed of their destination or responsibilities until they arrived at the scene where arrests were to be made.

In "ordinary" times with an unfettered press and no obvious reason for caution in the expression of one's opinion, the measurement of popular attitudes is an uncertain science. The limited quantity of documentation for the Vichy period of necessity undermines the confidence of the historian in an attempt to generalize about popular levels of anti-Semitism or opposition to it. Moreover, the motivations of those people who gave aid to the Jews might be mixed. For example, while Mayor Mille of La Bourboule castigated the Jews in blatant anti-Semitic terms and sought to avoid the designation of his town as a relocation center, the officials of St.-Nectaire (including representatives of organizations like the Légion, some of whose propaganda was openly anti-Semitic) wanted the prefect to choose their town in hopes that the coming of Jewish refugees might benefit the local economy that had suffered from the sharp wartime reduction in "curistes."[121] Patriotism, Christian charity, peer pressure, and factors other than ideological opposition to anti-Semitism were sometimes involved in a decision to shelter a Jewish family. It took only a handful of committed people to pass warnings effectively. So it is impossible to say conclusively how many people were directly or indirectly active in opposition to anti-Semitic policies.

Still, the survival of so many of those who were marked for destruction can only be understood in the context of a countryside where thousands of people offered food, shelter, refuge, or simply silence when questioned. If Vichy's anti-Semitism was the "blackest mark"[122] on its record, surely the response to those policies by a significant segment of the population in the Auvergne provides one of the most encouraging chapters in the history of those desperately tragic years.

6

Public Opinion at the Grass Roots

In normal times newspapers and other news media provide a major source of information concerning public opinion. In Vichy France, as with authoritarian regimes elsewhere, newspapers may be valuable sources for information of several kinds, and, used with care, they may tell us much about the regime in power, but their value for the interpretation of attitudes toward the government and its leaders is minimal. For Clermont-Ferrand the experience of Alexandre Varenne, founder and director of *La Montagne,* one of the three local daily newspapers at Clermont, offers a perfect illustration of this phenomenon. Varenne's private war with the censors and his consistent, though ultimately losing, battle waged in the interest of freedom of the press form the basis for a wonderfully entertaining "story within a story" concerning conditions under the Vichy regime that is at the same time instructive with regard to the issue of analyzing public opinion under authoritarian governments.

From the point of view of those charged by the Vichy regime with censorship of the press at Clermont-Ferrand, there cannot have been a more cantankerous, irascible 70-year-old man alive at Clermont in 1940 than Alexandre Varenne. Born in Clermont-Ferrand one month after the fall of the Second Empire and the proclamation of the Republic in Paris, Varenne's lifetime until 1940 had coincided with that of the Third Republic, a regime he had served with distinction in several capacities. Elected deputy from the Puy-de-Dôme between 1906 and 1936 with only one term's interruption, Varenne was also French governor general in Indochina for three years in the late 1920s. During World War I, at the urging of the Socialist Party, he had declined to accept a ministry in 1917 in Painlevé's government, but he had served the administration in the Censorship Office—the latter experience providing an invaluable store of references for some of his arguments with Vichy's censors. Trained as a lawyer, Varenne had turned to politics and journalism as a young man. In the 1890s he had helped organize the Socialist Party in the Puy-de-Dôme.

Varenne's journalistic credentials were impeccable. In addition to work for several regional newspapers and national journals of lesser stature, he worked with Jean Jaurès on *L'Humanité* from 1902 until 1918 when he founded his own paper, *La Montagne,* at Clermont-Ferrand. Differences with the party leadership over ministerial participation and support for national defense, and sympathy with some of the arguments of the "Neo-Socialist" faction led Varenne to break with the SFIO in the early 1930s, after which time he styled himself an "Independent Socialist" in much the same manner as his newspaper was labeled "Quotidien Populaire Indepen-dant." One thing is certain: Alexandre Varenne was very much his own man.

Inextricably bound up with the history of the Third Republic, Varenne had been stung sharply by the republic's collapse, but he was defiantly proud of the republic's many accomplishments, and he was unwilling to join with Vichy in casting the blame for France's fall on the institutions and leaders of the fallen republic. Acknowledging that some practices and structures might have been altered slightly to improve the edifice, Varenne was dismayed to see the whole system abolished; and as weeks and months passed, he was deeply distressed by the increasingly authoritarian drift of Marshal Pétain's regime. With the persistence of a gadfly, Varenne set about his self-appointed task, "with the only goal of being in my modest place useful to my country,"[1] offering his advice to Pétain on matters con-cerning government policy and its impact on France. From August 1940 until the spring of 1941, by which time he was convinced of the futility of this gesture, Varenne wrote Pétain at least seventeen personal letters in which he attempted to warn him about the harmfulness of government poli-cies that he believed to be disastrous for France and contrary to Pétain's proclaimed intention of fostering national unity and social harmony.

It would be difficult to imagine a more fervent and eloquent testimonial to French republicanism, or a firmer defense of civil liberties and justice, than was contained in these letters. Although inadequate to convey the richness of the correspondence, the following excerpts will suggest some of Varenne's principal concerns. Reflecting his experience in Southeast Asia and his special interest in that part of the world, on four separate occasions Varenne urged Pétain to make a strong stand against the Japanese in Indo-china, fearing that an abandonment of French sovereignty in Indochina would be but the first step in the dismemberment of the French empire, an invitation for others to follow. He was furious when Vichy's propaganda services in July 1941 tried to impose an article, "The origin of the Franco-Japanese agreement," suggesting that the Japanese had been obliged to move into Indochina to thwart American and British imperialistic designs on the area, asking Pétain: "Just how far will we descend into lying and disgrace?"[2]

Describing as a travesty of justice the arrest and imprisonment of former Education Minister Jean Zay and others who in June 1940 had sailed on the *Massilia* in hopes of continuing the battle from North Africa but who had been labeled "émigrés" and "déserteurs," Varenne warned Pétain:

> If this is not made right, if Lieutenant Jean Zay is forced to experience the Calvary of Captain DREYFUS, mark my words that sooner or later the truth will break through, besmirching your name, your government, even your work, compromising, as in times past, that national harmony to which you never cease to urge the French people.[3]

A month after Pétain's meeting with Hitler at Montoire and the announcement of the government's intention to embark on a path of collaboration, Varenne expressed his reservations about this decision. Had the Germans intended to treat France truly as an equal or as a major element in a new Europe organized for the benefit of all, there might be legitimate grounds for collaboration, but Varenne did not believe this to be Hitler's viewpoint: "For these gentlemen from Berlin we are at an inferior stage, a little above the yellow races, Negroes, and the Jews, at the rank they have decided to attribute to us in the hierarchy of the races, among which they occupy the superior echelon."[4] Although he did not have much faith in the policy announced at Montoire, Varenne agreed to insert whatever articles the government required concerning the new policy with the understanding that "we not be asked to be dazzled by a dawn which may only be a mirage," adding: "We will not accept to be chained to the cart of our conquerer."[5]

Three of the topics that recurred most frequently in Varenne's correspondence with Pétain were the abuse of police powers, constitutional changes, and, of most direct relevance to Varenne's livelihood, censorship of the press. Varenne referred to the imprisonment of Blum, Daladier, and the other leaders of the Third Republic charged with responsibility for France's defeat, and the incarceration by administrative decision of political opponents of lesser stature, as a return to "the Bastille of lettres de cachet, aggravated by the sequestering of men against whom . . . no formal charges have been made," asking:

> Frankly, Marshal, do you not realize that all of this lacks elegance, and that in having recourse to the worst abuses of the troubled epochs of our history, you risk accustoming the French people to the misuse of force and encouraging a taste for violence?[6]

In the late fall of 1940 the organization and training of a special police called "groupes de protection" with headquarters at Clermont-Ferrand brought a sharp note of condemnation from Varenne, particularly in view of the milieu from which they were recruited and their extreme right-wing political coloration.

> The principal offices are held by individuals formerly indicted in the so-called Cagoulard conspiracy, of which our city was for a time one of the centers. Regular policemen see in them the same persons they had been ordered to arrest three years ago, and I leave it to you to imagine what thoughts this unsettling competition suggests to them. . . . Are you allowing to be formed under your eyes a Gestapo, a fascist militia, an Iron Guard?[7]

As was often the case in his letters, Varenne tried to give Pétain some benefit of the doubt by suggesting that these policies were not really accurate reflections of the Marshal's intentions, urging him to straighten out the mistakes of his ministers before it was too late: "For the policies that *they are carrying out* too often *in your name* suggest a misunderstanding of certain fatal historical errors. They are taking us back to the White Terror of 1815. . . . You have launched the idea of a 'National Revolution.' That is not the same thing as the Restoration. That is the counterrevolution."[8] When the responsibility for the abuse of power was clearly Pétain's own, Varenne did not mince words. Pétain stated publicly, long before their trial at Riom, that Blum and the others blamed for France's defeat were guilty, and Varenne accused him of flagrant disregard for due process beyond anything Louis XI, Richelieu, or even the Sun King would have dared to try.

> What? Marshal, do you not draw back before the responsibility of deciding by yourself about the honor and liberty of men, without preliminary examination, without a law court, consequently without the possibility of defense? A Court-Martial with a single judge, judging without appeal, after a procedure with time limits and formalities decided by that judge, without hearing the defense or even listening to the suspect? . . .
> In truth, Marshal, this action is a judicial heresy. Is there not one jurist at the Hôtel du Parc, what am I saying, is there not even a beginning law student? He could have warned you against an initiative which may appear to you to be justified in terms of political necessity, but which defies good sense and the most elementary notion of justice.[9]

Varenne believed that the granting of full powers to Pétain had been the result of extraordinary circumstances, justifiable only on a temporary basis without prejudice for the regular constitutional system that should be established definitively only after the war and occupation were over. Any system imposed on France before that time would be "condemned to the provisional."[10] Above all, Varenne felt that France should avoid adopting Nazi models simply because of the momentary dominance of the Germans. According to Varenne, the "overwhelming majority"[11] of the French were both patriotic and republican. They were attached to their traditional liberties and offended by policies that divided the country or revived old quarrels. By early in 1941 "a large fraction of public opinion" was disturbed by the excessive use of the personal powers granted to Pétain. For them the republic had been not only, in the words of Thiers, "the regime that divides us the least. It was also, and above all, the one that was based on the law, tending to peace and Justice."[12] French democracy needed to be reformed and strengthened, not destroyed as Vichy's policies seemed intent on doing. Citing the opinions of his many contacts at all levels of society and of various political persuasions, Varenne admonished Pétain:

> It was not for these policies that France has given you its confidence. You were in her eyes, you could be nothing other than the man of national unity, the leader above parties, around whom, for the renewal of the country all well-intentioned people could rally. It was not to persecute the Jews and harass the Freemasons, and it was still less to conjure away the Republic that France has conferred upon you a mandate without limitation of power or of time.[13]

Only seven months after the creation of the Vichy regime, Varenne concluded sadly that little possibility remained that his letters might have any influence on Pétain's decisions: "Despite all that I have tried to tell you . . . it seems that you are committed to a path along which we will be unable to share any common ground."[14] Although many things, almost everything, about the Vichy regime had disturbed Varenne, it was an argument over the issue probably most dear to his heart, freedom of the press, that led to his decision to terminate abruptly his correspondence with Pétain in March 1941. Varenne's troubles with the censor at Clermont-Ferrand had begun immediately upon his return from his summer residence to that city in November 1940 when he resumed direct control over the production of his newspaper, *La Montagne*. The very first evening following his return, he objected to the censor's insistence that he devote several columns to a description of Pétain's trips to Toulouse, Clermont, and Lyon. As he explained to Pétain, these events were newsworthy and deserved to be covered, "but within reasonable limits."[15] Instead, the censor's office had flooded the newspapers with "grandiloquent and occasionally infantile reports in excessive volume."[16] Varenne argued: "The public hardly reads these long accounts which all look the same whoever the high dignitary involved. And this abundance of required copy threatens to give the public the impression of publicity controlled by the censor. Thus the effect that you wish to produce will be weakened or annulled."[17] In conversations with others, Varenne was less diplomatic: "No one reads that junk, and I have more interesting things to put in my newspaper."[18]

This was only the first in a long series of disputes with the censors. As documented by police records, by Varenne's lively correspondence with Pétain, Laval, Paul Marion, and others, and by a host of complaints from the censorship officials about the rebellious editor, Varenne was a nuisance of the first order. He never hesitated to direct his complaints to the highest authorities, and occasionally he succeeded in obtaining the reversal of a decision made at the local level. According to the local officials, these successes only made him more difficult to handle. Referring to one such case, an observer commented: "Moreover, the measure of clemency taken toward him does not seem to have calmed him down, for in a telephone conversation the 15th of this month, he violently criticized the censor at Clermont-Ferrand, warning him that 'things will change one day.' "[19] Before publication stopped entirely in August 1943, Varenne and *La Montagne* held the record among newspapers in southern France for the number of suspensions because of alleged violations of directives from the censorship services. A glance through the notices of suspension indicates that Varenne was relentless in testing the censor's patience. Among a host of possible examples the following may be cited: 6 July 1941, "Failure to follow governmental orders"; 10 January 1942, "Unfortunate article about the Germano-Russian war"; 2, 3, 4 March 1942, "Because of Constant nonconformity with the Censor's instructions"; 3, 4 August 1942, "Because of failure to publish an official German communiqué"; 27 March 1942, "Annoying presentation of information that provoked Italian protest"; 9 September 1942, "Particularly inopportune and annoying article"; 21, 22, 23 September 1942, "Article on Valmy"; 15 March 1943, "Publication of a Tendacious Headline"; 11 May 1943, "Title about terrorist attacks in Brussels constituting a provocation to murder."[20]

The wit tinged with sarcasm that accompanied many of Varenne's exchanges with those responsible for censorship suggests strongly that he enjoyed toying with them. In March 1941 he welcomed Paul Marion, spokesman for a violently anticommunist regime, to his new position as Secrétaire Général à l'Information by reminding him that they had something in common, namely, that "both of us were, some thirty years apart, editors for *L'Humanité*. My boss was a man named Jaurès. This is to say between us conversations can only be full of cordiality."[21] But if his methods seemed lighthearted at times, Varenne was deadly serious about freedom of the press.

From the beginning of the Vichy regime until he was forced to go into hiding after closing down *La Montagne,* Varenne pleaded with Pétain, Laval, Marion, and the others that the government recognize that it was in its own interest to adopt a liberal attitude toward the press, requesting a modicum of courtesy on the part of the censors: "It is much better to persuade than to rage."[22] In hopes of persuading Marshal Pétain that censorship was counterproductive, Varenne commented extensively on the government's attempt in February 1941 to impose on all the newspapers an article with the title, "No bananas for little French children," alleging that the English blockade in the Mediterranean was preventing the arrival in France of food from overseas. First, he stressed that the allegation was false, reminding the Marshal that despite the fact that Pétain had claimed he hated lies: "Well, Mister Marshal, people are still lying all around you." Moreover, argued Varenne, the whole procedure was simply "stupid," elaborating:

> When the reader sees the same information, above all with a polemical headline like that one, appear in all of the newspapers, he easily figures out that the article was imposed, and the effect is lost.
>
> But if the government wishes to be maladroit that is its business. What concerns me is that they dare to use outrageous procedures like this toward French newspapers who make a point of honor of not being subject to anyone: "Publish everything I send you, in the form that I require, or I will shut you down." Such is the system they are trying to impose upon us. This is a system of an occupying power, not of a regular government.[23]

Admitting that under foreign occupation some subjects would have to be forbidden and others treated with care, Varenne asked that the government trust editors to act responsibly. In a letter to Marion, he wrote:

> There can be recommended subjects. You indicate these to us in your "orientation notes." But "recommended" must not signify "imposed." Enthusiasm can not be decreed. We have enough good faith to praise spontaneously that which is praiseworthy. On the condition that we are allowed to criticize that which is blameworthy. At least that is the way that those journalists think—some of them remain—who refuse to submit themselves to the service of the authorities.[24]

No one in a position of authority at Vichy proved receptive to Varenne's reasoned eloquence. Although the forms of censorship changed from time to time—choices were occasionally given for selected articles rather than a single one, editors were allowed some liberty to express themselves *if their attitudes were correct,* and so forth—his inability to express his true opinion, and de Gaulle's decision in London that any paper continuing to appear under the German occupation would be banned at the liberation, led Varenne to decide shortly after the occupation of southern France that there was little purpose in continuing his unequal struggle with the censors. *La Montagne* continued to appear for several months after the arrival of the Germans, in part due to Léon Blum's request to Varenne that he keep the paper alive as a symbol of resistance. But the increasingly heavy hand of censorship officials who dictated titles, placement, length of articles, size of type—in short, virtually all of the content and tone of the newspapers—

meant that almost no distinctions could be detected in the French papers.[25] In any case, the public had long since turned to foreign radio or underground newspapers for their news. In these circumstances Varenne's last exchanges with Vichy authorities were increasingly sharp, bitter, and defiant. At the end of April 1943, he responded proudly to criticism of *La Montagne* from the Secrétaire Général à l'Information:

> "Your newspaper, you conclude, is the only one—among those which have not agreed to the accord—with which you must deal perpetually with problems of this sort." I am not too sure about that. I will continue nonetheless to defend for *La Montagne* the last vestiges of what was the liberty of the press, that liberty which was the adornment of our profession that I do not despair of seeing reborn one day, when our people will have finally recovered the right to think freely and to choose a government of its own choice.[26]

Having secured other employment for as many of his workers as possible and hidden away several tons of paper at Chamalières for use after the liberation, Varenne used the excuse of a disagreement with the censor to stop publication of *La Montagne,* the last issue published in occupied Clermont appearing 27 August 1943. A note was sent to all subscribers telling them that "difficulties of a professional order or of a technical nature have led us to suspend the publication of our newspaper,"[27] and offering to reimburse them for the balance of their subscription. The next edition of *La Montagne* was to appear 15 September 1944 with an editorial signed "Alexandre Varenne," and entitled "France Is Saved."

Just as Varenne's note to his subscribers gave little indication of the true reasons that had led to his decision to cease publication of *La Montagne,* so, because of the government's generally successful control over the content and presentation of news, only careful readers of *La Montagne* in 1941 and 1942 would have been able to detect hints of Varenne's opposition to the Vichy regime—for example, in articles celebrating Valmy or in descriptions of ceremonies presided over by Pétain or Laval that were relatively bland or less enthusiastic than articles in the other local newspapers. By 1943 virtually no room for maneuver or self-expression remained, except for those who chose to exceed the censor's requirements in praising the government. That (as Varenne had warned Pétain would be the case) this uniformity of the newspapers under Vichy thoroughly discredited the French press was confirmed by numerous reports from both French and German sources. As early as five weeks after the vote of full powers to Pétain in 1940, German observers with headquarters at Angers reported that the population had very little trust in French newspapers, "preferring to listen to British radio."[28] In November 1940 police at Clermont-Ferrand noted the same thing, adding that most people believed that the Germans censored everything on the radio and in the newspapers.[29] In May 1941, commenting specifically on public reaction to radio broadcasts of recent speeches by Pétain and Darlan and generally about popular response to information provided by the news media in France, the chef de la Sûreté at Clermont-Ferrand concluded: "To summarize, the public no longer attaches any significance to speeches. It would like a break from them, preferring action [to words]. It no longer believes in the press which it considers enslaved."[30] In other words, less than a year after the establishment of the Vichy regime, many French people believed very little that they were being told publicly by their own government.

Later reports indicate that this skepticism about the public statements of the government and information conveyed in the press persisted throughout the occupation. Listening to broadcasts of the BBC in public places was banned in November 1940, and Swiss newspapers were removed from circulation in France in 1942. Therefore, for more accurate news than they could obtain from French sources, each evening behind their closed shutters the Clermontois listened to the BBC or to Swiss radio, which was easier to receive in the area. René Payot's broadcasts from Geneva seem to have been particularly popular at Clermont. Police and administrative officials often complained about the French radio's lack of information and delays in reporting important developments, as well as its "lack of objectivity."[31] In addition to its inadequacy and untrustworthiness as a source of news, French radio was criticized occasionally for its insensitive choices of programming. According to the Ministry of the Interior, the prefect of the Bouches-du-Rhône had registered his disgust that "the very evening of the day that the fleet was sinking into the ocean at Toulon, the State radio stations were playing concerts of cheerful music."[32]

Alarmed by their reading of the drift of public opinion away from the Vichy regime and its leaders, Légion Propaganda Service officials argued late in 1942 that an infusion of 60 million francs to their coffers and transfer to them of exclusive control over propaganda would permit a reversal of the deplorable situation in which "it is Foreigners who are controlling opinion in France."[33] In addition to a remarkably frank admission that "the National Revolution 'which can only succeed if the people understand it and call for it' *is making hardly any progress,*" the Propaganda Service's appeal to Marshal Pétain that the Légion be designated solely responsible for propaganda in favor of the National Revolution contained this assessment of public opinion in France as of December 1942: "In France, not only is *public opinion, in large part, aroused against its government,* but the principal instruments of propaganda (press, radio) are completely discredited."[34]

The légionnaires' appeal to Pétain was based on twin fallacies, the questionable assumption that public opinion could be readily molded by an adjustment of propaganda techniques and an excessively optimistic notion that the Légion was capable of refurbishing Vichy's image despite the total occupation of France and the loss of its overseas empire. Nonetheless, the Légion's propaganda directors recognized something that has not always been made clear by historians and memorialists of wartime France. Accepted temporarily in a moment of extreme national crisis, the Vichy government had rapidly become unpopular in France.

Among the most persistent and the least justifiable myths concerning the Vichy regime has been the notion that for a long time—perhaps through two or three full years—Pétain's government enjoyed widespread popular support in France. A close examination of the evolution of public opinion at the grass-roots level will not support such an interpretation. The "reliable French informant" who told the British ambassador in Madrid in July 1940 that the Pétain government had left Clermont-Ferrand "precipitately in the space of two hours because of the threatening attitude of the local opinion, who are chiefly industrial workers"[35] almost certainly overstated the case. But it was true that the Vichy government *never* was able to rally the unanimity of opinion behind Pétain that it desired, and undeniable signs of hostility to the regime and even to the Marshal were apparent much sooner than has often been acknowledged.

Arguments from a variety of perspectives, presented with different levels of sophistication, and based on evidence of unequal value, have contributed to the propagation of the idea that Vichy enjoyed substantial popular favor for a long period. In the postwar era apologists for Vichy were naturally inclined to exaggerate the strength of the regime's following. Many accounts of the Vichy era have failed to distinguish adequately between attitudes toward Pétain himself and popular opinion regarding the government and its programs, and the reasons for the seeming longevity of faith in Pétain have not always been explored thoroughly. In recent years through diverse mediums, critics of the Gaullist idea of France as a "nation of resisters" who never accepted the defeat as final have stressed the extent of collaborationist sentiment in films such as *The Sorrow and the Pity* and *Lacombe Lucien* and in provocative books such as Bernard-Henri Lévy's *L'Idéologie française*. Although there is certainly merit in a reexamination of the Gaullist myth, as Stanley Hoffmann has noted,[36] there is a danger of the creation of a countermyth derived from a distorted image implying the existence of a "nation of collaborators." Having reached such a state, the pendulum of interpretation has swung far beyond a point that can be supported by convincing evidence.

From other vantage points, authors more favorably disposed to Gaullism, as well as essentially nonpartisan, dispassionate historians, have described the early years of Vichy in a manner that has supported the image of strong public support for Pétain's regime. Memoirs by resisters and accounts tracing the history of the resistance have underlined the isolation of the "real" resisters in 1940 and 1941, and have emphasized that active participation in the resistance even in 1944 represented only a small minority of the French population. In the most authoritative general history of the Vichy regime, Robert Paxton, while acknowledging the difficulty of measuring public support for authoritarian regimes, argued that the apathy, public lethargy, and acquiescence of most French people meant that they "were 'collaborators' in a functional sense." According to Paxton, public opinion "offered a broad basis of acquiescence within which active participation in the Vichy regime was made legitimate," and only in the spring of 1943 did opinion turn against the regime.[37]

Some of the arguments presented in earlier surveys of public opinion under the Vichy regime, particularly those stressing the limited extent of violent public resistance, are convincingly articulated if one accepts the authors' definition of terms such as *resistance* or *apathy*. But most treatments of public opinion of which I am aware fail to distinguish adequately between thought (opinion) and action, and—more crucially from a historian's viewpoint—serious reservations may be raised about the sources from which judgments concerning public opinion have been reached. Until very recently the most serious stumbling block to a reasonably accurate assessment of the evolution of public opinion during the occupation was the inability of researchers to obtain access to French archives that contain the most extensive and valuable documentation concerning this matter. If, as I believe to be the case, the discussion of public opinion under Vichy to be presented here is more satisfactory than some that have been offered previously, the primary reason resides in the superiority of the documentation that I have been fortunate enough to consult.

Biweekly and monthly reports by local police (in the case of Clermont-Ferrand for the whole city and for each of the distinct arrondissements) included a special section devoted to public opinion that formed the basis of monthly reports by the prefects to the government. At a national level the prefects' reports were combined into a "Synthèse" distributed periodically to administrative officials around the country by the Ministry of the Interior. The original sources for information provided in these reports included paid informants hired to observe particular groups or milieux (labor organizations, informal political circles, specific factories, or clubs, and so forth); under Vichy, police were encouraged to expand their networks of such spies in order to be able to head off unfortunate "surprises" for the government. Other information came from interceptions of postal, telephone, and telegraph communications, including random samplings and investigations of specific individuals, and, of course, from the personal contacts and observations of those officials involved in drafting the reports. One of the most striking, although perhaps predictable, patterns that emerges from an evaluation of information about public opinion is the manner in which reports were filtered and often watered down as they passed to each higher level of the bureaucracy. The problems of interpretation created for historians by this situation may be illustrated by the following examples.

In March 1942 Marshal Pétain, accompanied by Admiral Darlan, visited Clermont-Ferrand to preside over ceremonies inaugurating the Corporation Paysanne in the Puy-de-Dôme. Sounding very much like the government-controlled newspapers that had called on all Clermontois to decorate their houses and come out to cheer Pétain during his visit, the central police commissioner at Clermont reported to his superiors: "In all circles it [Pétain's trip] has been commented on favorably. No discordant note troubled this reception and despite the well-known coldness of the Auvergnats and the present difficulties, the Head of State was warmly applauded."[38] *Le Moniteur,* a newspaper owned by Laval, claimed that the enthusiasm for Pétain was "undescribable," demonstrating that Auvergnats "do not always deserve the reputation for coldness that they have."[39] Neither in the newspapers nor in the commissioner's report was there any indication of the reservations expressed by police at lower echelons who had described the day's events in more measured tones.

A representative of the Police des Sociétés Secrètes noted that violently anti-Pétain and anti-Darlan tracts had been distributed in Clermont the morning of the arrival of the two leaders of the Vichy regime. The police commissioner for the First Arrondissement acknowledged "the warmth of the applause that greeted the Marshal and numerous shouts from the crowd of 'Vive Pétain' and 'Vive la France' at the passage of the cortege." Indicating that he had verified his impressions in conversations with others who had had different vantage points for the parade and ceremonies, he added: "However, I did observe both at the arrival and the departure, for one thing that the acclamations were not unanimous, certain people remaining impassive, and for another that it was unable at any moment to detect a cheer for Admiral DARLAN."[40] The reader may recall (see Chapter 3) that it was for this particular visit of Pétain to Clermont-Ferrand that the members of the Légion Française de Combattants had been coached to cheer at appropriate moments. Obviously straining to put the best possible interpretation on the events, the commissioner for the largely working-class Third Arrondissement concluded that everyone had been happy with Pétain's presence even though his commentary on the visit suggested otherwise: "If *the crowd failed to express very much its joy* at receiving here the Head of State through vivas or cries of welcome, nonetheless a real satisfaction could be read on their faces. . . ."[41]

Of course, what one saw depended to some extent on what one was looking for. Thus, the prefect of the Puy-de-Dôme noted merely that people had listened "with interest"[42] to the notorious speech of 22 June 1942 in which Pierre Laval stated that he wished for a German victory to prevent the triumph of Bolshevism. Four days after that speech the central commissioner at Clermont-Ferrand went so far as to claim about Laval: "His return to Power is no longer criticized nor even discussed, but approved."[43] Were these officials trying to anticipate what their superiors might desire to hear? How else might one explain their ignoring the reports of their subordinates who had informed them pointedly that the speech had been poorly received: "President LAVAL has too clearly taken a stand as Head of the French Government in hoping for the German victory. . . ."[44] In this particular case the wave of protest from all over the country was apparently so strong that it could not be denied by the government, because the monthly "Synthèse" of prefects' reports acknowledged that the population had been upset by Laval's statement that he hoped for a German victory.[45] In most instances where one examines the monthly "Synthèse" in light of the original local description of events or reports on opinion, an attempt to put the most favorable possible interpretation on the situation is apparent as opinion is interpreted at each higher level.

A clear, and by no means unique, example of this process was provided in August 1942. On the basis of gendarmerie reports and inspection tours of the outlying communes of their district (including Laval's hometown of Chateldon), local officials and the subprefect at Thiers conveyed to the prefect of the Puy-de-Dôme a scathing indictment of Vichy policy as a reflection of the attitude of the local population (estimated to be 60 percent "if not Gaullist, at least favorable to the Anglo-Saxons," 10 percent "communiste" with only 30 percent loyal to the National Revolution or indifferent).[46] The prefect of the Puy-de-Dôme, who had visited personally the chief towns of the department, in turn conveyed to the regional prefect a summary of the outstanding complaints of the population, emphasizing specific economic grievances. But the regional prefect, in his report to Laval, chose to emphasize "the calm and good spirit of the populations visited, despite the difficulties of the present situation,"[47] claiming that the outstanding problems might be ameliorated by government action. Finally, the "Synthèse" for August 1942, while not entirely overlooking potential dangers (some hostility to the roundup of Jews in southern France was indicated), concluded that in spite of the "same symptoms of systematic distrust and indifference," the French people realized that present government policy was the only possible course, and the population was not *actively* or *violently* opposing the regime in significant numbers.[48]

From a certain perspective, the ministry's summary of public opinion was not *entirely* inaccurate—the Vichy regime was surely not confronted immediately by a massive revolutionary upheaval—but as a reading of the state of public opinion in southern France in the summer of 1942, the conclusions reached were highly misleading. In a similar vein, were it not for other police reports describing a "spontaneous" demonstration of 400 to 500 people on the place de Jaude at Clermont-Ferrand (people singing the "Marseillaise" and shouting, "Long live de Gaulle" and "Down with the Boches,"[49] and the government's firm orders forbidding "all public or private demonstrations, of any sort, susceptible to disturb public order," with specific reference to "incidents . . . that took place on the occasion of 14 July in several towns in the free zone,"[50] one might assume, as proclaimed by *Le Moniteur* on 15 July 1942, that "the National Holiday was celebrated with contemplation and dignity," as had been intended by the government.

These few examples should suffice to demonstrate why documentation from the grass-roots level is essential if one is to arrive at a satisfactory understanding of the evolution of public opinion under the Vichy regime. Obviously, conditions may have varied from town to town or region to region, and no claim is made that conclusions reached about public opinion at Clermont-Ferrand are directly transferrable to all of France. A definitive study of public opinion under Vichy must await the completion of similar investigations for all regions of France. Nonetheless, those studies completed so far, dealing with areas on both sides of the line of demarcation, indicate that while specific conditions may have varied from place to place, attitudes toward the occupation and the Vichy regime were not vastly different. Where conclusions have been well grounded in documentation from departmental or local archives, the main lines of the evolution of public opinion elsewhere seem consistent with my findings for Clermont-Ferrand.[51]

Although French archives contain the largest amount of valuable documentation for a consideration of public opinion, German, British, and U.S. sources are also available, and their differing perspectives and the observations they contain offer important clues for analyzing French attitudes under the Vichy regime. For Clermont-Ferrand and the Auvergne, German documents originating both from the economic control commission and, after November 1942, from the military occupation units have been preserved. As might be expected, the German reports reflect their origin and the particular concerns of the occupying forces with war production and the maintenance of order. Consequently, as will be developed more thoroughly in the next chapter, the German sources are far more helpful for such matters as the willingness of entrepreneurs to take up German orders and workers' attitudes toward working on war contracts, or the interest of the French in international developments (especially the course of the war) and their reactions to the occupation troops, than they are for questions concerning the National Revolution or French domestic issues in which the Germans were relatively less interested. Also, the particular status of each German observer affected the perception of events and attitudes. For example, whereas in the spring of 1944 the military officer might conclude that the situation, though tense, was well in hand and not seriously threatening to his combat troops, the economic officer's version, reflecting the extensive sabotage that was bringing industry to a standstill, would convey a sense of desperation, even panic, on the part of the occupation authorities.[52]

Contemporary British and U.S. evaluations of the evolution of public opinion in France, relying heavily on agents or intelligence informants within France and the comments of people who left France during the war, are by and large less reliable and certainly less systematic and complete than the French and German sources. In general, the British reports are more trustworthy than the American ones because of the far more direct and extensive operation of the British in France. The contacts of Admiral William Leahy, the American ambassador at Vichy, were restricted, and OSS intelligence surveys were highly uneven in quality, becoming more accurate as British and American policy became more closely coordinated in the last year of the occupation. Neither British nor American sources refer directly to Clermont-Ferrand or the Auvergne on a regular basis, although there are infrequent citations of interest. Consequently, the intelligence summaries they contain are most useful for their general comments about the evolution of opinion in all of southern France.[53]

For the historian the study of public opinion under any circumstances is a difficult proposition. How can one be confident about statements concerning the attitudes of a given individual or group, much less those of a town or country? The particular circumstances of the occupation in France exacerbate these difficulties. As Georgette Elgey has observed so perceptively, the dislocation caused by the defeat in 1940 and the subsequent occupation produced "an unprecedented trauma"[54] in France. The traditional framework for description was shaken by the disappearance or shattering of institutions and regular formalities of behavior:

> One could no longer speak of such or such a category, one could only evoke individual cases. History exploded into chaos. Only individual destinies counted . . . a population shocked in such a manner no longer reacts according to traditional criteria.[55]

From this perspective the most accurate history of France and French opinion under the occupation would be that of 40 million individuals; that of Clermont-Ferrand, the case studies of 100,000 Clermontois. One's ability to obtain food for the family, retain a job, visit relatives in other parts of France, and so on, often depended on personal contacts and carefully cultivated networks of acquaintances or inventive stratagems to bypass restrictive regulations.

Still, human beings over time seem to be amazingly resilient and adaptable to changed circumstances. The French pride themselves on their ability to *se débrouiller* ("make do") in much the same fashion as the British vaunt their persistence in "muddling through" the most difficult ordeals. With time the "exceptional" became "normal" or at least "regular." In the process, modified but recognizable groups emerged that can be distinguished in more or less traditional ways. While recognizing the difficulty of meaningfully lumping together all of the French, all workers, all Clermontois, and so on, in a satisfactory summary of attitudes toward the Vichy regime, its leaders, or particular policies, an examination of attitudes within certain identifiable segments of the population may help to refine the pattern of the evolution of opinion that will be offered as valid for Clermont-Ferrand and France in general.

Perhaps the simplest representation of the evolution of public opinion in France during the Vichy era would be to portray the swinging of a pendulum or the tipping of a scale from one extreme of massive support for Marshal Pétain and his government in the summer of 1940 to its opposite four years later: an overwhelming enthusiasm for Charles de Gaulle and the resistance in the summer of 1944. Complications arise immediately with such an image because some converts to the Gaullist camp in 1944 retained at the same time an admiration for Pétain, whom they believed to have been well intentioned but abused by the men around him. Conversely, a not inconsequential number of the French, notably among supporters of the Communist and Socialist parties, were never a part of the "unanimity" of opinion supporting Pétain in 1940 and had serious reservations concerning de Gaulle in 1944.

Probably more than any other factor, the "personalization" of power in the figure of Marshal Pétain has served to obscure the fact that he presided over a government that was highly unpopular from a surprisingly early date. Even in terms of the persistence of Pétain's personal popularity, too much has been made of the fact that he drew large crowds during visits to several cities in northern France in 1944. Yves Durand has explained that in Orleans and other towns many individuals came out on such occasions to sing the "Marseillaise" and exhibit their patriotism in defiance of the German occupation troops rather than to display any particular affection for Pétain, who was seen by many of those who did favor him as a symbol of protection versus the Germans *despite,* rather than because of, the actions of the Vichy regime.[56] Moreover, along with accounts of these apparently warm receptions, it should be remembered that projected visits by Pétain to Aurillac and Saint-Flour in the fall of 1943 were canceled because of the anticipation of hostile popular reaction.[57] This is not to deny that sympathy for Pétain, even widespread sympathy, continued to exist throughout the occupation. Indeed, in the 1980s it is still possible to find French people who bristle at what in their opinion was the "injustice" of Pétain's being put on trial and convicted of treason at the liberation. But one should distinguish clearly between sympathy for what were perceived to be the protective intentions of the legendary hero of Verdun, whose fame stemmed largely from his solicitous behavior toward the "poilus" of the Great War, and attitudes toward the Vichy regime. The longevity of active enthusiasm for Pétain as head of state should not be exaggerated.

For Clermont-Ferrand most sources concur that for the first few months following France's defeat in 1940, support for Pétain was exceptionally strong. If some individuals were troubled by Pétain's meeting with Hitler on 24 October 1940 at Montoire and the subsequent announcement of the government's policy of "collaboration,"[58] most of the French seemed happy at the news of the dismissal of Pierre Laval from the government a few weeks later, and Pétain's image was fortified by this action. Nonetheless, Pierre Etienne Flandin, whom Pétain named to succeed Laval as head of the government, was not a popular favorite because many people remembered the notorious telegram he had sent to Hitler in 1938 congratulating him on the peaceful settlement of the Munich crisis. As early as January 1941, the military commander for the Puy-de-Dôme expressed his fears that public opinion was not entirely behind the Marshal. No doubt most people favored Pétain, but the commander, Lieutenant Colonel Peragallo, believed that large numbers within the bourgeoisie were Gaullist, half of the students were Pétainist but the others were Gaullist or Communist, the workers were indifferent or hostile, and enthusiasm for Pétain even among veterans was not universal, especially among the soldiers of 1939–1940 who were not joining the Légion. The same officer reported that almost no workers showed up for the officially sponsored May Day ceremonies in 1941, and even among the "petits bourgeois" and others in attendance there was only meager applause for Pétain's speech. By June 1941, a few weeks before the end of the Vichy regime's first year, Peragallo, who had hoped that a few strong actions by the government would rally the hesitant behind Pétain, was seriously concerned about the inroads made by Gaullist propaganda in the region, noting: "Everywhere people are listening to the English radio." Although he believed the Gaullists to have had the

« J'ai été avec vous dans les jours glorieux.
Je reste avec vous dans les jours sombres.
Soyez à mes côtés. »

Ph. Pétain

Juin 1940.

Marshal Pétain, head of state

greatest success among students, the bourgeoisie and refugees from Alsace-Lorraine, he sensed a widespread feeling of discouragement.

> Malaise? Crisis? Something new and a little disturbing is beginning to appear in the population. . . .
>
> One is obliged to recognize in all milieux: elites and managers, middle classes, the masses also—a wavering in the attachment to the Marshal and numerous and occasionally violent criticisms of the Government.[59]

All contemporary witnesses responsible for following the evolution of public opinion and keeping the government informed of possible shifts in the public's mood did not detect this apparent drop in Pétain's popularity that so troubled Peragallo. Some observers (occasionally ignoring less optimistic opinions of their subordinates who had reported otherwise) continued to echo the words of the Puy-de-Dôme's gendarmerie commander who in April 1941 had written of Pétain: "The population of France has its idol and its prop, that which it was looking for without knowing it."[60] Paul Brun, the regional prefect at Clermont-Ferrand, claimed in March 1942, "The popularity of the Marshal remains intact and public opinion has absolute confidence in him."[61] Even as late as March 1944, a police official at Chamalières believed that Pétain still commanded a "unanimity of sympathies," although "people regret that he does not take a more significant personal action in the Government."[62] But the preponderance of evidence from French, German, and British sources reveals a pattern of steady decline in Pétain's prestige, less rapid but no less clear than that of the governments that served under him.

Interestingly, Peragallo, who felt that the problem was that Pétain had not acted in as forcefully authoritarian a manner as was desirable, and Varenne, who believed the opposite (too many traditional republican liberties were being destroyed), agreed that the beginning of this decline in enthusiasm for Pétain was evident by the first half of 1941. Sharing their conclusion, a diplomat who had served Vichy for a year before defecting to de Gaulle believed that Pétain's decision to beef up Vichy's police forces in April 1941 had seriously marred his standing, even among many bureaucrats at Vichy. Before he left France he had noted, "In the same salons where several months earlier people made a distinction between him and the government, people now do not refrain from mentioning his name and making allusions to his person." Pétain's authoritarianism had affronted "the sentiment of liberty to which the French are particularly attached." Although in view of his decision to join de Gaulle he may have overstated his case, the diplomat had this interesting observation to make about the pitfalls of estimating public attitudes toward Pétain and the Vichy regime on the basis of information culled from diplomatic sources at Vichy (was he thinking, possibly, of Admiral Leahy, the American ambassador?):

The Vichy government may well have received, moreover in abnormal circumstances, all the regular legal consecrations, it can indeed impose the display, in all stores, of the portraits of Marshal Pétain and of Admiral Darlan, it is nonetheless a government which has, in fact, no roots in the nation which submits to it but in its very large majority does not recognize it as its true expression. Living in the artificial and closed environment of Vichy, a certain number of foreign diplomats appear to have curious illusions about this matter.

The government of Vichy is, here and now, condemned, and wishing to persist in considering it, without a second thought, the normal government of France will not fail to have, sooner or later, very serious repercussions on the international political level.[63]

By the fall of 1941 agents for the Postal Control Commission charged with the random sampling of correspondence as one means of surveying public opinion reported that people in northern France had little confidence in Pétain and for the unoccupied zone, where there was somewhat more support for Pétain, the French had serious reservations about the Marshal's National Revolution, which they saw as a divisive policy, the revenge of certain groups, stating that "a Country that divides itself is a Country that will be unable to renew itself."[64] Although the strongest expressions of disapproval were directed toward his "entourage," according to the Postal Control officials, by September 1941 the Marshal was also the object of a growing criticism. On 1 September 1941 the chef de la Sûreté at Clermont-Ferrand commented that although Pétain's recent speeches had been fairly well received, they had not produced "the enthusiasm that the Government might have anticipated. . . . One still has the impression, as I have noted already in my earlier reports, that the public remains almost completely indifferent."[65]

We have already seen how reactions to Pétain and Darlan's visit to Clermont-Ferrand in March 1942 were not as uniformly enthusiastic as the government-controlled press and the reports of officials at the higher levels claimed. In Chapter 2 we revealed the findings of a survey ordered by the minister of the interior early in 1942 that determined that only thirteen of forty-seven leading notables in the Puy-de-Dôme could be termed certainly loyal to Pétain, with seven others believed to be loyal. Commenting on the visit of Pétain and Laval to Clermont-Ferrand in August 1942 for the second anniversary of the founding of the Légion Français de Combattants, Clermont's central police commissioner remarked that the two leaders had been cheered by those in attendance, but observed: "However, it appears that official demonstrations reach but a certain fraction of the population, in particular the rural and petit bourgeois part, but leave aside the truly popular masses."[66] In October 1942, stressing very serious opposition to the relève scheme, the police commissioner for the Second Arrondissement at Clermont-Ferrand reported that the word *République* was heard more and more often in his district, and noted: "People speak little or not at all about the Marshal."[67]

If a gradual drop in public support for Pétain is discernible over the first two years of the Vichy regime, the most dramatic and *definitive* loss of prestige for the Marshal accompanied the Anglo-American invasion of North Africa and the occupation of southern France in November 1942. After those events, very little respect remained for Pétain *as head of state,* although, for those who had convinced themselves that the Marshal was no longer responsible for what was happening in France, there remained a measure of sympathy for Pétain, the man, despite everything still the "Hero of Verdun." The outspokenly republican air force officer who left the Auvergne for England in January 1943 may have exaggerated a little when he said that "people now publicly spit on Pétain's portrait. He is generally recognized as a traitor except by about ten percent of the population."[68] But other witnesses who left France soon after the total occupation confirmed in less florid language that Pétain had lost "almost entirely the respect in which he was held before the occupation of the whole country."[69] Local authorities at Clermont-Ferrand, noting the telltale sign that during the past few days "Marshal Pétain's photograph had disappeared from numerous shops in the city of Clermont-Ferrand,"[70] reported strong criticism of Pétain because of the sinking of the fleet at Toulon and the temporary resistance offered by Vichy forces to the American landings in North Africa, an action that Pétain had castigated as a hostile aggression. According to police at Clermont, for the French public "there is still only one invader: the German."[71]

In contrast to some of the more sharply negative observations of others, in his first report following the German occupation of Clermont-Ferrand, the central police commissioner claimed that the recent events had revived images of June 1940 and the Marshal's popularity had risen as a result of this, but he added:

> Generally people figure that he has accomplished all of his duty as a soldier and an honorable man, but they consider that from now on his role is finished and that he has been definitively supplanted by President Laval. The latter appears more and more as the German's man, and the sincerity of his collaborationist sentiments is no longer doubted by anyone. His unpopularity is growing.[72]

Foreign witnesses corroborated the eclipse of Marshal Pétain in public esteem by the end of 1942. An officer with the German occupation forces at Clermont noticed that acts of attention to Pétain were merely "acts of politeness"[73] and observed no evidence of enthusiasm for the French government. Walter Stucki, the Swiss ambassador at Vichy, grousing about his obligation to return to Vichy for "the farce of the New Year reception of the Corps Diplomatique by the Marshal," told British diplomats in December 1942 that "there is literally no one behind Monsieur Laval and only a few simpletons still consider that Pétain is able to fool the Germans."[74] The day after Christmas 1942, the central police commissioner at Clermont-Ferrand concluded: "The public has the impression of no longer having an independent government. . . . The Marshal is respected but people believe him to be kept completely in the dark."[75]

If, because of the lingering of a sympathetic respect for Pétain, some ambiguity persists in the interpretation of popular attitudes toward him, no such problem exists for the analysis of public opinion with regard to the government's policies or for estimating the public standing of the other leaders of the Vichy regime. As has been suggested earlier in a discussion of the government's faltering attempts to implement the National Revolution at Clermont-Ferrand, there was *never* much enthusiasm in the Auvergne for the programs of the Vichy regime. Aside from Pétain, the principal political figures of the regime were the objects of derision, scorn, or hatred from a majority of the French public. When in 1941 Pierre Laval and Marcel Déat were the victims of assassination attempts, police at Clermont-Ferrand reported that these attacks "left people indifferent. They have very little concern for those whom they call 'political horse traders,' from now on the public wishes to place its faith only in men uncontaminated by this virus."[76] Ironically, the attempted assassinations of Laval and Déat, attributable to isolated individuals, may not have provided an accurate barometer of public opinion toward them because they were certainly *less* popular later when in the government.

A month-by-month analysis of police reports concerning public opinion at Clermont-Ferrand reveals an evolution in attitudes that corresponds closely to Yves Durand's schema proposed for a periodization of the Vichy regime.[77] Durand suggested that from the fall of 1940 through the summer of 1941, Vichy attempted to win support for its programs by persuasion, turning to more authoritarian means in the fall of 1941, by which time it was apparent that only a minority of the French were convinced of the virtues of the National Revolution. As early as November 1940, observers in the working-class districts at Clermont-Ferrand indicated that the workers, although hesitant to talk about politics for fear of repression, were still loyal to the left and distrustful of the government, especially of Laval.[78] In February 1941, one police official, signaling "an incontestable shift in favor of England," lamented: "Those who have not yet understood the new situation created by our defeat are very numerous."[79] By March the Socialist Party showed signs of regrouping, seeking to organize the workers and to "openly attack the Government."[80] More so than Pétain, by early 1941 other members of the government and the administration were the object of increasingly sharp criticism. In April the chef de la Sûreté at Clermont, underlining "a certain malaise," predicted (accurately) that most workers would boycott the government's official May Day celebration, adding: "In any case, those who will take part in the official ceremonies will do so only to demonstrate their sympathy and their thankfulness for Marshal Pétain alone."[81]

By the summer of 1941, the malaise detected in the spring had given way to direct and outspoken hostility from an increasing number of Clermontois. Under Darlan the government had edged toward fuller collaboration with the Germans, and this drift was clearly viewed with disfavor by a majority of the French. Reports based on postal interceptions indicated that Darlan and others were criticized especially for their failure to obtain the release of French prisoners of war.[82] In his monthly report on the state of public opinion at Clermont during July 1941, the chef de la Sûreté noted that "it would be false to say that it [the population] has good morale."[83] From that moment until the liberation in 1944, in scores of reports drawn up by various officials charged with the evaluation of public opinion, there was virtually no indication that from the viewpoint of the Vichy government, morale was anything but bad at Clermont-Ferrand.

On 1 August 1941, the central police commissioner for Clermont related the joy of the majority of the population that the Germans now were confronted by fierce adversaries in the Russians, claiming: "Even more than in internal politics people lack good judgment, almost forgetting our defeat and the occupation of two-thirds of the country." As to their attitudes toward interior developments, he remarked:

> The prewar mentality persists: permanent criticism of governmental actions, lack of confidence in the leaders, credence accorded too readily to the rumors of those who pretend to be well informed.

In summary: "Morale leaves much to be desired. Lack of confidence in the Government. Lack of courage and patience, exaggerated pessimism on the part of too many Frenchmen."[84] For the month of September 1941 the prefect of the Puy-de-Dôme, drawing his conclusions from visits around the department, believed conditions to be better in the countryside where food was more plentiful, but concluded: "The general impression appears to be very unfavorable to the Government."[85] For October the chef de la Sûreté observed: "On the whole, the population is discontented to a high degree. It no longer believes in much of anything."[86] According to most contemporary accounts, by the end of 1941 the general situation was dominated by malaise and anxiety. On New Year's Eve one witness wrote:

From one side and the other emerges the impression that the National Revolution has not attained its goal and has not produced the effects that were expected of it.

From all sides one senses the need for something to happen so that "things will change" because they can not stay the same without danger.[87]

In early 1942 prefects and other government officials seemed to take some solace in the fact that pressing concern with material problems, especially an obsession with obtaining adequate food for their families, had distracted most French people from potentially hostile political activism. Apathy and resignation were often emphasized in the prefects' reports to the government. But these sentiments were not mistaken for support of the regime. In February 1942, the police commissioner for the Second Arrondissement at Clermont-Ferrand stated: "Official speeches are no longer listened to on the radio or read in the press."[88] When Laval returned to the government in April 1942, even the minister of the interior's "Synthesis of the Reports of the Prefects of the Free Zone," despite attempting to interpret the situation in the most favorable manner possible, admitted that Laval was "incontestably" the person "who was received with the most reserve by the population."[89] Reporting for the same month, a police official in Clermont feared that "morale which has been rather resigned until now is now turning bad."[90]

By the spring of 1942 German Armistice Commission observers stationed at Royat were convinced that "the greatest part of the population"[91] was hostile to the French government. Laval's notorious public advocacy of a German victory to save Europe from Bolshevism only increased the government's unpopularity and the level of hatred for him. In October 1942 Clermont's central police commissioner stated in clear and simple language: "One thing is certain: *the government does not have the population behind it.*"[92] Although attitudes toward the government had deteriorated over time and would continue to do so during the remaining two years of the occupation, the commissioner's statement would probably have been valid for Clermont-Ferrand as much as a full year earlier.

The preceding cursory overview of the evolution of public opinion at Clermont-Ferrand demonstrates that the Vichy regime became generally unpopular much more rapidly than has often been suggested. Beyond this rough generalization, it was obvious that some segments of the population rejected Vichy sooner than others, and that some government policies were more widely unpopular than others. Among a variety of issues that might be explored in an attempt to refine our understanding of the evolution of public opinion, the following themes emerge most clearly from a study of the situation at Clermont-Ferrand.

Although the progressive erosion of sympathy for the government continued in a seemingly irresistible manner throughout the history of the Vichy regime, there were occasional fluctuations in public morale. Officials at Clermont-Ferrand noted, for example, that changes in weather often produced recognizable, if temporary, changes in spirit. In March 1942 the central police commissioner remarked: "The approach of good weather seems to have relaxed spirits and, in spite of the real difficulties the population must put up with, one can, without exhibiting an excessive optimism, note better spirits than during the preceding month."[93] Similarly, even after the alienation from the government of the majority of the population had been accentuated by the introduction of the forced labor draft (STO), visible hostility ebbed and flowed with the tide of the departures of French workers to Germany. Thus, in April 1943, even though describing the general tenor of opinion as "still deplorable," an observer claimed: "However, some appeasement has been produced . . . following less frequent and smaller departures for Germany."[94]

Even that most conspicuously unpopular of Vichy leaders, Pierre Laval, enjoyed fleeting moments of popular endorsement. (Perhaps more accurately, one may say that at times the public wished him well in specific endeavors.) A native of the region, Laval's reputation in the Auvergne seems to have been mixed. According to one witness, commenting in the fall of 1941, not all of his neighbors in the village of Chateldon cared for him.

> Some reproach him for his change of political attitude and the too rapid acquisition of a large fortune.
> Moreover, the liberation he obtained for eight prisoners of war from the commune aroused among the families in the area a strong jealousy and provoked unfavorable commentaries.[95]

As late as the summer of 1943, the central police commissioner at Clermont-Ferrand claimed that, "despite everything, President Laval possesses . . . above all in the Auvergne, a certain esteem."[96] The commissioner's use of the word *esteem* may imply an excessively favorable assessment with regard to Laval's public standing in wartime France, but there was some evidence of a certain grudging admiration for Laval's ability. In a colorful portrait of Laval as he knew him in the 1930s, the British journalist Alexander Werth described him as "un malin" and one who was "proud of being malin";[97] many Clermontois viewed Laval in this light. Consequently, when Laval returned to the government in the spring of 1942, despite the population's massive hostility to the idea of collaboration, hopes were raised that the government might finally obtain the liberation of the French prisoners of war, and many people believed Laval to be "crafty enough"[98] to bring this about. Afterward, when these hopes for a quick release of the prisoners were dashed, hatred of Laval would be all the more intense.

Just as the Vichy government experienced interludes of modest recovery in its flagging fortunes with regard to its public standing, so the Allies and the Gaullists faced occasional setbacks despite their generally rising stars. One police source claimed that 75 percent of the French "considered normal"[99] the British bombings of the Renault factory in Paris in early 1942, adding that local workers felt that it was unfortunate for the Parisian workers, but they should not have been working for Germany in the first place. But when the Michelin factory was the object of an air raid in the spring of 1944, resulting in civilian casualties as well as the destruction of property, several officials at Clermont recorded the "profound indignation" of local residents and claimed that many Clermontois had stopped listening to the BBC.[100] Another drop in enthusiasm for the Allies had been reported at the beginning of the winter of 1943–1944 because the much-hoped-for invasion of France had not taken place the preceding summer or fall. Still, these fluctuations in the public's temperament were not so much reversals of opinion as the expression of disappointment and frustration at the continuation of the war and occupation. As an official at Vichy noted, although the bombings had been upsetting to the French, they did not have "on the public the impact that the Press and Radio impute to them," and they were far from creating "a current favorable to the occupation authorities."[101]

We can safely say that nothing, except perhaps their departure from Clermont-Ferrand and from France, would have produced a favorable attitude toward the Germans. As the chef de la Sûreté at Clermont wrote in January 1942, "with regard to the Germans, the same position is always observed, which is to say people wish disaster for them."[102] The logical corollary to this staunchly anti-German attitude were widely held pro-British and pro-American sentiments. Although shortly after the Armistice most of the French were upset and dismayed by the British attack on part of the French fleet at Mers-el-Kebir, their immediate anti-British tack did not last very long. British intelligence evaluators monitoring French public opinion were satisfied by late fall 1940 that the French were overcoming rapidly their displeasure about the incident at Mers-el-Kebir and were heavily pro-British.[103] The Vichy government persisted for several years in a strongly anti-British propaganda campaign, but the periodic reports concerning public opinion at Clermont demonstrate that this propaganda fell on deaf ears. In March 1942, when the police commissioner for the Second Arrondissement at Clermont noted: "No one wishes to hear any more talk about Franco-German collaboration,"[104] he was only expressing what had been an almost universal sentiment at Clermont-Ferrand since the first weeks following France's defeat in 1940. Aside from an immediate indication of curiosity in business circles as to what impact the terms of the Armistice would have on commerce, there was almost no indication that, outside of an extremely marginal band of fanatical collaborators, anyone at Clermont-Ferrand was interested in dealings with the Germans beyond the strict requirements of the Armistice. Although not entirely fair to him, Laval was so widely detested in large measure because he was considered to be a creature of the Germans. Commenting on Laval's return to power in April 1942, the police commissioner for the First Arrondissement wrote: "I will not come back to French attitudes toward the Germans. Hostility is certain and unanimous in the working classes. But even in the wealthiest circles, numerous comments testify to this hostility."[105]

At the liberation and afterward much attention was focused on spectacular cases of collaboration for personal profit, but for a valid historical perspective, it should be remembered that such instances were the exception, not the rule. As will be demonstrated in the next chapter, which considers the occupation from a German viewpoint, the Germans themselves had no illusions about French attitudes toward them. If much of French industry worked for Germany, it did so out of the convictions that there was no reasonable alternative and no other way of preserving property intact or retaining a maximum number of French workers in France. According to one observer who left France in December 1941 to work at the Brookings Institute in Washington, it would be "wrong to suppose that all the big industrialists were prepared to collaborate purely for the sake of profit." With specific reference to Clermont-Ferrand, he added that "one of the strongest leaders of resistance in the country was Monsieur Michelin."[106]

The Sorrow and the Pity projects a striking image in the figure of a former Wehrmacht officer, who claimed: "People in Clermont liked us very much: our relations were good, and as far as they were concerned, there was no distinction between Frenchmen and Germans." The same officer added, in a more scabrous vein, that although the young women of Clermont would not look at German soldiers during the daytime, "Well at night, well it's a fact I must say—they were a great deal more friendly."[107] Aside from the self-serving and contradictory aspects of the officer's testimony, this severely distorted version of popular attitudes toward Germans at Clermont-Ferrand is in flagrant contradiction to all of the contemporary sources of both German and French origin.[108] No theme is more persistently documented, month after month, than the consistently hostile attitude of the overwhelming majority of Clermontois toward the Germans and toward the idea of Franco-German collaboration. Evidence of a modicum of civility in unavoidable daily contacts and those exceptional instances (which occurred at Clermont as elsewhere in France) in which a music-loving lycée professor attended a German concert, a young woman became romantically involved with a German soldier, or a cabaret owner was seen wining and dining German officers should not distract us from understanding that the dominant theme of popular opinion with regard to the Germans and collaboration was a current of resolute antagonism. In this respect, at least, the Clermontois more than lived up to their legendary reputation for "coldness."

There seems to have been a greater uniformity of opinion across the full range of society in terms of attitudes toward Germany and collaboration than was true for other issues. As suggested by the description offered earlier of the worker's passive resistance to Vichy's proposed Labor Charter, the working class as a whole formed the first and most unremitting body of opposition to the Vichy regime. We have seen that suspicions of police at Clermont-Ferrand in the fall of 1940 about the loyalty of workers toward the government were confirmed by their boycott of the first May Day ceremonies sponsored by the Vichy regime. Occasionally, their opposition took the form of playful jousting with local authorities, as exemplified by an exchange of letters between the Union Locale des Syndicats Ouvriers de la Ville de Clermont-Ferrand and Lieutenant Colonel Peragallo, the military commander of the Puy-de-Dôme. The union had requested the commander's permission to hold a meeting in June 1941, but Peragallo was not happy with the presentation of their request. As he explained to the prefect:

> This is not the first time that this Union or others have used old paper with "CGT" at the top of assorted letterheads. This time some progress was made, given that a square of white paper was glued over the forbidden insignia, and I acknowledge the good intentions of the secretary, but still the inscription is so easy to see by simple transparency, that I regret to say I will not be able to put my signature on such a paper.
>
> Let me suggest again the destruction of all stocks of paper with "CGT" at the top, or, in an understandable goal of conservation, removal with scissors of the upper left corner, and this not only for correspondence with the Authorities, *but above all for internal or external correspondence with other unions.*[109]

During the Riom trials, local authorities were surprised by their inability to detect "any hatred against those who were responsible for the misfortunes which have befallen our country"[110] and acknowledged: "In working-class circles people read, not without satisfaction, the declarations of Monsieur Léon Blum, still capable of flattering popular sentiments."[111]

With the imposition of the STO, the worker's opposition to the Vichy regime took on a much more active form, ranging from "symbolic strikes" of short duration, to failure to report for transfer to Germany, to acts of direct sabotage. When Laval tried to arrange for a French delegation to accompany German labor officials on an inspection tour of German factories, the local agent responsible for recruiting delegates was forced to report: "I was disappointed, and I must tell you that I found no volunteer for the trip to Germany."[112] Ultimately, the workers' representative had to be appointed and was forced to go against his will. It might be argued that the workers in general suffered proportionally more than other French people in the occupation era, and thus it may be only logical that they were the group most obviously unsympathetic to Vichy. In any case, their almost immediate and persistent opposition to the government stands out as one of the most striking themes of public opinion as recorded in the documents of the epoch.

If the workers were the earliest, most readily identifiable segment of the population to be classified as hostile to the Vichy regime, other groups did not lag far behind. Refugees from Alsace and Lorraine, attracted to Clermont-Ferrand by the transfer for the duration of the war of the University of Strasbourg to the city, as well as students in the lycées and at the University of Clermont-Ferrand, were among the first in the area to be described as Gaullist. Local authorities signaled the beginning of a Gaullist movement at Clermont as early as November 1940.[113] By early February 1941 the majority of university students, especially those at the Faculté de Strasbourg, were considered Gaullist, and a similar situation prevailed among younger students. In June 1941 police authorities informed the prefect of a "marked Gaullist tendency among the students at the Lycée of Clermont-Ferrand."[114] In May 1941 the chef de la Sûreté at Clermont, without labeling them Gaullist, noted: "The bourgeoisie, as well as the intellectuals, in its majority does not follow the government in matters of foreign policy." He felt that the "middle classes" were divided: "Many of them are seeking their path, without placing too much hope in one side or the other."[115]

Attitudes toward the Vichy regime were unquestionably influenced by factors other than politics or foreign policy. Many accounts stress the particular difficulties with food supply confronting residents of urban areas to explain why discontent with the Vichy government seems to have been first widely apparent in the cities. In May 1941 a police official at Clermont-Ferrand noted: "One can say without fear that the chief preoccupation of the public—and this will certainly have a vital importance—is the question of food supply."[116] Later that fall, the minister of the interior indicated that the same condition was evident in all parts of the country, reporting that the situation "is dominated essentially—certain Prefects go so far as to write in their reports 'uniquely'—by material preoccupations always concerning the same objects: food, heating, clothing, shoes."[117] The French countryside, even though its inhabitants were relatively better nourished, cannot be portrayed as a reservoir of enthusiastic support for the Vichy regime. As early as January 1942, the regional prefect at Clermont-Ferrand remarked: "In the rural milieu, an almost total indifference seems to reign with regard to the policies of the Government. One observes virtually no evolution from prewar mentalities."[118]

If it is thus abundantly clear that with slight differences in timing, virtually all identifiable groups within French society turned away from the Vichy regime at a relatively early date, it is not equally clear when or to what or to whom they turned as an alternative. Gaullism and communism, as the two most important catalysts of the organized resistance in France, were perhaps the most likely candidates. But most of the French, of course, were never actively involved in resistance movements, and very few indeed were committed to *active* resistance in 1941 or 1942 in spite of the emergence of substantial antipathy for the Vichy regime and its leaders. Shocked by the defeat of the French army in 1940, disoriented by the forced adjustment to a divided France and the oppressive difficulties of material conditions during the occupation era, most of the French would have devoted little time to systematic thought concerning the ideal kind of political regime or society they desired for France. Consequently, what the public disliked in the immediate circumstances (the Germans, the programs and leadership of the Vichy regime, and so on) was most apparent to contemporary commentators. Still, there were some rough indications of more positive sentiments, however lacking in precise or consistent form. Although the Third Republic had been thoroughly discredited by the defeat of 1940—and the massive popular vote against restoring it in 1945 would underscore this conclusion—resentment of Vichy's authoritarianism fostered the growth of an attachment to republican and democratic ideals in a general sense. In particular, the Riom Trials, staged to portray the Third Republic's leaders as villains responsible for France's collapse, served Léon Blum, Edouard Daladier, and others as an arena for a ringing defense of their actions and partially restored the republic's tarnished image.[119] Certainly, de Gaulle's public and unequivocal commitment to a republican ideal was crucial in rallying many politically conscious resisters to his cause.[120]

Estimates of the exact timing of shifts in public opinion with regard to the acceptance of Gaullism are at best precarious, not to say foolhardy. The principal cause of this difficulty is that Gaullism meant many things to many people, and observers during the 1940s often used the term casually, without definition. Although Clermont-Ferrand's central police commissioner in October 1942 spoke of "a thousand adherents in the department"[121] to describe those Gaullists who were actually members of resistance movements, he also cited "a Gaullist management class"[122] that was active in collusion with the workers to sabotage the relève. The following spring another police official at Vichy evaluated at 70 percent "the partisans of overbidding"[123] who followed Gaullist broadcasts on the BBC. Other sources vary widely from the letter writer who in September 1941 claimed that the Parisians were "99% anglophiles, 60% gaulliste,"[124] to the subprefect at Riom who estimated that 15 percent of the population was Gaullist in May 1941, and believed that those who, without being Gaullist, hoped for an English victory, represented the greatest single number of people.[125] The subprefect at Thiers believed the population in the spring of 1943 to be 60 percent "if not Gaullist, at least favorable to the Anglo-Saxons."[126]

In October 1942 the police commissioner for Clermont's Second Arrondissement expressed thoughtfully what seems to be a fundamental starting point for evaluating the importance of Gaullism during the Vichy epoch: "Gaullism seems to be for many persons a form of anti-German thought rather than a policy or a program."[127] Earlier, in March 1942, an observer, reporting to British authorities in Switzerland, claimed that de Gaulle and his movement

> have a very large prestige in France in large sectors of the population, above all among the workers and most of all among the youth of all social categories; in effect they symbolize refusal to accept the defeat, the will to fight, the defense of honor. If it were possible hundreds of thousands of young men would join de Gaulle. . . .[128]

According to the agreed views of representatives from all of the British military and diplomatic intelligence and information services, a marked change in French public opinion was discernible after the return to power of Laval in 1942. Until that time anti-German sentiments were evident, but passivity and apathy had been dominant. By the fall of 1942, although the *active* Gaullist following was still relatively small "a majority of Frenchmen" were said to support de Gaulle "as a symbol of resistance."[129] By then, Vichy police authorities considered de Gaulle's challenge to the regime's legitimacy to be serious. Obviously listening regularly to the BBC along with the vast majority of their compatriots, police at Clermont-Ferrand ordered the deployment of massive forces to deter the public from following de Gaulle's summons to participate in symbolic demonstrations on various patriotic occasions or national holidays. In this general, symbolic sense, it is appropriate to argue that by the time of the occupation of southern France in November 1942, Gaullism had already achieved substantial support in France, providing for most of the French an increasingly attractive alternative to the Vichy regime.

The shift in French public opinion away from Pétain and Vichy to enthusiasm for de Gaulle and the resistance that was well under way by 1942 did not mean that most French people had become active resisters. To be sure, for many of the French, more than any other single factor, the implementation of the STO in late 1942 and early 1943 produced the first and most important instance in which their dislike for the Vichy government was translated into outright opposition. By spring 1943 police officials at Clermont-Ferrand obviously were apprehensive about the growing potential for violent resistance. Some reports expressed satisfaction that no large, antigovernment demonstrations had taken place during the traditional workers' holiday, 1 May, but others warned: "With the passing of time the state of spirit of the population is becoming less good, the present calm seems uncertain, in order for public order to be maintained all incidents must be avoided."[130] Two months earlier, Clermont's central police commissioner, emphasizing the acute crisis created by the forced labor draft, had remarked:

> We are living through anxious times. People fear slanderous denunciations and vengeance. There is a complete moral disarray for which people blame the Government, which faces a marked hostility in all social classes. . . .
> The virtual totality of opinion is oriented more and more toward resistance by every means to what it considers "deportation." The social environment is marked by violence and threats. It would be imprudent not to recognize that a climate of civil war or insurrection is emerging from day to day.[131]

Nonetheless, four months later, the same official noted: "The French still remain in a wait-and-see phase submitting to their fate calmly with the hope that things will improve soon."[132]

If one defines "resistance" as active participation in a resistance organization, one can argue convincingly that the vast majority of the French remained throughout the occupation in this "wait-and-see phase." Difficulties posed by this limited definition of resistance will be considered later (see Chapter 8), but for now suffice it to say that because of the relatively limited extent of violent resistance before 1944, some historians of the Vichy era have been led to underestimate the rapid appearance and high level of hostility to Pétain and the Vichy regime. Therefore, in concluding this rapid survey of the evolution of public opinion in wartime France, it may be worth reiterating one of the most striking themes evident in contemporary British, German, and French reports concerning popular attitudes at Clermont-Ferrand. The majority of the population had lost much, if not all, of its sympathy for the Vichy regime long *before* what was by all accounts the regime's most unpopular act, the introduction of the forced labor draft. Therefore, to emphasize the *attentisme* ("wait-and-see attitude") of most French, their apparent indifference, apathy, and acquiescence under the Vichy regime, and to describe them as " 'collaborators' in a functional sense"[133] (particularly given the strongly emotional and ideological connotation of the term *collaborators*) fails to make sufficient distinction between thought and action and distorts the usual meaning of conventional language.

Might not apathy and indifference be better interpreted as *opposition* than *support* of a political regime, particularly one that was exerting itself on all fronts in an attempt to generate enthusiasm for its programs and leaders? If one were forced to choose a phrase to describe the sentiments of most French people under Vichy, *functional resisters* might be more apt than *functional collaborators*, but neither phrase would be really appropriate. Instead, whether or not they desired to stand aside from partisan strife, thousands of men and women were confronted, infrequently or almost daily depending on their residence and circumstances, with apparently simple choices, the consequences of which were exaggerated to the tragic or absurd by the peculiar conditions of the occupation. For example, when the local gendarme asked: "Have you seen Pierre X this week?" what was the baker, the postman, or the farmer's wife to say? How were they to know whether or not the question was the prelude to an invitation to share an apéritif or a summons for the STO from which Pierre was hiding? Was one really a "collaborator" or a "resister" in the France of 1943 because of the answer he or she might give to a gendarme's casual question? Perhaps we may understand something of the horror of the occupation for the French in perceiving that in this tragic era (potentially at least), there was no such thing as a casual question.

Police in the Auvergne complained frequently of a "veritable conspiracy of silence"[134] in which most Auvergnats were accomplices. It would be misleading to assert that their silence transformed them into active resisters, but this lack of cooperation with servants of the Vichy government bespoke popular opposition to, not support for, the regime. Certainly, the leaders of the regime understood the situation in those terms. The repeated laments from officials at all levels that the people had not understood the importance of rallying behind the government's programs, that they had been unwilling to make the right choices, and so forth, underscored the fact that most French people liked the Vichy regime less and less with each passing month. If many people had been thrown into disarray by the defeat in 1940 and were at first sharply critical of the Third Republic and desirous of a change, they were not ready for just *any* change. If they appeared temporarily apathetic and resigned, they had not stopped thinking, and what they were thinking was usually unfavorable to the Vichy government.

7

Clermont through German Eyes

Clermont-Ferrand was occupied twice by the Germans during World War II. The first occupation at the time of the fall of France in June 1940 lasted only one week, left few victims, and gave little indication of what was to come in 1942. When the German offensive was launched against France in May 1940, a German bomber had attacked the Etablissements Aubert et Duval at the Ancizes just outside of Clermont. Four persons were killed and fourteen others wounded in this raid, but the Auvergne was not the scene of major military operations. All told nineteen French and two German soldiers, buried in cemeteries of the Puy-de-Dôme, were killed in brief skirmishes in the vicinity of Clermont-Ferrand. Upon the arrival of the German troops 21 June 1940, one soldier, Louis Antoine Taillandier, was killed in the city itself at the corner of the rues La Sellette and Jacobins. During the week of 21–28 June, François Jean Longchambon from a small commune in the Puy-de-Dôme was shot at Montferrand and buried "secretly" by the Germans.[1] He was Clermont-Ferrand's only civilian casualty of the first occupation. Shortly after the departure of the German troops, the central police commissioner reported that aside from a few thefts and irregular requisitions by individual German soldiers, the temporary occupation had passed without incident. French police, after a symbolic surrender of their weapons, had had them returned and had accompanied German soldiers on patrols in order to help prevent any possible disorder.[2] A few days after the German withdrawal, the owner of a gas station on the rue de Montrognon thanked the prefect for interceding with a German officer who had seen to it that the merchant was paid for goods taken from his store by German soldiers.[3] Thus, the image of "correctness" that was to be one side of the German occupation strategy was present from the beginning.

Correct or not, the people of Clermont-Ferrand were happy to see the German troops leave the Auvergne after their brief visit in 1940. Those few German officers and enlisted men who remained as observers for the Armistice Commission took up quarters at the Hôtel Richelieu in Royat and were rarely seen by most Clermontois. Their presence did not seriously dampen the local residents' satisfaction at living in the "free zone" under French sovereignty. From the summer of 1940 until the return of German troops in November 1942, few incidents took place between the French and the German officials or soldiers at Clermont-Ferrand. During an Armistice Day commemoration in 1940 attended by Pétain, at the appearance of two German officers the crowd had sung the "Marseillaise" and shouted "Vive la France" several times, and the officers had been whistled at on the way to their hotel. Police reported that the Germans had not realized that the whistles were meant for them, and no confrontation had resulted.[4] From time to time the officers would be insulted or badgered by students, especially Alsatian students from the University of Strasbourg, which had been moved to Clermont at the outbreak of the war, and French police reported occasional problems with drunken soldiers discharging their weapons late at night or quarreling with a bartender who wanted to close his establishment.[5] Such occurrences were rare, however. The first highly publicized armed attacks by the French on German occupation troops at Bordeaux and Nantes in October 1941 generated a flurry of activity in police circles, producing local orders to tighten security measures for the guard of members of the Control Commission at Royat.[6] If the French authorities were apprehensive and anxious to prevent the recurrence of such attacks, German officials at Clermont-Ferrand, although reporting an increasingly hostile public opinion, do not seem to have been worried about their personal safety. Two months after the attacks at Bordeaux and Nantes, the control commissioners at Royat noted nonchalantly that for exercise they had hiked up the Puy-de-Dôme.[7] In our own times, an attempt by an overweight or out-of-shape tourist to hike up the 4806-foot (1465-meter) Puy-de-Dôme might be dangerous in itself; yet in December 1941 a German officer could plan such an outing through the Auvergnat countryside with little apparent threat to his well-being other than the stress of the exercise.

It would be an exaggeration to say that the presence of Germans in southern France before the total occupation in 1942 went unnoticed or was of no importance. As will be shown, the Control Commission personnel were actively laying the groundwork for an extensive French economic contribution to Germany's war effort. In addition to the staff headquartered at Royat, visiting delegations passed through Clermont with a variety of missions ranging from the purchase of horses to attempts to convince professors and students from the University of Strasbourg to return to Alsace.[8] In June 1942 the Office de placement de main d'oeuvre pour

APPEL A LA POPULATION

Les troupes d'occupation sont entrées dans Clermont, ville ouverte, et seront bientôt suivies de forces plus importantes.

Dans ces circonstances, nous demandons à tous de faire preuve de la discipline qu'exige le calme et d'observer la réserve que commande la dignité.

Nous avons pris l'engagement, en votre nom a tous, que l'ordre serait respecté ; nous sommes certains que vous faciliterez notre tâche par votre fermeté d'âme, votre tenue irréprochable et votre sentiment élevé du devoir.

Evitez tout attroupement et toute circulation inutile.

La vie publique continue, chacun doit demeurer a son poste et accomplir sa tâche.

Clermont-Fd. le 21 Juin 1940.

AUFRUF AN DIE BEVÖLKERUNG

Die Besatzungstruppen sind in Clermont, eine offene Stadt, eingezogen : Es werden grössere Truppenteile folgen.

Unter diesen Umständen bitten wir alle die Disziplin zu zeigen, die die Ruhe erfordert und die Zurückhaltung, die die Würde verlangt.

Wir haben uns im Namen Aller verpflichtet, dass die Ordnung aufrecht erhalten bleiben wird : Wir sind überzeugt, dass Ihr uns die Erfüllung unserer Pflicht erleichtern werdet, durch Euere Seelenstärke, Euere tadellose Haltung und Euer hohes Pflichtgefühl.

Vermeidet jede Zusammenrottung und jeden unnützen Verkehr.

Das öffentliche Leben geht weiter : Jeder muss auf seinem Posten bleiben und seine Pflicht erfüllen.

Clermont-Fd. den 21 Juni 1940.

L. DE PERETTI DELLA ROCCA,   Paul POCHET,

Gabriel PIGUET,   Antoine VILLEDIEU,

D GRASSET,   D VIMAL DE FLÉCHAC

Jean VÈZE.

Affiches MONT LOUIS - Clermont - Paris

German troops enter Clermont-Ferrand, June 1940; local dignitaries appeal for calm l'Allemagne (Office de Placement Allemand—OPA) established an office at Clermont-Ferrand to begin recruiting workers for German factories.[9] Despite these German intrusions into several domains, the French administration appeared confident that its authority in the south was unimpaired. Although apparently yielding somewhat "in a spirit of collaboration"[10] in the summer of 1942 when German control commissioners were permitted to see police duty rosters, the French were generally sticklers about the maintenance of their sovereignty.

In September 1941 the regional prefect at Clermont had ordered his subordinates to give no information about the police to German officials.[11] In December of the same year the minister of the interior alerted his prefects to a visit from a Doctor Scherberger, curator from the University of Strasbourg, who was on his way to Clermont with the intention of closing down the operations of the University of Strasbourg in its temporary home. The minister instructed the prefect not to cooperate with this official.

> You will act in such a manner that, while avoiding any incident, you will provide no assistance to Doctor Scherberger's mission, the goal of which may harm our sovereign rights over Alsace and Lorraine.[12]

Similarly, local officials were ordered to give no information whatsoever to the German Red Cross delegates about refugees from Alsace or Lorraine.[13] Beyond passive resistance to German requests, Vichy officials occasionally took modest steps of a more active sort. Alsatians who knew German well were employed as spies to keep watch over the Armistice Commission delegates at Royat.[14] A Frenchwoman, under suspicion because she was having an affair with a German officer assigned to the Control Commission at Royat, was assigned to residence at Chamalières so that she could no longer travel around the region with him.[15] As late as March 1942, the French army's Bureau des Menées Anti-Nationales proposed to arrest and intern a family that was openly pro-German. (The family avoided this fate by signing contracts to go to work in Germany in June 1942.)[16]

Thus, before November 1942, the Vichy government at least seemed to be master of its own house in the unoccupied zone. This situation was to change rapidly following the Allied landings in North Africa and the subsequent occupation of southern France by German troops. When elements of the 66th Reserve Korps arrived at Clermont-Ferrand on 24 November and three days later disarmed and dissolved the local units of the French Armistice Army, there could be little doubt that a new master had arrived. If officials at Vichy still had some illusions about the new state of affairs, their attitude was not shared by the Clermontois nor by most other French people. The German troops who had anticipated resistance to the disarma-

ment action—"This will be no picnic," they had been warned—were pleas-
antly surprised at the lack of opposition from the French and reported that
the old "Franc-Tireur spirit" seemed to be dead.[17] The German officers
noted that the French government, weakened by the loss of its North
African territories and the scuttling of the once proud and powerful navy
at Toulon, had little standing with the population.[18]

Be that as it may, the Vichy regime continued to exist until the bitter end
of the German occupation. Consequently, arrangements had to be worked
out between German and French officials to meet the new conditions of a
now totally occupied France. In their attempts to sort out a suitable relationship, Vichy's fervent desire to salvage what was possible of its sovereignty was evident. No less clear was the French government's failure to
obtain much in this regard. At least until the last desperate months of the
occupation, Germany had its way with France in virtually every substantial
matter. If the facade of French sovereignty was maintained, in practice the
reality of German power and control prevailed. In order to assess the German occupation of France from a German perspective, to view the occupation of Clermont through German eyes, one might best begin by asking
what German intentions were with regard to France. The files of the German Armistice Control Commission that was stationed at Royat provide
interesting insights into this question.

On Christmas Eve 1941, an inspector for the commission reported that
a new joke about Franco-German collaboration was popular in the area:
"The German says to the Frenchman, 'Give me your watch, and I'll tell
you what time it is.' " In other words, he went on to explain, "the Germans
are taking from the French all the most important things and giving them
in return only what is strictly necessary."[19] The joke and the German inspector's understanding of its meaning offer a perfect introduction to German policy and intentions with regard to occupied France during World
War II. Eberhard Jäckel has argued convincingly that Hitler never seriously considered the possibility of France becoming a full partner either
in the prosecution of the war or in the elaboration of a New European
Order.[20] What Hitler desired from the Vichy government was that it keep
the French people quiet and put the French economy to work to support
the German war effort. Therefore, an evaluation of the occupation of
France from a German perspective, among other things, requires a consideration of the two major themes of German policy, production and
pacification.

On a national scale, although everything did not turn out as the Germans
had hoped, they must have been pleased with the general results of this
"limited" collaboration. By the fall of 1943 some 40 to 50 percent of all
French industrial and agricultural production was going to Germany. By

that time France had become "the most important supplier of raw materials, foodstuffs, and manufactured goods to the German economy," and among the foreign labor force there were more male French workers in Germany than any other ethnic group.[21] Moreover, this unquestionable economic success had been obtained at a relatively small cost to Germany in terms of manpower and effort. Particularly in the interior, France was garrisoned by fairly small numbers of reserve troops, including several foreign and Volksdeutsche units of inferior battle quality.[22] The command centered at Clermont-Ferrand, the Hauptverbindungstab (HVS) 588, whose jurisdiction spanned ten departments in the Massif Central, normally had only 6000 men at its disposal.[23] Consequently, German military units were concentrated in strategically important localities, so that depending on their residence, some Auvergnats might never, or rarely, have seen a German soldier, while those in garrison towns saw them every day of the occupation. Even within a town, such as Clermont-Ferrand, one's exposure to German soldiers or police might vary substantially with regard to the location of housing or workplace.

Lacking sufficient forces to do everything themselves, in numerous matters, large and small, the Germans managed to have French officials carry out their work for them. In spite of the widespread hostility of the majority of the French people to them and the growth of an important resistance movement, the Germans were not driven out of France by the French. Although maquis bands and urban guerillas were extremely active in some parts of France in the months surrounding the Allied landings in Normandy, only on rare occasions of short duration did the German High Command consider them a serious threat to the maneuvering and withdrawal of the main body of German forces. In short, from a military perspective, the pacification of France had been generally successful, and the retreat of German troops from France was but one notable episode in the larger saga of German defeat at the hands of overwhelming Allied numerical and material superiority.[24]

A description of selected aspects of the German occupation experience at Clermont-Ferrand paints a striking picture of the extent to which the Germans were able to put France to work for the German war economy. At the same time, it should permit a more subtle appreciation than has been offered previously of the problems faced and the methods employed by the Germans in their attempt to pacify individual French communities.

The first and one of the most persistent problems the Germans encountered was the issue of French sovereignty. In some instances the Germans seemed to have ignored French prerogatives and run roughshod over what was left of Vichy's sovereignty. More typically, the occupiers sought to maintain a surface deference to the principle of French sovereignty, seeking thereby to induce the French to cooperate with them more willingly than might otherwise have been the case. The German military commanders asked for information about literally everything that went on in the region and obviously desired to have a finger in every pie in order to regulate matters in the best interest of the German troops. They were often satisfied, however, with discovering a problem, bringing it to the attention of the local French administration, and, although insisting on immediate attention to the matter, leaving it to the French to carry through the project.

Before examining several specific examples that may illustrate the general nature and the evolution of Franco-German relations at Clermont-Ferrand during the occupation, we should note that the German officials referred to in most of this discussion where negotiations are involved are those officers attached to the HVS 588 (housed at the Grand Hôtel on the place de Jaude) or the Armistice Control Commission (located in the Hôtel Richelieu at Royat). Although not always, their attitudes and certainly their behavior often differed sharply, even dramatically, from those of two other German organizations present and active at Clermont, the German police—the SD (avenue de Royat at Chamalières)—and the labor service agents of the OPA—or the Arbeits-Einsatzstabes Clermont-Ferrand (with headquarters on the place Delille). As will be shown, these last two organizations had far less consideration for the niceties of polite cooperation with the French. The bitter legacy of brutality and inhumanity burned into French memory by the German occupation was largely, although not entirely, a result of their activities. As was true of the French they encountered there, all Germans who came to Clermont-Ferrand were not alike. This fact afforded some opportunity for maneuvering on the part of the French, who could hope to find a more sympathetic ear among the regular military or the economic control officials, but such possibilities were limited. For example, these German officials might freely express their sympathy or even agreement with French officials about the Gestapo's arrest of an innocent man, but they would hasten to acknowledge their helplessness to intervene.[25]

Bearing in mind that comments concerning negotiated arrangements between the French and Germans do not apply as well to the German police and labor agents who acted in a much less restrained manner, let us turn to an investigation of the general pattern of relations between local French administrators and those German military and economic officials with whom they had most frequent contact.

Immediately upon their arrival, and again in the summer preceding their departure, the German troops that occupied Clermont-Ferrand displayed directly their power as conquerors through extensive use of requisitioning. Forty-two hotels, including all of the important ones, 198 private apartments and buildings, three cinemas, sixty-six parcels of farmland, twenty-one garages, seven schoolhouses, a prison, the municipal theater, several hospitals, one brasserie, two cafés, and one brothel were among those facilities taken over for the use of the occupying troops at Clermont-Ferrand, and similar requisitions occurred in adjoining Chamalières and Royat as well as in all communes of some importance in the region.[26] The local population was unhappy when the Germans took over the food stocks of the disbanded Armistice Army, and farmers were particularly upset by requisitioning of livestock, sometimes choosing to slaughter their animals early (and illegally), rather than risk losing them to the Germans.[27] A standard procedure was established to pay farmers for requisitioned livestock. Although possibly considered fair by the Germans because the rates were those set by the French government's agricultural services, the farmers realized those prices were below their real value—that is, what they might have obtained on the black market.[28]

Irregular requisitions occurred from time to time throughout the occupation. In March 1944, the Légion's Commissaire à l'Action civique noted with regret that the 40 dozen eggs collected for a picnic planned for children of local POWs could not be delivered because German troops had seized all of them, suggesting that in some circumstances no item was too small to escape German attention.[29] Normally, though, the requisitions involved pressing needs of the occupation forces. Thus, the most widespread use of requisitions was for housing and other facilities at the time of the original installation of the German units and the seizure of bicycles, motorcycles, and automobiles that were used to expedite the retreat in August 1944.[30]

Occasionally, French officials requested that the Germans accept substitutes for individual requisitions they had demanded, but apparently with little success. Colonel Gilbert Sardier, head of the local Légion Française de Combattants, whose apartment and garage were taken over for the use of a German officer, was told curtly that "the rank of a Colonel commanding a German Regiment takes precedence over Colonel Sardier's position as Head of the Légion."[31] In at least one case, the French apparently tried to head off some requisitions through the transfer of titles of vehicles and other material from the army to various public agencies, such as the forestry service, the police, the SCNF, and the PTT, or to private individuals. Several hundred vehicles were spread around the Puy-de-Dôme in this manner and thereby may have escaped wholesale requisition, even though the Germans still managed to carry off at least 146 vehicles of various types from French army stocks.[32] In general, Vichy authorities did not challenge the right of German commanders to impose requisitions. Instead, they hoped to ensure that all requisitions were accounted for and credited against French Armistice obligations to pay the costs of the occupation. Clinging to what in retrospect seems a chimerical pretense of sovereignty, but also in a desperate attempt to reduce the financial burden of the German occupation, just two days after the entry of German troops into southern France, Pierre Laval informed his prefects that they were not really witnessing an occupation. "The presence of axis troops in the free zone does not have the character of an occupation: French sovereignty will be maintained."[33] Two weeks later ministerial instructions forbade the use in southern France of the terms *occupation authorities* or *occupation zone*. Instead, *operational authorities* or *operational zone* were to be employed.[34]

Laval claimed that he had received confirmation that the "German military authorities should in no manner become involved in the civil administration of the free zone."[35] Accepting German reasoning that their troops were forced to move into southern France to guard against an Allied invasion from North Africa, the French insisted that troops utilized for this purpose were *operational* not *occupation troops,* and therefore France was not responsible to pay for their upkeep. French negotiators at Armistice Commission meetings in Wiesbaden and Paris reiterated this theme persistently, and local authorities kept careful account of requisitions and expenditures for German ends, hoping—vainly as it turned out—to be able to subtract these amounts from France's occupation payments.[36] Little impressed by legal technicalities or verbal gymnastics, the Clermontois were well aware of what the arrival of German troops in their city meant. The central police commissioner reported: "The population has few illusions about the term 'operational troops'; people are convinced that this is an occupation, pure and simple."[37] Local police and gendarmerie officials, forgetting or ignoring the interdiction against the use of such terms, in their reports repeatedly referred to the "occupation troops," indicating that they too had few illusions.[38]

Because the regime seems to have been so eager to grasp at even the slenderest straws in order to magnify its importance or to dignify some of its actions, sarcasm seems unavoidable in describing Vichy's pitiful pretensions to sovereign status after 1942. In September 1943, following conversations with the German police officials, René Bousquet, Vichy's Secrétaire Général à la Police, wrote to the regional prefects urging them to employ the greatest possible energy in the repression of strikes. They were ordered to inform the local German police immediately at the first sign of disorder, but, exulted Bousquet, the German authorities "have agreed to leave to the French police the complete initiative as to which measures to take," even if the strikes were in factories working for Germany.[39] In ex-

actly the same manner in February 1943, Laval had outlined to the prefects of the "free zone" the circumstances of the creation of the STO. Explaining that earlier, more limited schemes had failed to produce enough
workers so that the Germans had demanded the institution of a comprehensive, obligatory system, Laval stressed what he called the "essential
point: it is a matter of the government preserving the initiative in an operation that otherwise the German authorities would have been led to carry
out themselves."[40] So, as was true in so many matters, the French agreed
to do the Germans' work for them. Preservation of the facade of sovereignty remained all-important to Vichy's leaders even as its substance was
dissolving at every turn.

We have good evidence that in one area, at least, Vichy, to some positive effect, remained adamant in its assertion of French sovereignty. In the
face of repeated direct and surreptitious inquiries about refugees from
Alsace and Lorraine, from the beginning through the end of the occupation, the French government consistently ordered its servants at all levels
to refuse any cooperation with the Germans, insisting that anything to do
with Alsace or Lorraine was a purely French domestic concern.[41] Given
the significant size of the refugee community at Clermont-Ferrand, many
people there certainly were protected by the government's attitude in this
matter. But this one example of firmness on Vichy's part truly seems to be
the exception that proves the rule. In no other case was the government's
position so steadfast, nor was it so absolute in its refusal to compromise in
any other realm. At times, particularly during the first months following
the occupation of the south, local officials tried to prevent or restrain German intervention in French domestic affairs or to assert French prerogatives in areas such as police activities, civil defense, or management of the
economy. Some of these actions were the result of individual initiative, but
others had the backing of higher authorities at Vichy.[42]

One of the most common tactics employed by local officials was to delay providing information or services to the Germans on the grounds that
permission was needed from superiors at Vichy. Such withholding or re-
stricting of information became more difficult as time passed, but in some
quarters it continued nonetheless. The minister of the interior noted in
May 1944 that certain regional prefects had not shown their plans for the
preservation of order (in the event of an invasion of France) to German
authorities. He noted that the label "secret" on those plans did not mean
they were to be hidden from the Germans "from whom the Secrétaire
Général Maintien de l'Ordre has nothing to hide."[43] A different approach
was to be *too* helpful. In August 1944, the German Labor Service office at
Clermont asked the intendant de police to order the guard he had provided
at German request for the recruitment bureau to act and dress in a more

discreet manner. It seems that the gendarme in question, helmeted with rifle at the ready, had stood directly in front of the door, discouraging use of the sidewalk that passed before the office. The Germans complained that this was "counterpropaganda to the goal that we wish to attain" and insisted that the guard stand away from the door, adding that "the cap and revolver will be fully sufficient" for his duties.[44]

Temporizing tactics or deliberate misconstruction of German requests might result in momentary "victories" for French officials, but the contest was an uneven one, and the Germans would ultimately have their way in almost all matters of consequence. During the first months of the occupation of the south, French officials would attempt to refuse cooperation with the Germans, standing by the letter of the Armistice agreement or the text of a ministerial directive to argue that the matter was an exclusively French one, not subject to German purview. For example, when a German officer complained about the inadequacy of camouflage for civil defense at Mont-luçon and demanded that the French improve the situation, the regional prefect at Clermont-Ferrand was ordered to refuse requests by local German authorities to inspect or control civil-defense installations because in the south this responsibility was supposed to be exclusively French. Then, having proclaimed that they were in charge, the French hastened to carry out precisely those improvements deemed necessary by the Germans.[45] After the summer of 1943, the formal reticence of some French authorities to cooperate and such insistence on proper protocol became less frequent.

For one thing, the longer the Germans stayed, the more information they had and the more direct control they exercised over all aspects of life in the area. Consequently, the possibilities for maneuvering were reduced. Furthermore, changes in the Vichy government, steadily evolving in the direction of greater collaboration as the occupation dragged on, meant that some of those officials in place at the arrival of German troops were replaced by more cooperative men. At Clermont-Ferrand a few, including a police commissioner, the head of the gendarmerie, and several labor draft officials, had been arrested by the German police.[46] Probably more than anything else, the increasing importance of the German police explains why, if never entirely disappearing, obvious instances of obstructionism on the part of French officialdom were rare in the last year of the occupation—at least until the Allied invasion when such actions would reappear in vastly altered circumstances.

An important meeting was held in Paris on 18 April 1943, when SS General Karl Albrecht Oberg, chief of the German police in France, explained to regional prefects and police intendants for the southern zone the significance of an agreement he had reached that month with René

Bousquet. The French police in the south were to remain autonomous and to have independent responsibility for maintaining order and internal security. Against enemies including Jews, Bolsheviks, Anglo-Saxons, terrorists, Communists, and saboteurs, the French police were to act "in full independence, on their own initiative and under their own responsibility."[47] Bousquet saw in this agreement the confirmation of a brave order he had issued to his prefects the day after the Germans entered southern France: "Reminding you that all police operations can only and must only be undertaken by French police acting in full independence and in conformity to French instructions and French laws."[48] Bousquet, in vaunting the independence of the French police, was deceiving himself or perhaps had missed the most important point of Oberg's comments: "To the German Police falls the task of ensuring in all circumstances the security of the German Army."[49] Of course, the German police would be entirely free to determine when and by whom or by what the troops were threatened. What this meant at Clermont-Ferrand was that the local SD officers intervened in everything and did exactly as they pleased with total disregard for French law or the sensibilities of the French police services.

A French policeman recorded a telling incident that occurred in Clermont the night of 2–3 January 1943, about six weeks after the Germans had occupied the town. Pierre Breuer, a member of the local Gestapo (as the Clermontois called the SD), set up a temporary interrogation center in the Café du Globe on the boulevard Desaix, located just in front of Clermont's prefecture. Breuer had arrested a man alleged to be Jewish and started beating him. The French policeman who was present told Breuer that his actions were illegal, and that an arrest "could only be made in the free zone with a regular arrest warrant and by French policemen." Breuer replied with several nasty comments about the French police and declared that "the free zone was in reality occupied." The French officer reported that he had telephoned Captain Muller, a Wehrmacht officer assigned to the German military headquarters, who said that he would inform his superiors immediately; but the Frenchman acknowledged that he had been unable to prevent Breuer from taking away his "suspect," adding: "Not wishing to create an incident, I withdrew."[50]

By the summer of 1943 only the most obtuse or self-deluded French official could have failed to understand that the "free zone" was indeed occupied. In April 1943, the German police requested from the regional prefecture at Clermont-Ferrand monthly reports on the activities of the French police, and the local intendant de police was ordered by Vichy to comply.[51] In July the Interior Ministry instructed the prefects to reorganize their files concerning all foreigners in their regions and to make these files available to the local German police.[52] Despite the supposed independence and autonomy of the French police, they might become at any moment mere auxiliaries of the German police on the demand of the latter. The Germans dipped into the pool of French police manpower whenever they chose to do so. For example, in March 1943, when Colonel de la Rocque, prominent as the head of the right-wing Croix de Feu in the 1930s, and five of his friends were arrested at his home near Clermont, the Germans took along several French policemen although French police officials knew nothing about their mission.[53] It was clear from the first that in stating that the French and German police would "cooperate closely"[54] in the southern zone, General Oberg had had in mind a one-way collaboration.

The Germans decided how many French police units could be employed; they distributed permits for weapons to the French police, even requiring that they be written in German; and when, a few days after D-Day, they took direct executive power over all French forces who could take no action nor move units without German approval, this was only an official recognition of what had existed in practice for a long time.[55] French police had never been allowed to stop, search, or arrest Germans even if they were obviously involved in illegal activity. In early 1944 SS Hauptsturmführer Geissler, regional chief of the SD, had forbidden French gendarmes to make written reports to their superiors about operations they had participated in under the German police.[56] The German police virtually never gave information to the French about arrests they had made, even when the request for it came from the highest levels of French officialdom.[57] Légion, police, and gendarmerie officials all proclaimed their helplessness to obtain any information from the local German police. Summarizing scores of similar examples, Gilbert Sardier, head of the Légion at Clermont, replied to a request from a Monsieur Edmond Lavauzelle for information about a relative who had been turned over to the German police. "From that moment, all attempts to intervene become useless, because the occupying authorities maintain the most absolute silence, even when our requests are only for information. . . ."[58] Eventually, many French officials, convinced of the futility of such attempts, simply quit trying.[59] And finally, at the end of April 1944, they were ordered by Darnand, chief of Vichy's Milice, appointed Secrétaire Général au Maintien de l'Ordre, not to bother the Germans with requests for information or the release of prisoners except in extremely important cases; then the French were to expect an answer "only if the Germans felt like they could give one."[60] A further illustration of the distinctions between various German administrations is that the German military had little more success with the SD than did the French. Their reports indicate that they also knew only what the German police chose to tell them.[61]

Thus, particularly during the last year of the occupation as the SD with their French Gestapo and Milice underlings stepped up their activity, one looks in vain for the slightest vestiges of French sovereignty. Why, then, did most French civil servants continue to participate in the sham of preserving a French administration that in Clermont-Ferrand, as in towns all over France, did Germany's bidding in so many ways? After the war defenders of the Vichy regime claimed that Pétain, Laval, and the others had saved France from "Polandization"—that had the French authorities not continued to cooperate, France would have suffered a far harsher occupation. Robert Paxton has argued convincingly that this was not the case,[62] but many conscientious French civil servants remained at their posts *in the belief* that they might be able to protect their fellow citizens. As a leading newspaper editor at Clermont-Ferrand recalled, all so-called collaborators "were not bastards."[63] Some of them played crucially important roles in association with various resistance movements. Others may simply have stayed on because they saw no obvious alternative for employment. It seems probable that the reasons suggested by the German officials with whom they worked may have been valid for most of these French fonctionnaires.

In the first days of the occupation, the Germans were favorably impressed by the cooperative attitude of Paul Brun and Henri Guerrin, respectively the regional prefect and the préfet délégué for the Puy-de-Dôme, the two highest administrative representatives at Clermont of the Vichy regime. Their comportment throughout the occupation was signaled as correct and helpful.[64] When the Germans left Clermont-Ferrand in August 1944, the Rüstung (Armistice control) officials reported having exchanged cordial farewells with their French counterparts, and the prefect at Clermont-Ferrand was cited with those at Toulouse and Lyon as being among the most consistently cooperative in southern France. The German reports added that this record of loyal cooperation might even entail the death of these men in liberated France, a possibility of which they had been aware.[65] With the exception of the mayor of Chatel-Guyon, no French officials in the Auvergne are hinted to have had, as a reason for this cooperative action, a pro-German attitude. On the contrary, the Germans seem to have been convinced from an early date that the French officials definitely shared the negative attitudes of the general population toward the occupation forces. Occasionally, they seemed to "let the mask slip,"[66] as when they neglected to exchange salutes with German officers or appeared halfhearted in compliance with German requests for services or information. Rather than sympathy for Germany, their officially correct behavior reflected a fear of disorder, apprehensiveness about what might happen in the future, a genuine desire to protect French life and property, and, one might surmise, a sense of professional responsibility.[67] Although there is ample evidence that the regional prefect at Clermont-Ferrand was often very zealous in his pursuit of French resisters, whom he considered to be subversive outlaws, the German records from the occupation support Brun's postwar assertion that in his supervision of the French police he was "above all concerned to avoid trouble with the German police."[68] In fairness to hundreds of local administrative officials who served the Vichy regime, one should neither deny nor forget their intention to ease French suffering during the occupation. Still, few episodes in modern French history better illustrate the maxim that "the road to hell is paved with good intentions" than the attempts of French officials to coexist as peacefully as possible with the conquering Germans. A brief survey of those tasks undertaken by the French at German behest reveals to what a striking degree French cooperation contributed to the success of the occupation from a German perspective.

In flagrant contradiction to Pierre Laval's claim, in November 1942, that the "operational" troops would not meddle in French domestic affairs in the southern zone,[69] a listing of all the interests of the German command of the HVS 588 at Clermont-Ferrand would include virtually everything that went on in the region. Naturally, they were especially concerned with those things that most directly affected the security of the occupation troops and production for Germany. Thus, they energetically sought out the hidden arms depots of the Armistice Army, requested precise information about the location of explosives for mining or construction, ordered the collection and storage of hunting weapons, and closely regulated permits to bear arms. Services required of the French that were directly related to safety of the troops included posting guards for the German barracks and offices, plowing under fields immediately after harvest, strewing large boulders and digging trenches across unused landing fields that might welcome enemy planes, and making improvements in civil defense facilities. To help ensure the continuity of production and delivery of products from those industrial plants filling German orders, the French were required to provide guards for the companies, as well as for the power stations, high-tension lines, and transformers that provided the current to run the machinery and the railroad lines and locomotives that transported the goods to Germany.[70] Other German intrusions into French administrative affairs were less obviously connected with their military and economic goals. German commanders became involved in such diverse matters as film censorship, permits to take photographs, and the regulation of prostitution. The Germans complained that the incidence of venereal disease was much higher among prostitutes in the Auvergne than elsewhere in France and ordered better medical treatment and tighter controls.[71] German military officials called for campaigns to clean out sewers, reduce the rat population in public buildings, and combat *doryphores* (Colorado beetles). When Colonel von Massow urged local schoolchildren to help their families seek out and destroy these insects that attacked potato plants, proclaiming that with energetic actions the pest could be wiped out, he must not have known that *doryphore* was the slang expression the French had adopted for *German!*[72]

Without further belaboring the point, it should be clear that the German command at Clermont-Ferrand had a finger in every pie. Furthermore, the Germans were highly successful in using the French to carry out these multifarious tasks for them. German troops sometimes replaced or reinforced French guards, as in September 1943, when twenty heavily armed German soldiers began watching the transformer at Enval, supplier of electrical current to Michelin and other important factories that had been damaged several times in succession by the resistance.[73] Generally French manpower was employed to do whatever the Germans desired, enabling the German army to occupy France with a striking economy of force. The result of this situation for the French administration, particularly for the police, was that its resources were stretched to, and often beyond, the breaking point. Noting that serious problems of morale were exacerbated in the summer of 1943 by the exceptionally hot weather, "this dog-day's heat" (Clermont-Ferrand's temperature averaged about 2° centigrade above normal that summer, the hottest of the occupation), the chef de la sécurité publique at Clermont complained that the 350 policemen in the town were overwhelmed by the duties required of them. They were on duty an average of fourteen hours a day. Sports activity and professional training had been suspended because there was no longer time for it, and as many as one-quarter of the men were calling in sick.[74] The main reason for this state of affairs was the burden imposed on the French police for guard duty required by the Germans.

More than half of Clermont's police force was engaged at least part-time in static guard duty on German orders, while about one-third was used full-time, and the same was true for the gendarmerie in the Puy-de-Dôme with 258 gendarmes out of 630 so employed.[75] Local police complained that "more than elsewhere, the occupation authorities are demanding."[76] Admitting that the majority of its policemen were physically and mentally "worn out," in November 1943, after conversations with high German officials, Vichy attempted to remedy this increasingly serious problem by ordering the French police to refuse all future requests from local German authorities for such guard duty. Indeed, they were to cut back on those obligations already accepted by the substitution of patrols for static guard duty, the use of curfews, and so forth.[77] Five days after this order was issued by Bousquet, the intendant de police at Clermont-

Ferrand informed local German authorities that having already assigned twelve gendarmes to guard the Ateliers Industriels de l'Air and twenty-six others to Michelin, he could not provide men for the rubber and steel works of Bergougnan and the Ancizes.[78]

Although this attempt to draw the line for services increasingly beyond their capacity to perform may have brought a partial respite of a few weeks for the French police, the evidence suggests that any gains were temporary. The forces used for guard duty remained substantial, and in any case those police taken off of guard duty were shifted to other tasks (such as collection of information, escort of convoys, or actions versus the resistance) that served German purposes. In a meeting at Vichy in February 1944, the regional heads of the Services de Sécurité Publique complained that guard duty and other obligations imposed by the Germans on the urban police were preventing them from carrying out their normal task of ensuring public order. Their usual jobs of surveillance of the roads and patrols at night were being neglected with the result that "The cities are no longer watched over and terrorist attacks can take place in scandalously easy conditions."[79] Faced with increased resistance sabotage from month to month, far from reducing their demands, the Germans increased them. In addition to the police, hundreds of low-ranking civil servants, civilian draftees, STO recruits, and finally private companies were called on to produce guards for various Wehrmacht installations, industrial plants, explosives depots, rail and communication lines, and even farm machinery.[80] Aside from recognition of the persistent growth of resistance in the region, these measures contributed toward bringing more and more people into a network of support for the German occupation. In this sense, there is some truth in Pascal Ory's assertion: "At the limit, every Frenchman who remained on soil occupied by the German Army or dependent on its good will 'collaborated' with it to some degree."[81] Yet, this is at best a partial truth. Equally if not more important is the fact that such "collaboration" was given under constraint and against the will of most of those involved. German actions at the time and their reports on public opinion make it abundantly clear that they had no doubt about the hostility of the local population toward them.[82]

This situation confronted the occupation authorities with a substantial dilemma. How could they place arms in the hands of men they did not trust? But how could they ensure security without arming the guards? After months of hesitation, the German solution was to arm the guards, but only with light arms (usually shotguns or hunting rifles) and to allow each of them only ten rounds of ammunition.[83] In these circumstances, as several French officials pointed out, the guards could serve only as sentinels who might give an early alarm, but could not hold off a major attack by well-armed resisters; nor in fairness could they be held responsible for failure to stop such resistance actions.[84] Even Vichy's Milice, out of step with the general population in that many of its members were eager to fight the resisters, were armed meaningfully only in April or May of 1944 after having proved their worth in actions against the maquis.[85] Units of the GMR and the gendarmerie were considered so untrustworthy that they were disarmed in August 1944 and forced to volunteer for units serving directly under German command should they wish to continue the fight.[86] In the late spring and summer of 1944 many gendarmerie units in the Auvergne had become, in effect, arms suppliers to the resistance as one gendarmerie post after another was attacked, almost always surrendering without a fight, and occasionally deserting en masse to the maquis. One of the most spectacular of these episodes occurred at the Château de l'Oradou just outside of Clermont. A fictionalized account featuring 150 heavily armed resisters was conveyed to French and German officials, but the operation was in fact carried out by half that many men who found the gendarmes in no mood to contest the theft of their weapons.[87] As indicated by the notations in their reports about these events, describing surrenders before so-called superior forces,[88] the Germans were not fooled, but they could do nothing about it except try to seize the weapons before the resistance took them all. For what little satisfaction that might have brought them, the Germans could at least claim to have seen vindicated their suspicions about the reliability of French guards and the potential hazards of arming them.

These events took place in the summer of 1944 when everything was beginning to fall apart for the Germans. We should reiterate that, at least on the surface in dealings between French public officials and the occupation authorities, throughout most of the occupation relations were relatively good between the French and Germans. As we have seen, occasionally French officials dragged their feet or were less than forthright in complying with German wishes. Incontestable evidence of enmity toward the occupant was often present, as, for example, when no volunteers could be found among the teachers knowing German in local lycées to help with cultural functions or lessons for the German troops so that the French administration was forced to appoint someone.[89] According to the Directeur de Services de la Police de Sûreté, the majority of the French police felt "a genuine repugnance in turning over to the Germans a Frenchman, even if he were guilty."[90] An ironic comment might betray the inner feelings of a prominent official, as was the case when Clermont's central police commissioner, Monsieur Kastner, was asked to suggest a location for a German police post. Kastner suggested a building across from the mayor's office that previously had housed a funeral home, stating: "The location of this building seems entirely suitable to the goals envisaged."[91] Attempts were usually made to hide such attitudes from German view, though, and on both sides expressions of basic satisfaction with the local occupation arrangements were frequent.

French documents confirm German reports that however divergent attitudes might have been, relations were for the most part smooth. The regional prefect, the commander of the gendarmerie, and the central police commissioner at Clermont-Ferrand all testified that relations were "correct," and that serious incidents involving the occupation troops rarely occurred during the first several months of the occupation.[92] Even after the first German officer was killed in Clermont, the Germans were considered to be attempting to keep up "the most courteous relations" with the population; in May 1943, they had shortened the curfew and other restrictions originally imposed in reprisal for resistance attacks.[93] Later in the occupation the Clermontois expressed surprise at the relative moderation of German response to other resistance actions in or near the city, although there were some cases of severe reprisals.[94] Even though relations deteriorated noticeably in the second half of the occupation, two days before the Germans left Clermont-Ferrand the German authorities could still say that the behavior of Clermont's residents had been "up to this point very proper."[95]

While regular contacts between French and German officials remained formally proper throughout the occupation, from the summer of 1943 until the liberation, a steadily mounting tension recognizably strained Franco-German relations at Clermont-Ferrand. The major cause for this development was clear. In his monthly report for July 1943, the police commissioner for Chamalières/Royat wrote:

> It is worthy of note that the great number of arrests made by the German Police, very often for no reason, as well as the contemptible police methods they use, have led to the reprobation of all social classes. Everywhere, the good impression left by the propriety of the German military is obliterated by the German police methods that may begin to produce hatred.[96]

Hatred, yes—and also *fear,* the commissioner might have added. At Clermont-Ferrand the Gestapo (German members of the SD and their intimate associates, the so-called French Gestapo) fully lived up to its reputation for brutality and inhumanity. SS Hauptsturmführer Hugo Geissler, with headquarters at Vichy, was the head of the Gestapo for the Auvergne region, and suspects arrested at Clermont were frequently taken directly to Vichy for interrogation. But for the Clermontois the Gestapo's headquarters, 2 bis and 4, avenue de Royat, hold a special place in their memories of those dark years of the occupation. There, Blumenkamp, the local Gestapo chief, and his German colleagues, Roth, Eckhardt, Grunewald, Kugler, Kaltseiss, and Ursula Brandt (called "the Panther" because of the fur coat she wore), along with their French associates, Georges Mathieu, the brothers Vernière, Sautarel, Bresson, and others, beat, tortured, raped, or disfigured countless suspects, many of whom were innocent or had only the slightest connection with the resistance movements.[97]

Serge Fischer, a librarian for the University of Strasbourg and one of the leaders of the Front National, recalled that one thing that possibly helped him to survive repeated beatings without breaking was that Blumenkamp and the others kept asking him questions about a different organization of which he had little knowledge.[98] Three decades after the occupation, another leader of the Front National at Clermont commented that after all these years one of his strongest memories was of the absurdity of the arrest and deportation of all of those innocent French people while he did not even have to change his residence until the last months of the occupation.[99] The local Gestapo were not very good police in the sense of discovering evidence, following leads, and breaking up major resistance organizations. But they were savagely brutal and successful at instilling great fear in the population as well as in the ranks of their fellow Germans.[100] Theoretically, Blumenkamp was supposed to cooperate with the local military command, but he reported only to Geissler or higher police authorities in Paris, and according to one officer assigned to the military staff at the Grand Hôtel: "No one said anything, because everyone was afraid of them."[101] Similarly, Frenchmen who had been incarcerated in Clermont's military prison noticed that the moment a Gestapo agent appeared, the guards on duty lost any smile or trace of sympathy they might have shown before.[102]

Ample evidence in the wartime experience of Clermont-Ferrand substantiates what has become in our own day a literary and cinematic cliché of the evil German Gestapo officer versus the honorable, duty-bound military officer. Still, we should not stretch this image too far to explain all of the violence, hatred, and terror of the German occupation. Just as decisions of the Vichy government tended to involve many of the French in ever-widening circles of collaboration with the Germans, so the Gestapo, by calling on the German army from time to time for assistance in its operations, spread the exercise of terror far beyond the dark cells of their building on the avenue de Royat. Almost certainly, as the German military claimed at the time, relations with the French would have been much smoother had it not been for ill-advised and counterproductive actions by the German police.[103] We should remember that when the Gestapo ordered a major action against the University of Strasbourg at Clermont in November 1943, Kaltseiss, of the Gestapo, murdered Professor Paul Collomp in cold blood; but a regular soldier of grandfatherly appearance shot down Henri Blanchet, the 15-year-old boy incautiously running across the avenue Vercingetorix, near the cordon of German troops that had surrounded the university buildings. And regular soldiers as well as police hit, kicked, and jammed rifle butts into the backs of those students who dared to put down their hands before ordered to do so.[104]

The occupation's overall toll in terror for Clermont-Ferrand and the department of the Puy-de-Dôme was substantial. At least 238 persons were murdered or executed by the Germans; approximately 2000 others were arrested and deported to concentration camps; and a conservative estimate shows 250 instances of torture, 30 rapes, and 250 cases of pillage reported for Clermont-Ferrand alone.[105] These facts help us to understand why, in the last year of the occupation and afterward, many Clermontois refused to distinguish between the "bad" Nazis and the "good" Germans, as some major resistance newspapers attempted to do.[106] For the people of Clermont-Ferrand, the brutal face of German domination had too often broken through the mask of "correctness." Given these circumstances we should not be surprised to observe that beneath the formal propriety of contacts between official French and German representatives, day-to-day contacts between German soldiers and French citizens were not particularly friendly.

It is perhaps obvious, but may merit noting, that most Germans did not come to Clermont-Ferrand during the war to make friends among the French, and most did not. German soldiers felt that they were surrounded by a sea of hostility from the Clermontois, and this perception was accurate. The desire to see Germany defeated by the Allies, signaled by Armistice Commission personnel before the occupation of the south, was strengthened immeasurably with the arrival of German occupation troops at Clermont. Angry glares, jibes about Allied successes in Russia, North Africa, or Italy from personnel at the hotels where they lived or from people on public tramways, and boos or derisive laughter at the showing of newsreels featuring Hitler were the everyday fare of the German soldier at Clermont-Ferrand. The monthly reports of German units stationed in the area begin monotonously, month after month, with the phrase "still more hostile" so many times that the reader wonders how it was possible after January or February 1944 to be *still more hostile*.[107] To be sure, at Clermont-Ferrand as elsewhere in France a few exceptions were to be found. The major at Chatel-Guyon, a long-time proponent of Franco-German friendship, and the subprefect at Riom, from communes a few miles north of Clermont, frequently entertained the officers of the 159th Reserve Division.[108] Certain women struck up relationships with individual German soldiers. But these cases were exceptional and usually drew strong reprimands from neighbors. In April 1943, an officer of the 66th Reserve Korps, the main unit responsible for the occupation of Clermont-Ferrand, recorded a typical example. A young woman, employed by the Wehrmacht in an artillery casern, had been abused by French gendarmes at a roadblock. They told her that "any girl employed by the Germans or seen in their company would be called to account at the end of the war."[109] French and German sources concur emphatically that those rare ultracollaborationist organizations like the Milice had very little support in the region. Long before the Germans had arrived in force, outspoken collaborators and their property had been the object of bombing attacks by the resistance and were simply thought of as traitors by the population.[110]

Clermont-Ferrand was believed to be particularly hostile to the Germans because of the presence of students and faculty from the University of Strasbourg. Before the occupation of the Vichy zone, one German official described Clermont with its visitors from Alsace as "the main center of the anti-German movement in unoccupied France."[111] The Germans made several unsuccessful attempts to convince faculty and students to return to Alsace, and different German missions had tried to recover the university's library and other valuables that had been transferred to southern France in 1939.[112] Some German officials believed that if the faculty and students did not return of their own free will, they would provide possible sources of opposition to the New Order in Strasbourg, and so they were better left at Clermont. Others, notably the Gestapo chief at Clermont-Ferrand, felt that the best solution was a frontal attack "to finish with the University of Strasbourg once and for all."[113] Eventually, in 1943 when, beyond the generalized resentment of the population, the Wehrmacht was faced with armed attacks on its soldiers at Clermont, the University of Strasbourg often bore the main weight of the reprisals. Following earlier, less dramatic blows, on 25 November 1943, the grounds of the universities of Clermont-Ferrand and Strasbourg were surrounded and hundreds of students and faculty arrested. Despite some mistreatment, most were released within several days, but eighty-six were deported to German concentration camps.[114] From that fall of 1943 until the liberation, relations between the civilian population and the German soldiers were increasingly tense.

In March 1943 the first German soldier had been killed in a commune near Clermont-Ferrand. Following that incident, isolated attacks on soldiers or German police occurred in the area almost every month, although not always resulting in fatalities.[115] The most serious attack came on 8 March 1944, when grenades were thrown at a unit of Wehrmacht troops who were marching down the rue Montlosier to a motion picture theater in Clermont. One soldier was killed and thirty-two others wounded, five seriously.[116] Gone were the days of December 1941, when the members of the German Control Commission at Royat, for carefree exercise, could hike up the Puy-de-Dôme and back.

Still, what strikes the historian most about the occupation at Clermont-Ferrand in retrospect is that despite the pervasive hostility of the population and the steady growth of the resistance movements, until the summer of 1944 the Germans do not seem to have felt threatened in the sense of a challenge that might have prevented them from accomplishing their basic missions at Clermont, those of pacification and securing production for the German war economy. It cannot have been pleasant to feel hated by all of those French people, but as a matter of fact, before June 1944 few of the troops found themselves in life-threatening situations. They stayed to themselves in barracks or on training exercises, in part because their officers did not want them to have contact with French civilians. Attempts, particularly directed at the Volksdeutsche recruits, to encourage desertion were reported, and invitations to listen to the BBC in private homes at Riom were noted.[117] The local officers were dismayed by the difficulty in receiving German broadcasts at Clermont-Ferrand and feared that the troops were receiving most of their news of the front from enemy sources.[118] When contacts with the French were unavoidable, the German soldiers were enjoined to present a correct but firm appearance. According to directives issued concerning contacts with the local population, the Germans believed that the French might misinterpret kindness for weakness, but would respond to strength when handled properly.[119]

In fact, most of the soldiers' dealings with the population seem to have been proper. There were occasional incidents, but generally the French officials at Clermont-Ferrand acknowledged that the German soldiers, in sharp contrast to the German police, had behaved well. When asked after the war by the prosecutors at Nuremburg for evidence of war crimes in the area, the local authorities, although citing some of those Gestapo activities described earlier and certain measures against the Jews, for the most part admitted that the region had been spared the flagrant atrocities evident in the neighboring Limousin (Oradour-sur-Glane) and the Dordogne (Tulle).[120] Whether or not in response to the soldiers' comportment, or because, as some of the Germans suspected, they were simply trying to survive until liberated by the Allies,[121] the majority of Clermont's population did nothing in an active manner to harm the German army. The active resistance movements, among the strongest in all of France, still represented only a small part of the population. The same German officers who so consistently stressed the increasingly hostile attitudes of the Clermontois noted repeatedly that for a substantial majority such opinions had not resulted in active opposition of a violent sort.[122]

Because they had relatively few troops, the Germans decided to occupy only the larger towns, especially those along main lines of communication. Their goal was to keep open the major traffic arteries and communication networks so that goods for the German war economy and, if necessary, troops could move freely. The occupation troops watched as the maquis, continually nurtured by new recruits from among the STO deserters and aided by the widespread complicity of French officials and the local population, gradually took over the countryside in late 1943 and early 1944. As long as these bands stayed on the back roads around the smaller communes of the region, the army command seemed content to leave the problem of dealing with them to the French Milice and GMR and the German police forces.[123]

The occupation troops were stirred to offensive action against the resisters only when, at the time of the Allied landings in Normandy, large assemblies of maquis took place. What happened then demonstrates why the Wehrmacht had seemed to exhibit relatively little concern for their security. The most spectacular encounters between the forces of the German army and the resistance in the vicinity of Clermont-Ferrand occurred in June 1944 in the battles of Mont Mouchet and the Monts de la Margeride at the extreme south of the region of the Auvergne. An impressive museum and national monument to the resistance now stands at Mont Mouchet. We in no way detract from the courage and the sacrifice of the 200 French who died there by pointing out that in contrast to the glowing accounts in the literature distributed at this monument, the episode was a temporary disaster for the French resistance. In contradiction to the claims of those responsible for the poorly timed gathering of resistance forces, and despite some heavy fighting, the Germans sustained only light casualties and easily cleared the maquis from their strong points. With heavier armament, and usually much better training, regular units of the German army were always more than a match for resistance forces in open combat.[124]

Generally speaking, in military terms, until their withdrawal from the area the Germans never lost control over the situation. This did not mean that all German units were secure. Small troop detachments and isolated Rüstung control outposts, especially in the Cantal and parts of the Puy-de-Dôme and the Correze between Clermont and Limoges, fought their way out of the area only with great difficulty and incurred substantial casualties.[125] Insofar as one goal of guerilla warfare is to create a sense of insecurity in the enemy forces, the resistance was highly successful during the summer of 1944. Unable to contact superior officers because of sabotage of rails, telephone, and telegraph, unable to travel the roads without the help of heavily armed convoys sent to break them out, several units surrendered to resistance groups.[126] Shortly after D-Day, war production for the German economy was brought to a standstill by the combined effects of troop movements and resistance actions. At the time of their withdrawal in August 1944, the occupation forces at Clermont-Ferrand were no longer able to carry out their mission of keeping open the flow of French products to Germany. Preparations had been made to blow up the most important factories in the region, but, as one measure of the degree of resistance effectiveness, the local commander at Clermont-Ferrand agreed not to destroy the Michelin factory "in the interest of the retreating troops."[127] The French resistance eventually did pose a threat to the Germans, and in the end succeeded in stopping industrial production for Germany, but as they left Clermont-Ferrand the morning of 27 August 1944, the retreating Germans could pride themselves on having reaped enormous benefits from their stay in the Auvergne. We have seen how they succeeded in bringing French administrators to carry out many of their tasks for them. Perhaps the most striking illustration of the general success of the occupation from a German perspective was found in their exploitation of the local economy.

Even before the total occupation, important industries in the region had been geared to satisfy German needs. As a part of the Armistice arrangements, German Control Commissions to monitor industrial production had been established in the Vichy zone. One of these posts had its headquarters at Royat, a thermal center adjoining Clermont-Ferrand. The members of the Control Commission reported that before the entry of German troops in November 1942, the behavior of the local population, although certainly not friendly, was correct. More important for them, despite some obstructionism by French liaison officers, the local manufacturers were willing to consider German production contracts.[128]

Circumstances were such that some industries had very little choice about working directly or indirectly for Germany. For example, the rubber industry, the region's most vital industry, was from the fall of 1940 bound by a quota system agreed upon by the two governments and regulated from offices in Paris.[129] In exchange for making tires for Germany, the French would be supplied with "buna," the synthetic base product that was to be substituted for natural rubber since French supplies from Indochina were inhibited by British blockades. Thus, even a man as incontestably patriotic as Marcel Michelin (three of his sons joined Gaullist units in North Africa, his wife was arrested, and he and another son, Jacques, were deported by the Germans) was obliged to work for Germany or see his factory closed down entirely.[130]

The Vichy government did not oppose the French working for the Germans. Indeed, they hoped to benefit from German work orders, but the government wished to ensure that all production in the German interest would be duly credited toward the payment of the heavy occupation costs France bore.[131] Therefore, Vichy tried to regulate as closely as possible all contracts for production in the southern zone where its sovereignty was, in theory, still complete. This governmental intervention helps to explain why the Control Commission's inspectors sometimes complained that French government representatives were restraining the cooperation of individual manufacturers. The liaison officer assigned to the Control Commission at Clermont-Ferrand was accused of trying to influence entrepreneurs to answer only the precise questions asked of them by the Germans without further elaboration.[132] The Germans believed that the intervention of such men and possibly of higher officials had resulted in the loss of many possible contracts. They obviously felt that had they been able to deal directly with the businessmen, who appeared eager for contracts, their task would have been simplified.[133]

Whatever their problems with French officialdom, the German agents gradually succeeded in harnessing the local industry to the German war machine. After a somewhat slow start in 1941, the Control Commission reported that by the spring of 1942 the pace had quickened. The inspectors' work load was increasing as a result of the many new contracts and subcontracts.[134] When German troops in Russia needed chain saws, they were supplied from the French cutlery capital at Thiers, 25 miles east of Clermont.[135] At least as early as October 1941, representatives of Michelin and Bergougnan were negotiating contracts with the German authorities, and by May 1942, Michelin, Bergougnan, and Dunlop, the three largest rubber companies in the region, were sending prototypes of new tires made from buna to the Phoenix factory in Hamburg, and Ducellier at Issoire, 20 miles south of Clermont, was supplying parts to Bosch and to Ford-Köln.[136]

After a brief period of tension and some bitterness at the beginning of the total occupation, the Control Commission at Royat indicated that the French liaison officers were less troublesome than before and that the entrepreneurs were now "very willing" to take up German contracts.[137] The inspectors were under no illusion that this attitude represented a genuine change of heart in the sense of friendship toward Germany. Manufacturing difficulties of all sorts, including lack of raw materials, energy, and labor, had contributed to a desire to tap resources that could be had only, if at all, through the Germans. Above all, the manufacturers hoped to retain their workers in France and prevent their machinery from being carted off to Germany.[138] Consequently, the number of firms filling German orders rose dramatically after the occupation of the south. Late in 1943 when those companies considered vital to the German war economy were designated as *Speerbetriebe* (*S-Betriebe*), fifty-eight companies were noted in the department of the Puy-de-Dôme out of a total of one hundred in the Auvergne.[139] Most significantly, virtually every one of the enterprises with more than one hundred salaried workers was included, except for the Banque de France at Chamalières.[140] The Germans cannot have worried very much about this one exception since the 1700 employees there were busy printing French bank notes that, in any case, would find their way eventually into German coffers in payment of the daily occupation costs.[141]

Because of incomplete statistics and perpetual fluctuations caused by the forced labor draft (STO), it is impossible to measure precisely the percentage of workers directly involved in production for the German economy, but 60 percent of the workers at Clermont-Ferrand seem to have been in that category.[142] For the first seven months of 1944 over 30,000 workers in the Clermont region were employed in S-Betriebe, and thousands of others worked in armaments factories supervised directly by the German army and not included in these figures.[143] Control Commission statistics for the period of December 1943 through May 1944, after which time resistance sabotage reduced sharply the possibilities for supply and production, indicate that the monetary value of production from the regional economy for the German war effort averaged 3,406,532 reichsmarks (68,130,640 francs) per month, and the companies had outstanding orders to be filled for ten to fifteen times that amount.[144] Among a host of possible examples that might be cited, more than two-thirds of the region's aircraft factories were heavily engaged in production for Germany; the Ateliers Industriel de l'Air at Aulnat were producing 200 airplane motors a month; and in the month before it was shut down by Allied bombers, Michelin produced 727 tons of automobile tires, of which 80 percent went to fill German contracts.[145]

These raw figures are impressive in themselves, but they are best translated into the following general terms. When one considers that Germans also were major buyers for important local products not related directly to war products, such as conserved fruits, it is not too much to state simply that the region of Clermont-Ferrand was, in effect, integrated into the German economy during the occupation. The Control Commission at Royat had done its job very well indeed. One can speak of failures of the German economic officials only in the relative terms of what might have been. For there was one area in which German policy contributed incalculably to the reduction of potential French production, and for their blundering in this area the Germans had principally themselves to blame. Had it not been for the attempt to transfer French workers forcibly to factories in Germany, production of the local economy for German purposes would have been much higher.

The conflict between Fritz Sauckel and Albert Speer over priorities for foreign labor is well known and need not be related in detail here. Simply stated, Sauckel felt that foreign workers were more productive working in German factories, whereas Speer believed that higher overall levels of productivity could be obtained by leaving the workers where they were.[146] The impact of their high-level controversy was evident at Clermont-Ferrand

and manifested itself in discernible hostility among the servants of the various German bureaucracies in the region. Generally, the regular military and the economic control officials were on one side against the German police and labor agents on the other. There is no evidence of actual collusion between the Rüstung authorities and the French, but they agreed on one key issue. Attempts by the German labor service, and the exertions of its extremely active leader at Clermont-Ferrand, Doctor Westrich (one of the Germans most hated by local people), to round up young men for transfer to Germany, were responsible for driving workers out of the local economy and into the steadily growing maquis who thrived in the mountainous and thickly wooded terrain of the Auvergne.[147] Few Clermontois saw the STO as anything other than deportation. In these circumstances most men who were called up for the STO simply did not appear for physical examination or induction, and those who did were often given exemptions by sympathetic doctors. When Vichy and the Germans sought to eliminate exemptions by ordering the most cursory physical exams in the presence of both German and French physicians, thousands of workers simply disappeared into the hills at the first hint that they might be slated for examination.[148] German Rüstung officers cited numerous examples of massive desertions from the STO. At the news of a special measure concerning workers at the Luftwaffe motor factory located at Aulnat, Clermont's airport, all but 12 of the 120 men affected vanished into the countryside. Thus, complained a Rüstung official, not only were those 108 skilled workers not working in Germany, but they had had to be replaced at Clermont-Ferrand by unqualified workers who had no idea what they were doing. So Germany had lost on all counts.[149]

In these circumstances the Rüstung officials were constantly criticizing the actions of the German labor service, especially in the last months of the occupation when Westrich gathered together a private army of thugs, dubbed the Comité Pour la Paix Sociale, who arrested men at random, literally kidnapping them for deportation to German factories.[150] When Speer won Hitler's partial and wavering support for his viewpoint, local Rüstung authorities were happy to interpret in a liberal manner the agreements whereby workers in S-Betriebe were to be shielded from forced labor services. Although this arrangement was not systematically maintained—Sauckel was allowed in 1944 to "comb out" certain categories of workers—the results seem to have justified the Control Commission's belief that the French were not joining the maquis to avoid work *for* Germany; they were deserting to avoid work *in* Germany. When factories were protected from Westrich's carnivorous grasp, workers who had deserted earlier returned to their jobs, apparently without hesitation.[151] Indeed, there were notable advantages to working for Rüstung concerns for both management and labor. Not only did management profit from German contracts and protect its equipment from requisition; workers in the plants used the fact that they worked for S-Betriebe to obtain exemptions from after-hours guard duty along rail lines, or at supply depots, measures that were imposed on civilians working in other sectors of the economy. And the local German army commanders supported their refusal to comply with orders for guard duty, cleanup details, and other services demanded by French officials.[152]

Numerous German reports regarding the state of public opinion, the attitude of young men in the Chantiers de Jeunesse camps and of foreigners in labor units, as well as those concerning workers in local factories, attest to the German officials' conviction that without the threat of arrest for forced labor in Germany or for the TODT Organization along the Atlantic Wall, most men would have remained "correct" in their behavior, and would have continued working for German ends.[153] No doubt Germany for its own purposes exploited the economy of the region surrounding Clermont-Ferrand to a remarkable degree. Nonetheless, the failure to respond fully to appeals from the Rüstung inspectors for a more limited application of the labor draft prevented an even greater achievement in this domain.

Considering the overall record of their occupation of Clermont-Ferrand, the Germans might regret not having controlled the area's labor resources more completely, but on balance they cannot have been overly disappointed. If production was lower than it might have been, most of what was produced went to Germany. Most employed persons were working, directly or indirectly, for German ends. With a limited number of troops at their disposal, the Germans had managed to achieve many of their designs through utilization of the French administration and civil servants. If relations with the local population began to deteriorate seriously by the end of the occupation, for most of their stay in Clermont-Ferrand, the Germans had not been unduly worried about their security. Indeed, when one considers that the young troops rotated out of Clermont-Ferrand after training were destined for the Russian front or (in the case of those in flight school at Aulnat) for the air war against the increasingly successful American and English air forces, they may have looked back on their days in the Auvergne as having been relatively pleasant.

8

Resistance and Liberation

Clermont-Ferrand and the region of the Auvergne figured prominently in French resistance to the Vichy regime and the German occupation. Some German authorities considered Clermont-Ferrand to be *the* most active center of opposition to their control over southern France.[1] While the resistance in the Auvergne had certain distinctive features, in many ways it conformed to a pattern evident elsewhere in France. Issues that surfaced everywhere in France were played out in the Auvergne. A drive for unity around the symbol of Charles de Gaulle, competition between Communist and non-Communist groups, debates about appropriate levels of activism and the best tactics to use, and tensions between local and national or exterior (Gaullist and Allied) leaders influenced the growth and activities of the Auvergnat resistance. As was true elsewhere, the resistance in the Auvergne began with individual initiatives and embryonic groups of like-minded friends, relatives, or professional associates. As time passed, the major national movements, notably the Mouvement Unis de la Résistance (the MUR), the Front National, and the smaller and less activist Organisation de la Résistance Armée (the ORA), absorbed most of the smaller groups and controlled most of the organized resistance in the region. The Auvergnat resistance was characterized by a remarkable diversity and by its pervasiveness. Some organizations were small, specialized intelligence networks directed by British or Gaullist agents. Others concentrated on producing and distributing propaganda. The military components of the movements organized and directed the maquis in guerilla attacks and open combat against the Germans and the Milice, while the administrative wing of the resistance established a "shadow" government in preparation for the takeover of power at the liberation. In these activities the organized resistance was aided enormously by the complicity of many individuals who were not formally members of a resistance movement.

As was true everywhere in France, resisters in the Auvergne did not, on their own, drive the Germans out of their country. But the Auvergnat resistance contributed significantly to that process in sapping the morale of occupation troops, encircling isolated German units in a climate of insecurity, and harassing them relentlessly as they withdrew toward German soil. Only Thiers of the major cities of the Puy-de-Dôme was the scene of liberation through a clash of arms in a direct battle between resisters and Germans, and this, too, came in the circumstances of a general German order for retreat. Politically, the liberation revealed how well the resistance had done its work. The transition from the Vichy regime to the Provisional Government was smooth. Individuals approved by local resisters took over administration and government virtually without contest. The atmosphere at Clermont-Ferrand and in the vicinity was volatile for a few months following the liberation. The purge of collaborators and occasional unfortunate actions by maquis, slow to adapt themselves to the new conditions of legality, troubled those citizens who wished to return immediately to "normality." Recurrent bombings against suspected collaborators or their property after the regular police and judicial authorities had released them broke the calm and offered the most conspicuous exception to the general rule that all had been restored quickly to order and due process.

Within months of the liberation the first postwar elections confirmed what the resisters had claimed all along: France was ready for a change. A marked shift to the left provided a resounding endorsement for the resisters and the political parties that had benefited from their association with the resistance and its ideals. The eventual disappointment that many former resisters felt when the Fourth Republic fell short of the new society they had imagined—"all of their tomorrows did not sing"—was a product of the circumstances of a new era in which many resisters were no longer directly committed to political activism. Dismay with "politics as usual" did not shake their conviction that in what had been for the majority of them the most crucial and dramatic years of their lives, they had done what needed to be done, they had made the right choice.[2]

Anti-Vichy and anti-German tracts, slogans or symbols scribbled on walls or traffic signs, and underground newspapers were the first visible signs of resistance at Clermont-Ferrand. Throughout the occupation era, propaganda activity remained the chief concern of many resisters who believed that the pen was more powerful than the sword. In any case, swords were far more difficult to come by in 1940 and 1941, and during those years resisters channeled most of their energy into the production and distribution of the underground press. The products of this precocious opposition were detected by police at Clermont-Ferrand from a very early date.[3] In the fall and winter of 1940, the most frequently discovered propaganda was in the form of Gaullist Croix de Lorraine or "Vive de Gaulle" slogans handwritten on walls and Communist *papillons* (small leaflets of various shapes) stuck to walls or placed in mailboxes at night. General Cochet's famous *Conseils aux Occupées* were passed from hand to hand in the region before the major resistance movements had made their appearance. Along with occasional regional editions of *La Voix du Peuple* and *Bibendum,* produced by trade-unionists from the Michelin works, the underground *L'Humanité,* which had existed since the Communist Party was outlawed in 1939, was the only regular underground newspaper to appear at Clermont-Ferrand until late in 1941. By that time the southern zone's three major non-Communist resistance movements, Le Franc-Tireur, Libération, and Combat, after trial runs with ephemeral publications such as *France-Liberté, Petites Ailes,* and *Vérités,* had introduced newspapers bearing the names of their distinct movements. From early 1942 until the liberation, these newspapers, along with the Socialist Party's *Le Populaire* (from May 1942) and other serial publications such as *Témoignage Chrétien,* appeared in the Auvergne regularly each month, "malgré la Gestapo et la police de Vichy," as was proclaimed defiantly on *Le Franc-Tireur*'s masthead.

The major, and increasingly professional, underground newspapers were supplemented by more numerous and (in the early days) often crudely produced leaflets and tracts, mimeographed and distributed sporadically by the organized movements or by small groups of individuals unaffiliated with any particular resistance organization. Two examples will suggest the style and tenor of these leaflets:

> Confidence thanks to Pétain
> Hope thanks to Pétain
> French Resurrection thanks to Pétain
> Delivery to Germany thanks to Pétain

> I have spoken to you until now in the language of a Father
> Today I speak to you in the language of a Leader
> Ph. Pétain
> 30 Oct. 1940
> and Today in the language of a spoiled traitor[4]

Although much of the propaganda distributed in Clermont-Ferrand was produced locally, it occasionally arrived via the air. From time to time British planes flew over the region and dropped packets of literature that had been produced in London by the Gaullist or British intelligence services. According to one witness, local schoolchildren who were assigned the task of gathering up these leaflets (for example, the *Courrier de l'Air*) turned over only about one-fourth of their collection to the police or gendarmes, distributing the rest to family, friends, and neighbors in the vicinity.[5] As discussed earlier (see Chapter 6), encouragement to resist both

Vichy and the Germans also reached the Auvergne over the airwaves from BBC programs directed at occupied France and Europe. Police records leave no doubt that many Auvergnats took advantage of this opportunity and trusted much more readily what they heard on the BBC and on Swiss radio than what was broadcast by the officially controlled French radio stations.[6]

It is difficult to assess the impact of these varied forms of propaganda on the local population. Perhaps reflecting the academic bias of many of the Front National's leaders at Clermont-Ferrand, one representative of that movement claimed that written and spoken propaganda was extremely effective.[7] Noting the resisters' deficiency in armaments and pointing out that an attack on German soldiers, the type of action more characteristic of the later phases of the resistance, resulted only in one or two fewer soldiers and often brought with it severe reprisals, Alphonse Rozier believed that propaganda activities were in the long run of greater consequence. The Front National drew on the German language skills of students and faculty from the University of Strasbourg to produce tracts in German intended to convince the local occupation troops that the war was lost, and the resisters even managed to distribute these leaflets inside the German barracks.[8] Records of the occupation units stationed near Clermont-Ferrand indicate that there were several desertions every month. Some German officers commented that the Volksdeutsche troops were especially susceptible to hostile propaganda, but the available evidence is suggestive rather than conclusive, and one can only speculate about how direct the connection was, in fact, between resistance propaganda and the desertions.[9]

French officials seemed to have been of two minds about the influence of resistance and Allied propaganda. Most of their biweekly and monthly reports on public opinion stated that opposition propaganda had failed to disturb the calm resolution with which the people were going about their business. Yet those same reports detailed a steadily growing disenchantment with the Vichy regime and an unremitting hostility to the Germans. In one instance, an officer charged with a special investigation of attitudes in the metalworking industry at Clermont-Ferrand during the summer of 1943 asserted that political propaganda was not causing problems in the factories. In the next breath he added that should ringleaders of the resistance issue orders to the metalworkers, "one can assume that a very large number of them will slavishly obey the orders communicated to them. . . ."[10] Just possibly, instead of winning converts to their cause, the resisters' tracts and underground newspapers and the BBC's broadcasts simply reinforced in many Clermontois convictions they held already as a result of actions taken by Laval, Pétain, and the Germans, or in response to the rapidly degenerating conditions of life in occupied France.

Whatever the impact of resistance propaganda on others might have been, activities surrounding the production and distribution of clandestine literature were central to the early growth of the organized resistance. The typical resister's introduction to clandestine life began with participation in the procurement of materials, or the printing and distribution of illegal tracts or newspapers. The production of an underground newspaper in particular accomplished several objectives at once. Virtually everything (paper, ink, machinery) necessary for printing a newspaper was rationed and closely regulated by the Vichy regime. By November 1940 the prefect at Clermont-Ferrand had banned the sale without official authorization of ditto machines, stencils, and duplicating paper.[11] Consequently, the resisters had to obtain these materials surreptitiously. Production and distribution of underground newspapers demanded secrecy and attention to security. The networks of contacts and secure friends established in this process became a skeletal underpinning for the mature resistance movements. Clandestine methods thus learned were easily adaptable, with appropriate modifications, to the late-blooming military and administrative branches of the resistance. Sometimes—and this seemed to be true especially of the younger recruits—resisters were impatient to undertake more spectacular actions, notably to fight Germans. But, in the meantime, the production of underground newspapers, which rapidly gained an audience in all parts of France, gave the resisters a sense of belonging to a powerful national organization extending beyond their limited circle of comrades.[12]

By the last year of the occupation, despite retaining a measure of their original, individual character, and certainly hiding the behind-the-scenes quarrels that frequently disturbed relations among the resistance movements, the major underground newspapers were remarkably similar in content and tone. All were committed to the support of a provisional government under the leadership of Charles de Gaulle. All reflected the resisters' desire for a democratic and socially progressive republic in France after the war. Each journal took pride in highlighting sabotage exploits of the resistance and chronicled with evident satisfaction every German defeat on the major fronts of the war. And, of course, the papers' editors called on the French people to do everything in their power to contribute to the overthrow of the Vichy regime and the final defeat of Germany.[13] This seemingly uniform outlook, apparent in the underground press in 1944, obscured somewhat artificially the contrasting ideological and political views of the movements' founders.

The resisters' differing perspectives had been much more evident in early editions of the newspapers. The most obvious distinction, present at Clermont-Ferrand as elsewhere in France, was the division between the Communist and the non-Communist resistance. Participation of Communist ministers in the Provisional Government, substantial influence of Communist resisters in the National Resistance Council, and protocols of unity and cooperation at the regional and local level never entirely eliminated a fundamental tension between the two camps. Although ultimately sharing the same or similar goals, and agreeing that the immediate task of driving the Germans out of France overshadowed all other considerations, the leaders of the Communist and non-Communist resistance in the Auvergne had little meaningful contact and remained suspicious of one another throughout the occupation.

The core of these differences was the unshakable conviction of many non-Communist resisters that the French Communist Party was a puppet dancing to the pulls and tugs of a master puppeteer in Moscow, "a foreign nationalist party,"[14] in the words of Léon Blum. According to this non-Communist version, the French Communists only became truly active in the anti-German resistance after the Nazi invasion of the Soviet Union in June 1941. Although this description ignores the contradictory choices and actions of many individual Communists, the official party position was stated unequivocally in many Communist publications that were circulated in Clermont-Ferrand from the military disaster of 1940 through the spring of 1941. In November 1940, the *Voix du Peuple* ("Organe de la Région Communiste du Puy-de-Dôme") stated:

> The position of the French communists is clear: they are against de Gaulle, Agent of British imperialism, fighting to the last with the hides of others. They are against the Pétain-Laval Government, flunkies of Hitler who wish to drag France once again into the imperialist war.[15]

The war, according to the Communists, represented the ambitions of capitalists in Germany and Britain, as well as their allies in France, running the gamut from politicians on the extreme right to the Socialist Party. Only the Soviet Union and, in France, the Communist Party had opposed the war; in the present circumstances, only a "people's government" could assure "bread, peace, the independence and safety of our country."[16] As the months passed, Communist attacks on Pétain and the Vichy regime became increasingly virulent, but at the same time, as late as April 1941, Léon Blum, Vincent Auriol, Marx Dormoy, and Edouard Daladier were considered by *L'Humanité* to be the Marshal's "friends";[17] in that year's special May Day issue, the original Communist viewpoint seemed to have changed very little:

> For peace, for the international solidarity of workers and the fraternity of peoples against any participation of France in the imperialist war which is continuing, against the criminal recruitment of young Frenchmen, some

who are sent to the slaughter by the agents of de Gaulle in the service of British imperialism, others by Pétain, Darlan, and the Lavalians in the service of the German imperialists.[18]

It is not surprising then, that Gaullist resisters, noting that the disappearence of such attacks on de Gaulle coincided with the entry of the Soviet Union into the war, would believe that the Communist resistance had begun in earnest only after the summer of 1941.[19]

The Communists, of course, saw things in another light. For them, resistance was defined in a broad context of opposition to fascism that stretched back at least to the Popular Front and their opposition to the Munich agreement. The party had turned to clandestine activity on a large scale when it resisted repression by the Daladier and Reynaud governments. The defeat, the advent of the Vichy regime, and the German occupation opened a new phase in an unbroken struggle for liberty, popular sovereignty, and social justice. Passing over in embarrassed silence their early attitude toward Charles de Gaulle, Communist resisters claimed legitimately that they were the most outspoken critics of the Vichy regime at a time when editors of the newspapers produced by the non-Communist movements, emphasizing the anti-German character of their actions, hesitated to criticize Pétain too severely.[20]

Further, Communist militants certainly noticed that they were being arrested in large numbers by Vichy police (and in the north by the Germans) for actions the Gaullist resisters refused to acknowledge as "real" resistance. The Communists were the chief targets of police repression during the first years of the occupation. Many police authorities at Clermont-Ferrand and elsewhere considered Gaullist resisters to be misguided patriots, but were unwilling to extend such "tolerance" to the Communists. In the winter of 1940–1941, when police at Clermont-Ferrand sought to suppress "antinational" propaganda, four inspectors were designated to "concentrate particularly on *Communist* propaganda,"[21] and the special antiresistance units created in later years were modeled on preexisting anti-Communist groups. Only in August 1942 did René Bousquet, secretary general of Vichy's police forces, order the regional prefects to prosecute with equal severity "all those involved in . . . Gaullist-inspired propaganda."[22] Although distinctions began to blur by 1943 and 1944 when *all* resisters were treated with increasing severity, the memory of an uneven justice remained. In that context one can understand why former Communist resisters bristle at the suggestion that their party was a latecomer to the resistance in France.

An unintended consequence of Vichy's and the Germans' disproportionate attention to the Communist resistance might have been the eventual development of a security system in the Communist movements that was superior to that of the non-Communist organizations. Whether because they had had prior experience in clandestine activities or because they were forced to be more careful in view of the special attention they received from the police, the Communist resisters gained a reputation for tight security. This reputation may not have been justified in every case; thousands of Communists were arrested, deported, or executed in all parts of France, demonstrating that Communist security was not unbreachable. Still, circumstantial evidence for the Puy-de-Dôme supports the relative generalization. By the spring of 1943 local police were looking for Robert Huguet, Emile Coulaudon, Maurice Jouanneau, and other leaders of the non-Communist resistance in Clermont-Ferrand and the vicinity. By contrast, a year later Alphonse Rozier, head of the Front National's FTP for the region, was still living at his house in Clermont-Ferrand, unmolested by French police or Gestapo.[23]

The individual experience of Rozier, beyond its relation to the issue of security, is informative in several respects with regard to the resistance in the Auvergne. Rozier, an electrician, came to the resistance through his association with Guy Perilhou, general secretary of the PCF for the region of the Auvergne, and Henri Diot, general secretary of the departmental federation of metallurgists. Interestingly, Rozier was not a Communist. His friendship with the two men grew not out of political activism, but from a common interest in music and the theater. He met Perilhou, who had an excellent voice, after a musical performance the latter had given at a theater in Vichy. Frequent contacts at cultural events led to fairly regular discussions among the three friends over apéritifs. To Diot and Perilhou's occasional requests that he join them in the party, Rozier responded that he did not believe that he could be at the same time a good Catholic and a Communist. Nonetheless, he saw no conflict in being a good Catholic and a good friend. Therefore, when the Communist Party was outlawed by the Daladier government, Rozier agreed to serve as a courier for correspondence between Maurice Thorez, head of the Central Committee in Paris, and Perilhou, leader of the party in the Auvergne. On Rozier's return to Clermont-Ferrand after demobilization from the army in 1940, he agreed, in a logical continuation of his prewar assistance to his friends, to organize and direct the PCF's local section of the clandestine Organisation Spéciale (OS). Out of loyalty to his friends and because of his personal anti-Hitlerian convictions, he agreed to work with the party until France was liberated. Rozier's choice to join the resistance was similar to many other resisters whose original commitment came in the context of conversations with like-minded friends, family, or professional associates.[24]

Rozier's rise to leadership in the local resistance was rapid, and it mirrored a pattern typical of both Communist and non-Communist movements in France. Prominent politicians and union activists of the prewar era rarely played key roles in the resistance—not a surprising development in view of Vichy's antipathy to the Popular Front whose Socialist, Communist, and Radical supporters were designated for attentive police surveillance. Most of the leading Communists, in particular, were interned very early in the Vichy regime. This was true at Clermont-Ferrand of Perilhou, Diot, and Robert Marchadier, general secretary for the CGT at Michelin. Consequently, persons who were relatively unknown, such as Rozier, Emile Coulaudon, Robert Huguet, and Henry Ingrand (a stranger to the region) for the MUR, provided the leadership that more recognizable personalities could not have offered so easily. Thus when Etienne Neron, a parliamentary reporter for *L'Humanité* during the Popular Front era, was arrested in January 1941—as Rozier recalled, "He had not been suited for underground life"[25]—Rozier temporarily became responsible for Neron's assignment, editing and producing the Communist underground press. This job was in addition to locating materials for and distributing tracts and newspapers, the original task of the OS. Police at Clermont-Ferrand, who during 1940 and 1941 staged several sweeping raids leading to the arrest of dozens of real and alleged Communists, periodically celebrated having eliminated the sources of Communist propaganda, only to express shortly thereafter their astonishment that the propaganda was continuing despite the apparent success of their raids.[26] Their exasperation was in large part explained by the nature of recruitment for the early resistance movements. Communist propaganda was not being produced and distributed by Communists alone.

When in September 1941 police at Clermont-Ferrand discovered the first tracts circulated locally announcing the creation of the Front National,[27] that organization, although founded at the command of the Communist Party, included many more non-Communists than Communists. The members of Rozier's OS groups, transformed into the Francs-Tireurs et Partisans Français (FTP) under the Front National, were workers, Christian trade-unionists, and students. In addition to Rozier, who was eventually the secretary of the Front National and the chef d'état major of the FTP, the original directing committee of the Front National in Clermont-Ferrand included Serge Fischer, librarian at the University of Strasbourg, and four lycée or university professors, Marcel Dichamp, Yvonne Canque, Jean Pérus, and Henri Martin. They were later joined by several students, a journalist, and a former member of parliament. Significantly, when Rozier sought advice about a political issue, he looked for guidance to Alexandre Varenne, *La Montagne*'s defiant editor and an independent Socialist, rather than to his contacts in the Communist Party.[28]

A survey of the early membership of both Communist and non-Communist resistance movements in the Auvergne strongly belies Emmanuel d'Astier de la Vigerie's glib comments in *The Sorrow and the Pity* that one had to be "maladjusted" or a "failure" to join the resistance.[29] No doubt an occasional romantic adventurer was involved in the resistance, but most resisters, particularly in the early years, were serious individuals, convinced of the necessity to stand up for political liberty and personal freedom in the face of authoritarian government and foreign occupation. Police reports and the memory of former resisters concur that while people from all social categories could be found in the resistance at Clermont-Ferrand, most of the active resisters were at first students, teachers, and factory workers.[30] These individuals were responsible for producing and circulating the underground propaganda that was the principal activity of the resistance in southern France in 1940 and 1941. Of course, the makeup of resistance changed with the changing circumstances of the war and occupation. New conditions brought with them new methods and new recruits.

In 1942 the resistance in the Auvergne entered a second, more aggressive phase, broadening the scope of its earlier activities to include threats and bomb attacks against the property or person of outspoken partisans of Germany or the Vichy regime. Police at Clermont-Ferrand were first placed on alert with regard to the threat of violent resistance following the shooting of German soldiers at Nantes and Bordeaux in October 1941.[31] Orders were issued that month that all packages or bags brought into the prefecture were to be inspected at the entry for explosives.[32] In February 1942 national and local authorities, alarmed by frequent thefts of explosives, insisted on tighter security at locations where these materials were stored.[33] By May the Interior Ministry, noting that the pro-British resistance organizations had begun to coordinate their activities, announced plans to centralize actions against them from a command center at Lyon.[34] A month later the regional prefect at Clermont-Ferrand reported the creation of a fourteen-man special section under the Police Judiciare to deal with resistance affairs.[35] The motivation for this obvious and increasing concern of police and Vichy officialdom about the underground resistance was not difficult to understand. Prior to 1942 there had been virtually no evidence of armed or violent resistance in the Auvergne.[36] But from the spring of 1942 until the liberation, almost every month there was an escalation in the strength, variety, and visibility of opposition to the Vichy regime and the German occupation. As the example of Clermont-Ferrand illustrates, 1942 was the year that the French resistance became visible and explosive.

Some historians have cited demonstrations on May Day and Bastille Day 1942 as the first widespread evidence for mass resistance to the Vichy regime.[37] Thousands of people who were not active participants in the resistance movements had taken this opportunity to voice their opposition to the government. Bastille Day, 14 July, was marked by public demonstrations in most of the major cities of southern France, including Clermont-Ferrand. All of the local resistance movements were active in distributing tracts and newspapers encouraging the Clermontois to show their support for the resistance by assembling on the place de Jaude to sing the "Marseillaise" in defiance of the government's ban on such public gatherings. There may actually have been two separate demonstrations at Clermont-Ferrand, one at 6:30 P.M., as called for by BBC broadcasts, and another one earlier in the afternoon. Eyewitness accounts of what happened vary substantially. Estimates of the number of people involved range from 2000 down to 150.[38] Alphonse Rozier, who helped to plan the Front National's participation in the demonstration and was in the crowd that day, recalled his disappointment that only 150 persons had come out, and he remembered that no one had been arrested thanks in part to the vigorous reaction of several armed men who were former volunteers for the International Brigades in Spain. Police reports on the following day estimated the crowd at 500 and noted that eight persons had been arrested and one policeman injured in a scuffle with demonstrators.[39]

Whatever the exact size of the demonstration, the impact of the event was unmistakable. Within days the demonstration had grown to much larger-than-life proportions as accounts of it passed from neighbor to neighbor. In the weeks following the demonstration, Rozier, who had been dismayed by a smaller crowd than he had hoped for on 14 July, was encouraged by the increase around the town in comments sympathetic to the resistance. The Clermontois seemed impressed that the resistance was moving beyond underground propaganda to action.[40] The government's response left no doubt that it had been impressed by this public show of force. The minister of the interior, while attempting to play down the importance of the Bastille Day demonstrations, issued strict orders that no such demonstration should be allowed to occur again.[41] All available forces, including the police, gendarmerie, army, and even auxiliary recruits from the Service d'Ordre Légionnaire, were to be called on to maintain order where necessary. That these orders and the precedent of 14 July 1942 were taken seriously by the Vichy regime was evident in police files that indicate a careful monitoring of the BBC and the underground press for warnings of possible demonstrations. Every national holiday or patriotic date after 1942 produced directives for systematic police sweeps in the vicinities where demonstrations were likely to occur and the deployment of hundreds of police, gendarmes, and gardes mobiles (GMR) with strict orders to keep people away from potential assembly points—for example, Clermont's place de Jaude with its statue of Vercingetorix.[42] In these circumstances after 1942 the resisters generally played down this particular form of opposition and turned to other types of action.

Combat, a local section of which was organized and developed at Clermont-Ferrand under the guidance of Professor Albert Coste-Floret and others associated with the University of Strasbourg, was the largest and best-organized non-Communist resistance movement in southern France. In the spring and early summer of 1942, the movement made its presence felt at Clermont-Ferrand beyond the realm of propaganda. Letters signed "Centre Régional de Combat," ordering local proprietors to stop displaying German or collaborationist magazines and newspapers, were sent to bookstores and newstands. When owners refused to take these letters seriously, the groupes francs broke out windows in several stores as a further warning. In order to make their point still more emphatically, with the help of professors and students in the University of Strasbourg's chemistry laboratory, the resisters set off a series of bombs at the residences or places of business of individuals considered to be collaborators.[43] On other occasions the "bombs" could be less destructive, as when tear-gas canisters were lobbed into the conference hall at the Salle Saint-Genès in order to discourage attendance at public lectures staged by collaborationist organizations.[44] As one might suspect, these activities quickly caught the attention of local police. Unfortunately, in the late summer and fall of 1942, several dozen young resisters implicated in these actions became the first victims of arrests by Clermont-Ferrand's new "special section."[45]

Ironically, the misfortune of those arrested may have contributed indirectly to progress toward unification of the non-Communist resistance in the region. Encouraged by men such as Pierre Brossolette and Jean Moulin, who were to become legendary heroes of the resistance, in 1942 resistance movements in all of France had accepted the leadership of Charles de Gaulle, whom they recognized as the uncontested head of the French resistance. Within France the major movements had moved toward a coordination of their efforts. The three largest southern movements, Combat, Franc-Tireur, and Libération, formally became the Mouvements Unis de la Résistance (MUR) in January 1943. The following May all of the major resistance organizations in both south and north joined representatives of the clandestine political parties and trade unions in the National Resistance Council (CNR). The process of unification had required months of difficult negotiations. Mutual suspicions bred by clandestine conditions and pride in and loyalty to one's original organization meant that local resistance leaders were often reluctant to see their movements absorbed and subordinated to a distant regional or national hierarchy, even though they accepted the fundamental notion that strength lay in unity. Consequently, in all of southern France, long after leaders at the national and regional levels had agreed to unification of their movements, arguments readily traceable to conflicting ideologies or personalities in the original movements occasionally troubled the resistance.[46]

In this regard the resistance in the Auvergne, especially at Clermont-Ferrand and in the Puy-de-Dôme, was exceptional. The damaging arrests referred to earlier, which had temporarily set back the fortunes of the resistance at Clermont in the fall of 1942, coincided with the last stages of the creation of the MUR in southern France. By that date all three of the components of the MUR, Combat, Libération, and Franc-Tireur, had active organizations in the region. The original meeting of Emmanuel d'Astier de la Vigerie, Lucie and Raymond Aubrac, Jean Cavaillès, and Georges Zerapha that led eventually to the creation of Libération had taken place at Clermont-Ferrand in November 1940. Jean Rochon, a journalist at *La Montagne,* was Libération's first representative on the MUR's original directing committee for the Puy-de-Dôme. By the summer of 1942 Franc-Tireur had developed a strong local organization with several hundred members at Clermont-Ferrand divided between a branch centered around university students and faculty, headed by Marc Gerschel, Germain Sournies, and Robert Waitz, and a group of syndicalists concentrated at Michelin under the leadership of Gaston Jouanneau and Claudius Jeantet. Franc-Tireur, like Combat earlier, turned to the use of explosives in the fall of 1942 with similar consequences. Following a coordinated series of bombings in November at Clermont-Ferrand and Thiers, police arrested or drove into hiding all of the members of Franc-Tireur's directing committee. Thus, when Henry Ingrand, destined to become the regional chief of the MUR for the Auvergne and, in the liberation era, the Commissaire de la République, arrived at Clermont-Ferrand in the fall of 1942, he found the non-Communist resistance organizations in apparent disarray and Vichy's police on the offensive.[47]

Refusing to be stymied by these disheartening circumstances, Ingrand, Huguet, Coulaudon, Commandant Pierre Dejussieu, and other leaders of the Auvergnat resistance turned the situation to their advantage. Ingrand later recalled that he had wanted to "start from zero"[48] in rebuilding the resistance in the name of the MUR. Within months distinctions between the original movements seemed to have disappeared, and recruitment for the rapidly growing maquis was done in the name of the MUR only. Ingrand had been particularly concerned about security problems at the University of Strasbourg, the original mainstay of support for Combat at Clermont-Ferrand, and he decided to place a "cordon sanitaire"[49] around that center of resistance, limiting to a minimum any contact between the main organization of the MUR and the university, and preferring to base most of his action in the Auvergnat countryside. To ensure his personal security, his headquarters were located in small, out-of-the-way communes. Thus, from 1943 until the liberation, the main focus of MUR activity was on organizing the maquis and operations outside of the large cities, while the Front National, although supporting several maquis groups as well, continued active campaigns in the university community and among the urban workers.[50]

By the end of 1942 the Auvergnat resistance, by national standards, was characterized by a remarkable stability of leadership at the higher levels. While arrests and shifts of responsibility necessitated some changes, Ingrand, Coulaudon, and Huguet, to cite the most conspicuous examples, gradually extended their influence beyond the Puy-de-Dôme and retained key leadership positions until and even beyond the liberation. Ingrand's position as head of the Regional Liberation Committee, and as chief representative in the Auvergne of de Gaulle's Provisional Government, was acknowledged later by the Front National, as well as by the MUR.[51] For this reason, members of the directing committee of the MUR regularly cited R6 (the region of the Auvergne) as the area in which there were the fewest problems in terms of organization and control of the resistance.[52] In fact, as will be seen later, what was valid in terms of hierarchies or paper diagrams of chains of command sometimes covered up a much more turbulent situation in terms of actual control over the forces and actions of the resistance. For now, we may conclude that by early 1943 the resistance around Clermont-Ferrand was implanted seriously and was well on its way to unification.

In addition to the activities of resistance leaders, two important events in the fall of 1942 had a significant impact on the resistance in the Auvergne. Pierre Laval's announcement that all young men were to face the obligation of a national labor service and the occupation of southern France by German troops dramatically affected the size and intensity of French resistance to the Vichy government and the Germans. The relève scheme and later the STO provided the single most important spur in turning the resistance into a mass phenomenon. The number of persons participating directly in resistance formations (especially the maquis) and the network of popular complicity that helped to sustain them expanded several times over, as hundreds of thousands of people affected by the forced labor draft did everything they could to oppose its effective implementation. The arrival of foreign troops in the cities and countryside of southern France brought the previously sheltered southerners into the same immediate contact with the German occupation that people in northern France had experienced for more than two years, and this change made resistance more violent and more dangerous. In 1943 and until the liberation in 1944, public attention would focus primarily on the armed resistance, while at the same time and outside public purview, resisters concluded their secret preparations for the replacement of the Vichy administration by persons favorable to the resistance.

Surveying the Auvergnat resistance in this final phase, one is struck first and foremost by its pervasiveness. From thefts of equipment, clothing, ration coupons, and other resources needed to supply the maquis, to sabotage of communications and industrial production, to attacks on collaborators and German troops, the frequency of resistance activity in the realm of direct action was simply astonishing.[53] It would be impossible to list here every instance of resistance activity in the Auvergne, but among several possible choices, the following examples may suffice to illustrate the range and extent of these actions. One famous exploit of the Auvergnat resistance was "the escape from Pontmort" in August 1943. A corps franc unit from the MUR headed by Coulaudon and Huguet, who pretended to be a police commissioner, stopped a train at the station of Pontmort and freed Maurice Jouanneau and ten other recently arrested resisters who were being transferred out of the region by French police. Although the hapless guards who had been taken in by Huguet's ruse had nothing to do with the escape, they were arrested by Vichy authorities on charges of complicity with the resisters.[54] Along these same lines, mass prison escapes at Le Puy

Resistance sabotage of a factory in Clermont-Ferrand

Resistance weapons and sabotage materials discovered by police at Clermont-Ferrand

and Riom were engineered by Auvergnat resisters. One of the resisters' most spectacular coups occurred in February 1944 when a Front National team seized the so-called Milliard of the Banque de France in the train station at Clermont-Ferrand. Although the take from this robbery was not really a full billion francs, more than 900 million francs was a lot of money even in a seriously undervalued currency, and Front National units and their dependent families in all of southern France who were without other means of support benefited from the operation.[55] Still, in retrospect one is impressed not so much by the occasional, extraordinary robbery or sabotage as by the sheer volume and frequency of actions.

Naturally, the rhythm of resistance activity varied in view of weather, the location of German troops, Vichy police operations, and other factors. Guerilla operations and sabotage reached their most intense levels in the weeks immediately preceding and following the Allied landings in Normandy in June 1944; but during the last year and a half of the occupation, rarely did a day pass in the Auvergne without some action to attest to the presence of the resistance. Police dossiers concerning these actions include 1137 separate documents concerning attacks on mayoral offices from November 1943 through August 1944 in which the maquis took items such as ration tickets for food and clothing and stamps for the production of false papers. Files for the same months include 514 documents recording attacks on rail or communications lines, and those concerning the sabotage of electrical installations or factories contain 772 separate items. Of course, some of these reports referred to the same incidents, but the volume of administrative paperwork generated by resistance activity suggests the size of the problem confronting those responsible for maintaining law and order.[56] In just two months, 12 May to 13 July 1944, almost half (twenty-seven of sixty-two) of the tax collection offices in the Puy-de-Dôme, several of them more than once, had been visited by resistance groups and robbed of 1,841,436 francs; in approximately the same period, there were seventy-nine separate attacks on PTT bureaus, producing an additional 2,040,636 francs for resistance coffers.[57] These attacks on mayor's offices, post of-

Clandestine radio receiver/transmitter used by resisters

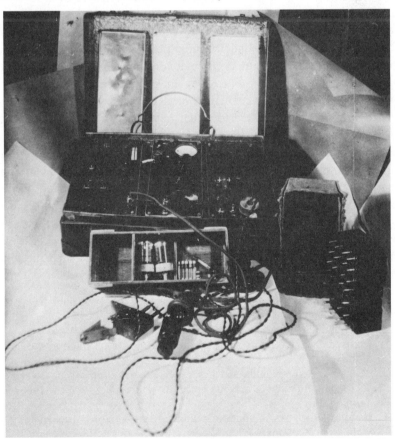

fices, banks, and tax offices were sometimes made under cover of darkness, but frequently they were carried out in broad daylight, even in the center of Clermont-Ferrand and other towns. Months before the liberation, from the perspective of the Vichy government, things were simply out of control.

From an early date, Vichy authorities, aware of the frequent disappearance of substantial quantities of explosives, gasoline, ration coupons, and other materials useful to the maquis, had tried to limit those losses by various means. Armed convoys were employed to guard the items in transit from one location to another. In repeated and increasingly strident orders for tightening security, guards and those responsible for supervising depots for explosives and gasoline were threatened with severe sanctions in the event of further losses. Because of the repetition of these directives, one assumes that they had been ineffectual. One local businessman noted that "it is not possible for a merchant to take the place of the forces of law and order."[58] The director of Mines de Brassac added that in view of the number of well-armed maquis active in the region, "we must admit that we cannot possibly stop a theft attempt that is seriously carried through."[59] In view of the refusal of the Germans to allow the arming of guards beyond hunting weapons with a meager allotment of ammunition, even an official high in the Vichy administration admitted: "It would seem difficult then to hold these communal civil servants responsible in the event of thefts in their communes, since they have not been provided with the means for defense."[60] On numerous occasions unarmed or lightly armed guards who had been drafted to watch railway lines were induced (more or less willingly) to help maquis units carry out the very sabotage they had been charged with preventing. As one guard from the commune of Cendre Orcet remarked to the man in charge of the watch: "What is the use of guarding these tracks? No one wants to take them away, they may well unbolt them, and we, we can do nothing but help them."[61]

Vichy authorities, clearly incapable of stopping thefts and sabotage by force, tried other methods. Hoping to reduce or eliminate thefts of gasoline, in February 1944 the prefect of the Puy-de-Dôme issued the following instructions:

1. Gas pumps that are open to the public are to be open only from 9:00 A.M. to 6:00 P.M.
2. When these stations are closed for lunch, the handle and hose are to be removed from the pump and locked in the garage or taken to the home of the owner.
3. At 6:00 P.M. the handles and hoses are to be taken to a gendarmerie or police station or to the mayor's office for safekeeping until the following morning.
4. Handles and hoses of inactive pumps are to be stored permanently at those same locations.[62]

Other steps had included reducing the quantities of gasoline, money, to-bacco, ration coupons, or other items stored in any one location in order to reduce the impact of thefts, and delivering these materials only on the day they were to be used or made available to the public. Ultimately, Vichy authorities admitted that they could not stop the thefts. At best their losses could be reduced slightly. Countless documents regarding these mat-ters testify to a remarkable turn of events. Long before German troops left the region, the Vichy regime was no longer master of its own house in the Auvergne.

Outside of the major centers of industry or communications held by German troops, in 1944 the French resistance controlled the Auvergnat countryside. As described in Chapter 7, this was not an enormous problem for the Germans.[63] At least in terms of their major objectives of keeping open the main lines of transportation and communications and maintain-ing the security of their troops, the Germans were largely successful. On the other hand, resistance sabotage certainly reduced their ability to ex-ploit the French economy in support of the German war effort. For the Vichy regime, the problem was of another order. Nominally the govern-ment of France, Vichy had completely lost its credibility with the French people. The administration was riddled with resistance agents and sym-pathizers, so that any action it planned was known in advance by the re-sistance.

German suspicions about the reliability of the regular French police and gendarmes were borne out at the liberation when large numbers of them went over to the resistance or (more frequently) allowed themselves to be disarmed by the maquis without a fight. On D-Day and the following week or so, almost 30 percent (575 of 1950) of the gendarmes, 16 percent (183 of 1125) of the urban police, and 11 percent (94 of 878) of the GMR in the region of the Auvergne left their posts, most of them to join the maquis.[64] Although one-third of these men returned to their homes in the next weeks, and police officials claimed they had left only because of misleading Gaullist radio broadcasts stating that all French police were going to be arrested by the Germans, it is noteworthy that almost all of those who returned came back *without* their weapons. Purge commissions after the liberation concluded that even those police who had remained on duty during the last months of the occupation undertook any action against the resistance with the utmost reluctance. Many of the younger GMR or police had joined those forces only to "seek a refuge in the Police in order to escape forced labor in Germany,"[65] and they had no desire to fight other young French, many of whom had joined the maquis for the same reason. In these circumstances the Vichy regime could rely only on the loyalty of a few GMR units and the Milice, viewed by the population as servile instruments of the German Gestapo and hated by resisters and regular French police alike.

Reflecting their impotence outside of an occasional punitive strike with concentrated forces of Milice and GMR, Vichy police authorities fell back on security plans that paralleled those of the Germans. In essence abandoning the countryside to the maquis, the Vichy regime concentrated its police forces in the major cities such as Clermont-Ferrand and Vichy, and left major antiresistance actions to the German police and military. In a directive issued shortly after D-Day, Lieutenant Colonel Hachette, commander of the uniformed security forces for the region of Clermont-Ferrand, acknowledged that the Puy-de-Dôme, the Cantal, and the Haute-Loire were "in large part occupied by the maquis,"[66] and stated that the mission of the French police was limited to holding Clermont-Ferrand and the immediate vicinity. The logbooks for the forces under his control from June until the liberation indicate that Hachette stuck close to his original statement of their mission, seldom venturing out into the countryside and refusing requests from the prefect of the Puy-de-Dôme that he adopt a more active posture by undertaking operations in other sectors of the department.[67]

Recalling the extraordinary number of thefts that had occurred in the region for more than a year, it was not surprising that in the summer of 1944 Vichy ordered suspension of all shipments of food, tobacco, and money in those areas held by "dissident organizations in order to avoid certain confiscation."[68] For the Puy-de-Dôme 46 percent (219 of 473) of the communes were deemed unsafe in June 1944, but several months before, in February, the transport of gasoline in the department had been forbidden unless heavily armed escorts could be provided.[69] If this condition was striking in the Puy-de-Dôme because of its proximity to the seat of government, it was by no means limited to the Auvergne. Other centers of maquis activity in southern France, such as the Savoie, the Haute-Savoie, the Jura, the Isère, and the Correze, experienced a similar phenomenon. An irony of the situation in the Auvergne was that long before the liberation, the "outlaws" (the resistance) had to a limited extent begun to restore the law and order that had vanished from the French countryside with Vichy's effective abdication. A "police of the maquis" was organized by the MUR that issued orders for the control of prices to try to restrain black-market activity and arrested resisters or "false resisters" who had committed robberies without the sanction of resistance hierarchies. Punishment was severe and might even bring execution on the spot.[70]

On several occasions during the last months of the occupation and in the liberation era, criminals hiding behind the guise of the resistance took advantage of the unsettled times for personal gain, and resistance leaders were determined to separate their cause from such actions. In most cases when resisters "confiscated" goods or money, they left receipts marked FFI, FTP, or MUR, noting that reimbursement would be made following the liberation of France. And, indeed, while insisting on careful investigations to ensure that the obligations were attributable to genuine resisters and not to "the impudence of vulgar highway robbers," the Provisional Government accepted the responsibility to make good on the resisters' promises.[71]

To this point our discussion of resistance activity in the last two years of the occupation has focused on areas that were principally within the purview of the Vichy government. More dramatic, and often more tragic in their consequences, were direct attacks on the German military or police personnel. Attacks on individual Germans or military units were much less frequent than sabotage, robberies, or attacks on French collaborators for several reasons. The resisters were never adequately trained or armed to contest German military units on an equal footing. Therefore, resistance units were always most effective in staging sudden guerilla attacks against isolated units, utilizing their mobility and superior knowledge of the local terrain. Planning and carrying out assassinations of individual soldiers or German police was also well within the capacity and resources of the resistance organizations. But killing individual Germans or attacks on German units brought severe reprisals, usually at the expense of the civilian population. Mindful of the inevitable German response to such actions, the resisters preferred engagements with German troops to take place outside of populated areas.

On several occasions at Clermont-Ferrand when shooting of German police or soldiers did occur, the killings were in the context of desperate escapes by entrapped resisters, not premeditated assassinations. The Germans, of course, did not distinguish between these different sets of circumstances. German police, military, or SS units vented their fury through reprisals whether the killings had been intentional or not. The tempo of resistance attack and German reprisal began slowly in the Auvergne, but increased rapidly during the last months of the occupation. Four months after the arrival of occupation troops, on 21 March 1943, the first German soldier was shot in the vicinity of Clermont-Ferrand at the Col de Ceyssat, west of the city near the Puy-de-Dôme.[72] The following month the staff medical officer, Doctor Schellen, was killed a mere 300 meters from the German barracks in Clermont-Ferrand. On 20 June two German staff officers were killed at Chamalières, and four days later two German police were shot when trying to apprehend a resistance suspect. In the succeeding months, this irregular pattern repeated itself. One month a grenade would be thrown into a German movie theater, the next month a bomb would explode at a restaurant frequented by German officers, or a railway car reserved for German troops might be raked with gunfire. Rarely did a month pass during the occupation of Clermont-Ferrand without some incident of that sort, and occasionally there would be two attacks in quick succession, some causing deaths or injuries, others misfiring. The bloodiest episode of this sort occurred on 8 March 1944 when a German column marching along the rue Montlosier to a movie theater was attacked by resisters with grenades, killing one soldier instantly and leaving thirty-four others wounded, most of them seriously. According to German records, between D-Day and the date of their withdrawal from the area (the three months when tension was most extreme), forty-eight German soldiers were killed in this type of "terrorist" ambush in the region controlled from headquarters at Clermont-Ferrand.[73]

Although local German commanders claimed that their reactions were moderate by comparison to the actions of German troops in Paris and elsewhere in France, their response to resistance attacks in the city of Clermont-Ferrand were swift and often severe. Curfews of varying duration followed each attack, and mass arrests often leading to deportation (particularly of Jews and students or faculty from the University of Strasbourg) followed several of the early attacks. In response to 8 March 1944 attack on the rue Montlosier, the soldiers fired immediately in the direction from which they suspected the attack had come. Five persons caught in their field of fire were killed or wounded, and at least one person died in an apartment building on the place de la Poterne in a fire set off by the gunfire. The soldiers arrested eighty persons on the spot and prevented the French firemen from extinguishing the fire their gunfire had caused. In the next few days German police and courts-martial stepped up the pace of executions and deportations of those accused of involvement in the resistance. As a matter of course the people of Clermont-Ferrand, Chamalières, and Beaumont were faced with another curfew for several weeks, during which all theaters, cinemas, restaurants, and other public "pleasure places" were closed at 7:30 P.M., and all movement of vehicles was forbidden between 9:00 P.M. and 5:00 A.M., except for physicians, firemen, and others who had passes from the proper authorities.[74]

Given the predictably harsh reaction of German soldiers and police to attacks of this kind, it was understandable that resistance groups hesitated to undertake them on a large scale. The resisters themselves rarely agreed about the desirability, utility, or moral implications of such actions. The public responded to them with apprehension. Police at Clermont-Ferrand, whose reports concerning public opinion in other respects documented a steady development of widespread support for the resistance, noted sharp criticism of assassinations and bombing attacks. Many Clermontois believed that these actions did nothing to end the war and that they "can only create trouble for all of the inhabitants."[75] Early in the occupation, when the Germans began mass executions of hostages in the Parisian area in reprisals for attacks on their troops, de Gaulle had attempted to discourage resisters from taking such actions. Consequently, most of the direct attacks on German soldiers or isolated troop units, especially in northern France, were attributable to the Communist FTP, whose leadership rejected the Gaullist stance as insufficiently activist. Interestingly, in the Auvergne this pattern was reversed in that the Gaullist MUR, with a larger following in the region, was more frequently involved in direct encounters with German troops than was the Front National.

Alphonse Rozier, regional chief of the FTP, had an argument with a delegate from the Front National's national directorate over this issue. Although the Front National at Clermont-Ferrand had decided, in April 1943, to kill a German soldier as an example and a warning to the local German command, Rozier believed that his units normally were much more productively employed in sabotage operations that were more harmful to the German war effort and less costly to the civilian population in France. Despite threats from the Front National's national delegate that he would be replaced at the liberation, Rozier (who, in any event, did not plan to remain active in political affairs after the occupation had ended) stuck to his decision that local FTP units would undertake only those operations for which their armament and capabilities best suited them.[76] Beyond the issue of direct attacks on German soldiers, this incident testified to a significant feature of resistance reality, common to Communist and Gaullist organizations alike. Local resistance chiefs, who had recruited, trained, and organized their own followers, demanded and enjoyed a wide degree of latitude in directing the operation of those units.

This condition was apparent in the events surrounding the battle of the Mont Mouchet, the largest single encounter between resisters and German troops in the Auvergne. On 20 May 1944 Colonel Gaspard (Emile Coulaudon), regional chief of the Forces Français de l'Intérieur (FFI) in the Auvergne, announced that an "Army of Liberation" was being constituted in the heart of the mountains of the Auvergne. He called on all resisters to join him and the FFI in the mountains of the Margéride.[77] Coulaudon was apparently convinced by earlier conversations he had had with British agents that the Allies were going to airlift troops into the Auvergne, which was to serve as a base for military operations to liberate southern France. All of the major resistance groups in the region had been informed of this possibility. In a meeting of 9 March 1944 at Chadeleuf, all had agreed to a unified command to include representatives of the Front National and the MUR. Several weeks later, on 30 April 1944, at the Voulte Chilhac

Henry Ingrand informed Alphonse Rozier (FN) and Pierre Girardot (representative of the Communist Party) that Robert Huguet was organizing a concentration of maquis in the Monts de la Margeride. On behalf of their respective organizations, Rozier and Girardot agreed to support this concentration with guerilla attacks on the rear of German units in conjunction with Allied plans for D-Day, on the condition that their units received adequate armament.[78] In a sense, then, all of the organized resistance in the Auvergne was involved with preparations for the concentration of maquis at Mont Mouchet. In fact, the decision to call for the immediate concentration of maquis in late May 1944 was made by Coulaudon alone, without orders from London, without reference to his nominal superior Ingrand, and without consultation with the theoretically "unified" command of resistance forces. Consequently, upon hearing about Coulaudon's proclamation, Rozier (on his own initiative) traveled around the area to order all FTP units in the region not to join the concentration. His organization had not been consulted, and his men had not received the arms that they had been promised.[79] Given the outcome of the battles at Mont Mouchet and La Truyère, Rozier's decision was probably wise.

In the Monts de la Margeride the Auvergnat resistance ignored the cardinal rules of guerilla warfare: surprise and mobility. Although his comments concerned maquis operations in all of southern France, the remarks of an American officer responsible for aid to the French resistance applied very well to the Mont Mouchet:

> The FFI could have been more effective if it had confined its efforts to continual guerilla warfare, harassing the enemy at every turn, instead of attempting to concentrate huge forces of Maquis into an Army for the liberation of large towns. In very rare instances were such liberations of tactical value, or even the result of much actual combat. The Germans held what they wanted as long as they wanted to. When they moved out, the FFI moved in and the town was proclaimed "liberated," with plenty of huge headlines. The FFI had neither the arms, discipline, training nor sufficient leadership to organize a large-scale operation against a determined enemy. Especially in the last months, many targets of very good opportunity for guerilla attack, were neglected in favor of more spectacular projects.[80]

The best scholarly account of the events at Mont Mouchet and La Truyère confirms the American officer's observation. In contrast to romanticized versions claiming, "This was the greatest victory won by the French maquis against the German Army,"[81] and greatly exaggerating the number and quality of German troops and the number of German casualties, Eugène Martres has demonstrated convincingly that the concentration of maquis at the Mont Mouchet was ill-advised and tragic in its consequences.[82] Although able to field roughly the same number of troops as the

Germans (2000 to 3000 men) for the actual battles, and holding the high ground, the maquis were inferior in training and equipment, even against soldiers who were not among the Germans' best combat troops.

An American weapons specialist who was present at Mont Mouchet as part of the Allied team (which bore the collective code name BENJOIN) remarked: "Earlier arrival in the field would have been preferable. . . . There was great need of instruction in the use of weapons and other basic field subjects. The Bazooka proved almost ineffective in the hands of inexperienced men. . . . Stens [with which many maquis were armed] were almost useless and caused many accidents."[83] As Martres concluded:

> The concentrations of resisters were barely accomplished when they became a burden for those who had created them or allowed them to form and were in charge. The events took a rapid and dramatic turn when the enemy seized the initiative; illusions collapsed when the concentrations were shattered.
>
> Should one speak of a succession of "disasters"? These were at the least grave setbacks. More than 350 French deaths from 10 June to 10 July in the Cantal and its bordering regions for 40 to 50 Germans, or a proportion roughly equal to that of the Vercors (1 to 8).
>
> Above all this combat had only feeble results on the German "war machine"; it did not relieve the Allied front; it hardly delayed the enemy units and destroyed not one of them. True, on another plane it had the effect of disturbing the German command and placing their soldiers in a climate of insecurity. But by the end of June the German military leaders had measured the fragility of these concentrations. They dispersed them but devoted only a few lines to them in their reports. In their overall strategy, these operations were only incidental mishaps. The communication lines, liaisons, the cities had much more importance for the German Army.[84]

Given the size and the spectacular nature of the confrontation between resisters and German troops in the Monts de la Margeride, much attention has understandably been focused on those events as a climax to the resistance in the Auvergne.[85] Certainly, in view of the sacrifices of the combatants, as well as those of the villagers in the surrounding area whose homes were burned and whose friends and relatives were executed in reprisals by the Germans, Mont Mouchet was the appropriate site of a national monument to the French resistance. Still, in concluding this discussion of the Auvergnat resistance, we should note that paying excessive attention to the Mont Mouchet may distort one's appreciation of the resistance in the Auvergne. After all, as we have seen, resisters were active in the region long before the forced labor draft drove many future maquis to the hills and mountains of the Auvergne. Hundreds of men and women involved in the production or distribution of the underground press and those who were preparing the takeover of the administration at the liberation had placed themselves in great danger, even though their actions remained less visible than those of the maquis. Moreover, it is arguable that by emphasizing the activities of the organized resistance movements, and describing the bombings, assassinations, robberies, sabotage, and guerilla attacks that dramatized their presence, one might understate the size and importance of French opposition to the Vichy regime and the German occupation.

In order to successfully convey the atmosphere or reconstitute the history of France under the German occupation, a reformulation of the definition of resistance is required. The notion of a small band of activist conspirators must be made to square with, or be incorporated into, a broader perspective that will account for the existence of an atmosphere in 1943–1944 in which resistance was nurtured by massive and widespread popular complicity, while collaboration, its polar opposite, was discouraged, and collaborators were made to feel like outcasts in their own land. The existence of an extensive network of sympathizers and accomplices beyond the framework of the organized resistance has sometimes been overlooked or underestimated in scholarly accounts of the Vichy period.[86] The problem at one level is simply one of counting, where documentation is incomplete and often unreliable. Beyond that basic consideration are problems of definition and interpretation. We know that many individuals who were not members of resistance movements committed acts of opposition to the Vichy regime or to the Germans. How many such actions were necessary for one to be considered a resister? Or was membership in an organized group required before acts of opposition could be described as resistance? A definition that is limited to active members of organized groups has the advantage of greater precision, but such a limitation may prohibit an adequate appreciation of the *phenomenon of resistance.* A broader construction of the term *resistance,* involving a concept of *active opposition* to the Vichy regime and the Germans, is admittedly unwieldy. But it is also truer to the complex reality of the resistance in France.

To illustrate the methodological and interpretative issues involved, let us consider the conclusions of one of the most objective and fair-minded general histories of the Vichy period. Starting with what seems to be an unchallengeable proposition that most people in France were neither active resisters nor active collaborators, and repeating an earlier scholarly estimate that perhaps 400,000 persons, or 2 percent, of the adult population of France belonged to the resistance, Robert Paxton has written that if one lumps together volunteers for the Milice, regular police, and French guard units, "it is likely that *as many Frenchmen participated in 1943–44 in putting down 'disorder' as participated in active Resistance,*" adding that "the overwhelming majority of Frenchmen, however they longed to lift the German yoke, did not want to lift it by fire and sword."[87] Other authors, taking their cue from Paxton, or following a similar logic, have posited the concept of a "Franco-French" civil war at the liberation.[88] According to this scenario, extremists on either side fought it out, while the vast majority of the population stood aside, uncommitted and uninvolved. Insofar as these perspectives have served to revise an earlier viewpoint—the myth that all the French were resisters during the Nazi occupation of France— they have served a useful purpose. Our study of Clermont-Ferrand and the Auvergne suggests that the revision has been overdrawn, that the idea of a "nation of resisters," while unquestionably an exaggeration, cannot be dismissed out of hand.

If one starts with Paxton's estimate of 2 percent of the adult population, there should have been approximately 13,000 resisters in all of the Auvergne and 5000 in the Puy-de-Dôme. Although an exact accounting of membership in resistance groups is impossible, a variety of sources suggests approximate totals for the upper and lower limits of participation in the organized resistance formations. After the liberation 35,000 persons signed membership cards with the Mouvement de la Libération Nationale (successor to the MUR) and another 6500 with the Front National. These figures included many sympathizers and some latecomers to the cause and were undoubtedly inflated in terms of active participation in resistance formations. One police report noted that 15,000 was a better estimate of the clandestine adherents of the MUR/MLN in the Puy-de-Dôme, and Alphonse Rozier testified that a figure of 5000 active members of the Front National for the Auvergne was closer to the truth than the 10,000 claimed by some members of that organization at the liberation.[89] If the higher estimate suggested by these figures were accurate, *17 percent* of the adult population would have been active in the resistance in the Puy-de-Dôme; according to the lower estimate, perhaps *7 percent*. If one considers only the men enrolled in regular FFI formations at the liberation (about 16,000 for the region, 10,000 for the Puy-de-Dôme), the totals are still higher than 2 percent, but much closer to Paxton's estimate for active participation in the resistance. One might conclude, then, that the slightly higher-than-average number of FFI in the Auvergne reflected simply the fact (generally acknowledged) that in view of its mountainous terrain, the region was among the most active centers of resistance in France. But to accept such a conclusion is to accept a definition of the resistance that is much too narrow. The FFI were by no means the only active participants in the resistance in the Auvergne or elsewhere.

Consider, for example, that at least 543 persons, not included in the preceding figures, were executed (*fusillés*) "for acts of resistance" in the Auvergne (238 in the Puy-de-Dôme, 120 in the Cantal, 27 in the Haute-Loire, and 158 in the Allier); more than 1000 persons were arrested by the Germans in the Puy-de-Dôme in 1943 and 1944; and at least 1171 were deported from the Puy-de-Dôme to concentration camps in Germany or central Europe for political motives or resistance, as were hundreds of other suspected resisters in the other three departments of the region.[90] If one adds several hundred persons the French police arrested on suspicion of Communist propaganda or "antinational" activity, many of whom were sent to internment camps, and recalls the massive opposition to the forced labor draft from which several thousand Auvergnats escaped by direct acts of disobedience, the total numbers of individuals *actively involved* in opposition to Vichy and the German occupation, although still a minority, becomes a substantial minority. Moreover, to this point we have dealt only with individuals who, after a great deal of painstaking research, could be identified and counted individually. What of those men and women who, while not found on the membership lists of a resistance formation, nor on the lists of deported, executed, or outlawed, contributed in a meaningful way to the resistance? Can one omit the doctors in the Puy-de-Dôme, who although not usually members of resistance movements, sabotaged the operation of the STO and the attempted requisition of men for railroad guard duty by signing hundreds of certificates of physical incapacity for individuals who the police complained continued "to pursue as usual their occupations"?[91] What of the village priests who were credited by the resisters with numerous acts of bravery in sheltering those sought by French and German authorities, or those men and women who gave work, food, and shelter to maquis groups or individuals forced to live off of the land?[92]

On Armistice Day 1943, in response to tracts signed by the CGT, MUR, the Front National, and the Socialist Party, hundreds of workers at Ollier, Bergougnan, Michelin, and the other major factories at Clermont-Ferrand stopped working for ten or fifteen minutes at 11:00 A.M. in a symbolic protest, and even the thirty saleswomen at Prisunic joined them by crossing their arms in silence.[93] Several months before that, when Marcel Michelin had been arrested by the Germans, all 7000 employees of the Michelin firm were preparing to go out on strike until the management convinced them that such an action might bring further harm to Monsieur Michelin.[94] Beyond such specific incidents, of which there are other examples, how can one quantify the amount of passive resistance involved in high worker absence from the workplace? Especially during the last months of the occupation, absence rates were 20 percent or more above normal in the mines and factories of the Puy-de-Dôme.[95] Although loud explosions were more likely to draw attention to resistance sabotage, some resisters believed that much had been accomplished by workers in silent, but more subtle actions, such as faulty wiring of precision parts for airplane motors that were machined ever so slightly under specifications. Interestingly, at

Clermont-Ferrand's most important industrial center, the Michelin works, management insisted that there be no sabotage in terms of inferior workmanship. The company was very concerned that Michelin uphold its reputation for making only "the best tires."[96] On the other hand, the company produced far fewer tires than it was capable of manufacturing and was able to hide fairly significant quantities of material from German overseers. And, of course, the resistance movements had contacts in the factory who informed them when shipments of tires were scheduled for delivery, so that large quantities of "the best tires" would not arrive in Germany.

One could continue to enumerate an impressive array of individuals responsible for actions not attributable to the organized resistance—the fifteen-year-old girl who on her own initiative burned the records of hundreds of young men scheduled to be drafted for the STO,[97] public employees charged with collecting and melting down metal statues who saved them from destruction by delays and falsification of records,[98] directors and staff at Clermont-Ferrand's central hospital who were suspected by police of "a tacit connivance" with the resisters and political prisoners who seemed to escape with a remarkable frequency when in treatment there,[99] or numerous PTT agents singled out for particular praise by resistance leaders because of their courageous and timely warnings concerning military or police movements by German or French forces.[100] A comprehensive listing would be at least as impressive as those more spectacular sabotage or guerilla actions of the organized resistance formations.

What was the cumulative impact of all of these isolated acts of opposition to the Vichy regime and the German occupation? In terms of "effectiveness" in hindering the German war machine, the value of such actions is impossible to calculate. Who knows how many, if any, airplane motors failed in flight or tanks broke down on the eastern front as a result of the sabotage of workers in factories at Clermont-Ferrand? We do know that factories in the city producing goods for Germany were constantly behind schedule in filling orders, despite the careful supervision of German officials.[101] No one would claim that the hundreds of thousands of French men and women who listened to the BBC or read and passed on to friends copies of underground newspapers were great heroes, no more than were those who participated in symbolic strikes of short duration or mingled anonymously among crowds that gathered in city squares for fleeting demonstrations on May Day or Bastille Day. Yet these actions were illegal under Vichy France, and they signified a choice consciously made, and never entirely without risk.

Eugène Martres has concluded that one in six persons in the Cantal was associated with the resistance in one way or another as a sympathizer or active participant, suggesting that there were perhaps ten sympathizers for every resister.[102] I have been unable to arrive at a satisfactory estimate of that kind for the Puy-de-Dôme, although resistance membership and the range of its activity was certainly higher there than in the Cantal. After more than fifteen years of research into the matter, I have become convinced that (short of a roll call in the hereafter) we will never have an entirely satisfactory statistical description of the French resistance. Even the rosters of FFI and lists of the various resistance medals awarded after the liberation are highly untrustworthy gauges for minimum calculations. For example, at Clermont-Ferrand when Alphonse Rozier was asked by the prefect of the Puy-de-Dôme to suggest members of the Front National who had been particularly distinguished in their service to the resistance, Rozier suggested the name of a young woman, killed by the Germans, who had been an intelligence informant for his organization, and was a prostitute. The prefect apparently felt that there was something undignified or improper about awarding a resistance medal to a prostitute, and consequently Rozier refused to submit other names or accept a commendation himself.[103] Therefore, the numbers of people active in the Front National are understated in "official" records of resistance membership. The problem, really, is not to add some names to one roster or subtract others where claims of resistance derring-do have been exaggerated. One must go beyond the ultimately insoluble issue of precise head counts to an appreciation of the general atmosphere, the climate in which resistance operated in the last two years of the German occupation.

Earlier chapters of this study have demonstrated the relatively rapid disenchantment of the Auvergnat population with Vichy's New Order and the patent failure of most of the regime's policies, the increasingly hostile reaction to German troops and occupation policies, the overwhelmingly negative response to genuine collaborationist groups, and the evolution of public opinion toward enthusiasm for a Gaullist political alternative. Therefore, it was not surprising that disgruntled police officers reported time after time that they were unable to obtain help from the local population in their efforts to fight resistance in the Auvergne. Gendarmes in the countryside cited "enormous difficulty in the search for information about the terrorists,"[104] and referred to "a veritable conspiracy of silence and a pretense of ignorance."[105] Their colleagues in the cities remarked that witnesses to robberies or sabotage never seemed to remember license numbers and were never able to describe vehicles used by resisters, and they noted "a tacit complicity on the part of the population."[106] Numerous documents originating from central police headquarters at Vichy indicated that this situation was not peculiar to the Auvergne—that "the individuals being sought often benefit from the sympathy of the population and start off with numerous accomplices."[107]

If one is looking for heroes, a choice to remain silent was certainly not comparable to full-time commitment to resistance activism. Still, in the conditions of occupied France, the cumulative weight of such decisions was significant. Moreover, when one considers the other side of the coin, the climate in which the "forces of order" were operating, the difference was striking. As surely as a simple enumeration of membership in the FFI understates the size of the resistance in France, calculations of the total number of Milice, GMR, and French police overstate the number of those *actively opposing* the resistance. First, effective Milice membership has often been greatly exaggerated. Instead of the more than 1000 adherents suggested by some accounts, no more than 250 men actually fought resisters in Milice formations drawn from the Puy-de-Dôme.[108] According to the careful records of the officer in charge of all uniformed security forces for the Puy-de-Dôme, with headquarters at Clermont-Ferrand, 2237 men and officers were available for duty in the summer of 1944.[109] Not only was this number well below the number of armed resisters in the department, but, for reasons that were discussed earlier in this chapter, these men were by no means reliable upholders of public order.

Not without reason had the Vichy regime begun to threaten its own servants with harsher and harsher penalties for failure to carry out the government's orders.[110] In addition to the desertions on D-Day of large numbers of police and gendarmerie units surrendering their arms to maquis units, the verdicts of postliberation purge committees for the police and gendarmerie offer another indication of how little substantial support the Vichy regime enjoyed in its last months. Since the commission included a significant number of resisters, lenient treatment of officers who had actively fought the resistance was unlikely. Individual notations concerning those police examined by the purge commission suggest that it was almost impossible to be maintained on the police force if one had fired a weapon in operations against the maquis. Officers who had participated in such operations, but had shown no zeal in action versus the resistance, were not usually penalized. Under that sort of careful scrutiny, only 244 policemen in the Auvergne were sanctioned by loss of their job, transfer to another region, or some other form of punishment.[111] In other words, aside from the Milice and a few GMR units, in the last months of the occupation resisters in the Auvergne did not find Vichy's "forces of order" to be serious threats, except, of course, when they operated in conjunction with German troops or the Gestapo.

No "Franco-French" civil war took place at the liberation in the Auvergne (nor for that matter elsewhere in France) because no one was left to fight for Vichy once the German troops had departed, taking with them the last diehard supporters of a French and European New Order. The liberation of France brought the establishment of the government of Charles de Gaulle without the widespread disorder and even chaos that some had predicted. No one should have been surprised. What a minority of French men and women had fought for during four long years was what almost everyone wanted—the Germans driven out of their country and freedom to choose their own way in the future. They had given scant aid and comfort to the enemy and little more to the government of Pétain and Laval. And when a skeptic asked, "What did you do when the Germans were there?" and thought that many seemed to embrace too eagerly the myth of a nation of resisters, most French people could answer honestly: "Our hearts were in the right place."

Epilogue: The Liberation

At 11:30 Sunday morning, 27 August 1944, two days after French troops under General Philippe Leclerc had entered Paris and one day after Charles de Gaulle's triumphal procession through the streets of the nation's capital, the last of the German occupation troops left Clermont-Ferrand. Within a few hours of the Germans' departure, FFI units were in control of the liberated city, having arrested the regional prefect, the prefect of the Puy-de-Dôme, and other high administrative officials, and having established their headquarters at the prefecture. The following afternoon Henry Ingrand, de Gaulle's Commissaire de la République, and the new prefect, Pierre Sauvanet, arrived. Both men addressed a crowd of 12,000 to 15,000 people from a balcony of the prefecture. They delivered their speeches without the aid of the microphone, which had broken at the last moment, but this did not diminish the spirits of those in the crowd who listened attentively and applauded enthusiastically. No doubt in this festive atmosphere it did not matter much that most of them could not hear the speakers. The celebration also included a rousing chorus of "It's a Long Way to Tipperary," sung in honor of a British officer who had arrived with the maquis. Certainly, as one observer noted, the liberation of Clermont-Ferrand was greeted with "a unanimously favorable welcome on the part of the population which visibly expressed its great joy."[112]

The new authorities, born of the resistance to Vichy and the Germans, were determined that the transition to the new regime would be carried out in order and with justice. Resolved to punish those guilty of serious acts of collaboration, the resisters did not wish the purge to become "a bloody farce."[113] Ingrand, reminding the Auvergnats that the war was not over, addressed the following appeal to the population:

> Justice will be done. Although happily few in number, too many Frenchmen have betrayed their country and their compatriots, or even simply

obeyed slavishly the orders of the enemy. They will be punished. But justice must not be revenge. Justice must be informed, deliberate, sanctioned, such matters cannot be carried out in one day. Know how to hold back your anger and restrain your impulses.[114]

Admitting that the circumstances required the retention of certain restrictions and the exceptional status of a state of seige, Ingrand promised that these measures would be temporary and added:

Rest assured that they will not open the door to arbitrary actions. Your reconquered liberty must be that of a politically mature people who know how to impose on themselves the momentary restrictions necessary for the preservation and extension of their liberty. May everyone in his place, by his labor and his discipline, *participate* in the still immense task of the French Resistance.[115]

News reaches the Auvergne that Paris has been liberated

PARIS
est libéré
par le PEUPLE de Paris

PARIS EST LIBÉRÉ,
Paris, cerveau de la France,
Paris, cœur de la France,
Paris libéré par le peuple de France, c'est la Liberté qui renaît dans le Monde. La Victoire est en marche.
Gloire à la Résistance !
Gloire à tous nos héros, à tous nos martyrs, à tous les combattants du Maquis et de la Rue !
Gloire à tous ceux qui, depuis septembre 1939, sont morts en défendant la Patrie !
Gloire aux Alliés Libérateurs !

PAVOISEZ !
En cette heure de triomphe, nous vous demandons, citoyens et citoyennes, de pavoiser pendant trois jours triomphalement.

VIVE LA FRANCE HÉROÏQUE ET LIBRE !...

Aurillac, le 23 août 1944.   Le Comité Départemental de la Libération du Cantal.

A LA POPULATION

Citoyens et Citoyennes,

Le COMITÉ DÉPARTEMENTAL DE LA LIBÉRATION, organe suprême de la Résistance dans le département, émanation des mouvements, partis et organisations de toutes tendances, qui dans la clandestinité ont lutté contre l'oppresseur, représente sur votre sol le Gouvernement provisoire de la République.

Il vous adresse à tous son salut patriotique. Il s'incline pieusement devant la mémoire de tous les martyrs, militants obscurs de la Résistance, combattants tombés les armes à la main, civils, victimes innocentes de la barbarie hitlérienne.

Il rappelle à tous qu'il n'y a désormais d'autre légalité française que la légalité qui émane du Gouvernement provisoire de la République Française, et qu'il n'y a d'autre fraternité française que l'unité patriotique de tous les Français groupés derrière le Conseil National de la Résistance.

Il vous demande de l'aider de toutes vos forces à la préparation de l'insurrection nationale qui seule, selon le mot d'ordre du Général de Gaulle, permettra la Libération Nationale.

Pour cela, aidez par tous les moyens en votre pouvoir l'action héroïque des glorieux combattants des Forces Françaises de l'Intérieur. Adhérez en masse aux Milices Patriotiques chargées d'assurer l'ordre public et de défendre la vie et les biens des citoyens.

Unissez-vous tous derrière vos Comités locaux et votre Comité Départemental de Libération.

Vive la France !
Vive la République !

Le Comité Départemental de la Libération.

The Departmental Liberation Committee calls on all citizens to help the resisters liberate France

These laudable counsels of moderation expressed intentions shared by most local resisters with de Gaulle and his associates in the Provisional Government. But, as was true elsewhere in France, some people refused to heed such advice, and a few weeks passed before the new authorities were able to bring all of their headstrong followers into line. Although an official court-martial for the Puy-de-Dôme was established at Clermont-Ferrand within two weeks of the liberation, at least thirty persons were executed in the Puy-de-Dôme without legal procedure of any sort.[116] Some "justice at the crossroads" was probably unavoidable. Authorities reported that at first the population accepted the executions as inevitable and often "justified" in the sense that many of the victims (torturers who had helped the Gestapo or those responsible for the deportation of resisters) might have received the same treatment from the court-martial or the Cour de Justice that succeeded it in mid-November.[117] But most of the population, along with most resisters, desired the establishment of due process as soon as possible.

When a small group of resisters, including Colonel Gaspard (Coulaudon) and his brother who edited a weekly newspaper, *Le MUR d'Auvergne,* upset by de Gaulle's policy of commuting death sentences of collaborators in the interest of political appeasement, began a vitrolic campaign for a harsher purge, they rapidly fell from public favor. In contrast to appeals from the Commissaire de la République, the prefect, the Departmental Liberation Committee, and editors of all the other local newspapers that "popular justice" give way to regular judicial procedures, the *MUR d'Auvergne* called on citizens to break into prisons where necessary to ensure justice by "the rope." Titles of editorials, such as "Justice? Non: Vengeance? Oui" and "Criminelle Indulgence" with reference to "light" penalties for certain collaborators suggested the paper's viewpoint.[118] At other times the threats could be less direct, if not exactly subtle. Referring to the Auvergnat tradition of slaughtering a pig at Christmas, and noting that a particular collaborator had gained nine kilos while in jail, the *MUR d'Auvergne* wrote:

> They say: "Jam for the pigs!" around here when the pigs are very fat, near Christmas. . . . But that's another story![119]

Although disenchantment with the purge was admittedly growing along with a general recognition that the later the trial, the lighter the penalty was apt to be, most Clermontois viewed these articles in the *MUR* as extremely provocative and ill-advised. Certainly, Coulaudon did not benefit politically from his position. Police predicted that resistance lists might suffer at the polls from the presence of Coulaudon, noting that his political adversaries claimed that "if one cannot guess who will be at the head of

AVIS
à la Population

PORT DES BRASSARDS DES F.F.I.

Seules les Forces Françaises de l'I· térieur sont autori-
sées au port du brassard.

Deux types de brassards sont prévus, l'un tricolore,
l'autre sur toile blanche, les deux brassards doivent porter la
mention F. F. I. et le cachet rouge · Vive de Gaulle ».

**Aucun autre brassard n'est auto-
risé.**

Les patriotes qui désirent être incorporés aux **Milices Patriotiques, réserve des F.F.I.,**
seront invités très prochainement à présenter leur demande
aux autorités compétentes.

**Le Comité Departemental
de la Libération**

Proclamation that only regular troops (FFI) are authorized to wear armbands
with Gaullist insignia

the list, one could hardly go wrong in affirming that Colonel GASPARD will
finish dead last."[120]

Local officials in the Auvergne intended the purge to be firm, rapid, and
fair, and the evidence suggests that on balance it was. Most suspects were
arrested by the police or the FFI within weeks of the liberation. Following
a scenario reenacted during the liberation era in cities all over France,
women accused of "sentimental relations with the enemy" were among
the first victims of the purge. In the week that followed Clermont-Ferrand's
liberation, a "commission for the examination of arrests" sitting at the
city's central police office ordered the release of seventy local women after
their heads had been shaven as a token of their "dishonor."[121] Of the 1809
persons arrested in the Puy-de-Dôme relative to "acts of collaboration,"
1413 were arrested within two months of the liberation, of whom more

than one-third (553) were released almost at once. Ultimately, more than one-half (56 percent) of the suspects were released unconditionally. Slightly more than one-third were brought before tribunals, either a court-martial, the Cour de Justice, or a Chambre d'indignité national. In keeping with evidence that active collaboration had been slight in the region, only 119 persons, including those judged in absentia, were condemned to death (of whom 54 had been executed by 15 February 1946), and another 123 were sentenced to forced labor.[122]

Of course, it is much easier for a historian, weighing the evidence in retrospect, to speak of the relative moderation and justice of the purge than it was for many persons at the time. The prefect of the Allier probably spoke for many Auvergnats when he commented that "the purge has satisfied no one."[123] Perhaps inevitably, some of the French felt the purge was too lenient, and others believed it too severe. Early consensus about the legitimacy of quick justice for the most conspicuous collaborators broke down as the process stretched out into months and then years. As local officials at Clermont-Ferrand admitted, mistakes were made—some that could be corrected, others that could not. For example, with regard to the arrests of persons suspected of membership in the Milice, the head of the Police Judiciaire at Clermont-Ferrand wrote:

> One must take into account that the various lists in possession of the Services must not be considered rigorously exact. As affairs have developed, some omissions have been discovered, as well as persons whose names were on the lists who, after investigation, are recognized as never having belonged to the Milice.[124]

Errors resulted from honest mistakes, but could also be the product of personal vendettas, finding an outlet in the highly charged atmosphere of the liberation. An investigation that police attributed to a neighborhood feud revealed that a sixteen-year-old girl accused of working for the Gestapo was completely innocent. The only piece of evidence produced as "proof" of her guilt had been the stub from a checkbook which read: "The amount for your collaboration in September 1943."[125] The "collaboration" in question was some typing the girl had done for a local publishing concern. In this case the young woman was fortunate to have undergone only the embarrassment of an investigation.

Ironically, the good intentions of the Gaullist government to restore republican legality swiftly at times led to tragic consequences for individuals facing the wrath of less scrupulous neighbors whose equanimity had been sorely tested by events during the occupation. Henry Ingrand was criticized by the minister of justice for retaining in custody several hundred persons who were suspected of collaboration, but against whom a legal case could not be made because of insufficient evidence. In reply Ingrand argued that prudence and wisdom should take precedence over legality in view of the circumstances (Ingrand had in mind popular attitudes at the moment of the return of deportees from German concentration camps or forced labor sites):

> . . . these measures probably would have the effect of avoiding most "punitive direct actions" or most of the "executions" because these persons, currently escaping Justice and not legally internable, occasionally pay with their lives for crime which, normally, would have cost them several months in prison.[126]

When making his case to the minister, the Commissaire de la République had on the desk before him a police report concerning a woman from Aigueperse, a small town north of Clermont-Ferrand. Released from custody in early June 1945, the woman had returned to her home. The day of her return the door of her house was blown open with explosives and she was taken out into the street and beaten up. The next day a crowd of 80 to 100 men and women dragged her from her home and hanged her from a railroad crossway. Police reported that news had reached Aigueperse that same day that Monsieur Bernard, a political deportee, and one of twenty-five persons arrested by the Gestapo in the vicinity of Aigueperse, had died. Popular belief that the woman had been responsible for his deportation was cited as the motive for the lynching, and the report concluded that "it does not seem exaggerated to say that it [the hanging] was favorably received by all of the population of Aigueperse which was indignant about the return of this person to the city."[127]

The incident at Aigueperse coincided with a renewed wave of bombing attacks in the Puy-de-Dôme at the homes of suspected collaborators for whose guilt there was no legally compelling evidence. As with the lynching at Aigueperse and several other executions in the Auvergne in the spring and summer of 1945, police emphasized that passions had been excited by the pitiful condition of returning deportees following the surrender of Germany.[128] Although striking, and certainly unsettling to most Auvergnats, these executions and bombings were only one aspect of the liberation era, and they should be viewed in perspective. As Charles-Louis Foulon has demonstrated in a superb study of the liberation, and as a particularly astute American observer who visited many liberated towns with the army noticed, most rumors of widespread disorder in France at the liberation were highly exaggerated.[129] Echoing what was, by and large, true elsewhere in the country, one month after the liberation of Clermont-Ferrand, the prefect of the Puy-de-Dôme reported to Ingrand:

> The arrival at Clermont-Ferrand of the FFI troops was greeted with an undescribable enthusiasm by the population. The correct bearing, as well as the decided and disciplined allure of all the military formations, strongly

impressed the public. The Clermontois had, from the first day, the sensation that the change of regimes would be carried out in order, in contrast to the fears expressed by many people. . . . This discipline and order, that we believe to be indispensable were thus attained more rapidly than one might have hoped for.[130]

To be sure, as elsewhere in France, in the first days following the liberation, residents of Clermont-Ferrand complained that young FFI were racing automobiles recklessly around the city. Before the resisters completed the establishment of the new administration, arrests and requisitions were carried out on questionable authority by individual maquis units and a variety of impromptu commissions. Years later, Ingrand recalled that some of his associates in the resistance were more difficult than others to control:

> In reality, nothing could better recapture the situation before and during the first days after the Liberation than to compare COULAUDON and his group to what we know about the Islamic students in Iran at the beginning of the revolution. That was why the rapid return to republican order did not always pass without incidents and the population rapidly judged the men involved.[131]

But as Ingrand noted in his monthly report two months after the liberation of Clermont-Ferrand, "one must know how to displease, even one's friends,"[132] and he was determined to restore normal conditions and regular government services as soon as possible.

In this ambition Ingrand was aided enormously by the fact that Robert Huguet agreed to serve temporarily as general police intendant for the region, and the prefect and leaders of the Departmental Liberation Committee were all well known to Ingrand from their shared experience in the resistance. In carrying out the most pressing immediate tasks—the purge, dissolution of the Milice Patriotique, incorporation of the FFI into the regular army, and restoring transportation, communication lines, satisfactory levels of economic production, and food supply—the administrators, confirmed in their powers by de Gaulle, and the resistance-born liberation committees generally agreed on what needed to be done and worked together smoothly. Although ultimate authority was vested by the government in the Commissaire de la République and the prefect, they were attentive to advice from the various commissions established by the liberation committees. This was true both because they had been ordered by the minister of the interior to consult the committees regularly and because, as Sauvanet told Ingrand regarding the situation at Clermont-Ferrand following the liberation, "in practice it is very difficult to reject" proposals from the liberation committee.[133]

Although both departmental and local liberation committees were desig-

nated "consultative organs," their recommendations carried the force of
law for several weeks. Moreover, despite occasional disputes over jurisdiction, the administration credited the committees with extremely valuable
assistance in several domains and appreciated the fact that the committees
"rounded angles and in difficult cases ameliorated the relations between
the civilian population and military elements from the FFI."[134] Describing
the active cooperation of the Departmental Liberation Committee with the
prefecture in the domains of food services, military-civilian relations, the
purge, and preparations for upcoming municipal elections, the prefect
claimed that "it would seem difficult, in this regard, to have obtained results more satisfactory than those realized in the Puy-de-Dôme."[135]

Some resisters in the Auvergne and elsewhere in France called for the
transformation of the liberation committees into permanent instruments of
government with extensive powers, but they were in a minority. In February 1945 the Departmental Liberation Committee of the Puy-de-Dôme
resolved to take a less active role in public affairs, "to work from now on
only in function of the role originally assigned to the Liberation Committees, as consultative organs."[136] Most of those former resisters interested
in active participation in politics soon drifted away from the mantle of
their respective resistance movements and returned to the fold of the established political parties. The slogans and actions of the Front National were
virtually indistinguishable from the Communist Party, and the majority of
the members of the MUR/MLN supported the Socialist Party. In July
1945 Ingrand noted that out of 35,000 members at the end of 1944, barely
2500 adherents of the MLN in the Puy-de-Dôme bothered to renew their
membership in 1945, concluding:

> It is easy to see that those few persons who come to the meetings of the
> FN or the MLN find themselves surrounded by a much more numerous
> attendance at the meetings of the communist or socialist parties.
> It appears that after the early enthusiasm that drew the public to the re-
> sistance movements, the voters have the sentiment that only the political
> parties have the material possibility of realizing their aspirations.[137]

In the aftermath of four bitter years of hardship, suffering, and terror,
what were their aspirations? Writing in September 1944, the day after
50,000 people had joined a demonstration at Clermont-Ferrand to com-
memorate the anniversary of the first French republic, the prefect of the
Puy-de-Dôme speculated: "The population of the Puy-de-Dôme will not
be frightened by a hardy social policy, but a wise one, one which should
moreover assure for our Country the respect and friendship of other nations," and concluded that the great majority hoped for "a strong, democratic Republic, enamored of progress and equitable for all."[138] In political
terms, these sentiments translated into votes for parties of the left. In line

with the pattern for the country at large, both national and local elections in 1945 in the Auvergne reflected "a very noticeable push to the left."[139] The major beneficiaries of this trend were the Communist and Socialist parties, although many candidates elected in the first elections ran on resistance (rather than party) tickets. The Radical Party, traditionally the dominant party in local elections in the region, and the conservative parties lost much of the substantial support they had enjoyed before the war. According to Ingrand's report on the municipal elections of April 1945:

> In the region, and more especially in the Puy-de-Dôme, it appears that men who come from the resistance have consolidated their political situation only in the measure that they have rejoined the traditional political parties. Then they have carried these parties by their influence and shared their prestige with them.[140]

Within a year after the liberation, politics were back to normal (or almost). As Alexandre Varenne, the widely respected editor of *La Montagne,* now Clermont-Ferrand's leading newspaper, had written months earlier: "The storm is passing by. . . . France has not forgotten the enemy to pursue, the injuries to be salved, the ruins to rebuild," but at the liberation the country had avoided "the horrid sacrilege of civil war . . . the head-chopping Revolution."[141] Perhaps Varenne's hopes were never entirely fulfilled. He had longed to "see once again the peaceable France that we knew when public order had as its defenders four gendarmes in the canton with their brigadier and for each church steeple a simple rural policeman armed with his badge of office."[142] Official observers indicated that at the liberation many Clermontois were guilty of confusing hopes with realities in anticipating an immediate return to a life of plenty, when the war was yet to be won and disruptions created by resistance sabotage or enemy destruction had still to be overcome.[143]

Still, a year after the liberation, the only German soldiers in the Auvergne were those prisoners of war employed on forestry or construction projects in the region. The Michelin plant was rapidly approaching prewar production levels, supplied with raw materials and filling orders for the U.S. army. Offices that formerly housed the headquarters of the resistance movements were closed, and bombings at the homes of suspected collaborationists were tapering off. Police turned their attention to traffic accidents and petty larceny, the everyday chores of officers-of-the-law in peacetime. Liberty and freedom of expression had returned to the political arena. A page was turning in the history of the Auvergne, and of France. On 18 October 1945, some 180 Indochinese workers marched through the streets of Thiers to protest the arrest of their fellow nationals at Paris and Marseilles for distribution of "subversive tracts."[144] Stopping to observe the curious spectacle of Vietnamese workers demonstrating in the heart of the Auvergne, only the most prescient among the crowd of half-interested on-lookers might have realized that they were witnessing an ever-so-small step toward the end of the Fourth Republic. The occupation and the liberation, if receding from view, were still fresh in everyone's mind. The years of "sorrow and pity" would not be easily forgotten, but new problems were at hand that would require the Clermontois, Auvergnats, and all of the French to make new choices.

Notes

Chapter 1

(N.B. The following abbreviations will be used throughout these notes: Cl-Fd (Clermont-Ferrand), PdD (Puy-de-Dôme), and Rü.K.K. (Rüstungskontroll-kommission). Unless specified otherwise, all references to dossier numbers are to documents found in the Archives départementales du Puy-de-Dôme, Clermont-Ferrand.)

1. *La Montagne,* 23 October 1978.
2. For example, *Le Moniteur,* 23 March 1942. In this particular case, the reference was to reactions to Pétain's visit to Clermont-Ferrand. The editor claimed reactions contrasted sharply to typical attitudes of indifference. *La Montagne* and *L'Avenir,* two other local newspapers, as well as many periodic police reports, used the same phrases repeatedly with reference to public attitudes at Clermont-Ferrand. See *M05670,* Rapport, Le Commissaire de la Rèpublique, Période du 15 au 30 Juin 1945, for an example of the same sentiment in the liberation era: ". . . on connaît le caractère froid et peu démonstratif des Auvergnats . . ."
3. *La Montagne,* 1 July 1940.
4. Although political considerations played some role in the choice of location for the new government (Lyon, for instance being considered the fiefdom of Edouard Herriot, as Clermont-Ferrand was considered to be under Laval's influence), the rejection of Clermont was based primarily on considerations of convenience and accommodations. Robert O. Paxton, *Vichy France* (New York: Alfred A. Knopf, 1972), p. 18, and Henri Michel, *Vichy: Année 40* (Paris: Robert Laffont, 1966), pp. 57–58, mention the political factors.
5. *Le Moniteur,* 1 July 1940.
6. *La Montagne,* 2 July 1940.
7. *Le Moniteur,* 3 July 1940.
8. *La Montagne,* 1 July 1940.
9. *T01532* is a dossier concerning supplementary food distributions to school children in the Puy-de-Dôme. Among the correspondence in this file is a letter from the departmental delegate of the Secours National to the Inspecteur d'Academie at Clermont-Ferrand stating: "Le Département du Puy-de-Dôme est un des plus riches de France et l'un des mieux ravitaillés.

Il n'a pas été sinistré, ou tellement peu." After the liberation, weighing evidence of several cases of harsh reprisals for resistance activity, investigators concluded that German police and military repression had been more savage in other parts of France.

10. *R01522,* 4 March 1943, Général Fève, Chef du Service départemental des prisonniers de Guerre à M. le Préfet du Puy-de-Dôme; *R01522,* 4 October 1942, Prefecture PdD, "Le Paquet du Soldat" notes a minimum of 16,500 POWs at that time. See also *M03950,* 2 October 1943, Gilbert Sardier, Chef Départemental, Légion Française des Combattants, à M. le Préfet Régional, Cl-Fd. Dossiers *R01521* and *R01532* include the results of a census of POWs from the PdD taken in December 1941, and a nominative list of all POWs from Cl-Fd.

11. See Chapter 5.

12. The reader should be aware that statistical information in this study, whether involving POWs, refugees, deportation, population censuses, economic conditions, or anything else, is drawn from a variety of often contradictory documentation. The author has attempted to establish the most satisfactory possible extrapolation from the data available (sometimes as many as fifteen or twenty different figures are given). The circumstances of the era were such that individuals refused to cooperate with census takers and other statisticians, and officials often falsified figures to protect themselves or others. Therefore, less precision than might be desirable is inevitable when dealing with numbers.

13. Simon Mathew Karter, "Coercion and Resistance—Dependence and Compliance: The Germans, Vichy, and the French Economy." Diss., University of Wisconsin at Madison, 1976; see especially Chapters 2 and 4.

14. *M07191,* 24 March 1943, Rapport Mensuel, Kastner, Commissaire Central à M. le Préfet Délégué.

15. Among others, Paxton, *Vichy France;* Karter, "Coercion and Resistance"; Alan S. Milward, *The New Order and the French Economy* (Oxford: Oxford University Press, 1970); and A. Sauvy, "Démographie et Economie de la France au Printemps 1944," paper presented at the International Colloquium on the Liberation of France, Paris, 1974.

16. Milward, *The New Order,* pp. 277 and 283.

17. *M07871,* Comités Sociaux des entreprises (1943–1944). A survey of the industrial establishments at Cl-Fd in late 1943 and early 1944 noted that Michelin's economic situation was "50% de ce qu'elle était auparavant," but the situation varied from month to month, and a 40 to 50 percent figure seems reasonable for the entire period of the occupation.

18. *M05755,* Questionnaire #4, Légion Française (1942?); *M06536,* 16 January 1943, Commissaire Principal Renseignements Généraux à M. le Préfet Délégué; compare statistics in Institut National de la Statistique et des Etudes Economiques, *Annuaire statistique* for 1939 and vol. 56, covering 1940–1945.

19. *M06619,* 20 December 1943, Rapport de l'Ingénieur des T.P.E. (Mines).

20. Sauvy, "Démographie et Economie," pp. 13–14, notes that for food products the shortages from lower productivity were twice as important as German requisitions.

21. *M07191,* 25 September 1942, Commissaire de Police de Chamalières-Royat à M. l'Intendant Régional de Police, Rapport Mensuel; 22 Septem-

ber 1943, Commissaire de Chamalières-Royat à M. le Commissaire Central, Rapport Mensuel; *M06378,* 22 September 1942, Maire de La Bourboule à M. le Préfet Régional, Cl-Fd; *M07196,* 25 May 1943, Commissaire Principal Chef du Service des Renseignements Généraux du PdD à M. l'Intendant Régional de Police; *M07170,* 25 November 1941, Hôteliers et Commerçants de St.-Nectaire à M. le Préfet du PdD; *M07199,* 7 April 1943, Maire de Chatel-Guyon à M. le Sous-Préfet de Riom.

22. *M08761,* 8 February 1940, Secrétaire d'Etat à la Production Industriel et au Travail à M. le Préfet, PdD; *M07191,* 27 February 1942, Commissaire Central à M. l'Intendant de Police, Rapport Mensuel; *M07871,* "Conchon-Quinette"; *M07871,* "Manufacture de chapeaux (Maison A. Maury Benech et Maury, fils)"; *M07191,* 25 August 1942, Commissaire du 1° Arrondissement à M. l'Intendant de Police; *M07761,* P.V. de la Commission Départementale des Textiles et Cuirs, 1941 (?); *M03822,* 30 September 1941, Commissaire de Police, Chef de la Sûreté à M. le Préfet du PdD, Rapport Mensuel; *M07191,* 25 April 1942, Commissaire de Police, 1° Arrondissement, à M. le Commissaire Central; *M07191,* 15 December 1942, Renseignements Généraux, Cl-Fd, à M. le Directeur des Renseignements Généraux, Vichy; *M07191,* 24 July 1943, Commissaire Central à M. le Préfet Délégué, Rapport Mensuel; *M07191,* 24 March 1942, Commissaire de Police du 1° Arrondissement à M. l'Intendant de Police; *M07191,* 22 December 1942, Commissaire Divisionnaire Renseignements Généraux à M. le Directeur Renseignements Généraux (Vichy); and *M07164,* March 1944, Commissaire de Police du 3° Arrondissement à M. le Commissaire Central.

23. *M06355,* 12 May 1942, Circulaire #102, Georges Hilaire, Sec. Gén. pour l'Administration, Ministère de l'Intérieur, à M. les Préfets Régionaux; *M07188,* Note, 24 June 1942, Tous Services de Police; *M03823,* 31 October 1941, le Commissaire de Police, Chef de la Sûreté, à M. le Préfet Régional; *M03811,* 3 July 1941, Rapport, M. Pic, Inspecteur Départemental du Travail; *M07871,* Rapport, "Imprimerie Banque de France-Chamalières; Milward, *The New Order,* pp. 59–64, includes a chart indicating the sharp rise in the fiduciary issue.

24. Milward, *The New Order,* p. 59.

25. *M07037–M07055* contain extensive records accounting for the expenditures of prefectures, communes, and so forth; *M06472,* 9 July 1942, Guerrin, Préfet Délégué à M. le Ministre de l'Intérieur; *M06472,* Visites Administratives du Secrétaire Général, 1942–43, 4 March 1943, Guerrin, Préfet Délégué, à M. le Préfet Régional.

26. *M07849,* "Compte Rendu Intégral de la Réunion des Présidents des Régions Economiques de la Zone Non Occupée," Lyon, 11 May 1941, submitted to the prefect by M. Dousset, Président de la Région de Cl-Fd, 17° région économique (Cantal, PdD, and l'Allier).

27. *M03822,* 2 December 1940, Le Préfet du PdD à Sec. d'Etat à l'Intérieur, Rapport Mensuel.

28. *M07191,* 27 January 1942, Commissaire de Police du 1° Arrondissement à M. l'Intendant de Police, Cl-Fd.

29. *M06670,* "Rapport du Comité Charbonnier Départemental," 1942; the same file contains several other reports on the fuel situation.

30. *M08761,* 26 August 1941, Préfet du PdD aux Maires. The prefect noted

that rationing required difficult and delicate choices. While there were no fixed rules, the mayors were urged to use good sense and equity and told that *need* must be the key criterion.

31. *M07191*, Commissaire Central à M. le Préfet du PdD, Rapport Mensuel, 25 June 1943.

32. Z4509/52/17 PRO, France No. 32, 30 March 1943, from Lisbon, Political Intelligence Department, "Conditions in Clermont-Ferrand." The report was based on information provided by Jean Mousset, who, from May 1941 to November 1942, was secretary general for the *Journal des Débats*, published at Cl-Fd. This and other British documents cited in this study were consulted at the Public Record Office (PRO), Kew Gardens, England.

33. Z1927/81/17, 20 February 1942, Mr. Hoyar Millar, British Embassy, Washington, D.C., to Mr. Mack, PRO (Kew).

34. See Chapter 7.

35. *M07191*, 25 April 1942, Commissaire de Police du 1° Arrondissement à M. l'Intendant de Police; see Chapter 7 for greater detail on the German involvement in the local economy.

36. *M08302*, "Dossier: Comité de Confiscation des Profits Illicites" contains hundreds of documents relative to economic collaboration and black-market profiteering; others are in *M08276*.

37. *M07191*, 25 May 1943, Commissaire Principal de Police, 1° Arrondissement, à M. le Commissaire Central.

38. *M06357*, folder June, July, August 1943, Renseignements Généraux N° 4618, Commissaire Principal, Chef du Service des Renseignements Généraux du PdD à M. le Commissaire Divisionnaire, Chef Régional des Renseignements Généraux à Cl-Fd, "Objet: Enquête dans les usines métallurgiques du secteur de Clermont-Ferrand."

39. *M03822*, 29 May 1941, Rapport Mensuel, Commissaire de Police du 2° Arrondissement à M. le Préfet.

40. *M03823*, 13 November 1941, Ministre de l'Intérieur à MM. les Préfets, Synthèse de Rapports Mensuels pour Novembre.

41. Marcel Ophuls, *The Sorrow and the Pity* (New York: Outerbridge & Lazard, 1972), pp. 28–29.

42. *M07191*, 25 August 1943, Commissaire Central à M. le Préfet Délégué, Rapport Mensuel.

43. *M06508*, 13 March 1941, Commission Départemental d'Etudes sur le coût de la vie.

44. *M06485*, "Note: Sur l'organisation des soupes dans les établissements d'enseignement secondaires de Clermont-Ferrand," 5 October 1942, le Recteur de l'Academie de Cl-Fd.

45. The American Red Cross also sent packets of clothing and paid for several hundred children to spend a month at summer camp.

46. *M05648*, 29 April 1943, Cl-Fd, Rapport sur l'activité du Service médical . . . pendant . . . Mars 1943.

47. *M06619*, Rapport de l'Ingénieur des T.P.E. (Mines), 20 December 1943; *M06619*, 5 December 1943, Renseignements Généraux, Commissaire Principal à M. le Préfet du PdD.

48. *M07788*, 1 February 1942, Paul Brun, Préfet Régional, Rapport Mensuel d'Information.

49. *M07191*, 24 June 1943, Situation Générale du District . . . de Vichy, Rapport Mensuel/Situation Morale et Economique.
50. A complete description of the system is found in a twenty-five page document, "Food Rationing in France," PRO (Kew), FO 371 31945 X/N 09947.
51. *M03770*, 8 March 1941, René Kastner, Commissaire de Police du 2° Arrondissement à M. le Préfet.
52. *M04860*, 24 January 1942, N° 115 Pol. Cab., le Ministre Sec. d'Etat à l'Intérieur à Messieurs les Préfets Régionaux de la Zone Libre.
53. Documents in files *M06565*, *M07149*, and *M07191*.
54. *M06422*, Secours National, la campagne d'Hiver, 1942.
55. *M06565*, 10 June and 12 June 1943. Commissaire Central Kastner à M. l'Intendant de Police, and several other reports in the same file.
56. *M07193*, 4 October 1943, Commissaire Divisionnaire, Chef Régional de la Sécurité Publique à M. l'Intendant de Police, Cl-Fd.
57. *M06373*, Télégrammes 1943, 28 January 1943.
58. *M07191*, 27 January 1942, Commissaire de Police du 1° Arrondissement à M. l'Intendant de Police, Cl-Fd; *M07788*, Brun, Préfet Régional, Rapport Mensuel d'Information, February 1942; *M07191*, 22 December 1942, Commissaire Divisionnaire Renseignements Généraux à M. le Directeur Renseignements Généraux (Vichy); *M07191*, 15 December 1942, Renseignements Généraux (Cl-Fd) à M. le Directeur Renseignements Généraux (Vichy).
59. *M07191*, 24 October 1942, Commissaire de Police du 2° Arrondissement, Cl-Fd, à M. le Préfet; *M05756*, 4 March 1943, Gilbert Sardier, Chef de la Légion Française des Combattants, Département du PdD, à M. le Préfet Régional.
60. Sardier, op. cit.
61. *T01455*, in "L'Ecole et la Famille," attached to 21 September 1943, Préfet Délégué à M. l'Inspecteur d'Académie.
62. *M03823*, 13 November 1941, Ministre de l'Intérieur aux Préfets Zone Libre, Synthèse Mois d'Octobre 1941.
63. *M07191*, 25 August 1942, Commissaire Central à M. l'Intendant de Police.
64. *M07191*, 24 October 1942, Rapport Mensuel, Commissaire Central à M. l'Intendant de Police.
65. *M07191*, 15 December 1942, Commissaire Divisionnaire, Chef Régional des Renseignements Généraux à M. le Directeur des Renseignements Généraux (Vichy).
66. *M07191*, 25 May 1943, Kastner, Commissaire Central à M. le Préfet Délégué, Rapport Mensuel.
67. *M07164*, 25 March 1944, Commissionaire Central, Repport Mensuel.
68. *M07164*, 24 March 1944, Commissaire de Police du 2° Arrondissement à M. le Commissaire Central.
69. Reports in 1942 and 1943 indicated that as much as one-half the milk, cheese, and potatoes being produced found their way onto the black market. *M05770*, 13 January 1942, Le Chef de District Principal Leune, Chef du Service du Contrôle des Ressources à M. l'Intendant, Directeur Départemental du Ravitaillement Général du PdD; and *M05756*, Sardier,

Chef Départemental de la Légion Française des Anciens Combattants, "Rapport sur l'activité à la commission du Ravitaillement."

70. Z4509/52/17 France N° 32, 30 March 1943, from Lisbon, Political Memorandum to Political Intelligence Department from Ridley Prentice, "Conditions in Clermont-Ferrand," PRO (Kew).

71. Attached to the police commissioners' monthly reports in *M07191* are statistics for the activity of the Police Economique. See also folders *M05538-40*, *M07881*, and especially *M07154* containing statistical information, directives and regulations for the Police Economique, and a series of dossiers of individuals involved in the black market.

72. *M07164* contains a file for January–March 1943 concerning Maupoint.

73. *M06615*, 27 March 1942, N° 104 CT, Darlan à M. le Secrétaire d'Etat à l'Intérieur for transmission to the prefects; *M06665*, 29 June 1942 and 2 July 1942, Sec. Gén. à la Police, René Bousquet aux Préfets.

74. *M03822*, 5 October 1941, Ch. Chevreux, Préfet, Rapport Mensuel d'Information.

75. A sampling of the sources related to the problems of farmers and the black market includes: *M03822*, 5 October 1941, Ch. Chevreux, Préfet, Rapport Mensuel d'Information; *M05755*, "Enquête sur les Bases du Ravitaillement," Légion–Agriculture Commission (1943?), and Questionnaire #4 (1942?); *M06473*, N° 433, 4 August 1942, Sous-Préfet de Thiers à M. le Préfet Délégué Cabinet; *M07191*, Commissaire Central à M. le Préfet Délégué, 24 July 1943, Rapport Mensuel; and Z4449/52/17, a copy of an interrogation of a French student who arrived in Great Britain, 15 March 1943, after farming for the past two years near Etroussat.

76. *M07188*, 8 August 1942, Intendant de Police à M. le Maire de Cl-Fd.

77. *M07191*, 24 March 1942. Commissaire du 1° Arrondissement à M. l'Intendant de Police. Other sources for this problem include *M07191*, 24 August 1942, Commissaire du 3° Arrondissement à M. l'Intendant de Police; and *M03822*, 30 April 1941, Commissaire de Police, Chef de la Sûreté à M. le Préfet du PdD.

78. *M03954*, 14 January 1942, Paul Brun, Préfet Régional, à Messieurs les Maires.

79. *M03954*, 24 February 1942, draft of prefect's notice to newspaper editors, and interviews with Alphonse Rozier. When these letters were signed, the names of their authors were often turned over to the resistance by postal workers. There is, of course, no way to verify the exact numbers of *authors* of such letters. Recently, André Halimi, a French journalist, has published hundreds of examples of letters of denunciation in his book, *La Délation sous l'occupation* (Paris: Alain Moreau, 1983), but has reference to three million letters of denunciation, as claimed by German police, seems excessive.

80. Paxton, *Vichy France*, p. 366. The OPA office in Clermont-Ferrand was located at 16, place Delille.

81. *M06372*, 13 May 1942, Note "Pour le Préfet Régional," Directeur du Cabinet, De Peretti Della Rocca.

82. *M07788*, 5 July 1942, Honoré Guerrin, Préfet Délégué, Rapport Mensuel Régional d'Information, 1942.

83. *M07191*, 19 January 1943, Lt. Col. Blachère, Cmdt. 13° Légion de Gen-

darmerie à M. le Chef du Gouvernement et à M. le Préfet Régional, Rapport sur la Physionomie Morale, Economique et Industrielle.

84. *M07188*, 19 October 1942, Ingénieur en Chef de l'Aéronautique (Insp. Gl. de la Production Industrielle Cl-Fd) à M. le Préfet Régional; and *M07183*, 4 November 1942, Préfet Régional (Directeur de Cabinet) à M. l'Intendant de Police.

85. *M07191*, 24 October 1942, Commissaire de Police du 2° Arrondissement Cl-Fd à M. le Préfet du PdD; *M07191*, 25 March 1943, Rapport Mensuel, Kastner, Commissaire Central, à M. le Préfet Délégué; *M07191*, 23 February 1943, Commissaire Central Cl-Fd à M. le Préfet Délégué.

86. *M07191*, 25 November 1942, Commissaire Central à M. le Préfet Délégué; *M07191*, 12 December 1942, Commissaire Divisionnaire Renseignements Généraux (Cl-Fd) à M. le Directeur Renseignements Généraux (Vichy).

87. *M07191*, 24 October 1942, Commissaire Central à M. l'Intendant de Police, Rapport Mensuel; *M07191*, 24 October 1942, Commissaire de Police du 2° Arrondissement Cl-Fd à M. le Préfet du PdD.

88. *M06357*, 12 March 1943, Renseignements Généraux #785.; *M07183*, 18 March 1943, Kastner, Commissaire Central à M. le Préfet Délégué.

89. *M07788*, 5 February 1943, Paul Brun, Préfet Régional de Cl-Fd, Rapport Mensuel.

90. Ibid.

91. *M07183*, "Relève Departs," 17 February 1943, Commissaire Principal des Renseignements Généraux de l'Allier à M. le Préfet de l'Allier.

92. *M03816*, "Réunion des Préfets des départements de la région de Clermont-Ferrand, 30 Decembre 1942."

93. Milward, *The New Order*, pp. 121–124.

94. *M07191*, 26 December 1942, Commissaire Central Cl-Fd à M. le Préfet Délégué.

95. Ibid.; see also *M07191*, 23 February 1943, Commissaire Central à M. le Préfet Délégué, Rapport Mensuel.

96. *M07191*, 24 October 1942, Commissaire Central à M. l'Intendant de Police, Rapport Mensuel.

97. *M05668*, September 1944, "Rapport sur l'activité des Services de la Main d'oeuvre—Départ des travailleurs en Allemagne," noted that the phrase "2% seulement de départs, bravo Clermont!" had led to much closer surveillance by the German police of local STO operations, and helped to account for the fact that by the end of the occupation 73 percent of the male personnel of the Service de la Main d'oeuvre had been arrested.

98. *M07301*, "P.V. de la réunion du 2 Août 1943," in which Préfet Régional Brun met with the Préfet Délégué Guerrin and all police commissioners and STO directors, describing his meeting in Paris, 30 July 1943, with top German and French labor officials. A new series of strict orders for a crackdown on STO deserters followed the meeting. Police officers and others were threatened with arrest and deportation for the STO if they did not cooperate fully. Obviously, the government suspected that many of them had not been doing so in the past.

99. *La Montagne*, 18 February 1979, summarizes a lecture by Professor G. A. Manry, "Volontaires et réfractaires chamalièrois sous la Révolution et l'Empire."

100. Emmanuel Le Roy Ladurie and Paul Dumont, "Quantitative and Carto-
graphical Exploitation of French Military Archives, 1819–26," pp. 74–76
and 94, in *Historical Studies Today* (New York: W. W. Norton, 1972),
edited by Felix Gilbert and Stephen R. Graubard.
101. *M07191*, 25 August 1943, Commissaire Central à M. le Préfet Délégué,
Rapport Mensuel; see also *M07157*, 5 April 1944, Commandant Sect.
d'Ambert, Gendarmerie, Rapport; and *M07191*, 25 May 1943, Commissaire de Police de Beaumont-Aubière à M. le Commissaire Central.
102. *M05664*, 26 August 1943, Deutsche Regional Werbestelle, Cl-Fd, Nachtigall (Le Directeur Régional) à M. le Préfet Régional; *M07191*, 25 August
1943, Commissaire Central à M. le Préfet Délégué, Rapport Mensuel; and
M06496, 24 August 1943, Deutsche Regional Werbestelle, Cl-Fd, à M. le
Préfet Régional.
103. *M05647*, 5 October 1943, Le Commissaire Général à la Main d'oeuvre
(Robert Weinmann) à MM. les Commissaires Régionaux; *R01719* includes what sems to be a complete set of all instructions issued for the
operation of the STO, and *M06496* includes telegrams supplementing the
general regulations and directives.
104. Paxton, *Vichy France,* Milward, *The New Order,* and other standard ac-
accounts concerning the Vichy regime at the national level include good
accounts of this rivalry between German administrations; see Chapter 7
for a discussion of local repercussions of this high-level bickering.
105. *R01720*, 30 October 1944, Préfet PdD à M. le Ministre de l'Intérieur, and
M05668, September 1944, "Rapport sur l'activité des Services de la Main
d'oeuvre—Départ des travailleurs en Allemagne" contain the two best
overall summaries of the impact of the STO in statistical terms. The latter
arrives at a total of *3240* workers but does not include the *relève* departures in late 1942, while the former documents concludes that *3718*
French workers left the PdD for Germany in both *relève* and STO operations; neither estimate includes foreign workers, who made up a substantial percentage of the total contingents of workers deported from the region. Eugène Martres, "La Main d'oeuvre Cantalienne en Allemagne au
cours de la deuxième guerre mondiale," *Revue de la Haute Auvergne* 45
(Janvier-Mars 1976), 363, calculates that 39.2 percent of those drafted
for labor from the Cantal were foreigners. Because the mass of contradictory statistics available for the Puy-de-Dôme (some totals include
foreigners, others do not, and many give no indication one way or the
other), I am uncertain about the percentage of foreigners drafted in the
Puy-de-Dôme and for all of the Auvergne, but an estimate of 30 percent
seems reasonable and may be too low. Certainly, the government's intent
was to draft foreigners instead of Frenchmen whenever possible.
106. *M05646*, 8 January 1944, Le Commandant Militaire en France (ave.
Kléber, Paris) au Commissariat Général à la Main d'oeuvre.
107. *R01719*, 5 April 1944, Secrétaire Général à la Main d'oeuvre à MM. les
Préfets Régionaux.

Chapter 2

1. *M06484*, 28 December 1940, Préfet du PdD à M. le Maire de Cl-Fd. This
process had been instigated by a directive from Minister of the Interior

Peyrouton, dated 22 October 1940 that had specified names of people related to the PCF or the Third International. The mayor had pointed out to the prefect that the Third International had had no influence whatsoever on the naming of streets at Cl-Fd, but he had sent a list of all the streets, marking those that might be questionable. These included streets named Locarno, Proudhon, Severine, and Grand Bretagne, as well as the three ordered changed by the prefect. See letters of 9 November 1940, Préfet à M. le Ministre à l'Intérieur, 14 November 1940, M. le Maire (Cl-Fd) à M. le Préfet, and 26 November 1940, Préfet (PdD) à M. le Ministre à l'Intérieur; all in *M06484,* which also includes similar correspondence regarding other towns in the Puy-de-Dôme.

2. *Le Moniteur et L'Avenir,* 28 June 1940, a special issue of the two newspapers, publishing jointly on the orders of the German troops occupying the town, citing Pétain's speech of 25 June.

3. *M04288,* N° 15, Rapport au Centre Départemental d'Information, à Cl-Fd, received at the prefecture, 18 July 1940.

4. *M06501,* 18 September 1940, Préfet aux Maires ou PdD. The law permitting revocation of such *fonctionnaires* had been decreed 17 July 1940, one week after the vote of full powers to Pétain.

5. Henri Michel, *Le Procès de Riom* (Paris: Albin Michel, 1979), p. 126.

6. *M06484,* 7 December 1940, Préfet du PdD au Sous-Préfet de Thiers.

7. Yves Durand, *Vichy 1940–1944* (Paris: Bordas, 1972). Although a slender volume, only 174 pages, this is in my opinion one of the very best assessments of the Vichy regime.

8. 15 January 1941, Alexandre Varenne à Monsieur le Maréchal. Copies of this and other correspondence between Varenne and Pétain were kindly provided me by Alphonse Rozier.

9. *T01455,* Affiche attached to, 28 June 1943, Ministre, Secrétaire d'Etat à l'Education Nationale aux Recteurs et Inspecteurs d'Académie.

10. For the PdD, 235 conseils municipaux were predominantly Radical, 60 URD, and 83 Républicain de Gauche, compared to 43 SFIO and 52 Independent Socialists. Of a total of 1537 conseilleurs municipaux, 690 were Radical Socialists, 205 Républicains de Gauche, 199 URD, 7 Conservateurs, compared to 110 Radical Independents, 30 Socialistes de France, 61 Républicains Sociaux, 211 SFIO, 5 PCF, and 19 Démocrates Populaires. By comparison, the complexion of local government in the department of Allier was predominantly Socialist, the Haute-Loire was more conservative, dominated by the URD and the Républicains de Gauche; while the Cantal, although more heavily agricultural and rural, was similar to the PdD in political persuasion.

11. Georges Potut, in *Le Gouvernement de Vichy 1940–1942* (Paris: Armand Colin, 1972), p. 104. This volume represents the published proceedings of a colloquium, "Le Gouvernement de Vichy et la Révolution nationale (1940–1942)," held at the Fondation Nationale des sciences politiques, 6 and 7 March 1970. Introduction and conclusion by René Rémond.

12. Ibid., p. 88; Michel Dupouey, Chef de bureau au Secrétariat Général à la Jeunesse.

13. See dossiers in file *M06752, M07852,* and *M07059.*

14. *M06752,* 31 October, 1940, Préfet PdD à M. le Ministre, Secrétaire d'Etat à l'Intérieur.

15. Dossiers in file *M06752*.
16. *M07852*, "Procès-Verbal," Conférence des Préfets Régionaux, Friday, 16 January 1942.
17. *M07059*, 6 January 1941, Peyrouton aux Préfets.
18. *M07059*, Intérieur à Préfet, télégramme N° 054644, 14 January 1941.
19. *M06692* contains many police reports on political meetings and rallies during the 1930s. These are especially numerous for 1936 and 1937.
20. *M07182* notes 231 different documents concerning these events, entitled "Grève générale, 30 Novembre 1938," that were sent by the prefect at Cl-Fd to be used as evidence against the defendants at the Riom trials.
21. *M06752*, "Loi du 17–7–40. Dossiers individuels du Personnel relevé de ses fonctions"; *M07184*, 19 August 1941, Intendant de Police à M. le Commissaire Divisionnaire de la Police Spéciale; *M03842*, 19 October 1940, Le Préfet à M. Secrétaire d'Etat à l'Instruction Publique et à la Jeunesse; and *M03842*, 30 October 1940, Préfet à M. le Garde des Sceaux, Ministre, Sec. d'Etat à la Justice.
22. *M07852*, Procès-Verbal de la Conférence des Préfets Régionaux de la zone occupée et de la zone non-occupée, 6 July 1942.
23. *M07852*, 29 May 1942, Procès-Verbal de la Conférence des Préfets Régionaux de la zone occupée et de la zone non-occupée.
24. *M06426*, Préfet du PdD, response to letter of 3 June 1941, Directeur du Cabinet, Darlan, Sec. d'Etat à l'Intérieur, à M. le Préfet du PdD.
25. *M07185*, 25 September 1941, "Note"—Intendant de Police à M. le Sec. Gén. Préfecture, Cl-Fd.
26. *M06426*, "Notice de Renseignement" concerning Raymond Perrier, a Socialist member of the Municipal Council at Cl-Fd.
27. In defining reasons for dissolving and reconstituting municipal councils, Laval listed first among the principal causes "l'hostilité manifeste et soutenue à l'oeuvre de rénovation nationale" (*M07059*, 22 June 1942, Pierre Laval aux Préfets Régionaux); the phrase, "hostilité . . . à l'oeuvre de rénovation nationale," was one of those most commonly employed in describing Socialists believed to be opposed to the government.
28. *M06777*, 14 October 1941, Sous-Préfet/Thiers à M. le Préfet/Cl-Fd. This file and others concerning the reorganization of municipal councils leave no doubt as to which ones were considered "good" or "bad" politically by the Vichy regime. "Bad" was in most cases clearly on the left of the political spectrum.
29. See *Le Gouvernement de Vichy 1940–1942*, Section 1, "Les Institutions," especially the article by James Steel, William Kidd, and Daniel Weiss, "Les Commissions Administratives Départementales," pp. 55–64.
30. *M07852*, 10 January 1942, Secrétaire d'Etat à l'Intérieur à M. le Préfet Régional, Cl-Fd. It was later decided that associates under the Ministry of the Interior could elect their officers subject to the prefect's endorsement, but the Post, Telephone, and Telecommunications Ministry and the Ministry of Education would use a separate process under the control of their ministers.
31. *M07852*, Procès-Verbal de la Conférence des Préfets Regionaux de la zone occupée et de la zone non-occupée, Friday, 29 May 1942; also Procés-Verbal of a later meeting of 6 July 1942.
32. *M06439*, 8 January 1942, Préfet du PdD à M. le Chef du Gouvernement,

Ministre à l'Intérieur. The prefect indicated that the need for secrecy had made it extremely difficult to obtain precise information.

33. *M03822*, 30 April 1941, le Commissaire de Police, Chef de la Sûreté, à Monsieur le Préfet du PdD.

34. *M07191*, 24 April 1943, Commissaire Divisionnaire/Vichy à M. le Sous-Préfet de Vichy, Rapport Mensuel.

35. *T01455*, "L'Ecole et la Famille," published by the Office de Propagande Générale, Paris. This booklet was sent in late September 1943 to all teachers in the PdD with instructions to include the message conveyed to students on the family question.

36. Ibid.

37. *M04288*, 9 July 1940, Président Conseil et Ministre Travail à Préfet, Cl-Fd.

38. *M05657*, Robert Weinmann, Commissariat Général au STO aux MM. les Préfets Régionaux, Paris, 29 June 1943.

39. *M05657*, 17 March 1944, N° 9/T/5, "Objet: Mise au travail des femmes," Pierre Laval, Le Chef du Gouvernement.

40. *M07155*, 17 March 1942, Pucheu aux Préfets.

41. *M07191*, 24 June 1943, Rapport Mensuel de Police, Vichy.

42. *T01455*, "L'Ecole et la Famille," published by the Office de Propagande Générale, Paris.

43. *T0873*, 11 April 1942, Guerrin, Préfet du PdD à M. le Ministre, Secrétaire d'Etat à l'Intérieur, a report on "l'état d'esprit du corps de l'Enseignement Primaire."

44. *M03842*, 12 March 1941, Commissaire Spécial Haudressy au Commissaire Divisionnaire de Police Spéciale à Cl-Fd.

45. *M03841*, 8 January 1941, Secrétaire d'Etat à l'Instruction Publique à l'Inspecteur d'Academie du PdD.

46. *T0874*, Folder labeled "Enquêtes sur differents instituteurs, institutrices," 1942–1943; *M07852*, Conférence des Préfets Regionaux de la Zone Libre, Friday, 20 March 1942, Procès-Verbal. Of the primary teachers, a government spokesman noted: "Le Gouvernement est en droit de compte sur leur loyalisme et il appartient aux Préfets d'user de leur autorité pour assurer leur ralliement."

47. *M03841*, 17 January 1941, Inspecteur de la Sûreté Bellon, Robert, à M. le Commissaire de Police, Chef de la Sûreté.

48. *T0873*, 11 April 1942, Guerrin, Préfet du PdD, à M. le Ministre, Secrétaire d'Etat à l'Intérieur, a report on "l'état d'esprit du corps de l'Enseignement Primaire." See also, *M07788* Brun, Préfet Régional, 1 February 1942, Rapport Mensuel d'Information.

49. *T01455*, 13 October 1941, Ciculaire, Secrétaire d'Etat à l'Education Nationale et à la Jeunesse (Jerome Carcopino).

50. Ibid.

51. Ibid.

52. *T01455*, 18 June 1942, Inspecteur d'Academie aux Messieurs les Inspecteurs primaires.

53. *T01455*, 13 May 1942, Circulaire, Abel Bonnard, Ministre, Secrétaire d'Etat à l'Education Nationale.

54. *T01455*, Allocution aux Instituteurs Primaires à la Radiofusion Nationale, 27 August 1942, Abel Bonnard.

55. *T0872*, Rapport Annuel sur la Situation de l'Enseignement Primaire dans le PdD pour l'Année 1944–1945, p. 12, V–*Education Morale et Civique* (Rubrique naguère d'une rédaction rédoutable et rédoutée . . .). Dossiers *TO2546–48* contain individual files of the teachers investigated at the liberation because of the compromising position in which their situations sometimes had placed them. It is clear from these files that because of such frequent contact with local people, teachers rarely, if ever, could hide their true opinions.

56. *T01524*, 23 December 1940, l'Inspecteur d'Academie, rapport au Secours National.

57. *T01570*, 10 February 1941, Ministre de l'Education Nationale aux Messieurs les Recteurs d'Academie.

58. *T01570*, 8 December 1941, Secrétaire Général à l'Information aux Messieurs les Recteurs.

59. *T01455*, Croquis for "La France que nous aimons" and instructions for their use, 28 September 1942, Ministre, Secrétaire d'Etat à l'Education Nationale aux Inspecteurs d'Academie.

60. *T01570* and *T01455*, 23 September 1942, Ministre Secrétaire d'Etat à l'Education Nationale aux Messieurs les Inspecteurs d'Academie; see also related documents in these files.

61. *M06135*, undated note concerning propaganda for "Le Calendrier du Maréchal."

62. *M03887*, 10 February 1941, "Note," le Chef du BMA.

63. *M03796*, 6 December 1940, Sous-Préfet de Thiers à M. le Préfet du PdD.

64. *M03954*, a note of 17 July 1941 in the files of the Préfet du PdD.

65. *M05755*, Arrêté, 26 July 1943, and 4 August 1943, Préfet du PdD Délégué aux Maires du PdD, concerning the repression of illegal dances.

66. *M03945*, 5 October 1943, Rapport, Renseignements Généraux. This file contains numerous examples of investigations of individuals who had asked Pétain for special favors.

67. *M07185*, 15 October 1941, P. Pucheu à M. l'Intendant de Police, Cl-Fd (italics in original).

68. *M07184*, 28 July 1941, Intendant de Police aux Messieurs les Commissaire de Police, which noted previous orders to this effect were not being obeyed; *M07185*, 23 October 1941, Intendant de Police à M. le Préfet du Haute-Loire, repeats the same theme.

69. *M07186*, 13 November 1941, Intendant de Police à M. le Cmdt. Pillon, GMR d'Auvergne.

70. *M04871* N° 4336, 27 May 1944, Le Commissaire Principal, Chef du Service des Renseignements Généraux, PdD, à le Préfet du PdD Délégué.

71. *T01456*, Dossier "Révision des catalogues des bibliothèques scolaires et post-scolaires 1941–1945." 24 April 1941, Préfet du PdD à M. l'Inspecteur d'Academie; lists of books to be withdrawn and other information relative to this issue in *M06551*.

72. Ibid.

73. *M06551*, 12 January 1942, Ministre de l'Intérieur aux Préfets. This letter was sent with the third list of books to be withdrawn.

74. *T01456*, 16 July 1941, Note du Service, Inspecteur primaire à M. l'Inspec-

teur d'Academie du PdD; lists of books to be purged and notations as to reasons, when given, in *M06551*.

75. *M06370*, 18 August 1943, Ministre de l'Intérieur, Conseilleur d'Etat (Sec. Gén. à la Police) aux Messieurs les Préfets.

76. *M06531*, 9 May 1942, Note of Préfet délégué Guerrin authorizing the re-establishment of the Orchestre du Globe. Other documents in this dossier indicate that jazz was ordered excluded from offerings at least as early as March 1941.

77. *T01458*, 20 July 1913, L. Barthou, le Président du Conseil, Ministre de l'Instruction Publique et des Beaux-Arts, aux Messieurs les Recteurs de l'Academie. Quotation of Ferry's comment in same file.

78. Ibid. Dossiers *T01458–60* contain evidence for the review of books in the PdD from the origins of the Third Republic.

79. Durand, *Vichy 1940–1944*, p. 67.

80. *Annuaire Statistique, 1940–1945*, vol. 56; and *Annuaire Statistique Régional Rétrospectif* (Auvergne).

81. *La Semaine Religieuse de Clermont*, #10, 8 March 1941, with reference to the law of 6 February 1941.

82. *T01420*, 2 April 1941, Préfet PdD à M. le Sous-Préfet de Riom, concerning a complaint from the director of an Ecole Libre at St. Ours, where the Conseil Municipal had refused to pay for heating the school. Other documents in this file and in *T01419* report similar incidents elsewhere.

83. *T01419*, "Extrait des délibérations du Conseil Départemental," May 1943. Clermont 1°, *1400*–privé *0;* Clermont 2°, public *1200*–privé *100*. (Numbers refer to francs.)

84. *M07852*, Procès-Verbal, Conférence des Préfets Régionaux, 20 February 1942.

85. *M07852*, Procès-Verbal de la Conférence des Préfets Régionaux, Paris, 6 July 1942: "Rapports entre l'autorité préfectorale et le clergé catholique."

86. *La Semaine religieuse de Clermont*, 72° Année, N° 1, 6 January 1940, and N° 21, 25 May 1940.

87. Ibid., N° 27, 6 July 1940.

88. Ibid.

89. Ibid., N° 40, 5 October 1940.

90. Ibid., N° 42, 19 October 1940.

91. Ibid., 73° Année, N° 7, 15 February 1941.

92. Ibid., N° 16, 19 April 1941.

93. Ibid., N° 35 et 36, 6 September 1941.

94. Ibid., 76° Année, N° 1, 1 January 1944.

95. Ibid., 75° Année, N° 11, 13 March 1943; 73° Année, N° 30, 26 July 1941; and 75° Année, N° 8, 20 February 1943.

96. Ibid., 74° Année, N° 11, 14 March 1942, and 76° Année, N° 13, 25 March 1944. The bishop's comment about the Allied bombing of the Michelin factory was cited as an indication that civilization was going backward toward barbarism.

97. Ibid., 75° Année, N° 27, 3 July 1943.

98. Ibid., 73° Année, N° 25, 21 June 1941.

99 *T0885;* dossier includes several reports concerning these protests and describing responses to them, as well as the text of Piguet's communiqué of 26 September 1942 denouncing the mixed schools.

100. *T0885,* 24 December 1942, Ministre de l'Education Nationale, à M. le Préfet du PdD.
101. *M05670,* Commissaire de la République, Région de Cl-Fd, Période du 15 au 31 May 1945, "Vue d'Ensemble–Etat de l'Opinion." The counter-demonstration did not materialize.
102. *M09464;* undated report, but probably February 1945, written at the Préfecture, PdD, following a request from A. Tixier, dated 4 December 1944. Similar conclusions found in *M06360,* 26 May 1945, Nᵒ 2978, Renseignements Généraux; 15 May 1945, Nᵒ 2726, Renseignements Généraux; and *M09462,* 5 February 1945, Rapport (origin unclear but probably Préfet, PdD).
103. *La Semaine Religieuse de Clermont,* 73ᵉ Année, Nᵒ 20, 17 May 1941; Nᵒ 27, 5 July 1941, reported that the bishop had told the government's Délégate à la Jeunesse pour le PdD that Catholic youths who wanted to participate in the "service unique rural" could do so only with their parents' permission and after arrangements regulating their participation had been made with the JAC.
104. *T0764,* 20 November 1941, Délégué Régional pour l'Auvergne et le Bourbonnais à M. le Préfet du PdD.
105. *T01570* contains a whole series of letters and other documents relating Bonnard's instructions to the Recteurs and Inspecteurs d'Académie, and the responses from schools in the PdD to them. W. D. Halls, *The Youth of Vichy France* (Oxford: Oxford University Press, 1981) is a study of all of Vichy's programs directed toward French youth. Halls's conclusions for all of France are consistent with my own for the Auvergne: with regard to Vichy's ambitions to control French youth, its programs were failures.
106. *M05648,* 8 May 1943, Dr. Charles Rohmer à M. le Préfet Régional.
107. *M07149,* 16 February 1942, orders from the minister of the interior about the exchange of salutes between police officers and personnel of the Chantiers de la Jeunesse.
108. *T02548/2,* 21 August 1942, A. J. Payen, Chargé de Mission: Province d'Auvergne, à M. Jean Delage, Chef de la Section Chantiers, Direction Générale de la Propagande. Roger Austin, "The Chantiers de la Jeunesse in Languedoc, 1940–44," *French Historical Studies,* No. 1 (Spring 1983), 106–126, studying another region, reaches similar conclusions about the Chantiers' failure in the realms of ideology and politics.
109. *M07191,* 24 June 1943, Vichy, Rapport Mensuel de Police.
110. Halls, *The Youth of Vichy France,* p. 13, notes that the Révolution Nationale was "largely a spent force by mid-1942, blown off course by more pressing priorities and the changing circumstances of war." "The educational corollary to these ideas [i.e., the Révolution Nationale] was never fully worked out and certainly never realized."

Chapter 3

1. *M07856,* "Appel des Anciens Combattants," for release to newspapers 19 June 1940, signed Jean Vèze, Jacquemin, Dr. Grasset, and Dr. Vimal.
2. Copy of welcome in *M03954.*

3. *M05776*, 15 July 1940, Grasset aux membres du C.A. de l'U.F. en Zone Libre.
4. *M05776*, numerous letters in Grasset's correspondence convey acceptance in principle, but disagreement in practice.
5. Reports concerning the political persuasion of Légion officials are in *M07858*.
6. *M05776*, 14 January 1941, Dr. R. Grasset à M. François Valentin, Dir. Gén. de la Légion Française des Combattants.
7. Ibid.
8. Ibid.
9. Ibid.
10. Jean-Paul Cointet, "Les Anciens Combattants. La Légion Française des Combattants," in *Le Gouvernement de Vichy 1940–42* (Paris: Armand Colin, 1972), p. 136; and see the same author's "La Légion des Combattants," in *Le Journal de la France* (de l'Occupation à la Libération) no. 127 (October 1971), 877–886.
11. *M07858*, Légion Française des Combattants, PdD, Rapport Mensuel, 10 September 1941.
12. Cointet, *Le Gouvernement de Vichy,* p. 135.
13. Cointet, "La Légion des Combattants," pp. 884–885, notes the difficulty of recruitment among the older veterans' organizations during the Légion's early months. For the PdD, 52 percent of those eligible joined in those communes for which I was able to find statistics.
14. *M06474*, 4 March 1943, Dossier "Visites Administratives du Secrétaire Général 1942–43," Guerrin à M. le Préfet Régional.
15. *M06475*, 16 November 1942, Sous-Préfet d'Ambert à M. le Préfet du PdD Délégué.
16. *M05774*, Text of speech by Raymond Grasset, Président Départemental du PdD, 3 November 1940, "Légion Française des Combattants, Assemblée Générale Constitutive de la Légion du Puy-de-Dôme, à Clermont-Ferrand."
17. *M05776*, 2 February 1941, Dr. Vimal de Flechac, Membre du Directoire, Légion Française des Combattants à M. X. Vallat, Secrétaire Général des Anciens Combattants.
18. *M06598*, 3 July 1942, Instructions sur les liaisons entre les pouvoirs publics et la Légion, signed Laval, Pétain, and Lachal; see also Cointet, "Les Anciens Combattants."
19. Ibid.
20. *M06598*, 21 July 1942, Pierre Laval aux MM. les Préfets régionaux et départementaux.
21. *M05774*, Text of speech by Raymond Grasset, Président Départemental du PdD, 3 November 1940, "Légion Française des Combattants, Assemblée Générale Constitutive de la Légion du Puy-de-Dôme, à Clermont-Ferrand."
22. *M07191*, 24 July 1943, Commissaire Central à M. le Préfet Délégué, Rapport Mensuel.
23. *M05776*, Ecrits du Président Grasset, "Comprendre l'Etat d'Esprit des Paysans."
24. *M05756*, Extraits du rapport de propagande, Section Veyre-Monton, in correspondance of Gilbert Sardier.

25. *M05758;* see, for example, a letter of 15 February 1944 from Gilbert Sardier to a man who has resigned from the Légion because his son had been taken for the STO. Shamed by Sardier's letter, citing a number of sons of Légion directors who had gone to Germany, the man withdrew his resignation.

26. *M03823,* Synthèse du 15/11/41, 13° Division Militaire, E. M. Coordination des Contrôles.

27. Documentation in folder *T01503.*

28. *M06422,* 17 March 1942, Grasset, "3° Circulaire Spéciale," concerning ceremony of 22 March 1942 at Cl-Fd.

29. *M05757,* 21 December 1942, a complaint from the Courpière section about numerous resignations from the Légion, in folder, Légion Correspondence, PdD.

30. Letters and police reports in *M06357.*

31. *M06357,* folder "Mars, Avril–Mai 1943," letter to Sardier. Evidence of other denunciations is in *M07199, M07184, M07185, M05756,* and *M06224.*

32. Ibid.

33. *M07191,* 24 February 1942, Rapport Mensuel, Kastner, Commissaire de Police, 2° Arrondissement, à M. le Préfet.

34. Engène Martres, "Le Cantal de 1939 à 1945." Thèse, Faculté des Lettres, Université de Clermont-Ferrand, 1974, p. 265.

35. Ibid. As Martres comments: "Tout est dit dans ce texte d'un connaisseur."

36. *M03822,* 28 April 1941, Rapport Mensuel, Commissaire du 2° Arrondissement à M. le Préfet s/c de M. le Commissaire Central.

37. *M07191,* 27 February 1942, Rapport Mensuel, Commissaire Central à M. l'Intendant de Police.

38. *M06135,* 23 July 1942, Ministre de l'Information, Circulaire N° 1 aux Délégués à la Propagande Ouvrière.

39. *M03804,* 18 December 1943, Commissaire Principal à M. le Préfet, N° 8554.

40. *M07871,* folder "Michelin," one of a large file of reports concerning the appointment and operation of the Comités Sociaux in companies located in the PdD.

41. *M07191,* 25 March 1943, Rapport Mensuel, Commissaire Central à M. le Préfet Délégué.

42. Jacques Julliard, "La Charte du Travail," in *Le Gouvernement de Vichy 1940–1942;* Paul Farmer, *Vichy, a Political Dilemma* (New York: Columbia University Press, 1955).

43. *M06422,* Extraits de la presse, 23 March 1942, reporting on Pétain's visit to Cl-Fd for ceremonies in favor of the Secours National.

44. *M05755,* "Enquête sur les Bases du Ravitaillement," Légion, Commission Agricole.

45. *M05755,* "Questionnaire #4," in Légion folder.

46. Eugen Weber, *Peasants into Frenchmen,* (Stanford: Stanford University Press, 1976).

47. *M03822,* 30 September 1941, Le Commissaire de Police, Chef de la Sûreté, à M. le Préfet du PdD.

48. *M05755,* 25 March 1943, Commission Agricole de la Légion, Rapport, Visite à l'office de l'Intendant des Affaires Economiques.

49. Copy in *M05770.*
50. Ibid.
51. *M05755,* 1 May 1943, Rapport, "Une Loi à Réviser," Le Président de la section pomologique de la Corporation paysanne du PdD.
52. *M05770,* R. Grasset, "Etude psychologique concernant le rapport du ravitaillement et la Paysannerie."
53. *M05758,* 3 February 1944, A. Mallet to M. Vasseur, Délégué à Propagande, Sauxillanges, and to the Président de la Légion à Champeix, in dossier containing correspondence of G. Sardier.
54. Ibid.
55. *M05755.* Troisième Anniversaire de la Légion, Un Appel de François Valentin, Ancien Directeur Général de la Légion Française des Combattants, Quelque part en France, Août 1943, Edité et diffusé par les Mouvements de Résistance Unis.
56. Durand, *Vichy 1940–1944,* p. 105.

Chapter 4

1. *M05756,* 29 October 1943, "La Légion, Suprême Espoir," in Correspondence, G. Sardier.
2. Pascal Ory, *Les Collaborateurs 1940–1945* (Paris: Editions de Seuil, 1976), especially Chapter 11, "Le Don de sa personne. La Collaboration armée," which suggests the interesting thesis that all collaboration ultimately evolved toward military or police actions in league with the occupying power.
3. For example, Ory, *Les Collaborateurs,* and the excellent general survey of collaborationist groups of Bertram Gordon, *Collaborationism in France during the Second World War* (Ithaca: Cornell University Press, 1980).
4. Ory, *Les Collaborateurs,* p. 271: "Compte tenu du gonflement comprehensible des deux chiffres—et compte non tenu des nombreuses exécutions sommaires—, il n'y eut guère moins d'affaires de collaboration soumises aux tribunaux *ad hoc* de la Libération (160,000) que de cartes distribuées à la même époque de 'combattant volontaire de la Résistance' (170,000)." Gordon, *Collaborationism,* pp. 326–327, estimates that 150,000 to 200,000 persons were involved in movements of collaboration. If research in local archives of other regions parallels my findings for the Auvergne and those of researchers (cited later) who have used other departmental archives, this estimate is much too high.
5. For example, Monique Luirard, "La Milice Française dans la Loire," *Revue d'Histoire de la deuxième guerre mondiale,* 25, no. 91 (1973), 77–102; in that same issue, devoted to collaborationism, see the articles by P. Gounand, "Les Groupements de Collaboration dans une ville française occupée: Dijon," 47–56, and Yves Durand and David Bohbot, "La Collaboration politique dans le pays de la Loire Moyenne," 57–76. Jean-Marie Guillon, "Les Mouvements de collaboration dans le Var," *Revue d'histoire de la deuxième guerre mondiale,* no. 113 (1979), 91–110; Michel Chanal, "La Collaboration dans l'Isère," *Cahiers d'histoire* [Lyon] 22, no. 4 (1977), 377–403; Martres, *Le Cantal de 1939 à 1945.*
6. *M03958,* 27 November 1937, Commissaire Divisionnaire à M. le Préfet.
7. *M07191,* 23 February 1943, Rapport Mensuel, Commissaire Central à

M. le Préfet Délégué; *M07184,* 4 August 1941, Intendant de Police, Cl-Fd, à M. Demay, Cabinet du Maréchal, Hotel du Parc: "Pas plus que les mois précédent, les partisans de la collaboration n'ont augmenté." This statement was typical of comments made consistently throughout the occupation by observers at Cl-Fd.

8. *M07160,* 19 April 1943, Commissaire de Police Leclère à M. le Commissaire Divisionnaire, Chef Régional des Renseignements Généraux, Cl-Fd, "Rapport de l'activité du P.P.F. à Clermont-Ferrand."

9. *M06536,* 15 February 1943, Commissaire Principal Renseignements Généraux à M. le Préfet Délégué.

10. *M07187,* 15 May 1942, L'Inspecteur Bellon à M. le Commissaire Principal de 1° Classe, Chef du Service des Renseignements Généraux du PdD, #1.963; and 16 May 1942, Note pour le Préfet, R. Baulard (Secrétaire Général à la Préfecture).

11. Ibid., Note pour le Préfet.

12. *M07161,* 3 June 1942, Haudressy, Chef de Service, Commissaire Principal des Renseignements Généraux; *M04228* contains a complete report on the meeting of 3 June 1942, Le Commissaire de Police, Chef de la Sûreté à M. le Préfet du PdD.

13. *M07160,* 19 April 1943, Rapport de l'activité du PPF à Cl-Fd, Commissaire de Police Leclère à M. le Commissaire Divisionnaire, Chef des Renseignements Généraux, Cl-Fd; and *M06536,* 15 February 1943, Commissaire Principal des Renseignements Généraux à M. le Préfet Délégué.

14. Several reports of these activities are in *M07160.*

15. *M07160,* 12 December 1942, police report on activity of LVF officials at Clermont; *M07191,* 26 December 1942, Commissaire Central Cl-Fd à M. le Préfet Délégué, Rapport Mensuel.

16. *M07160,* 9 August 1942, Note pour le Chef de Service Régional des Renseignements Généraux, Activité du PPF, signed Baulard, who quotes Laval in 24 July 1942 meeting with regional prefects and intendants de police at Vichy.

17. *M06357,* 23 July 1943, Renseignements Généraux, #4614; 31 July 1943, Renseignements Généraux, #4827; and 5 August 1943, Renseignements Généraux, #4922.

18. *M07191,* 23 February 1943, Rapport Mensuel, Commissaire Central à M. le Préfet Délégué.

19. *M07858,* Copy of Darnand's speech of 4 October 1942, as published in *La Légion* (Bulletin Officiel de la Légion Française des Combattants et les Volontaires de la Révolution Nationale," 15 October 1942.

20. *M07858,* 9 July 1942, Commissaire des Renseignements Généraux Haudressy à M. le Commissaire Principal des Renseignements Généraux du PdD. This is a report on a Légion meeting at Orcines in which Vimal de Flechac criticized the government's shift toward an apparently willing collaboration.

21. *M07191,* 24 October 1942, Rapport Mensuel, Commissaire Central, Cl-Fd, à M. l'Intendant de Police; and *M07191,* 24 October 1942, Commissaire de Police, 2° Arrondissement, Cl-Fd, à M. le Préfet du PdD.

22. *M07857,* 30 October 1942, Commissaire Central de la Ville de Cl-Fd à M. le Préfet Délégué.

23. Ibid.

24. *M07191*, 15 December 1942, Renseignements Généraux, Cl-Fd, à M. le Directeur des Renseignements Généraux, Vichy.

25. *M05822*, CDL Purge Commission file on the Milice.

26. J. Delperrie de Bayac, *Histoire de la Milice 1918–1945* (Paris: Fayard, 1969), p. 181. In one of the best available overviews of the collaborationist movements, Gordon, *Collaborationism in France*, p. 184, acknowledges the difficulty of determining membership with precision, but says 30,000 has been widely accepted. This is close to the figure of 30,412 cited by the Germans, but ignores the warning contained in a special report on the Milice drawn up by German Armistice Commission officials ("Sonderbericht Nr. 9: betr. die französische Miliz," 1 December 1943; Copies are in RW 34, V. 77, Kontrollinspektion der DWStK, Kontrollabteilung Az. 20, N° 2983/43g, Militärarchiv, Freiburg, W. Germany; and in Captured German Documents, National Archives, Washington, D.C., T77-R829 F 556063-77.) The document, p. 9, notes: "(The statements of the regional and departmental leadership concerning the membership numbers now and then meet with strong objections with regard to their reliability. At various times totally different statements were made, which are not consistent with one another and cannot be cleared up through the questioning of the local leader.)" Several monthly reports for 1943 and 1944 written by German Armistice Commission officials that discuss Milice membership estimates are in the Militärarchiv, Freiburg; Gordon, *Collaborationism*, pp. 355–356, Appendix A, reproduces membership figures by department, based on the microfilms of some of these German records in the National Archives. The best sources for Milice membership in the PdD are in dossiers *M05822* (including the CDL Purge Commission file on the Milice), *M06611*, *M07221*, *M07318*, *M09321*, *M09322*, and *M09328* (a *fichier* of Milice for the four departments of the Auvergne).

27. Guillon, "Les Mouvements de collaboration dans le Var," *Revue d'histoire de la deuxième guerre mondiale*, no. 113, (1979), 107.

28. *M06611*, 27 December 1944, Inspecteur Rouchy, Renseignements Généraux à M. le Commissaire Principal des Renseignements Généraux. *M09321* and *M09322* also contain files describing the circumstances in which various individuals joined the Milice.

29. *M07172*, 8 August 1942, Le Chef Départemental SOL à M. l'Intendant de Police.

30. See Hans Umbreit, "La Stratégie Défensive de l'Allemagne," a paper presented to the colloquium "La Libération de la France," Paris, 1974.

31. *M06648*, 28 July 1944, Direction Michelin à M. le Préfet Régional, and several other documents relative to the incident in this same folder.

32. Most of the information regarding Milice actions in the PdD is to be found in the documents relating to the postwar purge trials, as in the Rapport Milice, 15 May 1945, in *M07221*, and other information may be gleaned from Delperrie de Bayac, *Histoire de la Milice*.

33. *M07191*, 23 February 1943, Commissaire Central, Cl-Fd, à M. le Préfet Délégué.

34. "Sonderbericht Nr. 9: betr. die französische Miliz," p. 8.

35. *M06133*, Achon à M. Pierre Prier, Délégué Régional à l'Information, 21 July 1944.

36. *M07172*, 3 July 1944, Joseph Darnand aux Préfets Régionaux, Direction Général de la Gendarmerie Nationale, etc.
37. Paxton, *Vichy France*, p. 227, and his conclusion, "A Moral Balance Sheet," pp. 380–382.
38. *M06134*, 25 June 1944, N° 2, Délégate Régionale du Ministère de l'Information, la DCB (Bulletin de défense contre les bobards).
39. *M03823*, 31 October 1941, Le Commissaire de Police, Chef de la Sûreté, à M. le Préfet Régional, Rapport Mensuel.
40. Paxton, *Vichy France*, pp. 240–241, for example, considers the spring of 1943 to be the date at which opinion "turned decisively against the regime."

Chapter 5

1. *M04860*, 9 October 1941, P. Pucheu, Secrétaire d'Etat à l'Intérieur, N° 396. Pol. 4.
2. *M06615*, 2 December 1944, annex to directive of A. Tixier, Ministre à l'Intérieur, concerning operations of the Services des Contrôles Techniques de l'Etat.
3. See reports on such activities for 1943 and 1944 in *M07177*. Also *M05560*, 7 August 1943, l'Intendant de Police à M. le Commissaire Divisionnaire, Chef de la Sécurité Publique.
4. *M03954*, 14 January 1942, Paul Brun, Préfet Régional, à Messieurs les Maires; and 24 February 1942, draft of Préfet's notice to newspaper editors concerning denunciations. See also denunciations and reports relative to them in *M06369*.
5. *M07157*, 2 June 1943, Secrétaire Général à la Police, René Bousquet, aux Préfets, ordered the establishments of new *listes S* that would permit quicker action than under legal formalities required for the Carnet B. This file also contains copies of the *listes S* for Cl-Fd as verified 30 October 1943, as well as those for neighboring communes in the PdD.
6. *M03775*, 19 September 1941, Le Sous-Préfet à Thiers à M. l'Intendant de Police (Cl-Fd), and 15 December 1941, Le Sous-Préfet à Thiers à M. le Préfet délégué (Cl-Fd).
7. *M07184*, 25 August 1941, Intendant de Police à M. Picard, René, cantonnier-électricien, "Les Echevettes," Saint-Nectaire. This was not an isolated case. Numerous similar warnings were sent to other individuals, especially in 1941.
8. *M05538–40*, Liste des Internés Administratifs sous le Régime de Vichy dont les dossiers sont détenus à la I° division.
9. *M07184*, 24 July 1941, Intendant de Police à M. le Secrétaire Général pour la Police.
10. *M07196*, 24 February 1943, Préfet Régional aux 4 Préfets. See also *M07196*, 1 March 1941, Circulaire from H. Chavin, Secrétaire Général pour la Police aux Préfets.
11. *M07149*, 25 February 1942, Ministre à l'Intérieur aux Préfets.
12. *M04861*, 22 September 1943, René Bousquet, Sec. Gén. à la Police pour le Chef du Gouvernement aux Préfets.
13. *M07149*, 31 January 1942, Pierre Pucheu, Ministre à l'Intérieur aux Préfets Zone Libre. The correspondence of the prefect and the intendant

de police in *M07184* reveals that almost all of the requests for release from internment were refused.

14. *M04866,* 10 September 1943, Le Garde des Sceaux, Ministre Secrétaire d'Etat à la Justice à Monsieur le Chef du Gouvernement à Vichy.
15. *M05538–40,* 9 December 1944, Circulaire, A. Tixier, Ministre de l'Intérieur à Messieurs les Commissaires Régionaux et Messieurs les Préfets, S.N.E.P. 13–N⁰ 152.
16. *M07157,* 19 October 1942, Pour le Chef du Gouvernement, Sec. d'Etat à la Police, Bousquet aux Préfets. A circular (N⁰ 444 S.G. Cir) of 27 July 1942, Le Chef du Gouvernement, Ministre Secrétaire d'Etat à l'Intérieur à Monsieur le Préfet Régional de Cl-Fd, had stated emphatically: *"Le Gouvernement décide d'interdire, de façon formelle, toute manifestation publique ou privée, de quelque nature que ce soit, susceptible de porter atteinte à l'ordre public"* (his italics).
17. *M05655.* Several letters and telegrams June–July 1941 refer to these events. See *M07166,* 4 January 1944, "Note sur le Régroupement des Anglo-Américains effectué en février et mars 1943."
18. *M07160,* 10 February 1943, Pierre Laval aux Préfets Régionaux in file "Intendance de police–Cabinet, Activité politique 1941–1944."
19. *M07291,* 5 March 1942, "Note," Ministre à l'Intérieur, in files of the intendant de police.
20. *M03792,* 8 January 1929, André Tardieu aux Messieurs les Préfets, Confidentiel.
21. *M03770,* 9 August 1939, Préfet, PdD à M. le Ministre à l'Intérieur. *M03785,* 14 June 1940, report concerning workers at Usines Ducellier in Issoire.
22. FO 371 File #65, pp. 5295–7263 (24310), C 5372/65/17 11 April 1940, Sir R. Campbell (Paris) to Central.
23. *M06741,* 27 February 1940, Préfet du PdD à Ministre à l'Intérieur; *M06741,* 14 December 1939, Préfet du PdD à Ministre à l'Intérieur; *M03796* includes several reports concerning authorizations for union organizations to hold meetings, indicating that the chief criterion was the attitude of the organization toward the Nazi-Soviet pact. *M03766* includes a file concerning press control.
24. *R01391,* 17 October 1939, Rapport of Inspecteur Principal Adjoint Lamboursin à M. le Commissaire de Police, Chef de la Sûreté, and 13 and 30 October 1939 and 8 February 1940, Le Commissaire Divisionnaire de Police Spéciale à M. le Général Commandant la 13° Région.
25. *M03883,* 17 May 1940, Préfet du PdD au Ministre à l'Intérieur.
26. F0 371 French 1943 France File #52, pp. 6297–7794 (36018) Z6306/52/17, "Political Forces in France: Communism," F0 Research Department French Handbook paper, 26 May 1943.
27. *M03785,* 12 November 1939, Rapport, Deuxième Bureau, Etat-Major du Commandant Militaire du 13° Région.
28. Geoffrey Warner, *Pierre Laval and the Eclipse of France, 1931–1945* (New York: Macmillan, 1968), pp. 300–303, discusses the significance of Laval's speech. All of the police reports from Clermont-Ferrand about public opinion emphasize the dramatic impact Laval's words had and the negative popular reaction to them. See Chapter 6.
29. *M06650,* "Règlement Général sur l'organisation de la Milice Française."

30. *M06581,* Explanation of a law of 2 June 1942, appended to a directive of 18 August 1942, Ministre à l'Intérieur aux Préfets Régionaux. Actions against foreign agents and the black market received lower priorities.

31. *M03882,* 7 August 1940, le Colonel L'Huillier, Commandant p.i. le Département des B-Alpes à M. le Général Commandant le Département du PdD.

32. *R01388,* 16 August 1940, A. Marquet Ministre Sec. d'Etat à l'Intérieur aux Préfets and subsequent instructions, Préfet du PdD, L. Peretti Della Rocca à M. le Commissaire Central (Cl-Fd). As early as 17 July 1940, the Commissaire Divisionnaire de Police Spéciale reported (*M03785*) that on local initiative following discussions between the préfet and the commanding general for the PdD, the police were ordered to be watching for the release of "particularly dangerous" communists returning from the Army. Their current attitudes were to be investigated and, if desirable, propositions should be made for security measures against them.

33. *M03882,* 20 August 1940, le Préfet du PdD à Monsieur le Commissaire Central.

34. *M03882,* 22 July 1940, Inspecteur Lamboursin à M. le Commissaire de Police, Chef de la Sûreté.

35. *M07214,* 4 June 1941, Rapport Secret Nᵒ 19, "Parties et Groupements Politiques." The report noted that another 1000 *internés administratifs* were in three prisons in the northern zone.

36. *M07159,* 15 December 1942, Secrétaire Général à la Police, "Etat Nominatif des Individus Internés en Afrique du Nord pour Menées Anti-Nationales."

37. F0 371 French 1943 France File #52, pp. 6297–7794 (36018) Z6306/52/17 "Political Forces in France: Communism," FO Research Department French Handbook paper, 26 May 1943.

38. *M03883,* 5 January 1941, Rapport, Commissaire de Police, Chef de Sûreté à M. le Commissaire Central.

39. *M07159,* 13 October 1941, Rapport, Le Commissaire de Police Judiciaire Pigeon, and many other documents in same file.

40. *M07167,* 26 June 1943, Kastner, Commissaire Central, à M. le Préfet Régional in folder Intendance de police, cabinet, "Opérations importantes de police 1943." Similarly, in *M07196* there are lists of "Internés Politiques, Hommes Astreints à résider dans des Centres de séjour, considerés comme nettement dangereux en raison de leur activité passée"; where if a motive is indicated, it is most frequently "Militant Communiste."

41. *M07191,* 23 February 1943, Rapport Mensuel, Commissaire Central à M. le Préfet Délégué.

42. *M07159,* 20 August 1942, René Bousquet Sec. Gén. à la Police au Préfet Régional Clermont-Ferrand.

43. Ibid.

44. Ibid.

45. Testimonies in file *M05551,* 18 October 1944, "Déclaration du Commissaire Loridan, René," concerning an officer named Trotta.

46. Interview, Alphonse Rozier.

47. *M03766,* 25 March 1939, Préfet PdD à M. le Ministre de l'Intérieur. This dossier contains several reports and letters concerning censorship of information allowed to be given the Spaniards.

48. *M010402*, 28 November 1938, Ministre à l'Intérieur à M. le Préfet du PdD.

49. Louis Stein, *Beyond Death and Exile* (Cambridge: Harvard University Press, 1979), depicts vividly the hardships faced by the Spanish refugees, but seems at times a bit too harsh in his verdict on the French, who may have been individually and collectively more charitable than he suggests.

50. Elizabeth A. Lindquist has written an excellent dissertation on the Spanish in the Auvergne, "The Experience of the Spanish Republicans in the Auvergne, 1936–1946" (Diss., University of Kansas, 1984).

51. *MO10433–M010436*, GTE "Rapports trimestriels," 1942, 1943, and 1944.

52. *M06742*, 13 November 1942, Conseiller d'Etat, Sec. Gén. à la Police, Cado aux Préfets.

53. *M010433*, 18 August 1943, "Rapport sur le Moral et l'activité des Travailleurs Etrangers."

54. *M06566*, 16 October 1941, "Note" in dossier "Télégrammes 1942," and *M06372*, 13 May 1942, Pour le Préfet Régional, Directeur du Cabinet, De Peretti Della Rocca.

55. Ibid.

56. *M05657*, 5 April 1943, N° 11-c-4, "Prélèvement de travailleurs pour l'Allemagne."

57. *M07167*, 1 October 1943, "Note" Préfet Régional (Cl-Fd) à M. le Préfet Régional Limoges; also 7 July 1943, Préfet Régional de Cl-Fd à M. le Chef du Gouvernement "Objet: ramassage des Espagnols."

58. *M05654*, dossier entitled "Application aux étrangers de la procédure des mutations." Also *M06491*, 5 June 1944, Consul d'Espagne (Lyon) à M. le Préfet du PdD.

59. *M07167*, 7 July 1943, Préfet Régional de Cl-Fd à M. le Chef du Gouvernement.

60. *M05657*, 12 January 1944, "Télégramme," Préfet Cantal au Préfet Régional Cl-Fd.

61. *M010433*, 12 July 1943, Rougier Chef du S/Groupement départemental de la MOE à M. le Chef du Groupement N° 1 de la MOE Vic-le-Comte.

62. Ibid.; see various other reports in *M010433*.

63. *M010433*, 27 October 1943, Préfet Délégué à M. le Chef du Gouvernement.

64. *M010433*, 3 July 1944, GTE report, Rougier; and 23 June 1944, Renseignements Généraux à M. le Préfet Délégué.

65. Michael R. Marrus and Robert O. Paxton, *Vichy France and the Jews* (New York: Basic Books, 1981), originally published as *Vichy et les Juifs* by Calmann-Lévy, is the best overall study of Vichy's policy toward the Jews.

66. *M09982*, 12 March 1941, Chevreux, Préfet du PdD aux Maires du département. See also Préfet du PdD aux Maires, 15 October 1941, in *M06219* for a further explanation of the law's application. See Adam Rutkowski (ed)., *La Lutte des Juifs en France à l'époque de l'occupation* (Paris: Centre de Documentation Juive Contemporaine, 1975) for documents relative to the application of various measures taken against the Jews.

67. *M010501*, 9 August 1941, Maire, Cl-Fd au Préfet PdD. This file includes the individual declarations for each Jewish family from all communes in the PdD.

68. *M07169*, 8 May 1943, Intendant Régional de Police de Cl-Fd à M. le Chef de la délégation de Police Allemande (Vichy); from other evidence in *M07199*, a list for the PdD with 214 names and addresses, mostly of Polish Jews, was turned over to the German police 7 May 1943.

69. *M07169*, 9 December 1942, le Préfet Délégué du PdD à M. le Commissaire Central de Cl-Fd; *M010511* includes the text of an affiche, "Avis aux Juifs résidant dans le Puy-de-Dôme," ordering them to report to the police or gendarmerie stations before 14 January 1943 to have their papers stamped. *M07169*, 18 January 1943, Kastner, Commissaire Central Cl-Fd, à M. l'Intendant de Police, includes lists of the 259 foreign and 670 French Jews who came into the police stations at Cl-Fd.

70. *M07184*, 28 July 1941, Intendant de Police à M. G. Sardier, Chef Départemental de la Légion, and *M07185*, Intendant de Police à M. Lefebvre, Dir. Gén. du Personnel, Vichy.

71. *M010432*, "Demandes d'autorisation de séjour dans le Puy-de-Dôme refusés."

72. Letter of 7 April 1941, file F-L, in *M010446*. This file includes some requests that were approved. In each case it is clear that the individual had to have a guaranteed work contract or means of support to be allowed in, and even these did not guarantee acceptance. See *M010432*, "Demandes d'autorisation de séjour dans le Puy-de-Dôme refusés."

73. *M010253–M010254* contain documentation concerning *Passeports*, 1939–1946; *M010287* and *M010441* contain documentation concerning *Visas de Sortie*.

74. *M07173*, dossier on racketeers at Vichy and Chatel-Guyon making fortunes off of Jews who sought passage out of France.

75. *M07153*, 19 August 1941, Ch. Chevreux, Préfet PdD à M. le Ministre à l'Intérieur.

76. 1 December 1941, Intendant de Police, Cl-Fd, à M. Fougeron, Sous-Préfet de Riom (my italics).

77. *M010494*, Compte-rendu of "Réunion de la Sous-Commission pour l'expulsion des Israélites de la Région Administrative de Clermont-Ferrand," 15 June 1942 at Hotel de Parc, Vichy; *M07149*, Préfet Régional de Cl-Fd aux Préfets de la Région, describing application of the measure originally decided upon in May. *M010507*, 20 May 1942, V-Admiral Platon à M. le Secrétaire d'Etat à l'Intérieur; *M010494*, 20 May 1942, Platon à Secrétaire Général pour la Police. This dossier also includes "Etat des Travaux de la Commission Dept. de Révision des Permis de Séjour," I° Division, 4 September 1942; other relevant information in *M010504*, *M010506*, and *M010508*.

78. *M010494*, 17 October 1942, Platon à M. le Chef du Gouvernement, and a "Note" of 20 May 1942, Platon à M. le Sec. Gén. pour la Police. Other documents relative to this operation are in *M07149* and *M010504–508*.

79. Accounts of the later meetings are in *M010494*, *M010504*, *M010505*, and *M010506*.

80. *M010494*, 13 July 1942, U.G.I.F. à M. le Préfet PdD; also in *M010494*, a request from the Préfet Délégué à M. le Dir. Gén. Pol. Nat. to order other prefects that these Jews no longer be "systematically forbidden to establish themselves in new homes," and 23 July 1942, Cado aux Préfets

zone non-occupé, directed them not to put obstacles in the way of resettlement for these displaced persons.

81. *M07169,* "Projet de mesures à prendre pour le changement de résidence des juifs"; early spring, 1943? *M010504,* the notices signed by those affected only rarely indicated their destination. *M010494,* in files of Préfet Délégué PdD is a "Note" of 29 July 1942 with reference to a phone call from 9th Bureau Police Nationale, in which the police authorities at Vichy admitted that the failure to assign destinations had been unfortunate.

82. *M07196,* copy of law of 18 November 1939 authorizing camps and a fourteen-page "Instruction secret aux préfets: N° 12" from A. Sarraut, Minister of the Interior, 14 December 1939, explaining the exceptional nature of this procedure and warning against abuses of power. Pétain's decree is in Law of 4 October 1940, *Journal Officiel* of 18 October 1940.

83. *M07196,* Annexes N° I et N° 1 Bis à la circulaire N° 127 Pol. Cab. du 31 Jan. 1942, and *M05538–40,* "Camps d'internement et les centres de hébergement surveillé," 31 January 1942.

84. It is difficult to obtain a precise figure because of overlapping jurisdictions and uneven reporting, but certainly tens of thousands were interned in these camps. In 1943 German reports talked of 28,000 in all of the GTE; perhaps 35,000 political opponents (almost all Communists or alleged to be) were interned by Vichy. For the PdD alone there were four labor camps, four rehabilitation or family centers, and at least three or four temporary camps of various sorts in addition to the relocation centers. The number of those interned or assigned to residence in the PdD during the occupation was probably at least 4000.

85. *M07199,* Circulaire of 3 November 1941, Ministre à l'Intérieur aux Préfets Régionaux. A whole series of *Instructions* spelling out in detail this process are in *M07199.* The most important are the *circulaires* of 3 November and 14 December 1941; and 2 and 5 January, 30 March, and 18 April 1942.

86. *M010512,* 29 November 1941, Préfet PdD à M. le Commissaire Central de Cl-Fd; and 29 November 1941, Préfet Régional Cl-Fd aux 4 Préfets Départmentaux.

87. *M010514,* 25 March 1942, Préfet Régional à M. le Ministre à l'Intérieur.

88. Forty were foreign and twenty-one French. See *M07199,* 12 March 1942, Commissaire de Police, Riom, à M. l'Intendant de Police, Cl-Fd; and *M07168,* 6 February 1942, Arrêté by Préfet Régional, Paul Brun, ordering thirty-four of these persons to the departmental center of surveillance at Chateauneuf-les Bains.

89. Various documents in *M07153, M010450, M010512,* and *M06372* describe this process.

90. *M07191,* 3 June 1943, Commissaire Divisionnaire, Chef de Service Régional de Police de Sûreté à M. l'Intendant de Police, Cl-Fd; *M010494* includes several additional reports to the intendant relevant to these operations in June 1943.

91. *M09982* contains arrêtés ordering expulsion and letter of 28 May 1943, Sous-Préfet Riom à M. le Préfet PdD. See also *M07199* and *M07170,* Commissaire de Police Riom à M. l'Intendant de Police, Cl-Fd, admitting that "the real goal" of an earlier action at Chatel-Guyon had been to

make room for government employees. For the events at Puy-Guillaume, *M07185*, 30 September 1941, Intendant de Police à Cmdt. Michelet (Gendarmerie).

92. Interview and correspondence with Dr. Cecile Wechsler, to whom I am indebted for graciously sharing her memories and numerous documents with me.

93. Evidence for at least seventeen different operations or incidents that led to deportations are documented in the Archives départementales at Cl-Fd. My estimate of the number of people deported is drawn from over fifty different dossiers. Some of the most important files include *R01807*, *R01808*, *M06370*, *M07162*, *M07163*, *M07169*, *M010507*, and *M010512*. See also *De l'université aux camps de concentration: Témoignages Strasbourgeois* (Paris, 1954).

94. *M07199*, 22 May 1942 and 25 June 1942, M. Suramy, Directeur Régional du Service de l'Aryanisation Economique, Cl-Fd, à M. l'Intendant de Police; *M06913*, "Liste des Affaires juives, pourvus d'un Administrateur provisiore, dont les dossiers sont déposés, par ordre alphabetique aux Archives Départementales."

95. *M07169*, 3 October 1942, Intendant de Police aux Commissaires de police de la région.

96. *M07169*, 18 February 1942, Monsieur Suramy, Directeur . . . Aryanisation Economique à M. l'Intendant de Police (Cl-Fd), "Exposé Sommaire sur l'Activité du Service de l'Aryanisation Economique."

97. *M06548*, 20 July 1942, Procès verbal de réunion de coordination des Chefs de Services Régionaux.

98. *M06370; M05823*, Dossier Général Gestapo-Clermont; *M07221*, Rapport Milice, 15 May 1945; *M07173*, dossier on racketeers at Vichy and Chatel-Guyon making fortunes off of Jews who sought passage out of France; *M07798* and *M07169* also document various blatant extralegal acts of extortion, theft, and so on, against Jewish families.

99. Interview with Jean Ulmann, 24 January 1979.

100. *M06445*, 18 September 1944, Commissaire de la République à M. le Préfet; *M09483*, Administration des Biens Juifs. Unfortunately, the directeur of the Archives Nationales in Paris rejected my request to see files there that would have allowed a comparison of the situation in Cl-Fd to other cities in the South. Therefore, I cannot estimate how representative this situation might have been for France as a whole.

101. *M07188*, 7 August 1942, Intendant de Police à M. le Directeur . . . Sociétés Secrètes; and *M07191*, 2 April 1942, Le Délégué Régional de la Police des Sociétés Secrètes à M. le Préfet Régional.

102. *M07152*, folder entitled "Police de Questions Juives, Police des Sociétés Secrètes."

103. *M07169*, (especially Délégué Régional de la SEC Q.J. à M. l'Intendant de Police (Cl-Fd), 22 June 1943) and *M07199* (2 April 1943, Directeur de la SEC . . . Cl-Fd à M. l'Intendant) provide particularly good illustrations from which the quotations are taken, but many examples of the same phenomenon are throughout the files relative to Jewish affairs.

104. Azier had been criticized by the SEC for too readily signing travel permits for Jews. As with many of those arrested by the Germans, no explanation for his arrest was given to the French authorities.

105. *M010507*, 27 August 1942. This situation clearly was not exceptional. Lists of Jewish fugitives to be arrested were soon circulated by prefectures from all over southern France (see *M010511*). Literally thousands of Jews were hiding out to escape deportation. This suggests that the Jews in southern France did not accept deportation passively.

106. *M07169*, 25 August 1943, Gendarmerie Brigade de Billom, Rapport, "Sur incidents au cours de ramassage de Juifs." On the back of this report Capt. Rouanes, Cdt. la Section de Cl-Fd, added: "This case is not the only one. Very frequently those to be rounded up are aware of the operation a long time before the gendarmerie."

107. *M07169*, 24 August 1943, Commissaire de Police de la Ville d'Issoire à M. le Commissaire Divisionnaire Chef de la Sûreté Publique. Other examples are in *M010512*. The Germans were convinced that Jews allowed to work in the office of the GTE were passing warnings. See Monatsbericht Nr. 9, Kontrollinspektion der DWStK, Kontrollabteilung Az 20 Bourges, 8 Jan. 1944, Militärarchiv, Freiburg.

108. *M07153*, "Ramassage des Israélites étrangers"; *M07169*, "Ramassage Israélites Todt"; *M05664*, 5 August 1943, Nachtigall (OPA) to Préfet Régional. In his response the prefect said that the French director of the STO could not imagine how that could have happened. It may not be entirely unrelated to these events that Mr. Houzel, the French official involved, resigned his post a few weeks after this incident with the German labor draft official.

109. *M010512*, 16 November 1941, Maire de La Bourboule à M. le Préfet du PdD. See *M07858* and *M06369* for examples of denunciations; *M06764* and *M03770* for reports of broken windows; *M05776* for Légion complaints; and *M03955* for speech of the mayor of Saint-Gervais on his installation as mayor, in which he decries the activity of "la Juiverie internationale"and "la puissance judéo-maconnique." (Incidentally, this particular mayor was shot by a resistance firing squad before the liberation.)

110. Varenne to Pétain, 20 February 1941. Varenne had first protested against the Vichy regime's anti-Semitic policies in an earlier letter to Pétain, 4 December 1940. I am indebted to Alphonse Rozier for sharing with me his copies of the Varenne-Pétain letters.

111. Walter Laqueur, *The Terrible Secret* (Boston: Little, Brown, 1981) demonstrates that although much information was available from an early date about the mass murder of Jews, many people (both Jews and non-Jews) were unable or unwilling to believe it was happening.

112. *La Semaine religieuse de Clermont-Ferrand*, #11, 13 March 1943.

113. A copy of the appeal is reproduced in *Ville de Toulouse, Bulletin Municipal*, numéro spécial consacré à la libération de Toulouse, October 1944 (Marseille: Imprimerie Gaussel & Cie.) p. 28.

114. *M07191*, Groupement N° 1 de la MOE Vic-le-Comte, "Rapport Mensuel sur l'Etat du Moral: mois de Juillet 1942."

115. *M07152*, "Synthèse" August 1942.

116. *F0 892/155*, "Summary of Events in France from the 17th August to the 6th September," and "Summary of Events in France from the 6th to 19th September (1942)." PRO (Kew).

117. Georges Wellers, *L'Etoile jaune à l'heure de Vichy* (Paris: Fayard, 1973), pp. 263–264, argues that popular disapproval forced Laval to back down

from harsher treatment of the Jews in France, and the evidence for Clermont-Ferrand supports his contention.

118. *M010511*, 11 September 1942, Préfet du PdD délégué à M. le ——."
119. Several letters in *M010511*.
120. *M07153*, 25 March 1943, Intendant Régional de Police à M. le Commandant du G.M.R. d'Auvergne.
121. *M07170*, 25 November 1941, Hôteliers et Commerçants de St.-Nectaire à
M. le Préfet du PdD.
122. Paxton, *Vichy France*, p. 173.

Chapter 6

1. Varenne to Pétain, 22 November 1940. Alphonse Rozier has kindly made
available to me copies of Varenne's letters to Pétain and introduced me to
Francisque Fabre, director of *La Montagne*, who provided me with copies
of Varenne's correspondence with censorship officials in Clermont-Ferrand
and at Vichy.
2. Varenne to Pétain, 31 July 1941.
3. Varenne to Pétain, 2 November 1940.
4. Varenne to Pétain, 29 November 1940.
5. Ibid.
6. Varenne to Pétain, 10 December 1940.
7. Ibid.
8. Ibid. (my italics).
9. Varenne to Pétain, 13 February 1941.
10. Varenne to Pétain, 26 December 1940.
11. Varenne to Pétain, 6 January 1941.
12. Varenne to Pétain, 15 January 1941.
13. Varenne to Pétain, 6 January 1941. Varenne's comments reflected his own
opinions and prejudices, of course, but given his dual function of politician
and journalist of several decades experience with a widespread network of
contacts in the region, he was particularly well placed to understand the
mood of the population. In a sense both as politician and journalist it was
his *business* to keep up with shifts in popular attitudes. His views were
those of only one man, but they were those of a particularly well-informed
man.
14. Varenne to Pétain, 13 February 1941.
15. Varenne to Pétain, 22 November 1940.
16. Ibid.
17. Ibid.
18. *M03824*, 19 November 1940, Conseiller de Préfecture chargé de la liaison
avec les Commissions de contrôle postal, télégraphique, téléphonique de
Cl-Fd à Monsieur le Préfet.
19. *M03824*, 17 January 1941, Conseiller de Préfecture chargé de la liaison
avec les Commissions de contrôle postal, télégraphique, et téléphonique de
Cl-Fd à Monsieur le Préfet.
20. Notices of suspensions in *M06376* and in telegrams given to me by Francisque Fabre.
21. Varenne to Marion, 3 March 1941.
22. Varenne to Pétain, 29 November 1940.

23. Varenne to Pétain, 28 February 1941.

24. Varenne to Marion, 9 March 1941.

25. Philippe Amaury, *Les Deux Premières Expériences d'un "Ministère de l'Information" en France* (Paris: Librairie générale de droit et de juris-prudence, 1969) provides an excellent demonstration of this phenomenon on the national level. Sarah Dobin Shields, "A Case Study of Press Censor-ship in Vichy France" (M.A. thesis, University of Kansas, 1978) has writ-ten an insightful account of the situation at Cl-Fd based on a careful com-parison of *La Montagne* with other local newspapers.

26. Varenne to Monsieur le Secrétaire Général à l'Information, 28 April 1943.

27. *M05755,* notice dated 9 September 1943.

28. Militärverwaltungsbezirk B, Lagebericht für die Zeit vom 11. bis 19.8. 1940, O.U. den 19/8/40. In file RW 35/1254 V.1070, Militärarchiv, Freiburg.

29. 25 November 1940, Commissaire de Police du 3° Arrondissement à Mon-sieur le Préfet du PdD, Rapport moral mensuel d'ordre général, N° 3765, and 11 November 1940, Préfet à Monsieur le Ministre à l'Intérieur. Both in *M03822.*

30. *M03822,* 27 May 1941, le Commissaire de Police, Chef de la Sûreté, à Monsieur le Préfet du PdD.

31. *M07191,* 24 June 1943, Rapport Mensuel (Situation Morale et Econo-mique) Police, Situation Générale . . . de Vichy. A host of reports testi-fied to a general absence of faith in the French news media throughout the occupation years.

32. *M07191,* 15 December 1942, Ministère de l'Intérieur, "Synthèse des Rap-ports des Préfets de la Zone libre pour le mois de November 1942."

33. *M05756,* 28 December 1942, Rapport au Maréchal Pétain, attached to Rapport du Commissaire Légionnaire à la Propagande, Assemblé du 5 January 1943.

34. Ibid. (my italics).

35. Hoare at Madrid to FO, 27 July 1940, in Political Central France, FO 371 (24312), c 8003/65/17, PRO, Kew.

36. Stanley Hoffmann, Introduction to *The Sorrow and the Pity* (New York: (Outerbridge & Lazard, 1972).

37. Robert O. Paxton, *Vichy France* (New York: Alfred A. Knopf, 1972), pp. 235, 240–241.

38. *M07191,* 27 March 1942, Rapport Mensuel, Commissaire Central à Mon-sieur l'Intendant de Police.

39. *Le Moniteur,* 23 March 1942.

40. *M07191,* 24 March 1942, Commissaire 1° Arrondissement à Monsieur l'Intendant de Police.

41. *M07191,* 25 March 1942, Commissaire de Police, 3° Arrondissement à Monsieur l'Intendant de Police (my italics).

42. *M07788,* 5 July 1942, Rapport mensuel régional d'information, Honoré Guerrin, Préfet du PdD, "Opinion publique."

43. *M07191,* 26 June 1942, Commissaire Central Ville de Cl-Fd à Monsieur l'Intendant.

44. *M07887,* 24 June 1942, Commissaire Divisionnaire des Renseignements Généraux, "Note de Renseignement." Similar comments in *M07191, 25* June 1942, Commissaire 1° Arrondissement à Monsieur l'Intendant de

Police, and 23 June 1942, Commissaire 3° Arrondissement à Monsieur l'Intendant de Police.

45. American and British intelligence evaluations stressed the sharp impact of Laval's speech. Among the most interesting of numerous documents concerning this issue to be found in the Public Record Office, Kew, are z 6140/81/17, a report dated 27 July 1942, including references to a telegram from the U.S. Embassy at Vichy; z 7673/81/17, a paper on "French Morale," 7 October 1942, contains the combined views of FO, PWE, MEW and the three Service Departments that with the return of Laval a marked change was observable from an earlier anti-German but passive attitude with "apathy" the main characteristic to a "considerable wave of resentment." The report concluded that although de Gaulle's active following was still small, a majority of French supported de Gaulle as a symbol of resistance. According to one informant, Laval's speech of 22 June 1942: "a produit l'effet d'une véritable rupture entre le Gouvernement et l'opinion éclairée du pays, venant s'ajouter à celle qui existe depuis longtemps déjà entre les dirigeants de Vichy et le peuple." z 6214/81/17, 4 July 1942, Brugère in Vichy to Sir Ronald Campbell, English ambassador in Portugal.

46. *M06473*, 4 August 1942, N° 433, Sous-Préfet du Thiers à Monsieur le Préfet Délégué.

47. *M06474*, 31 July 1942, Guerrin à Brun, and 3 August 1942, Brun à Chef du Gouvernement, Ministre à l'Intérieur.

48. *M07152*, "Synthèse," August 1942.

49. *M07188*, 22 July 1942, Intendant de Police à Monsieur le Gén. Conquet, "Compte-rendu mensuel"; 14 July 1942, Préfet Régional à Monsieur le Chef de Gouvernement, "Compte-rendu Journée du 14 July"; and Intendant de Police à Monsieur le Préfet Régional; *M07161* Dossier "14 Juillet."

50. *M04861*, 27 July 1942, le Chef du Gouvernment Ministre Secrétaire d'Etat à l'Intérieur à Monsieur le Préfet Régional de Cl-Fd.

51. For example, Eugène Martres, "Le Cantal de 1939 à 1945" (Thèse, Université de Clermont-Ferrand, 1974). The overview of the evolution of public opinion presented in Yves Durand, *Vichy 1940–1944* (Paris: Bordas, 1972), is grounded in specialized research in the departmental archives of the Loiret. Marcel Baudot, *L'Opinion publique sous l'occupation* (Paris: Presses Universitaires de France, 1960), focusing on the Eure, includes numerous excerpts concerning public opinion from the local archives.

52. The records of the German occupation forces at Cl-Fd are preserved in the Militärarchiv, Freiburg. Among the most important sources for public opinion are the Kriegstagebuch of the Rüstungkontrollkommission (Rü.K.K.) covering 1941 through August 1944, and various partial series of Lageberichte and monthly reports of the military units stationed in the vicinity. I have also consulted the Captured German Documents in the National Archives, Washington, D.C.

53. Unfortunately, SOE files are not open for research, but much relevant information is to be gleaned from the Foreign Office records at the PRO (Kew) (London). With State Department clearance, the OSS records may be consulted in the National Archives, Washington, D.C.

54. Georgette Elgey, Preface to Françoise Renaudot, *Les Français et l'occupation* (Paris: Robert Laffont, 1975), p. 38.
55. Ibid.
56. Intervention, 29 October 1974, Colloque: La Libération de la France, CNRS, Paris.
57. Martres, "Le Cantal de 1939 à 1945," pp. 270–271.
58. In his radio speech of October 30, 1940, explaining his actions and calling on the French people to follow him ("cette politique est la mienne. Les ministres ne sont responsables que devant moi. C'est moi seul que l'Histoire jugera. Je vous ai tenu jusqu'ici le language d'un père. Je vous tiens aujourd'hui le language du chef. Suivez-moi. Gardez votre confiance en la France éternelle!"), Pétain acknowledged himself that his actions had "provoqué des inquiétudes." *Le Moniteur,* 31 October 1940.
59. *M03822,* 22 June 1941, "Bulletin Economique et Social," Commandant Militaire du Département du PdD; 23 May 1941, "Bulletin Economique et Social," Commandant Militaire Peragallo; and 25 January 1941, "Bulletin Economique et Social," Lt. Col. Peragallo, Commandant Militaire du Département du PdD.
60. *M03822,* Rapport, 3 April 1941, Michelet, Chef d'Escadron, Commandant de la Gendarmerie Nationale, 13° Légion.
61. *M07788,* 1 March 1942, Brun, Rapport Mensuel d'Information.
62. *M07164,* March 1944, Commissaire de Police Chamalières à Monsieur l'Intendant de Police, Rapport Mensuel.
63. FO 371 French 1942, France File #81, Document z 960/81/17, PRO (Kew), letter to FO dated 26 January 1942 from Mr. E. Lancial, Minister Plenipotentiary (appointed representative to Bolivia for de Gaulle's French National Committee). All quotations in this paragraph from this letter.
64. *M03822,* 10 October 1941, "Rapport Périodique, Commission de Contrôle Postal de Clermont-Ferrand," N° XXVII, p. 7.
65. *M03822,* 1 September 1941, Le Commissaire de Police, Chef de la Sûreté à Monsieur le Préfet du PdD. The Postal Control Commission's report of hostility to the Marshal as well as his entourage is in *M03822,* 1 September 1941, Commission de Contrôle Postale, "Rapport périodique 1 Août–1 Septembre 1941."
66. *M07191,* 25 September 1942, Commissaire Central Cl-FD à Monsieur l'Intendant de Police.
67. *M07191,* 24 October 1942, Commissaire de Police 2° Arrondissement Cl-Fd à Monsieur le Préfet du PdD.
68. France File #52, Report: Morale in France, z 4059/52/17. Interrogation by War Office in March 1943.
69. z 4170/52/17 PRO, 20 March 1943, Ridley Prentice, British Embassy Lisbon to Central Dept. FO—political memorandum based on interviews of people leaving France.
79. *M07191,* 15 December 1942, Commissaire Divissionaire Chef des Renseignements Généraux à Monsieur le Directeur des Renseignements Généraux (Vichy).
71. *M07191,* 25 November 1942, Rapport Mensuel, Commissaire Central (Kastner) à Monsieur le Préfet Délégué.
72. Ibid.

73. Cl-Fd, 27 Nov. 1942, Rü.K.K.I, Stimmungs-bericht zum Monatsbericht für November 1942, Militärarchiv, Freiburg.

74. FO 371, France File #7 (35995), z 7/7/17, Berne to FO, 30 December 1942, report of conversations with Stucki in Berne.

75. *M07191,* 26 December 1942, Rapport Mensuel, Commissaire Central à Monsieur le Préfet Délégué.

76. *M03822,* 30 September 1941, Rapport Mensuel, Commissaire de Police, Chef de la Sûreté à Monsieur le Préfet du PdD.

77. Durand, *Vichy 1940–1944,* pp. 104–105. Marcel Baudot's account of public opinion in the Eure (*L'Opinion publique sous l'occupation*) suggests a similar pattern.

78. *M03822,* 25 November 1940, Commissaire de Police 3° Arrt. à Monsieur le Préfet du PdD. #3765 Rapport mensuel d'ordre général.

79. *M03822,* 26 February 1941, Commissaire de Police de 2° Arrt. à Monsieur le Préfet, #1638.

80. *M03822,* 19 March 1941, Rapport Mensuel Gendarmerie National PdD.

81. *M03822,* 30 April 1941, Le Commissaire de Police, Chef de la Sûreté, à Monsieur le Préfet du PdD.

82. *M03822,* Weekly synthesis of interceptions through PTT control, #140, 23 May 1941.

83. *M03822,* 30 July 1941, Commissaire de Police, Chef de la Sûreté, à Monsieur le Préfet du PdD.

84. *M03822,* 1 August 1941, Le Commissaire Central de la Ville de Cl-Fd à Monsieur le Préfet du PdD.

85. *M03822,* 5 October 1941, Ch. Chevreux, Préfet du PdD. Rapport Mensuel d'Information.

86. *M03823,* 31 October 1941, Le Commissaire de Police, Chef de la Sûreté, à Monsieur le Préfet Régional, Rapport Mensuel.

87. *M03823,* 31 December 1941, Rapport Mensuel d'Information, Le Commissaire des Renseignements Généraux, Chef de Service.

88. *M07191,* 24 February 1942, Rapport Mensuel, Commissaire de Police 2° Arrondissement à Monsieur le Préfet.

89. *M07152,* Synthèse des Rapports des Préfets de la Zone Libre, April 1942.

90. *M07191,* 24 April 1942, Rapport Mensuel, Commissaire du 2° Arrt.

91. Rü.K.K.I, Cl-Fd, 5 June 1942, Monatsbericht vom 1 bis 31 May 1942.

92. *M07191,* 24 October 1942, Rapport Mensuel, Commissaire Central à Monsieur l'Intendant de Police (italics in original).

93. *M07191,* 27 March 1942, Commissaire Central Ville de Cl-Fd à Monsieur l'Intendant de Police.

94. *M07191,* 24 April 1943, Rapport Mensuel, Commissaire Central à Monsieur le Préfet Délégué.

95 *M07185,* 1 October 1941, Préfet Régional de Cl-Fd à Monsieur l'Intendant de Police.

96. *M07191,* 25 August 1943, Rapport Mensuel, Commissaire Central Cl-Fd à Monsieur le Préfet Délégué.

97. Alexander Werth, *The Twilight of France* (New York: Howard Fertig, 1966; original edition Harper, 1942), p. 37.

98. *M07191,* 24 April 1942, Rapports Mensuels, Commissaires de Police, 2° et 3° Arrondissements, Cl-Fd, à Monsieur le Commissaire Central et Monsieur l'Intendant de Police.

99. *M07191*, 2 April 1942, Le Délégué Régional de la Police des Sociétés Secrètes à Monsieur le Préfet Régional.

100. *M07164*, March 1944, Rapport Mensuel, Commissaire de Police, 3° Arrondissement, Cl-Fd.

101. *M07191*, 24 April 1943, Rapport Mensuel, Commissaire Divisionnaire de Vichy à Monsieur le Sous-Préfet de Vichy.

102. *M07191*, 31 January 1942, Chef de Sûreté à Monsieur l'Intendant de Police.

103. FO 371 Political Central France File #65, pp. 11239–12824, 1940 (z 4314). Marginal notes on several reports in October, November, and December 1940 convey this assessment. See also FO 371, 1942 France File #81 (31942), z 6117/81/17, 28 July 1942, a report by W. McStewart on the evolution of Jacques Bardoux with regard to opinion toward England.

104. *M07191*, 24 March 1942, Rapport Mensuel, Commissaire du 2° Arrondissement à Monsieur le Préfet.

105. *M07191*, 25 April 1942, Commissaire de Police, 1° Arrondissement à Monsieur l'Intendant de Police.

106. Document z 1927/81/17, British Embassy, Washington, Hoyar Millar to Mr. Mack, 20 Feb. 1942, PRO (Kew).

107. *The Sorrow and the Pity* (New York: Outerbridge & Lazard, 1972), pp. 96, 100.

108. Reports by French police as well as German economic and military officials are in complete agreement on this point. See Chapter 7 for further elaboration.

109. *M03794*, 17 June 1941, Lt. Colonel Peragallo, Commandant Militaire du Département du PdD à Monsieur le Préfet du Département du PdD (italics in original).

110. *M07191*, 24 March 1942, Commissaire 1° Arrondissement à Monsieur l'Intendant de Police.

111. *M07191*, 27 February 1942, Commissaire Central à Monsieur l'Intendant, Rapport Mensuel.

112. *M06576*, 4 October 1943, J. de Goer, CSPF Union Départementale des Syndicats professionals Français du PdD et du Cantal à Monsieur le Préfet Délégué; and several related documents in the same file.

113. *M03822*, reports of 11 November 1940 and 2 December 1940, Préfet du PdD à Monsieur le Ministre, Sec. d'Etat à l'Intérieur.

114. *M03822*, CCCP/2.816/M.A., 19 June 1941, Nº 4 à Monsieur le Préfet.

115. *M03822*, 27 May 1941 Commissaire de Police, Chef de la Sûreté, à Monsieur le Préfet du PdD.

116. *M03822*, 29 May 1941, Rapport Mensuel, Commissaire de Police, 2° Arrondissement à Monsieur le Préfet.

117. *M03823*, 13 November 1941, Ministre à l'Intérieur aux Préfets "Synthèse" of monthly reports for October 1941. Similar reports in 1942 indicate that this preoccupation with material concerns remained strong. For example, *M07788*, 1 March 1942, Brun, Préfet Régional, Rapport Mensuel d'Information, and *M07191*, 28 April 1942, Rapport Mensuel, Commissaire Central à Monsieur l'Intendant de Police.

118. *M03823*, 3 January 1942, Paul Brun, Préfet, Rapport Mensuel d'Information.

119. Henri Michel, *Le Procès de Riom* (Paris: Albin Michel, 1979).

120. See Chapter 3 of John Sweets, *The Politics of Resistance in France 1940–1944* (DeKalb: Northern Illinois University Press, 1976).

121. *M07191*, 24 October 1942, Rapport Mensuel, Commissaire de Police à Monsieur l'Intendant de Police.

122. Ibid.

123. *M07191*, 24 June 1943, Rapport Mensuel Vichy.

124. *M03822*, 1 October 1941, "Rapport Périodique, Commission de Contrôle Postal de Clermont-Ferrand," no. XXVII, 1 September–1 October.

125. *M03822*, 29 May 1941, Sous-Préfet Riom à Monsieur le Préfet du PdD.

126. *M06473*, 4 August 1942, Sous-Préfet Thiers à Monsieur le Préfet Délégué.

127. *M07191*, 24 October 1942, Commissaire de Police 2° Arrondissement, Cl-Fd à Monsieur le Préfet PdD.

128. z 3116/81/17, Berne Chancellery to French Department, 8 March 1942, a report from M. Viple on tendencies in France, PRO (Kew).

129. FO 371, 1942 France File #81, z 7673/81/17, 7 October 1942 "French Morale" (Reporting agreed views of FO, PWE, MEW and the 3 Service Departments). In the same file z 6129/81/17, a note of 3 August 1942, signed W. Strang, relates the British view that by that time de Gaulle already commanded a substantial following. "At the outset, at any rate, General de Gaulle will probably be the predominant French authority in liberated territory in Metropolitan France."

130. *M07191*, 25 May 1943, Commissaire de Chamalières/Royat à Monsieur le Commissaire Central.

131. *M07191*, 25 March 1943, Rapport Mensuel, Kastner, Commissaire Central à Monsieur le Préfet Délégué.

132. *M07191*, 24 July 1943, Rapport Mensuel, Commissaire Central à Monsieur le Préfet Délégué.

132. *M07191*, 24 July 1943, Rapport Mensuel, Commissaire Central à Monsieur le Préfet Délégué.

133. Paxton, *Vichy France*, p. 235.

134. *M06357*, 5 June 1943, Renseignements Généraux N° 2711, Folder for June, July, August 1943; and *M07191*, 25 August 1943, Rapport Mensuel, Commissaire Central à Monsieur le Préfet Délégué.

Chapter 7

1. *M03893*, Préfet du Puy-de-Dôme à M. le Ministre de la Défense Nationale, 10 May 1940; *M03785*, Rapport, 22 July 1940; *R02074*, "Liste Nominative des Victimes Civiles décédé, par suite d'actes de violence de l'Ennemi"; and *M03770*, Le Commissaire Central de la Ville de Cl-Fd à M. le Préfet du PdD. The night before the German entry into Cl-Fd, four other civilians had been killed at Lempes and Dallet, small communes along the route from Thiers to Clermont.

2. *M03770*, 3 July 1940, le Commissaire Central de la Ville de Cl-Fd à M. le Préfet du PdD.

3. *M06764*, 7 July 1940, L. Chevalier, Huiles et Essences, 5, rue de Montrognon à M. le Préfet. Other evidence that the area was spared from pillage at this time is found in later reports of 27 December 1940 and 23

January 1941 (in *M09027*) noting that very few cattle had been carried off by the occupation troops.

4. *M06438*, 11 November 1940, Préfet du PdD à M. le Ministre à l'Intérieur.

5. *M07185*, report of incident 14 October 1941; *M07188* and *M07191*, reports of incidents 25 June 1942; and *M07188*, 22 July 1942, M. le Général Conquet—Compte-rendu mensuel.

6. *M07158*, 28 October 1944, Commissaire des Renseignements Généraux, Haudressy à M. l'Intendant-Directeur de la Police Régional, Cl-Fd.

7. Kriegstagebuch, Rü K.K., entry for 6 December 1941. All German documents cited in this chapter are in the Militärarchiv, Freiburg.

8. *M09020*, 5, 6, 7 April 1942, "Commission Allemand: Achats de Chevaux"; *M07860*, several letters and reports relative to the University of Strasbourg; and *M07186*, 17 December 1941, Inspecteur Principal des R.G. Reitter à M. le Commissaire des R.G. (Cl-Fd).

9. *M07188*, 9 June 1942, Note pour M. le Commissaire Central, 6 June 1942, Note pour M. le Préfet Régional, and 3 June 1942, Préfet Régional à M. le Préfet de l'Allier.

10. *M0561*, Le Conseiller d'Etat, Sec. Gén. à la Police à M. les Préfets Régionals *zone libre*, 8 July 1942.

11. *M07185*, 16 September 1941, Préfet Régional et Préfet de PdD aux Préfets de la région.

12. *M07860*, 21 December 1941, Ministre Sec. d'Etat à l'Intérieur, Sec. Gén. pour la Police L. Rivallaud à M. le Préfet Régional de Cl-Fd.

13. *M06507* includes several telegrams to this effect in 1941.

14. *M03785*, 10 August 1940, "Note."

15. *M07204*, 24 October 1941, Note of assignment to residence and explanation for it.

16. *M06369*, 22 March 1942, "Opinion du B.M.A., Général de Division Lenclud, Cmdt. la 13° Div. Militaire, 13° Division Militaire Bureau M.A."

17. LXVI Rs.K. 27922/1, "Die Entwaffnung der französischen Wehrmacht."

18. RW 35/1315 Kommandant des Heeresgebietes Sudfrankreich, Abteilung Verwaltung u. Wirtschaft, Schlussbericht.

19. RüK.K. I, Cl-Fd, 24/12/41, Monatsbericht—23/11–22/12/41.

20. Eberhard Jäckel, *La France dans l'Europe de Hitler* (Paris: Fayard, 1968). The original German edition, *Frankreich in Hitlers Europa,* was published in 1966 (Stuttgart: Deutsche Verlags-Anstalt).

21. Alan S. Milward, *The New Order and the French Economy* (Oxford: Oxford University Press, 1970), pp. 135–136 and passim. Another important discussion of the economic consequences of the occupation is available in Simon Mathew Karter, "Coercion and Resistance—Dependence and Compliance: The Germans, Vichy and the French Economy." Diss., University of Wisconsin, Madison, 1976 (Ann Arbor, University Microfilms, #76–20, 902).

22. Eugène Martres, "Les Troupes allemandes dans le Massif Central," *Cahiers d'histoire* [Lyon] 22, no. 4 (1977), 405–420.

23. Ibid.

24. Various documents in dossier RH 19 IV/141 Militärarchiv, Freiburg, and *Kriegs-Tage-Buch de l'Etat-Major Principal de Liaison N° 588 de Cler-*

mont-Ferrand (French translation, Chateau de Vincennes: Commandant Even, Service Historique de l'Armée de Terre, 1975).

25. RW 35/1315 Kommandant des Heeresgebietes Sudfrankreich, Abteilung Verwaltung u. Wirtschaft, Schlussbericht; *M06648*, 7 August 1944, RüK.K. de Cl-Fd à Royat à M. le Préfet; and 159 Res. Division Nr. 363/43 geh. An Gen. Kdo LXVI Res. Korps. 27 February 1943.

26. *R01869* includes a "Registre des Immeubles réquisitionnés" for Cl-Fd, Chamalières, Royat, and Thiers, and other documents relative to requisitions.

27. *M07191*, Kastner, Commissaire Central, Ville de Cl-Fd à M. le Préfet Délégué, Rapport Mensuel, 26 December 1942; Commissaire de Police, Vichy, Rapport Mensuel, 24 June 1943; and Commissaire Divisionnaire R.G. à M. le Directeur des R.G. (Vichy).

28. *M09024*, "Evaluation Provisoire des dommages agricoles causés par la Guerre."

29. *M05758*, 22 March 1944, Coustet (vu Sardier) à M. Millet.

30. *M05667* and *M06748* contain numerous documents relative to requisition of vehicles in 1944.

31. *M06761*, 23 December 1943, Col. Picard à M. le Préfet Délégué, and 26 May 1944 Picard à M. le Préfet. Sardier lost his garage in 1943 and the apartment in 1944, and Colonel Picard insisted that the mayor should find another apartment for him.

32. *M07178*, "Etat des Matérials ayant appartenu à l'Armée sur le Département du PdD," and 24 July 1943, Le Directeur Général de l'Enregistrement des Domaines et du Timbre à M. le Directeur à Cl-Fd, ordering regularization of the transfers of title.

33. *R02023*, Telegram 13/11 22h15, Laval aux Préfets Zone Libre.

34. *M07188*, 18 November 1942, Intendant de Police: Note aux Commissaires Divisionnaires, etc.

35. *M07302*, 27 November 1942, P. Laval à M. le Préfet Régional. Also found in *M07165*.

36. Karter, "Coercion and Resistance," pp. 453–460.

37. *M07191*, 25 November 1942, Rapport Mensuel, Commissaire Central, Cl-Fd à M. le Préfet Délégué.

38. *M04860*, 5 January 1943, Direction Générale de la Gendarmerie Nationale à M. le Colonel Commandant de la 13° Légion de Gendarmerie; *M07191*, 23 August 1943, Rapport Mensuel, Commissaire Divisionnaire, Chef de la Sécurité Publique.

39. *M07149*, 25 September 1943, Bousquet à Messieurs les Préfets Régionales. Apparently misfiled in dossier titled "Circulaires Ministerielles 1941–42."

40. *M07851*, "Réunions des Préfets de la zone libre 1942–1944: Compte-rendu séance 23 February 1943."

41. *M010.372*, 8 March 1944, Préfet Régional Cl-Fd à Préfet Délégué.

42. *R01730* contains various ministerial instructions from Vichy to local officials concerning recommended behavior for direct contacts with occupation officials. *M0671*, "Rélations Franco-Allemandes 1942–1943," especially 12 February 1943, Sec. d'Etat à la Guerre aux Commissaires Régionaux à la Guerre; *R02070* contains several documents relative to "passive resistance" of French bureaucrats, notably in service of industrial production whose local officials are instructed not to refuse to give Germans information,

but to say they must ask Paris for statistics, etc. Also included are complaints from the EMPL 588 on 12 May 1943 and 6 July 1943 about such delays.

43. *M06707,* 23 May 1944, Intérieur aux Préfets.
44. *M07172,* 1 August 1944, Arbeitseinsatzstab Cl-Fd, Place Delille à M. l'Intendant de Police, Cl-Fd.
45. *R02070,* 7 May 1943, "Démandes EMPL 588: Sec. Gén. à la Police à M. le Préfet Régional de Cl-Fd." See *M04860,* 5 January 1943, Direction Générale de la Gendarmerie Nationale à M. le Colonel Commandant de la 13ᵉ Légion de Gendarmerie, for a similar assertion of independence of action.
46. *M07162–64* contain individual notices for those persons arrested by the Germans, 1943–1944.
47. *M07165,* 1 June 1943, "Circulaire, Pour M. le Chef du Gouvernement, Ministre Sec. d'Etat à l'Intérieur," signed Bousquet.
48. *M07302,* 12 November 1942, Intérieur Police Cabinet aux Préfets. After the April agreement with Oberg, Bousquet recirculated his earlier note but with the important addition: "Toutefois le concours de la Police Française peut être accordé aux autorités allemands si celles-ci demandent à être accompagnées dans une opération," *M07165,* 19 April 1943, "Note: Intendant de Police, Cl-Fd."
49. *M07165,* 1 June 1943, "Circulaire, Pour M. le Chef du Gouvernement, Ministre Sec. d'Etat à l'Intérieur," signed Bousquet. Paxton, *Vichy France,* pp. 295–298, contains a good, brief discussion of relations between French and German police in both zones.
50. *M07164,* report in files of intendant de police for January 1943.
51. *M07192,* 17 April 1943, Délégation der Deutschen Polizen Vichy an der Regionalpräfektur in Cl-Fd, and 27 April 1943, Sec. Général à la Police à M. l'Intendant régional de Police.
52. *M07153,* 12 July 1943, "Circulaire Chef du Govt, Sec. d'Etat à l'Intérieur," signed H. Cado, Sec. Gen. adjoint.
53. *M07164,* 10 March 1943, Commissaire Principal, Chef de Service Régional de Police de Sûreté à M. le Directeur des Services de la Police de Sûreté.
54. *M07165,* 1 June 1943, "Circulaire, Pour M. le Chef du Gouvernement, Ministre Sec. d'Etat à l'Intérieur," signed Bousquet.
55. *M07172,* 20 June 1944, "Note de Service: sur les communications à faire aux autorités allemands," Lt. Col. Hachette, Groupement des Forces du Maintien de l'Ordre de Cl-Fd. *M07212,* "Conférence des Secrétaires Généraux pour la Police, des 12 et 13 Décembre 1944"; text outlines history of the GMR/CRS noting that Vichy had planned to form 180 groups of the Gardes Mobiles de Reserve, but were allowed only 57 (40 in the south) by the Germans.
56. *M07165,* 4 April 1944, "Note."
57. Rü.K.K., Cl-Fd, 5 February 1943, Monatsbericht an die Rüs K. Inspektion Bourges.
58. *M05758,* 6 January 1944, Sardier à M. Lavauzelle; dozens of similar letters are scattered through numerous dossiers, including letters from Laval, Pétain, Mme. Giscard d'Estaing, and other local dignitaries.

59. *M03956*, 6 May 1944, Le Chef d'Escadron Durieux, Gendarmerie Nationale PdD à M. le Préfet Régional.

60. *M07165*, 29 April 1944, Sec. Gén. au Maintien de l'Ordre aux Préfets Régionaux.

61. 159 Res. Division Nr. 363/43 geh. 27 February 1943, Monatliche Meldungen an Gen. Kdo. LXVI Res. Korps.

62. Paxton, *Vichy France.*

63. Interview, 10 February 1979, Francisque Fabre.

64. LXVI Rs.K. 27922/1, "Die Entwaffnung der französischen Wehrmacht"; Abschrift 4 September 1944, Dr. Schmidt-Ewig MV-Obberrat, Verw. Gruppenleiter der OFK Cl-Fd (H.V.S.T. 588), "Bericht: Letzte Tätigkeit im Einsatzgebiet."

65. RW 34/V.76, Kontrollinspektion der D.W.St.K. Kontrollabteilung Az 20 Nr. 1212/44g 12 September 1944, Monatsbericht Nr. 17; and RW 35/1315 Kommandant des Heeresgebietes Sudfrankreich, Abteilung Verwaltung u. Wirtschaft, Schlussbericht.

66. Generalkommando LXVI Res. Korps. Abtl. Ic Nr. 3447/43 geh. 2 August 1943, Lagebericht für Monat Juli 1943.

67. RW 34/1315, Kommandant des Heeresgebietes Sudfrankreich, Abteilung Verwaltung u. Wirtschaft, Schlussbericht; also scattered comments in the monthly Lageberichte of the LXVI Res. Korps.

68. *M05551*, transcript of interrogation of ex-Préfet Régional Paul Brun, 13 October 1944, in connection with investigation of ex-Commissaire Divisionnaire Moritz. Generalkommando LXVI Res. Korps. Abtl. Ic Nr. 4073/43 geh. Lagebericht für Monat August 1943 states: "One has the impression that the authorities only do that which is necessary to avoid clashes with the German authorities."

69. *M07302*, 27 November 1942, P. Laval à M. le Préfet Régional. Also found in *M07165*.

70. Dossiers *M04862*, *M04870–72*, *M05230*, *M05645*, *M05758*, *M06357*, *M07172*, *M07174*, *M07190*, *M07193*, *R01778*, *R02009*, and *R02070* contain extensive documentation on these and other services required of the French.

71. *M07191*, Préfet Régional de Cl-Fd Intendance de Police, Rapport Mensuel de Fevrier 1943.

72. *R02070*, 24 June 1943, EMPL 588 Von Massow à M. le Préfet. Explanation of use of term *doryphore* by Roger Tounze in film *Le Chagrin et la Pitié.*

73. *M07172*, 11 September 1943, "Note" Préfet Délégué à M. le Préfet Régional.

74. *M07191*, 23 August 1943, Rapport Mensuel—Mois d'Août 1943, Police Régionale d'Etat de Cl-Fd, Intendance Régionale de Police Service de la Sécurité Publique.

75. *M07190*, 16 November 1943, Mayade à M. le Chef du Government "Effectives de Gendarmerie d'Auvergne utilisés à des services statiques permanents"; 28 December 1943, Intendant de Police de Cl-Fd à M. le Col. Krassmann, Commission Allemande de Controle; and M07191, Police Régionale d'Etat de Cl-Fd, Intendance Régionale de Police, Rapport Mensuel-Mois de Juillet 1943.

76. *M07191*, 23 August 1943, Rapport Mensuel—Mois d'Août 1943, Police

Régionale d'Etat de Cl-Fd, Intendance Régionale de Police Service de la Sécurité Publique.

77. *M04860*, 12 November 1943, Nº 477 SG/Pol Circu. STMO Le Conseiller d'Etat Secrétaire Général à la Police à Messieurs les Préfets Régionaux.

78. *M07190*, 17 November 1943, Mayade, Intendant de Police, Cl-Fd à M. le Col. Krassmann.

79. *M07214*, 8 February 1944, "Conférence d'Information des Commissaires Divisionnaires Chefs Régionaux des Services de Sécurité Publique tenue à Vichy, le 28 Janvier 1944."

80. See dossiers cited in note 70.

81. Pascal Ory, *Les Collaborateurs 1940–1945* (Paris: Editions du Seuil, 1976), p. 10.

82. Lageberichte of the LXVI Res. Korps.

83. *M04870*, 12 May 1944, Préfet Régional à M. le Préfet Délégué.

84. *M07181*, 18 March 1944, Préfet du Cantal à M. le Préfet Régional, and *M05230*, 14 Février 1944, Le Maire de la Ville de Thiers à M. le Préfet du PdD, Service des Rélations-Franco-Allemandes.

85. RW 34/V.77 Kontrollinspektion der DWStK Kontrollabteilung Az 20 Nr. 2983/43g "Sonderbericht Nr. 9," Bourges, 1/12/43, pp. 5–14; RW 34/48 Abteilung II; Französichen Miliz, 4 March 1944, Paris Deutscher Waffen-stillstandkommission Aussenstelle Paris Abt. I Nr. 76/44g an Kontrollin-spektion Bourges; and letters of General Bridoux Sec. d'Etat à la Défense à M. le Général Représentant à Vichy le Commandant en Chef 'Ouest,' dated 24 June 1943 and 29 July 1943. (in RW 34/48). RW 34/V.77.4, April 1944, Kontrollabteilung Az 33d Nr. 423/44g "Erganzungs- und Abshlussbericht zu Sonderbericht Nr. 9 betr. die französiche Miliz."

86. *M07172*, 13 August 1944, Télégramme, signed Darnand.

87. Interview, Alphonse Rozier, 5 March 1979.

88. RW 34/V.96 12/12/43 Kontrollkommission Cl-Fd, Befh Nr 527/43g an Kontrollinspektion der D.W.St.K. RW 34/V.94, 8 December 1943, Kom-mandant des Heeresgebietes Sudfrankreich Abt Ic/Qu. an Mil. Bef. im Frankreich, Paris, "Lager des französischen Arbeitsdientes," indicates that the camps of the Chantiers de Jeunesse were being raided with impunity by the maquis and meeting with no opposition from the French authorities.

89. *T01552*, 10 July 1942, Le Proviseur du Lycée Blaise Pascal à M. l'Inspec-teur d'Académie; 12 June 1944, Kommandant Kraftfahr-Park 688, Zweigstelle Cl-Fd à M. l'Inspecteur d'Académie de Cl-Fd.

90. *M07192*, 16 February 1944, Buffet, le directeur des Services de la Police de Sûreté à M. le Directeur du Personnel, du Budget et du Contentieux de la Police.

91. *M07165*, 20 November 1942, Kastner, Commissaire Central à M. le Préfet Délégué.

92. *M07191*, Paul Brun, Préfet Régional, Rapport Mensuel February 1943, "Rélations avec les Autorités d'Opérations"; Kastner, Commissaire Cen-tral à M. le Préfet Délégué, Rapports Mensuels for March, April, and May 1943; and 19 January 1943, 13° Légion de Gendarmerie "Rapport sur la Physionnomie Morale, Economique et Industrielle."

93. *M07191*, 26 May 1943, Rapport Mensuel—May 1943, Kastner, Commis-saire Central à M. le Préfet Délégué.

94. Rüstungskontrolloffizier III, Cl-Fd Tgb. No. 280/43, 30/12/1943, Monatsbericht Dezember 1943.

95. *M07856,* 25 August 1944, "Note" concerning the evacuation of buildings that had been requisitioned by the Germans.

96. *M07191,* 23 July 1943, Commissaire de Police de Chamalières-Royat à M. le Commissaire Central: Rapport Mensuel.

97. *M09309* contains enough evidence of what went on in Gestapo headquarters at Chamalières to turn the strongest of stomachs.

98. Serge Fischer, "A la prison militaire du 92," in *De l'Université aux Camps de Concentration: Témoignages Strasbourgeois,* 2nd edition (Paris: "Les Belles Lettres," 1954).

99. Interview, Alphonse Rozier, March 5, 1979.

100. René Cormand (pseud.), *La Vie d'une famille française face à la Gestapo* (Montreux: 1972), offers a dramatic and insightful image of the atmosphere at Clermont, particularly for those families whose relatives had been arrested by the Gestapo.

101. *M07318,* Text of "Audition," 47 typed pages of interrogation of Gustav Wilkens, Sonderfuhrer à le Feldkommandatur 588 à Cl-Fd.

102. Cormand, *Une Famille française,* and H. Baulig in *Témoignages Strasbourgeois,* "Au '92,'" pp. 21–37.

103. RW 35/1315, Kommandant des Heeresgebietes Sudfrankreich, Abteilung Verwaltung u. Wirtschaft, Schlussbericht.

104. Ernest Hvepffner, "La Rafle du 25 Novembre 1943," in *Témoignages Strasbourgeois,* and interviews, Paulette and Alphonse Rozier, March 12, 1979.

105. *M07244,* 17 October 1944, Commissaire Divisionnaire, Chef Régional des Renseignements Généraux au Secrétaire Régional pour la Police; 24 January 1946, Renseignements Généraux: "Statistique des crimes par les militaires allemands au cours de l'occupation, dans la commune de Clermont-Ferrand"; *R01807* contains a "repertoire" of arrests by the Germans in the PdD listing 1007 names, but only for those officially reported to French authorities. *R01807–01808* include lists and individual fiches for arrests including names not listed on the repertoire. A "Statistique de la Déportation" for the PdD by M. Martin was published in the *Bulletin* (N° 200, July–August 1972) of the Comité d'histoire de la deuxième guerre mondiale. Martin notes 1689 deportees, but his figures do not include several hundred Jews and foreigners. My estimate of 2000 arrests and deportations is a minimum figure. Because of conflicting reports in various documents, it is impossible to be precise in this matter, but the figure of 7000 deportees sometimes cited after the war is clearly an exaggeration. An undated report, drawn up in 1946 or 1947 by an official in the prefect's office, noted approximately 4000 arrests; but this document is often in error on many other points, and I would calculate that 4000 is the maximum possibility.

106. Henri Michel, *Les Courants de pensée de la Résistance* (Paris: Presses Universitaires de France, 1962), pp. 119–144.

107. Monthly reports are preserved at Freiburg for the 66 Reserve Division, the 189 Reserve Division, and the 159 Reserve Division, the three major units stationed in or around Cl-Fd. Occasionally differing on specific points of detail, they are substantially in agreement about the hostility of the general public.

108. 159 Res. Division, Monatliche Meldungen for January and February 1943.

109. LXVI Res. K. 36093/2, Bericht für März 1943, 2 April 1943.

110. Various French police files—for example, the monthly reports of the Commissaires de Police at Cl-Fd, *M07191*—make the attitudes toward collaborators clear. A special report on the Milice drawn up by the Germans in the fall of 1943 is in RW 34/77.

111. Rü.K.K., Kriegstagebuch, entry for 4 September 1942.

112. *M07186*, 17 December 1941, "Inspecteur Principal des Ren. Gen. Cl-Fd"; and numerous documents in dossier *M07860*.

113. This was Blumenkamp's view according to Georges Mathieu, a leading member of the French Gestapo at Cl-Fd. Mathieu testified in his postwar interrogation that the Jews and members of the University of Strasbourg were always selected as the first targets following "terrorist" attacks. Transcript of his interrogation in the papers of Henri Ingrand, Archives, Comité d'histoire de la deuxième guerre mondiale, Paris.

114. French police reports, in *M07164, M07165, M0671, R02069;* see also *Témoignages Strasbourgeois.*

115. A resistance "Chronologie" for the Puy-de-Dôme established by the Comité d'histoire de la deuxième guerre mondiale, Paris, lists 63 attacks or disturbances of various sorts that were cited in German reports. Although not a complete accounting, this document suggests the scope and frequency of attacks on German troops and installations.

116. LXVI Res. K. 48874/2, Lagebericht für Monat März 1944, Nr. 1917/44 geh., 3 April 1944.

117. Various reports from LXVI Res. K. See also Jacques Natali, "L'Occupant allemand à Lyon de 1942 à 1944 d'après les sources allemandes," *Cahiers d'histoire* [Lyon] 22, no. 4 (1977). Natali has consulted many of the German sources I have used, and his comments about Lyon often apply equally well for Cl-Fd.

118. Generalkommando LXVI Res. Korps, Abt. Ic Nr. 2352/43 geh. Bericht für Monat Mai 1943 and especially Generalkommando LXVI Res. Korps Atl Ic Nr. 3447/43 geh. Lagebericht für Monat Juli 1943.

119. LXVI Res. K. "Verkehr mit französischen Behorden und mit der Zivilbevölkerung im neubesetzten Teil Frankreichs," 2 November 1942.

120. Dossier M07244, especially Commissaire Divisionnaire, Chef du Service des Renseignements Généraux à M. le Secrétaire Général à la Police, Cl-Fd, 26 September 1945.

121. This idea is conveyed in various reports from both the Rüstung officials (Kriegstagebuch, Rü.K.K. I, Royat in RH 19 IV/141) and the military (Monatsberichte and Lageberichte of 66 Res. Div., 189 Res. Div. and 159 Res. Div.).

122. Ibid.

123. Martres, "Les Troupes allemandes."

124. There are numerous accounts of the events at Mont Mouchet, many of them highly romanticized and inaccurate, but recently Eugène Martres has produced an excellent analysis in his doctoral dissertation for the Faculté des Lettres at the University of Clermont-Ferrand, "Le Cantal de 1939 à 1945" (Clermont-Ferrand, 1974).

125. RW 34/1315 Kommandant des Heeresgebietes Sudfrankreich, Abteilung Verwaltung u. Wirtschaft, Schlussbericht; 4 September 1944, Abschrift

Dr. Schmidt-Ewig, MV-Oberrat Verw. Gruppenleiter der OFK Cl-Fd (H.V. St. 588), "Bericht: Letzte Tätigkeit im Einsatzgebiet"; and 26/9/44, Rüstungskommando Cl-Fd, Abwicklungsstelle, "Bericht uber die Lage im Rü-Bezirk Clermont-Ferrand in Monat August bis zum Abmarsch und Verlauf des Marsches."

126. Ibid.

127. Rü.K.K. Cl-Fd., Abwicklungsstelle, "Bericht uber die Lage im Rü-Bezirk Clermont-Ferrand im Monat August bis zum Abmarsch und Verlauf des Marsches."

128. Dossier RW 24/271–282 includes the Kriegstagebuch of Rü.K.K. I, Royat, which covers the period 1 October 1941–September 1944, plus appended documents. This is an extremely rich collection.

129. *La Délégation Française auprès de la Commission Allemande d'Armistice* (Paris: Alfred Costes, 1947) tome I, pp. 249–251; interviews with M. Jean Roger and M. Louis Bailly, former Michelin executives, Cl-Fd, 1978.

130. Such cases were to pose perplexing dilemmas for the members of purge committees at the liberation and for historians since: who was a collaborator?

131. Milward, *The New Order,* and Karter, "Coercion and Resistance."

132. Rü.K.K. I, Cl-Fd, "Monatsbericht vom 23/12/41–31/1/42," 3 February 1942.

133. This sentiment is expressed directly and indirectly throughout the Kriegstagebuch and appended documents, Rü.K.K., Cl-Fd.

134. Kriegstagebuch, Rü.K.K., entry for 15 April 1942.

135. Rü.K.K., Cl-Fd., Monatsbericht, 23/11–22/12/41, 24 December 1941.

136. Kriegstagebuch, Rü.K.K., entry for 29 May 1942, and entry for 4 March 1942. *M03823,* 31 October 1941, Commissaire de Police, Chef de la Sûreté à M. le Préfet Régional.

137. Rü.K.K., Cl-Fd, Monatsbericht vom 1–31 Jan. 1943, Gruppe Heer, 3 February 1943.

138. Ibid.

139. French documents relative to the S-Betriebe are found in Dossiers *R01722, M05755, M05653, M05664,* and *R02070.* A list of those companies employing more than 100 workers is in *M07871.*

140. Ibid.

141. Milward, *The New Order,* and Karter, "Coercion and Resistance."

142. My estimate of the percentage of workers in industry employed for German purposes is in part based on figures from the *Annuaire Statistique Régional Retrospectif: Auvergne* (Chamalières: I.N.S.E.E., 1964), p. 104. Also *M05659,* "Note: L'Inspecteur divisionnaire du travail adjoint, June 1943: Nombre de Salaires Employés dans la région de Clermont-Ferrand."

143. Averages from statistics reported in a series of Lageberichte, Rü.K.K., Cl-Fd., December 1943–May 1944.

144. Ibid.

145. RW 24/278, Rü.K.K., Cl-Fd., 12 May 1944, Abschrift; and RW 24/275, Rü.K.K., Cl-Fd., 18 March 1944, Abschrift: "Bericht über den Luftangriff auf das Werk Michelin. . . ."

146. Both Milward, *The New Order,* and Jäckel, *La France,* deal with the general debate.

147. RW 24/276 Rü.K.K., Cl-Fd., 12 July 1944, "Darstellung der rüstungswirt-schaftlichen Entwicklung un der Zeit vom 1.4 bis 30.6.1944."

148. The files of the Commissaires de Police at Cl-Fd, *M07191,* make numerous references to the popular view of the STO as equivalent to deportation. Similar observations are scattered through the Rüstung materials.

149. Mu. Os., Cl-Fd., Monatsbericht des Gruppe III für August 1943, 30 August 1943.

150. Dossier *M05668* includes the French government's complaint about West-rich to the German High Command in Paris, Secrétaire Général à la Main d'Oeuvre à M. le Commandant Suprême des Forces Allemandes en France, Hotel Majestic, Paris, 11 July 1944. The document notes that more "volunteers" had left Clermont for Germany since the official stop-ping of requisitions than in the corresponding period before, and concludes that the psychological benefit that Laval and the Germans had hoped to gain by ending the STO "est totalement annihilé par l'action du Docteur Westrich, laquelle augmente encore la méfiance de la population."

151. RW 24/278 Rü.K.K., Cl-Fd., Lagebericht für den Monat November 1943, 15 December 1943, and Schilderung der Lage im Bezirk des Rü-Kdos, 8 June 1944.

152. Correspondence concerning this problem in 1943 and 1944 in M05227.

153. In addition to the Kriegstagebuch and appended documents, see RW 34/76 Kontrollabteilung Az 20, Nr. 890/44 geh. 7 July 1944, Bourges, Monats-bericht Nr. 15: 1–30 June 1944, and reports in RW 34/98.

Chapter 8

1. Rü.K.K. I, Cl-Fd, 4 September 1942, Monatsbericht vom 1 bis 31 August 1942. Militärarchiv, Freiburg.

2. In interviews with dozens of former resisters for this book and my earlier study of the *Mouvements Unis de la Résistance,* I was struck by the fre-quency with which the same phrase recurs in the comments of leaders and militants of resistance groups: "We only did what had to be done, that's all."

3. Numerous reports by police and military officials in files *M03822, M03823, M03887,* and elsewhere document an active Gaullist movement at Cl-Fd by the fall of 1940 that authorities consider to be principally the work of students.

4. These and other tracts are found in file *M07184.* These particular exam-ples were distributed at Cl-Fd in May 1941.

5. Z4449/52/17, Public Record Office, Kew (London), copy of the transcript of an interrogation of a French student who arrived in Great Britain in March 1943. He had spent the past two years farming in the Allier near Etroussat.

6. See Chapter 6.

7. Interview, Alphonse Rozier, 24 April 1979.

8. Ibid., and records of the LXVI Reserve Korps; numerous Lageberichte and Tätigkeitsberichte for 1943 and 1944 refer to propaganda activities and often include translated copies of tracts in French. The majority of these materials found in the files of the LXVI Reserve Korps stationed at Cl-Fd are of Front National or Communist Party origin.

9. Reports in records of the LXVI Reserve Korps, and Jacques Natali,

"L'Occupant allemand à Lyon de 1942 à 1944 d'après les sources allemandes," *Cahiers d'histoire* [Lyon] 22, no. 4 (1977), 441–464.

10. *M06357*, 7 August 1943, Commissaire Principal de I° Classe, Chef du Service des Renseignements Généraux du PdD à M. le Commissaire Divisionnaire, Chef Régional des Renseignements Généraux à Cl-Fd, "Objet: Enquête dans les usines métallurgiques du secteur de Clermont-Ferrand." See also reports of police officials in series *M07191*, cited frequently in Chapter 6.

11. *M03883*, 23 November 1940, Préfet du PdD à M. le Ministre à l'Intérieur.

12. *Témoignage* of Claude Bourdet, Comité d'histoire de la deuxième guerre mondiale, Paris, as quoted in John Sweets, *The Politics of Resistance in France, 1940–1944* (DeKalb: Northern Illinois University Press, 1976), p. 43; René Cerf-Ferrière, *Chemin clandestin* (Paris: Julliard, 1968), the memoirs of an editor of *Combat,* are an excellent guide to issues involving the underground press.

13. Ibid. See also H. R. Kedward, *Resistance in Vichy France* (Oxford: Oxford University Press, 1978); and especially Henri Michel, *Les Courants de pensée de la Résistance* (Paris: Presses Universitaires de France, 1962).

14. Léon Blum, *A l'échelle humaine,* vol. 5 of *L'Oeuvre de Léon Blum* (Paris: Editions Albin Michel, 1955), p. 457.

15. Dated 25 November 1940, Nouvelle Série N° I, this paper as well as the national edition of *L'Humanité* was distributed in Montferrand the night of 21–22 November 1940. Copy in *M03824*.

16. *M03883*, *L'Humanité,* no. 96, 20 February 1941.

17. *M03883*, *L'Humanité,* 6 April 1941.

18. The same viewpoint was expressed in *Voix du Peuple,* "Organe de la Région Communiste du Puy-de-Dôme," nouvelle série N° I, 25 November 1940 (in *M03824*), and in other issues of *L'Humanité,* such as 20 February 1941, 6 March 1941, and 17 May 1941 (in *M03883*).

19. Bitter polemics about the date of entry of the Communists into the resistance have often served to obscure the more important issue of different definitions and conceptions of resistance.

20. Sweets, *The Politics of Resistance in France,* pp. 50–51.

21. *M03883*, 5 January 1941, report, Commissaire de Police, Chef de Sûreté, à M. le Commissaire Central, Cl-Fd (my italics).

22. *M07159*, 20 August 1942, René Bousquet, Secrétaire Général à la Police, à M. le Préfet Régional, Cl-Fd.

23. *M07157* contains several reports concerning active searches for Huguet, Coulaudon, Jouanneau, and others. Rozier is convinced that he was forced to flee his home just before the liberation only because of the carelessness of certain leaders of the MUR who had lost documents that mentioned his name.

24. Interviews, Alphonse Rozier, 12 August 1975, 31 January and 24 April 1979.

25. Interview, Rozier, 31 January 1979.

26. Documents related to this issue are in *M03822, M03882, M03883, M07152, M07159, M07184, M07185, M07188, M07191,* and *M07199.*

27. *M01785*, 10 September 1941, Intendant de Police à M. le Ministre, Secrétaire d'Etat à l'Intérieur, noted that a tract, "Front National de lutte pour l'indépendance de la France," was distributed at Cl-Fd the night of 7–8

September. *M03822*, 30 September 1941, Commissaire du 3° Arrondissement à Préfet, cited another tract, "Le Front National de Lutte pour l'Indépendance de la France est constitué," also circulated in September in the city.

28. Interview, Rozier, 29 March 1979.

29. *The Sorrow and the Pity* (New York: Outerbridge & Lazard, 1972), p. 118.

30. *M03823*, 3 January 1942, Paul Brun, Préfet, Rapport Mensuel d'Information. *M03822*, 25 January 1941, Lt. Col. Peragallo, Cmdt. Mil. du Département, PdD, "Bulletin Economique et Social"; 4–5 February 1941, Vichy, Inspection Générale des Services de Police Administrative, "Note sommaire sur la situation dans le département du Puy-de-Dôme"; lists of those arrested for resistance activities in January, May, July, and September 1942 in dossiers *M07187* and *M07191* reflect the prominence of those groups named.

31. *M07158*, 28 October 1941, Commissaire des Renseignements Généraux à M. l'Intendant Directeur de la Police Régionale à Cl-Fd.

32. *M04860*, "Additif au Plan de Surveillance de la Préfecture lors de la venue de Hautes Personnalités," undated, but in file with documents for October 1941.

33. *M07149*, 9 February 1942, Brun Préfet Régional aux Préfets de la Région; *M03812*, 9 February 1942, Circulaire no. 5, Préfet Régional de Cl-Fd à ——.

34. *M07283*, Note, 25 May 1942, Secrétaire d'Etat à l'Intérieur, Directeur Général de la Police Nationale aux Préfets.

35. *M07188*, 22 June 1942, Préfet Régional à M. le Chef du Gouvernement.

36. See, for example, file *M07157*, documenting resistance activities before 1942.

37. Kedward, *Resistance in Vichy France,* pp. 215–219. In my opinion the numbers involved in these demonstrations are exaggerated by Kedward, who bases his estimates of participation on the underground press, but his general point is well taken.

38. Dominique Veillon, *Le Franc-Tireur* (Paris: Flammarion, 1977) pp. 198–200; letter to the author, Rozier, 14 January 1981; *M07161* contains several police reports on the demonstration; also *M07188*, 14 July 1942, Préfet Régional à M. le Chef de Gouvernement, and 22 July 1942, Intendant de Police à M. le Général Conquet.

39. Ibid.

40. Rozier, letter, 14 January 1981.

41. *M04861*, 27 July 1942, Le Chef du Gouvernement, Ministre Secrétaire d'Etat à l'Intérieur à Monsieur le Préfet Régional de Cl-Fd.

42. *M06357*, "Service d'Ordre Prévu pour la Soirée du 18 Juin 1943"; *M06133*, Press Communiqué from Directeur des Operations du Maintien de l'Ordre dans la Région de Cl-Fd, forbidding any sort of demonstration for 14 July 1944.

43. File *M07158*, "Attentats 1941–1944"; also numerous documents in *M07157, M07187, M07188,* and *M07191.*

44. *M04228*, 3 June 1942, Le Commissaire de Police, Chef de la Sûreté, à M. le Préfet du PdD. In this particular instance, the hall was aired out before anyone arrived, and the meeting was not disturbed.

45. *M07188*, 5 July 1942, Intendant to Chef Régional de la Police Judiciaire; 31 December 1942, Préfet Régional à Monsieur le Chef du Gouvernement; and *M07191*, 16 June 1942, Intendant Régional de Police à M. le Général Conquet, Commandant d'Armes Délégué.

46. For a detailed description of the unification of the French resistance, see Henri Michel, *Jean Moulin l'unificateur* (Paris: Librairie Hachette, 1964), and Sweets, *The Politics of Resistance in France.*

47. See Kedward, *Resistance in Vichy France;* Veillon, *Le Franc-Tireur;* and Marie Granet and Henri Michel, *Combat* (Paris: Presses Universitaires de France, 1957) for details about the early activities of the movements. Henry Ingrand, interview with the author, 11 March 1970, recalled his first impression of the situation in the Auvergne.

48. Interview, Ingrand, 11 March 1970.

49. Ibid.

50. Rozier (Interview, 24 April 1979) believed that the benefits derived from the German language ability of students and faculty from Strasbourg far outweighed any security risk, and stated that the Front National's security system worked well among the university community.

51. Rozier, letters to the author, 3 April 1980, and 14 January 1981.

52. Sweets, *The Politics of Resistance in France,* p. 64.

53. A "Chronologie de la résistance, Puy-de-Dôme," established by the Comité d'histoire de la deuxième guerre mondiale, Paris, lists 61 different actions based on various German documents, attributable to the resistance in the PdD and suggests something of the variety of resistance activity, but it is nothing approaching a complete record. The records of the German occupation units (both military and economic) preserved at Freiburg, and French police files make it clear that the resistance was extremely active in the Auvergne. It would be difficult to cite a day in 1943 or 1944 that passed without a note of some sabotage or guerilla attack in the region.

54. *M07191*, 24 August 1943, Rapport Mensuel Intendance, Police de Sûreté; *M06357*, 4 August 1943, report in folder labeled "Juin-Juillet-Août 1943." See also Henry Ingrand, *Libération de l'Auvergne* (Paris: Hachette Litterature, 1974), p. 30, and Gilles Lévy and Francis Cordet, *A nous, Auvergne* (Paris: Presses de la Cité, 1974), p. 89–90.

55. Lévy and Cordet, *A nous, Auvergne,* pp. 164–165; letter, Rozier to the author, 14 January 1981.

56. The literally thousands of documents reporting sabotage, robberies, and guerilla attacks are too numerous to cite, but among the richest dossiers are *M04870*, *M06617*, *M06618*, *M06745*, *M07181*, *M07773–M07780*, *M07190*, and *M07214*. Box BI Puy-de-Dôme in the Archives of the Comité d'histoire de la deuxième guerre mondiale, Paris, contains a list of all the attacks on railways in the PdD in 1944.

57. See relevant documents in *M06745*, especially 27 July 1944, Directeur des PTT, PdD à Monsieur le Préfet, and 17 July 1944, Le Trésorier Payeur Général à Monsieur le Préfet Délégué.

58. *M04869*, 27 April 1944, Maison Allait à Monsieur le Préfet; similar comments from officials at Michelin, directors of mines, and other industry representatives in this file and in *M04870*.

59. *M04870*, 20 July 1944, Le Directeur, Mines de Brassac à M. le Préfet du PdD, Cl-Fd.

60. *M07181,* 18 March 1944, Préfet du Cantal à M. le Préfet Régional (Cl-Fd).

61. *M05229,* 19 July 1943, N° 126B, Rapport du Brigadier Comdt, la Brigade 89 de Cl-Fd.

62. *M04869,* 23 February 1944, Le Préfet du PdD délégué, H. Guerrin, à Messieurs les Directeurs des Dépôts de Carburants. In the same file, 15 February 1944, Le Préfet du PdD délégué, *Objet*-Protection des dépôts de carburants, is Guerrin's earlier order for the establishment of teams of armed night watchmen, and installation of better alarm systems.

63. In addition to Chapter 7, "Clermont through German Eyes," see Eugéne Martres, "Les Troupes allemandes dans le Massif Central," *Cahiers d'histoire* [Lyon] 22, no. 4 (1977), 405–419.

64. Lists of deserters and comments on the situation in *M07175* and *MO7300.*

65. *M07172,* 26 June 1944, Commandant GMR "Auvergne" à Monsieur le Col. Cmdt. le Groupement des Forces du Maintien de l'Ordre de la Région de Cl-Fd.

66. *M07172,* 17 June 1944, Note de Service, Lt. Col. Hachette.

67. Ibid.; logbooks and other documents related to the Groupement des Forces du Maintien de l'Ordre are in this same file, *M07172.*

68. *M06745,* 1 July 1944, Préfet Régional Brun transmits for application the orders of Raymond Clemoz (Vichy).

69. *M06740,* 22 February 1944, Secrétaire Général au Maintien de l'Ordre à M. le Préfet, PdD.

70. Interview, Ingrand, 11 March 1970; Eugène Martres, "Le Cantal de 1939 à 1945." (Thèse, University of Clermont-Ferrand, 1974), pp. 376–387.

71. See *M09457* for several claims for reimbursement. The quotation is from 4 September 1944, Trésorier Payeur Général à Monsieur le Commissaire de la République.

72. Kriegstagebuch, Rü.K.K. I, Cl-Fd, entry for 21 March 1943, in file RW 24/271, Militärarchiv, Freiburg.

73. Dr. Schmidt-Ewing, MV-Oberrat, Verw. Gruppenleiter der OFK Cl-Fd (H.V.St. 588), Bericht! Letzte Tätigkeit im Einsatzgebiet, Marburg, 4 September 1944, RW 35/1318; German report on 8 March attack in LXVI Reserve Korps, 48874/2, 3 April 1944, Lagebericht für Monat Marz 1944. All attacks on German troops are noted in both the military and economic records of the occupation authorities stationed at Cl-Fd (in Militärarchiv, Freiburg), and, of course, they are described in French police files as well.

74. Files *M05224, M06370, M07155, M07169,* and *M07191* all contain information on various curfews following resistance attacks on German troops.

75. *M07191,* 25 August 1943, Commissaire Central à M. le Préfet Délégué, and *M07164,* reports from police in all districts of Cl-Fd following the 8 March 1944 attack.

76. Interviews, Rozier, 12 August 1975 and 24 April 1979.

77. Copy of Coulaudon's proclamation in Lévy and Cordet, *A nous, Auvergne,* pp. 320–321.

78. Interview, Rozier, 24 April 1979, and letter to the author, 14 January 1981.

79. Ibid.

80. 20 September 1944, Grenoble, no. 987, Major Alfred T. Cox, "OSS Aid to the French Resistance in World War II," Operations in Southern

France, Operational Groups, p. 9. This and other documents regarding Mont Mouchet are found at the library of the J.F.K. Special Warfare Center, Fort Bragg, N.C.

81. *M05849,* "Grandes pages de l'histoire de la résistance en Auvergne."

82. Martres, "Le Cantal de 1939 à 1945," section entitled "Les Grands Affrontements," pp. 521–698. This is by far the most satisfactory account of the Mont Mouchet engagement. Lévy and Cordet, *A nous, Auvergne,* although capturing well the spirit of the maquis in the Auvergne, is untrustworthy on many points of fact and interpretation.

83. No. 979, Missions, BENJOIN, 10 November 1944, London, "Activity Report of 1st Lieutenant Le Baigue." J.F.K. Special Warfare Center, Fort Bragg, N.C. Le Baigue was the American member of the Allied mission Benjoin. He was the weapons specialist.

84. Martres, "Le Cantal de 1939 à 1945," pp. 686–687.

85. This is the viewpoint that is conveyed by works like *A nous, Auvergne* and, of course, the type of literature distributed at the monument at Mont Mouchet; it tends to identify resistance with the maquis, overlooking or underemphasizing other equally significant forms of resistance.

86. My own book, *The Politics of Resistance in France,* can be faulted on this score.

87. Paxton, *Vichy France,* pp. 294–95 (my italics).

88. For example, Bertram M. Gordon, *Collaborationism in France during the Second World War* (Ithaca: Cornell University Press, 1980) pp. 326–327, and the less scholarly Milton Dank, *The French against the French: Collaboration and Resistance* (Philadelphia: Lippincott, 1974).

89. For estimates of membership in resistance groups, see *M06336,* 25 January 1945, Note d'Information, Renseignements Généraux, concerning the integration of former FFI into the regular army; see also several documents related to pay for FFI units in *M09457,* and the monthly reports of the prefect and the Commissaire de la République following the liberation; letter from Alphonse Rozier to the author, 14 January 1981. The *Annuaire Statistique Régional Retrospectif* (Clermont-Ferrand: Institut National de la Statistique et des Etudes Economiques, 1964) provides basic population statistics used in my calculation of percentages involved in the resistance.

90. Lists of persons and statistics related to those executed, arrested, or deported are found in *M06643, M07244, M09361,* and *R01807-08;* also Daniel Martin, "Statistique de la Déportation," Département de PdD, de Juin 1940 à Août 1944.

91. *M04869,* 22 December 1943, Le Préfet du PdD Délégué à Messieurs les Médecins assermentés du Département. The letter stated, "Dans certaines communes, le nombre d'exemptées pour raison de santé dépasse le tiers des personnes susceptible d'être requisés."

92. *M05538–40* contain documents regarding persons sheltering STO deserters; *M09462,* Rapport, Préfet du PdD, 5 February 1945, discusses the actions of the clergy.

93. Relevant documents in *M07161.*

94. *M06357,* 6 July 1943, Renseignements Généraux, no. 4284.

95. *M05787,* statistics and comments concerning production; RW 24/275, 11

April 1944, Rüstungskommando Cl-Fd, "Darstellung der rüstungswirt-schaftlichen Entwicklung in der Zeit vom 1.1. bis 31.3.1944."

96. Interview, Louis Bailly, 1978.
97. Letter to the author, Rozier, 14 January 1981.
98. Numerous documents in *M05794.*
99. *M06357,* 27 December 1943, No. 38007, Commissaire Central à M. l'In-tendant Régional de Police.
100. *M05843,* Comdt. Martial, noted the PTT deserved a citation "très élo-gieuse."
101. Production records of the Rüstungskommando Cl-Fd in series RW 24, Militärarchiv, Freiburg.
102. Martres, "Le Cantal de 1939 à 1945," pp. 301–302.
103. Interview, Rozier, 24 April 1979.
104. *M07157,* 5 April 1944, Rapport Comdt. Sect. d'Ambert de la Gendarm-erie.
105. *M06357,* 5 June 1943, Renseignements Généraux, No. 2711.
106. *M06371,* numerous documents related to November–December 1943; quo-tation from *M07191,* 25 May 1943, Commissaire de Chamalières-Royat à M. le Commissaire Central, Cl-Fd.
107. *M07167,* 18 July 1943, René Bousquet, "Instruction sur la Préparation et la conduite des opérations de police ayant pour but la capture de groupes armés tenant la compagne." See numerous related documents in *M07157, M07167,* and *M04872.*
108. See Chapter 4.
109. *M07172,* 11 July 1944, Lt. Col. Hachette, Cl-Fd, Effectifs, Armement, Véhicules.
110. *M05561,* Extrait du J.O. du 2 Février 1944, Loi No. 56 du 1 Février 1944.
111. Extensive documentation of the purge process in files *M05552, M05548, M05549, M07214,* and *M09468;* see also Henry Ingrand, *Un an d'activité,* in particular Chapter 2, "Epuration et Répression." This was his summary of activity as Commissaire de la République for the Auvergne at the lib-eration.
112. *M06358,* 30 August 1944, Commissaire Principale à Cl-Fd, à M. le Direc-teur des Renseignements Généraux à Vichy. The liberation of the city was described in *M06353,* 24 September 1944, "Rapport sur la situation dans le Département," Préfet du PdD à M. le Commissaire de la République de la Région de Cl-Fd; *M06358,* 28 August 1944, S.G. No. 6883; *M09464,* Commissariat des Renseignements Généraux, 5 December 1944, "Situa-tion dans le Département du Puy-de-Dôme." The last actions of the Ger-mans in the city are described in files *M06358, M06659,* and *M07856,* and in *Kriegs-Tage-Buch de l'Etat-Major Principal de Liaison No. 588 de Cler-mont-Ferrand,* texte traduit et annoté par le Commandant Even du Service Historique de l'Armée de Terre, Chateau de Vincennes: 1975.
113. Yves Farge, *Rebelles soldats et citoyens* (Paris: Editions Bernard Grasset, 1946), p. 226. Farge was the Commissaire de la République at Lyon.
114. *M06791,* En Auvergne, 24 July 1944, "Appel du Commissaire de la Ré-publique de la région de Clermont-Ferrand."
115. Ibid. (my italics). Ingrand crossed out the now heavily stigmatized *colla-bore* of his first draft and substituted the word *participe.*

116. *M07252*, 4 July 1946, Renseignements Généraux, Cl-Fd, "Au sujet des exécutions sommaires ayant eu lieu lors de la libération du territoire."

117. *M07327*, dossier Epuration, 13 March 1946, "Enquête sur l'épuration et sur les réactions de l'opinion publique à cet égard dans le département du Puy-de-Dôme." This 23-page document overstates the number of summary executions (claiming, without evidence to support the claim, that there were 100 executions in the PdD), but otherwise it offers an extremely thorough discussion of the purge and reactions to it.

118. Ibid. Microfilm of the *MUR d'Auvergne* is available from the Bibliothèque Nationale, Paris.

119. Quoted in *M06361*, 22 August 1945, Note d'Information.

120. *M07268*, 24 April 1945, RG/SR No. 484; The prediction was almost correct. Coulandon was in fact elected twenty-seventh out of twenty-eight. Several letters and reports in *M0722* document scuffles and brawls in which Coulaudon, his brother, and some of their friends were involved, including an attempt to force a female café owner to contribute more than she had given toward the maquis monument at Mont Mouchet. Charges were not brought against Coulaudon because of his service to the resistance.

121. *M09464*, 1 October 1944, Secrétaire Régional pour la Police, Rapport sur l'activité du Secrétaire Régional pour la Police, Rapport sur l'activité du Secrétariat Régional pour la Police, Cl-Fd, Période 27/8/44 à 27/9/44.

122. The purge in the PdD is very well documented in the departmental archives. The best dossier for statistical information is *M06655*, Statistiques relatives à la répression des faits de collaboration 1945–1946. The minister of the interior called on the prefects to submit reports on the purge in March 1946. Those for the region of the Auvergne are in *M09369*.

123. *M09369*, 15 March 1946, Préfet d'Allier à M. le Ministre de l'Intérieur.

124. *M06611*, 21 November 1944, No. 15.152, le Commissaire Divisionnaire Chef du Service Régional de Police Judiciaire à M. le Préfet.

125. *M07245*, Dossier Renseignements Généraux, 1944–1946, Notes émanants de la Surveillance du Territoire, 16 December 1944.

126. *M09426*, 11 June 1945, Commissaire de la République, Cl-Fd à M. le Ministre de la Justice. Files *M06359, M06553, M07224, M09270,* and *M09320* contain other information related to the central government's push for "regularization" of justice and the local government's desire to take into account practical obstacles to that policy.

127. *M09426*, 9 June 1945, Rapport, Inspecteur de Police Judiciaire.

128. Interestingly, as gleaned from their reports on many of the bombing incidents (for example in *M06361*), the police did not seem to treat these actions as serious criminal matters, often noting in their reports that the attacks had been *provoked* by the victim's wartime attitudes.

129. Charles-Louis Foulon, *Le Pouvoir en province à la libération* (Paris: Armand Colin, 1975); and Crane Brinton, "Letters from Liberated France," *French Historical Studies* 2, nos. 1 and 2 (Spring and Fall 1961), pp. 1–27 and 133–56, respectively.

130. *M09462*, 24 September 1944, Préfet du PdD à M. le Commissaire de la République.

131. Letter, Ingrand to the author, 17 December 1980; see *M09462,* containing the Rapports Hebdomadaire du Préfet du PdD au Commissaire de la Ré-

publique (24 September 1944 to 18 February 1945) for an ongoing account of specific problems.

132. *M05671*, 3 November 1944, Commissaire de la République à M. le Ministre de l'Intérieur.

133. *M06353*, 24 September 1944, Rapport, Préfet du PdD à M. le Commissaire de la République.

134. *M06653*, 21 September 1944, Secrétariat du C.D.L. sur l'activité des Comités locaux de libération à M. le Commissaire de la République.

135. *M06353*, 24 September 1944, Rapport, Préfet du PdD à M. le Commissaire de la République. There is abundant documentation concerning the activities of the Comité départementale de la libération in *M06353*, *M06359*, *M07062*, *M09295*, and *M09319*.

136. *M06359*, 24 February 1945, Renseignements Généraux, no. 907.

137. *M09464*, 16 July 1945, Commissariat de la République, "La Vie Politique."

138. *M06353*, 24 September 1944, Rapport, Préfet du PdD à M. le Commissaire de la République.

139. *M07058*, 2 May 1945, Préfet du PdD à M. le Ministre de l'Intérieur, Compte-rendu des élections municipales du 29 Avril 1945 dans le département du PdD. *M07295* contains two interesting reports on the political situation in early 1945: 25 January 1945, Renseignements Généraux du PdD à M. le Commissaire Divisionnaire Chef Régional des Renseignements Généraux à Cl-Fd, and 30 January, Commissaire Principal R.G. du PdD à M. le Commissaire Divisionnaire Chef Régional des R.G. For further reports and statistics concerning the political situation in 1945, see dossiers *M06361*, *M06362*, *M06434*, *M06573*, *M07058*, and *M07060*.

140. Ingrand, Commissariat de la République, Région de Cl-Fd, Période du 15 au 30 Avril 1945, in PI (3), Archives, Comité d'histoire de la deuxième guerre mondiale, Paris.

141. *M06353*, 9 October 1944, Renseignements Généraux, No. 1026/SR, quotations from *La Montagne*.

142. Ibid.

143. *M06353*, 23 September 1944, "Note."

144. *M06361*, 18 October 1945, Gendarmerie nationale, 13° Légion, Section de Thiers, No. 913/2; *M06373*, Télégrammes, 9 October 1944, Intérieur/Paris à Cl-Fd.

Bibliography

The principal sources for this book were archival collections in France, Germany, and England. The most extensive documentation was found in the Archives départementales du Puy-de-Dôme at Clermont-Ferrand. The most valuable records were contained in Série M, where the regular reports of the police and gendarmerie officers and the monthly prefects' reports were especially useful. Série R contains documents originating with the military, and Série T includes information on education. In Freiburg, Germany, the Militärarchiv has important holdings concerning economic and military aspects of the occupation. The specific file numbers and dossiers from these collections and the documents consulted at the Public Record Office in Kew (London), England, and at the National Archives in Washington, D.C., are too numerous to list here, but many of them are cited in the notes. Although most of my work is drawn from these primary sources, I am indebted to a substantial body of secondary literature. The following list is a selective sampling of books and articles concerning wartime France that were helpful in the preparation of this work or are of related interest.

Books

Amaury, Philippe. *Les Deux premières expériences d'un "Ministère de l'Information" en France*. Paris: Librairie générale de droit et de jurisprudence, 1969.

Azéma, Jean-Pierre. *De Munich à la Libération 1938–1944*. Paris: Editions du Seuil, 1979.

Baudot, Marcel. *L'Opinion publique sous l'occupation*. Paris: Presses Universitaires de France, 1960.

de Bayac, J. Delperrie. *Histoire de la Milice 1918–1945*. Paris: Fayard, 1969.

de Bénouville, Guillain. *Le Sacrifice du matin*. Paris: Robert Lafont, 1946.

Billig, Joseph. *Le Commissariat général aux questions juives (1941–1944)*. Paris: 1957, 1959, and 1960.

Blumenkranz, Bernhard (ed.). *Histoire des Juifs en France*. Toulouse: Privat, 1972.

Bourdrel, Philippe. *Histoire des Juifs de France*. Paris: Editions Albin Michel, 1974.

Cerf-Ferrière, René. *Chemin clandestin*. Paris: Julliard, 1968.

Closon, Francis Louis. *Le Temps des passions*. Paris: Presses de la Cité, 1974.

Cordet, Francis, and Gilles Lévy. *A nous Auvergne*. Paris: Presses de la Cité, 1974.

Cormand, Reine (pseud.). *La Vie d'une famille française face à la Gestapo dans la France occupée, novembre 1943–juin 1945*. Montreaux: privately printed, 1972.

Courtois, Stéphane. *Le PCF dans le guerre*. Paris: Ramsay, 1980.

De l'Université aux camps de concentration: Témoignages Strasbourgeois. Paris: n.p., 1954.

Durand, Yves. *Vichy 1940–1944*. Paris: Bordas, 1972.

Fauvet, Jacques. *Histoire du parti communiste français*. Vol. 2. Paris: Fayard, 1965.

Foulon, Charles Louis. *Le Pouvoir en province à la libération*. Paris: Armand Colin, 1975.

Frenay, Henri. *La Nuit finira*. Paris: Robert Laffont, 1973.

Friedlander, Saul. *Quand vient le souvenir . . .* Paris: Editions du Seuil, 1978.

Gordon, Bertram. *Collaborationism in France during the Second World War*. Ithaca: Cornell University Press, 1980.

Le Gouvernment de Vichy 1940–1942. Paris: Armand Colin, 1972.

Granet, Marie, and Henri Michel. *Combat*. Paris: Presses Universitaires de France, 1957.

Hallie, Philip. *Lest Innocent Blood be Shed*. New York: Harper & Row, 1979.

Halls, W. D. *The Youth of Vichy France*. Oxford: Oxford University Press, 1981.

Hyman, Paula. *From Dreyfus to Vichy: The Remaking of French Jewry, 1906–1939*. New York: Columbia University Press, 1979.

Ingrand, Henry. *Libération de l'Auvergne*. Paris: Hachette Littérature, 1974.

Jäckel, Eberhard. *La France dans l'Europe de Hitler*. Paris: Fayard, 1968.

Karter, Simon Mathew. "Coercion and Resistance—Dependence and Compliance: The Germans, Vichy, and the French Economy." Diss., University of Wisconsin, 1976.

Kedward, H. R. *Resistance in Vichy France*. Oxford: Oxford University Press, 1978.

Kriegel, Annie. *Les Communistes français*. Paris: Editions du Seuil, 1970.

Kriegs-Tage-Buch de l'Etat-Major Principal de Liaison N° 588 de Clermont-Ferrand. French translation, Commandant Even, Chateau de Vincennes: Service Historique de l'Armée de Terre, 1975.

Laqueur, Walter. *The Terrible Secret*. Boston: Little, Brown, 1981.

Lecoeur, Auguste. *Le Parti communiste français et la Résistance*. Paris: Plon, 1968.

Lemeunier, Pierre. "L'Opinion publique et le début de la Résistance dans le Puy-de-Dôme." Thèse, Université de Clermont-Ferrand, 1969.

Lévy, C., and R. Tillard. *La Grande Rafle du Vel d'Hiv'*. Paris: Robert Laffont, 1967.

Lindquist, Elizabeth A. "The Experience of the Spanish Republicans in the Auvergne, 1936–1946." Diss., University of Kansas, 1984.

Marrus, Michael R., and Robert O. Paxton. *Vichy France and the Jews*. New York: Basic Books, 1981.

Martres, Eugène. "Le Cantal de 1939 à 1945." Thèse, Université de Clermont-Ferrand, 1974.

Michel, Henri. *Les Courants de pensée de la Résistance*. Paris: Presses Universitaires de France, 1962.

———. *Jean Moulin l'unificateur*. Paris: Librairie Hachette, 1964.

———. *Paris allemand*. Paris: Albin Michel, 1981.

———. *Pétain, Laval, Darlan: Trois politiques?* Paris: Flammarion, 1972.

———. *Le Procès de Riom*. Paris: Albin Michel, 1979.

———. *Vichy: Année 40*. Paris: Robert Laffont, 1966.

Milward, Alan S. *The New Order and the French Economy*. Oxford: Oxford University Press, 1970.

Noguères, Henri. *Histoire de la Résistance française de 1940 à 1945*. 5 vols. Paris: Robert Laffont, 1967–1981.

Novik, Peter. *The Resistance versus Vichy*. New York: Columbia University Press, 1968.

Ophuls, Marcel. *The Sorrow and the Pity*. New York: Outerbridge & Lazard, 1972.

Ory, Pascal. *Les Collaborateurs 1940–1945*. Paris: Editions du Seuil, 1976.

Paxton, Robert O. *Vichy France*. New York: Alfred A. Knopf, 1972.

Renaudot, Françoise. *Les Français et l'occupation*. Paris: Robert Laffont, 1975.

Rossi, A. (pseud. for Angelo Tasca). *Les Communistes français pendant le drôle de guerre*. Paris: Les Iles d'Or, 1951.

———. *La Guerre des papillons: Quatre ans de politique communiste, 1940–1944*. Paris: Les Iles d'Or, 1954.

Rutkowski, Adam (ed.). *La Lutte des Juifs en France à l'époque de l'occupation*. Paris: Centre de Documentation Juive Contemporaine, 1975.

Schnerb, Madeleine. *Mémoires pour deux*. Llauro: privately printed, 1973.

Shields, Sarah Dobin. "A Case Study of Press Censorship in Vichy France." M.A. thesis, University of Kansas, 1978.

Stein, Louis. *Beyond Death and Exile: The Spanish Republicans in France, 1939–1955*. Cambridge: Harvard University Press, 1979.

Sweets, John F. *The Politics of Resistance in France*. DeKalb: Northern Illinois University Press, 1976.

Tiersky, Ronald. *French Communism 1920–1972*. New York: Columbia University Press, 1974.

Veillon, Dominique. *Le Franc-Tireur*. Paris: Flammarion, 1977.

Vistel, Albin. *La Nuit sans ombre*. Paris: Fayard, 1970.

Warner, Geoffrey. *Pierre Laval and the Eclipse of France, 1931–1945*. New York: Macmillan, 1968.

Weinberg, David H. *A Community on Trial: The Jews of Paris in the 1930s*. Chicago: The University of Chicago Press, 1977.

Wellers, Georges. *L'Etoile jaune à l'heure de Vichy*. Paris: Fayard, 1973.

Articles

Austin, Roger. "The Chantiers de la Jeunesse in Languedoc, 1940–44." *French Historical Studies* 13, no. 1 (Spring 1983), 106–126.

Bohbot, David, and Yves Durand. "La Collaboration politique dans le pays de la Loire Moyenne." *Revue d'histoire de la deuxième guerre mondiale* 23, no. 91 (July 1973), 57–76.

Chanal, Michel. "La Collaboration dans l'Isère." *Cahiers d'histoire* [Lyon] no. 4 (1977), 377–403.

Gounand, P. "Les Groupements de collaboration dans une ville française occupée: Dijon." *Revue d'histoire de la deuxième guerre mondiale* 23, no. 91 (July 1973), 47–56.

Guillon, Jean-Marie. "Les Mouvements de collaboration dans le Var." *Revue d'histoire de la deuxième guerre mondiale* 29, no. 113 (1979), 91–110.

Luirard, Monique. "La Milice française dans la Loire." *Revue d'histoire de la deuxième guerre mondiale* 23, no. 91 (July 1973), 77–102.

Martres, Eugène. "La Main d'oeuvre cantalienne en Allemagne au cours de la deuxième guerre mondiale," *Revue de la Haute Auvergne,* 45 (January–March 1976).

———. "Les Troupes allemandes dans le Massif Central." *Cahiers d'histoire* [Lyon] 22, no. 4 (1977), 405–420.

Natali, Jacques. "L'Occupant allemand à Lyon de 1942 à 1944 d'après les sources allemandes." *Cahiers d'histoire* [Lyon] 22, no. 4 (1977), 441–464.

Revue d'histoire de la deuxième guerre mondiale (numéro spécial sur la condition des juifs), 6, no. 24 (1956).

Singer, Barnett. "France and Its Jews in World War II." *Contemporary French Civilization* 2, no. 1 (1977), 1–23.

Index

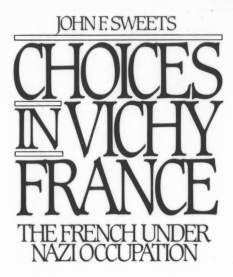

JOHN F. SWEETS

CHOICES IN VICHY FRANCE

THE FRENCH UNDER NAZI OCCUPATION

Films like *The Sorrow and the Pity* and *Lacombe Lucien,* as well as recent scholarship, have replaced the old Gaullist myth of Nazi-occupied France as "a nation of resisters" with a new myth of "a nation of collaborators." John F. Sweets's compelling and provocative reassessment overturns both stereotypes.

From evidence gathered at Clermont-Ferrand, the largest town near Vichy, the occupation capital, Sweets found the French far less devoted to Pétain and the Vichy regime than some have argued, and far more supportive of de Gaulle and the values he stood for than has been suspected. The New Order was emphatically rejected by most of the French, he concludes, and the numbers involved in the Resistance were larger than has been recognized by previous accounts. In addition, the author's archival research in Germany enabled him to reconstruct the wartime experience from the perspective of the occupiers as well as the occupied. He devotes individual chapters to the way the New Order was set up and the response it